Species Domain

スピーシーズドメイン

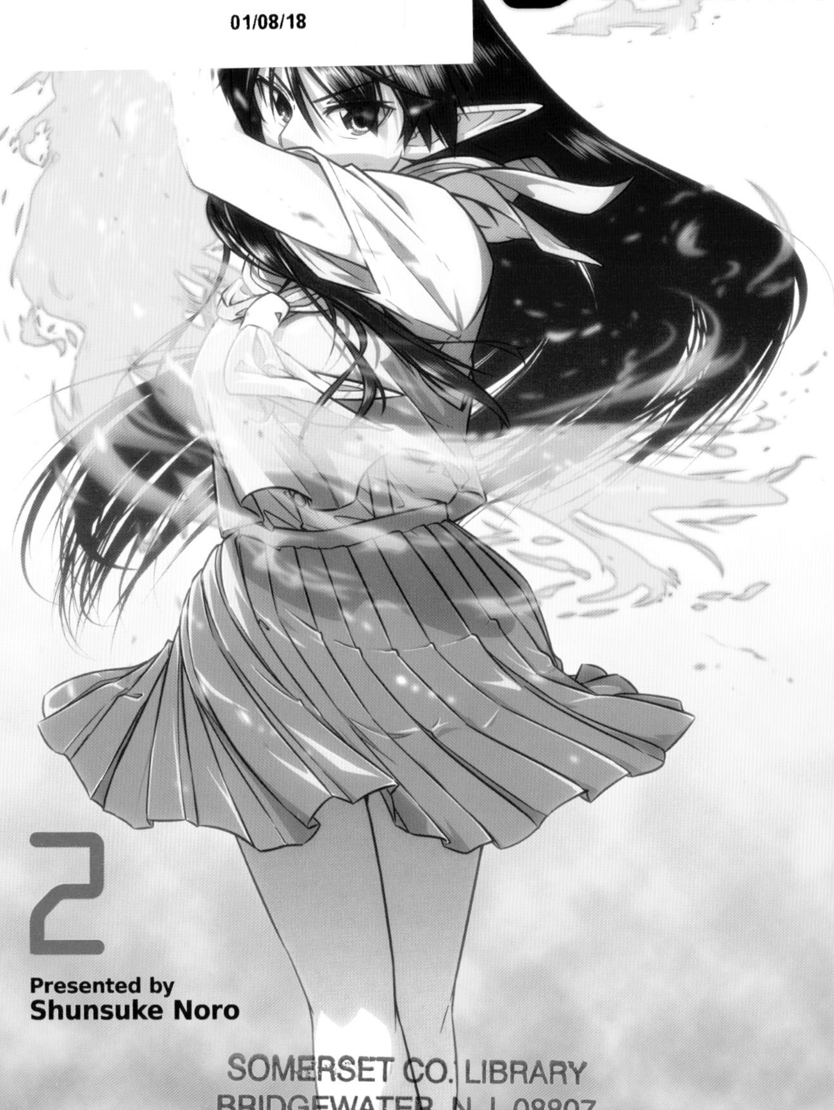

2

Presented by
Shunsuke Noro

Species Domain
スピーシーズドメイン

2

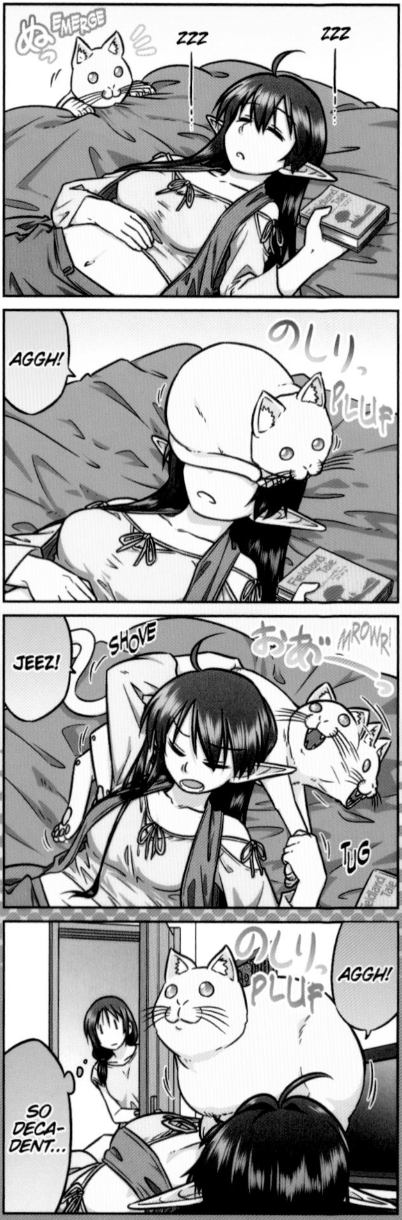
ぬっ
EMERGE
ZZZ
ZZZ
AGGH!
のしり
PLUF
JEEZ!
SHOVE
おあ
MROWR!
TUG
のしり
PLUF
AGGH!
SO DECA-DENT...

What will happen once she finds a boyfriend?

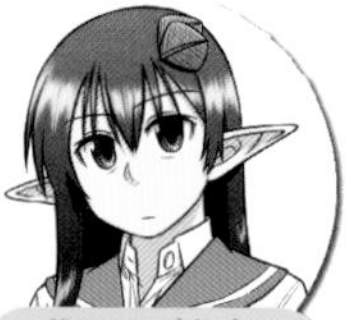

Kazamori Itoko
Elf. Wants to use magic but can't.

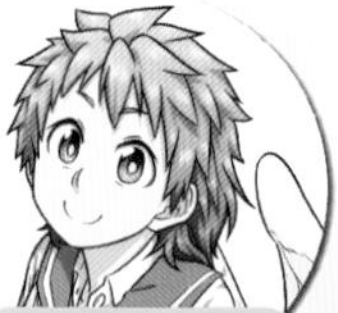

Hanei Minē
Icarus. Kind-hearted and large-breasted.

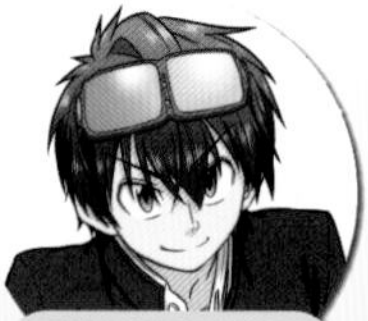

Ohki Hatsuhiko
Human. A science nut.

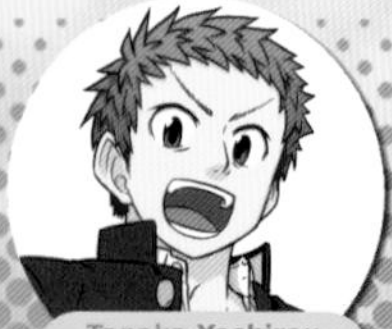

Tanaka Yoshirou
Human. Life of the party.

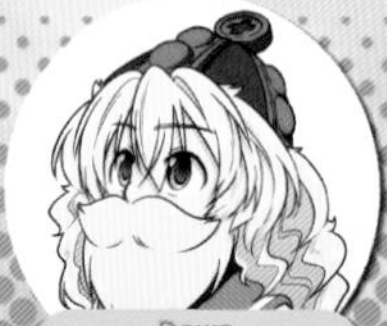

Dowa
Dwarf. A girl with a beard.

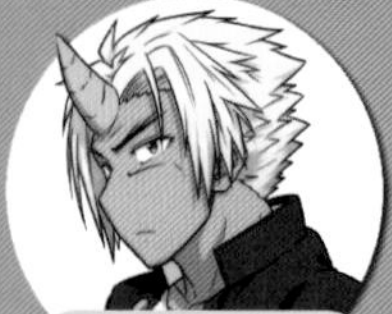

Mikasagi
Ogre. A young tough guy.

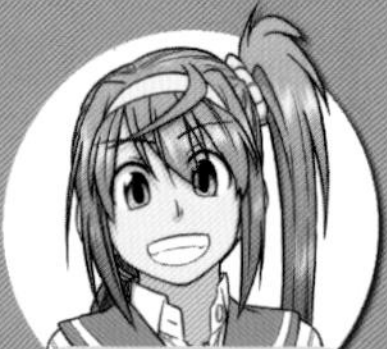

Hotarugi Rikka
Human. Tanaka's childhood friend.

Cover Design: 5Gas Design Studio

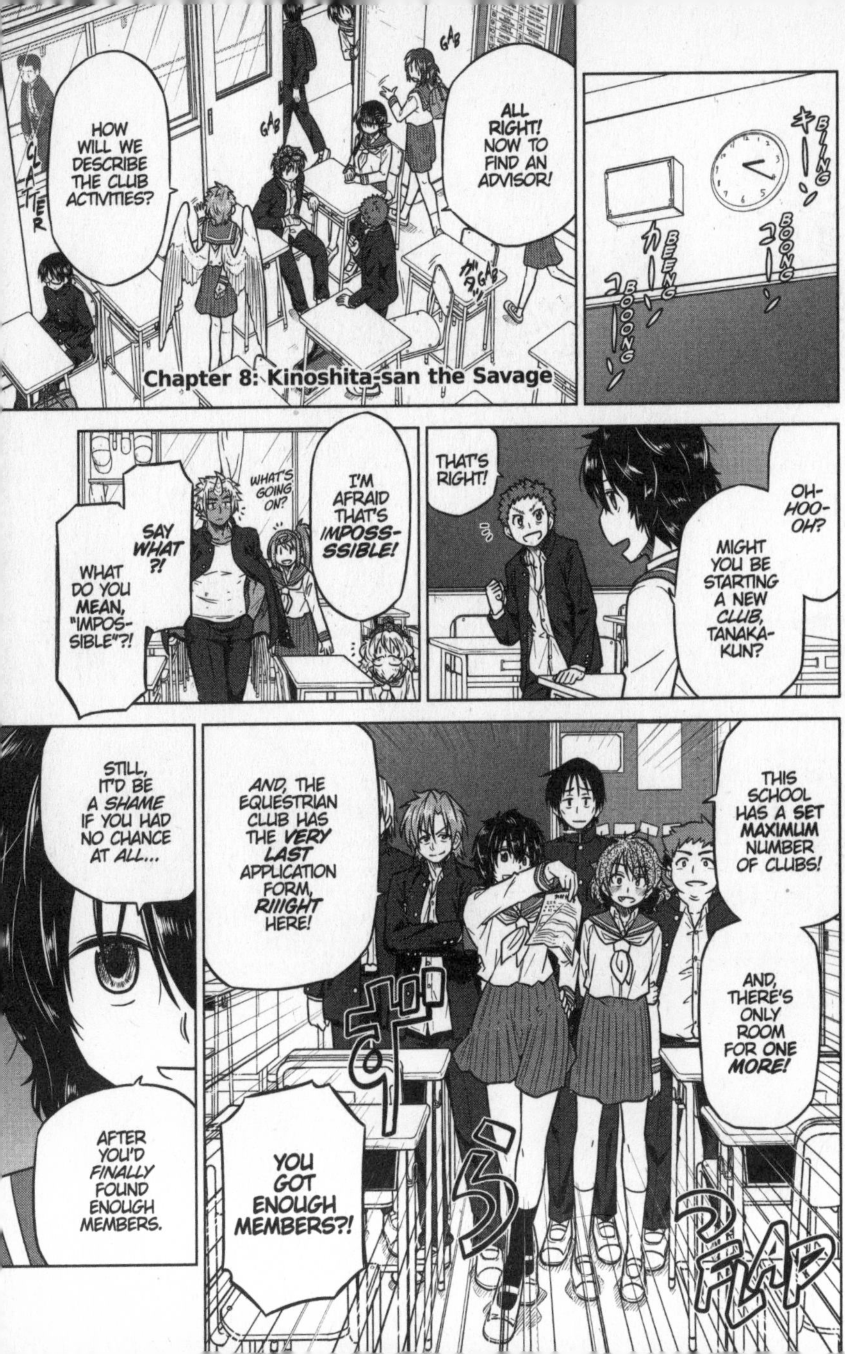
BIING
BOONG
BEENG
BOOONG
ALL RIGHT! NOW TO FIND AN ADVISOR!
GAB
GAB
GAB
HOW WILL WE DESCRIBE THE CLUB ACTIVITIES?
CLATTER
Chapter 8: Kinoshita-san the Savage
OH-HOO-OH? MIGHT YOU BE STARTING A NEW CLUB, TANAKA-KUN?
THAT'S RIGHT!
I'M AFRAID THAT'S IMPOSSSSIBLE!
WHAT'S GOING ON?
SAY WHAT?! WHAT DO YOU MEAN, "IMPOSSIBLE"?!
THIS SCHOOL HAS A SET MAXIMUM NUMBER OF CLUBS!
AND, THERE'S ONLY ROOM FOR ONE MORE!
AND, THE EQUESTRIAN CLUB HAS THE VERY LAST APPLICATION FORM, RIIIGHT HERE!
FLAP
YOU GOT ENOUGH MEMBERS?!
STILL, IT'D BE A SHAME IF YOU HAD NO CHANCE AT ALL...
AFTER YOU'D FINALLY FOUND ENOUGH MEMBERS.

Chapter 8: Kinoshita-san the Savage

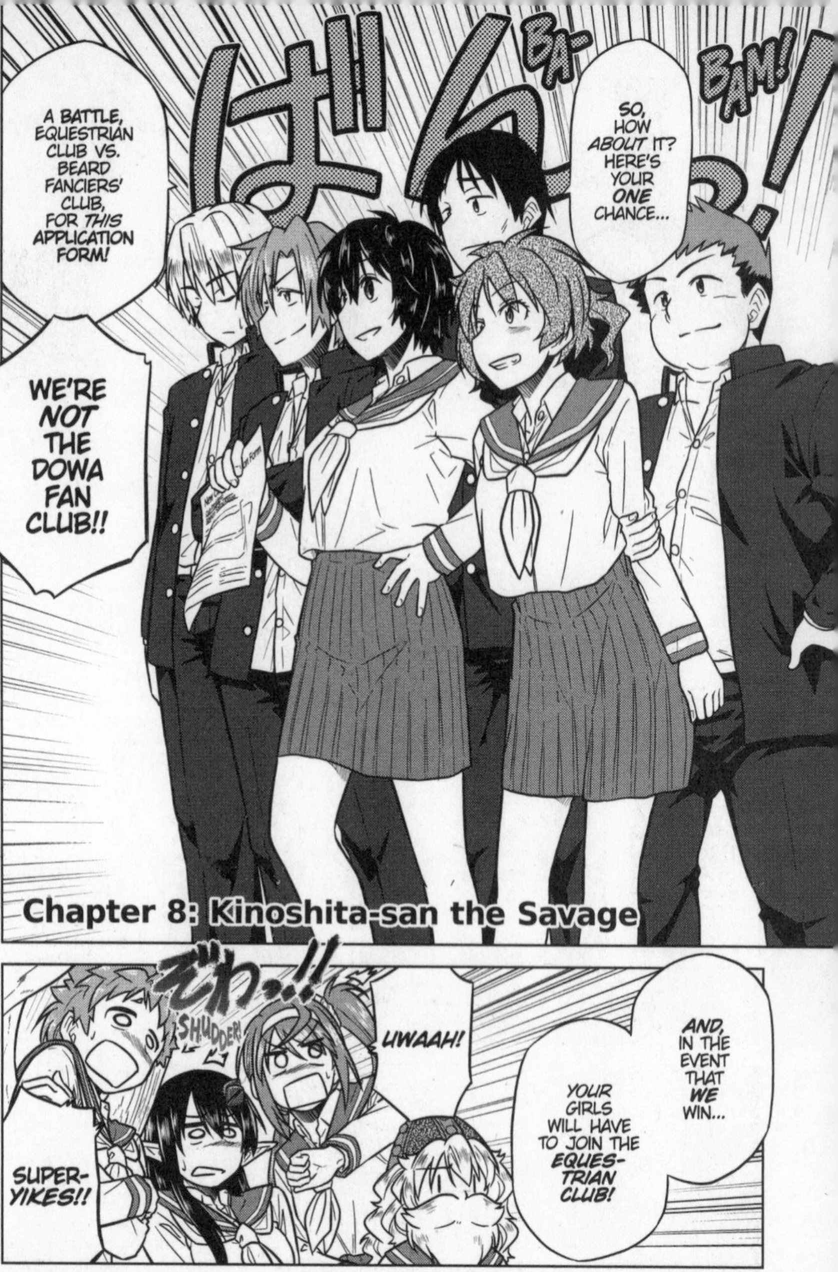

BA-BAM!!
SO, HOW *ABOUT* IT? HERE'S YOUR *ONE* CHANCE...
A BATTLE, EQUESTRIAN CLUB VS. BEARD FANCIERS' CLUB, FOR *THIS* APPLICATION FORM!
WE'RE *NOT* THE DOWA FAN CLUB!!
AND, IN THE EVENT THAT *WE* WIN...
YOUR GIRLS WILL HAVE TO JOIN THE *EQUESTRIAN CLUB!*
SHUDDER!
UWAAH!
SUPER-YIKES!!

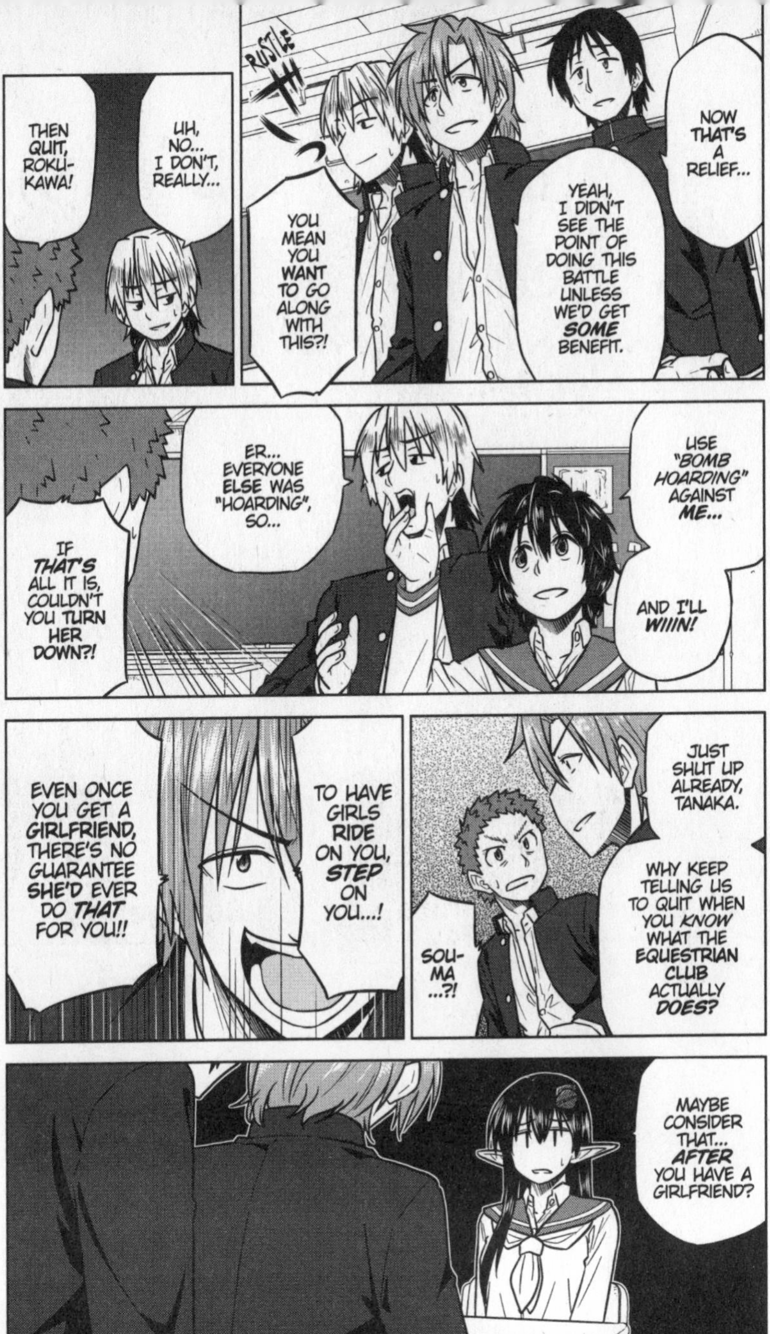

RUSTLE
NOW THAT'S A RELIEF...
YEAH, I DIDN'T SEE THE POINT OF DOING THIS BATTLE UNLESS WE'D GET **SOME** BENEFIT.
YOU MEAN YOU WANT TO GO ALONG WITH THIS?!
UH, NO... I DON'T, REALLY...
THEN QUIT, ROKU-KAWA!
USE *"BOMB HOARDING"* AGAINST ***ME...***
AND I'LL ***WIIIN!***
ER... EVERYONE ELSE WAS "HOARDING", SO...
IF ***THAT'S*** ALL IT IS, COULDN'T YOU TURN HER DOWN?!
JUST SHUT UP ALREADY, TANAKA.
WHY KEEP TELLING US TO QUIT WHEN YOU *KNOW* WHAT THE EQUESTRIAN CLUB ACTUALLY ***DOES?***
SOU-MA...?!
TO HAVE GIRLS RIDE ON YOU, ***STEP*** ON YOU...!
EVEN ONCE YOU GET A GIRLFRIEND, THERE'S NO GUARANTEE SHE'D EVER DO ***THAT*** FOR YOU!!
MAYBE CONSIDER THAT... ***AFTER*** YOU HAVE A GIRLFRIEND?

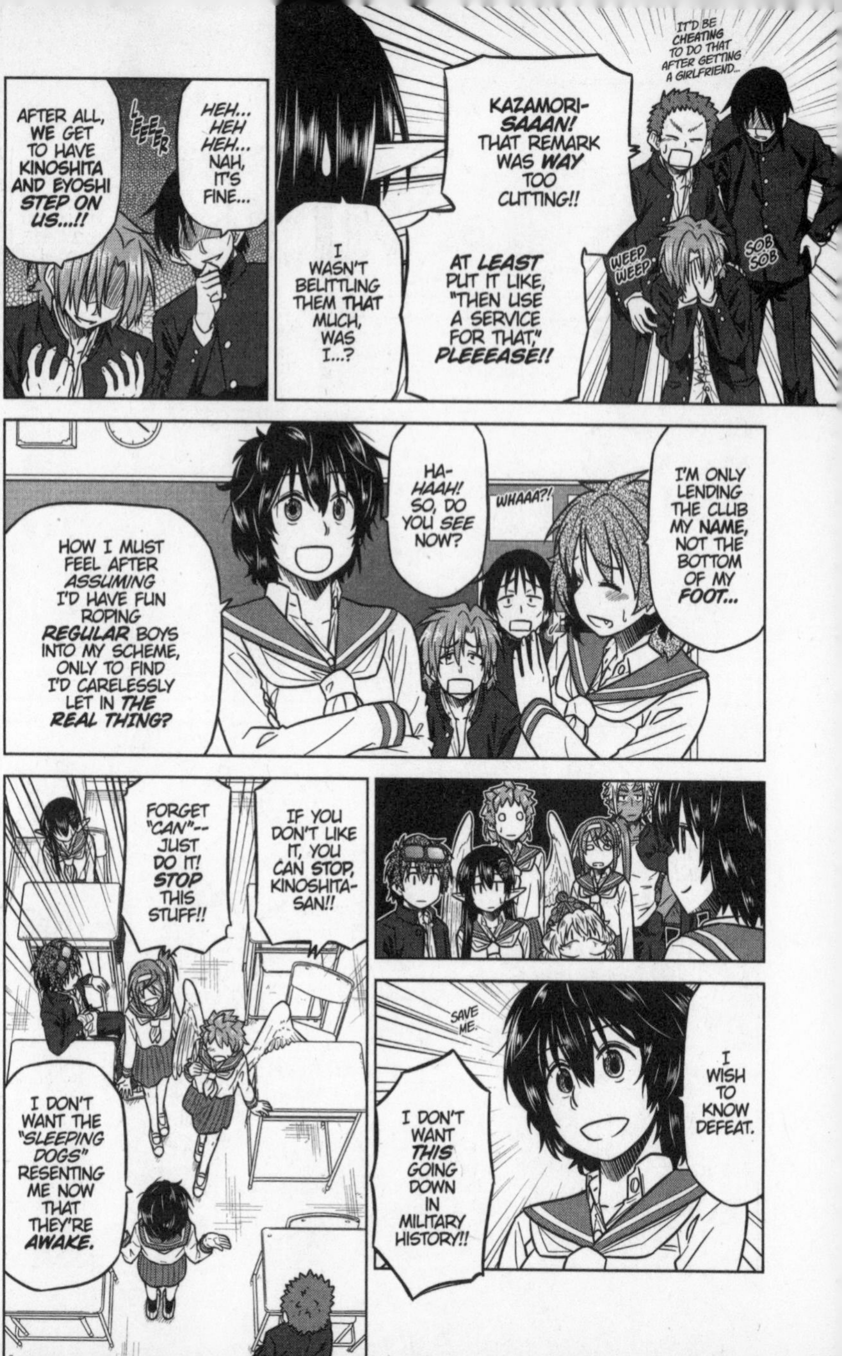

IT'D BE CHEATING TO DO THAT AFTER GETTING A GIRLFRIEND...
KAZAMORI-SAAAN! THAT REMARK WAS WAY TOO CUTTING!!
AT LEAST PUT IT LIKE, "THEN USE A SERVICE FOR THAT," PLEEEASE!!
WEEP WEEP
SOB SOB
I WASN'T BELITTLING THEM THAT MUCH, WAS I...?
HEH... HEH HEH... NAH, IT'S FINE...
LEEEER
AFTER ALL, WE GET TO HAVE KINOSHITA AND EYOSHI STEP ON US...!!
I'M ONLY LENDING THE CLUB MY NAME, NOT THE BOTTOM OF MY FOOT...
WHAAA?!
HA-HAAAH! SO, DO YOU SEE NOW?
HOW I MUST FEEL AFTER ASSUMING I'D HAVE FUN ROPING REGULAR BOYS INTO MY SCHEME, ONLY TO FIND I'D CARELESSLY LET IN THE REAL THING?
SAVE ME.
I WISH TO KNOW DEFEAT.
I DON'T WANT THIS GOING DOWN IN MILITARY HISTORY!!
IF YOU DON'T LIKE IT, YOU CAN STOP, KINOSHITA-SAN!!
FORGET "CAN"-- JUST DO IT! STOP THIS STUFF!!
I DON'T WANT THE "SLEEPING DOGS" RESENTING ME NOW THAT THEY'RE AWAKE.

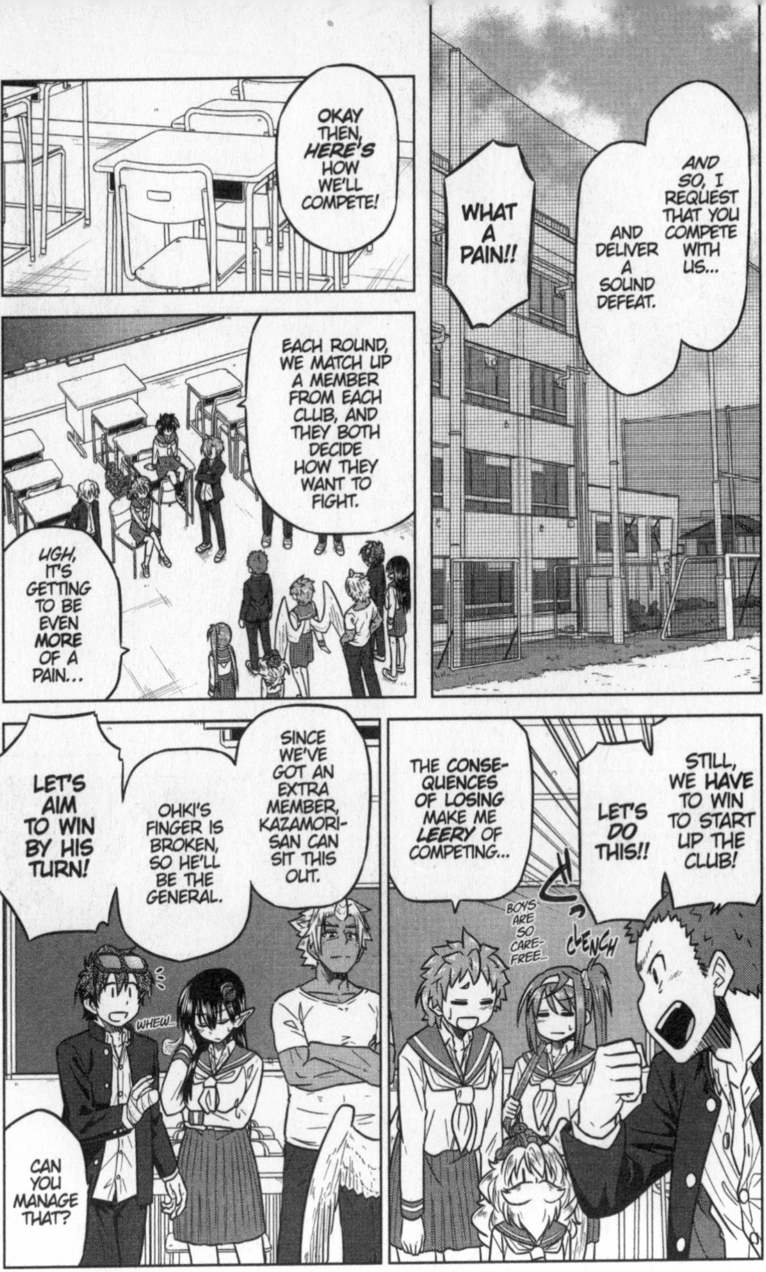
AND SO, I REQUEST THAT YOU COMPETE WITH US...
AND DELIVER A SOUND DEFEAT.
WHAT A PAIN!!
OKAY THEN, *HERE'S* HOW WE'LL COMPETE!
EACH ROUND, WE MATCH UP A MEMBER FROM EACH CLUB, AND THEY BOTH DECIDE HOW THEY WANT TO FIGHT.
UGH, IT'S GETTING TO BE EVEN MORE OF A PAIN...
STILL, WE HAVE TO WIN TO START UP THE CLUB!
LET'S *DO* THIS!!
CLENCH
BOYS ARE SO CAREFREE...
THE CONSEQUENCES OF LOSING MAKE ME *LEERY* OF COMPETING...
SINCE WE'VE GOT AN EXTRA MEMBER, KAZAMORI-SAN CAN SIT THIS OUT.
OHKI'S FINGER IS BROKEN, SO HE'LL BE THE GENERAL.
LET'S AIM TO WIN BY HIS TURN!
WHEW...
CAN YOU MANAGE THAT?

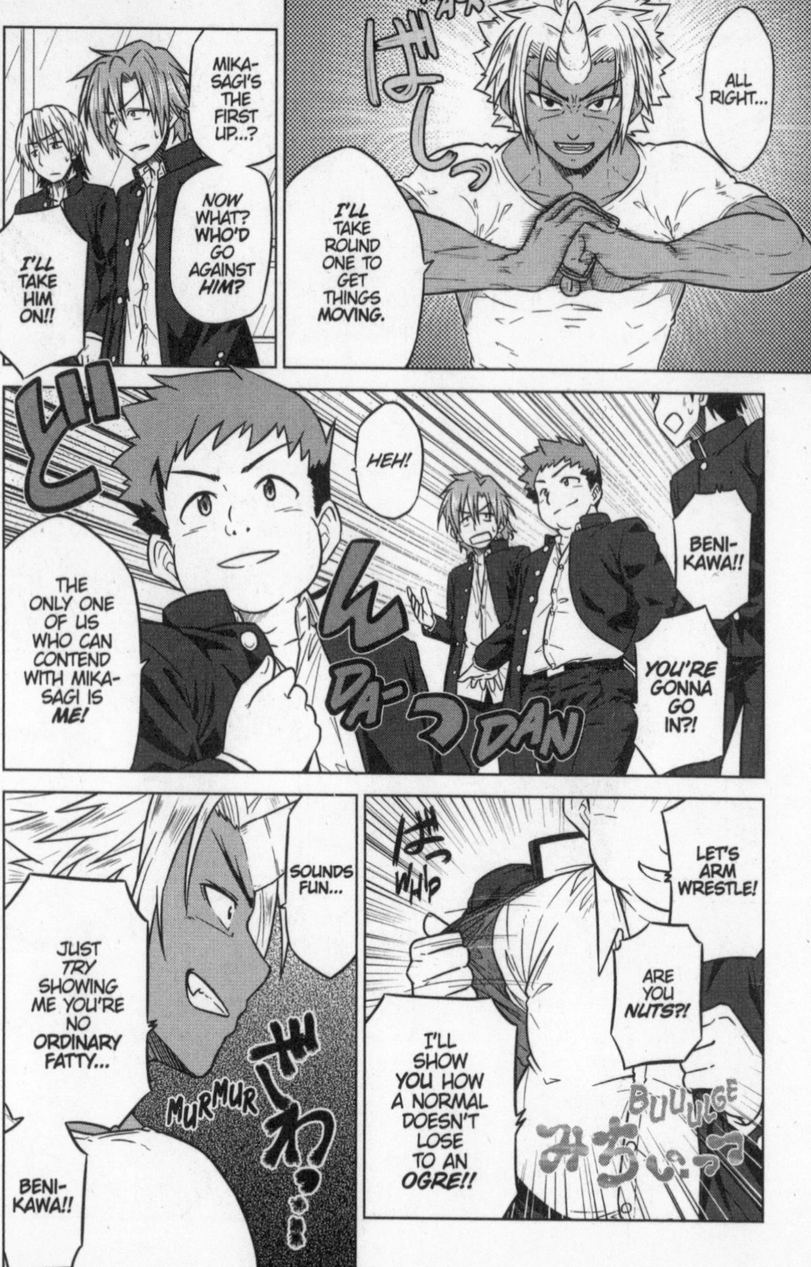
SMACK
ALL RIGHT...
I'LL TAKE ROUND ONE TO GET THINGS MOVING.
MIKA-SAGI'S THE FIRST UP...?
NOW WHAT? WHO'D GO AGAINST *HIM*?
I'LL TAKE HIM ON!!
BENI-KAWA!!
YOU'RE GONNA GO IN?!
HEH!
THE ONLY ONE OF US WHO CAN CONTEND WITH MIKA-SAGI IS *ME!*
DAN
DA-
LET'S ARM WRESTLE!
WHIP
ARE YOU *NUTS?!*
I'LL SHOW YOU HOW A NORMAL DOESN'T LOSE TO AN *OGRE!!*
BUUULGE
SOUNDS FUN...
JUST *TRY* SHOWING ME YOU'RE NO ORDINARY FATTY...
MURMUR
BENI-KAWA!!

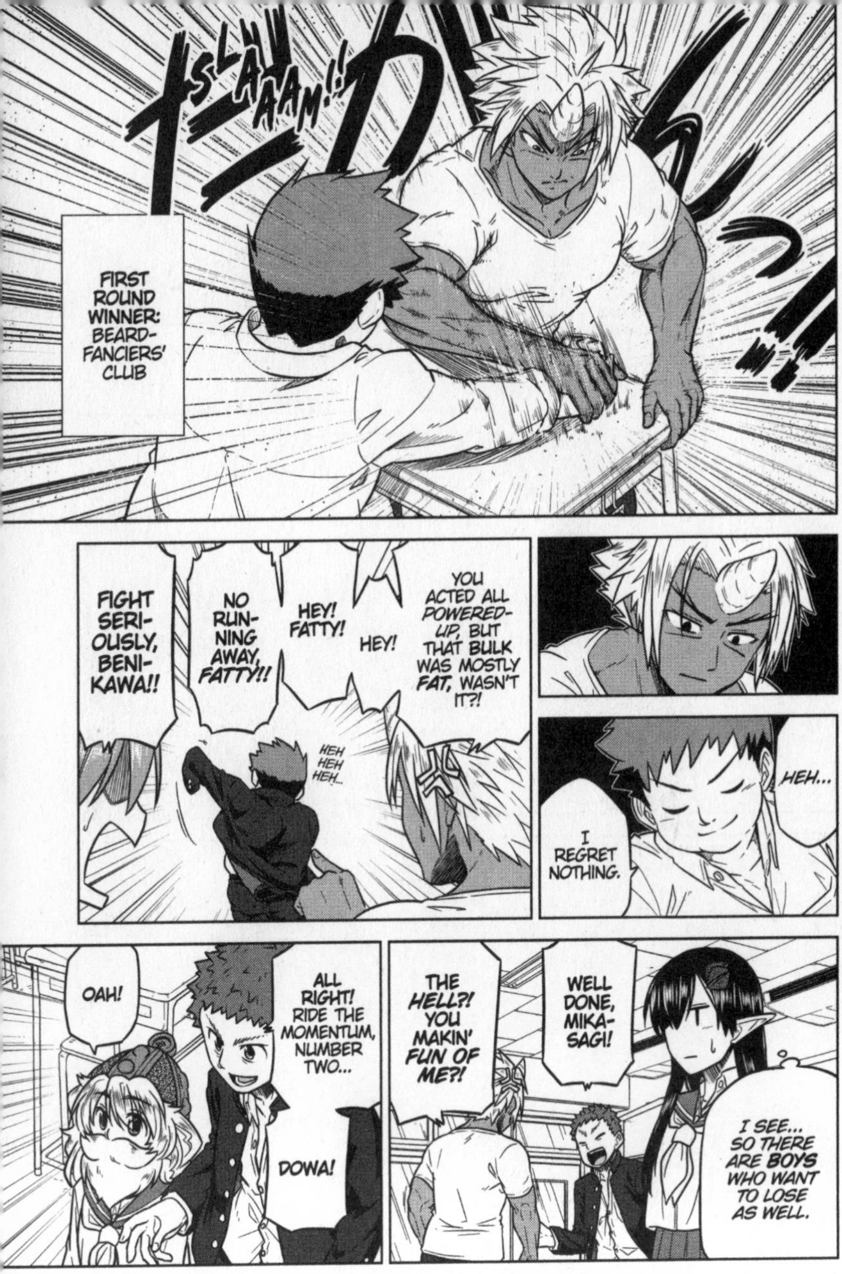
SLAAAAM!!
FIRST ROUND WINNER: BEARD-FANCIERS' CLUB
HEH...
I REGRET NOTHING.
YOU ACTED ALL POWERED-UP, BUT THAT BULK WAS MOSTLY FAT, WASN'T IT?!
HEY!
HEY! FATTY!
NO RUNNING AWAY, FATTY!!
FIGHT SERIOUSLY, BENIKAWA!!
HEH HEH HEH...
WELL DONE, MIKASAGI!
THE HELL?! YOU MAKIN' FUN OF ME?!
I SEE... SO THERE ARE BOYS WHO WANT TO LOSE AS WELL.
ALL RIGHT! RIDE THE MOMENTUM, NUMBER TWO...
OAH!
DOWA!

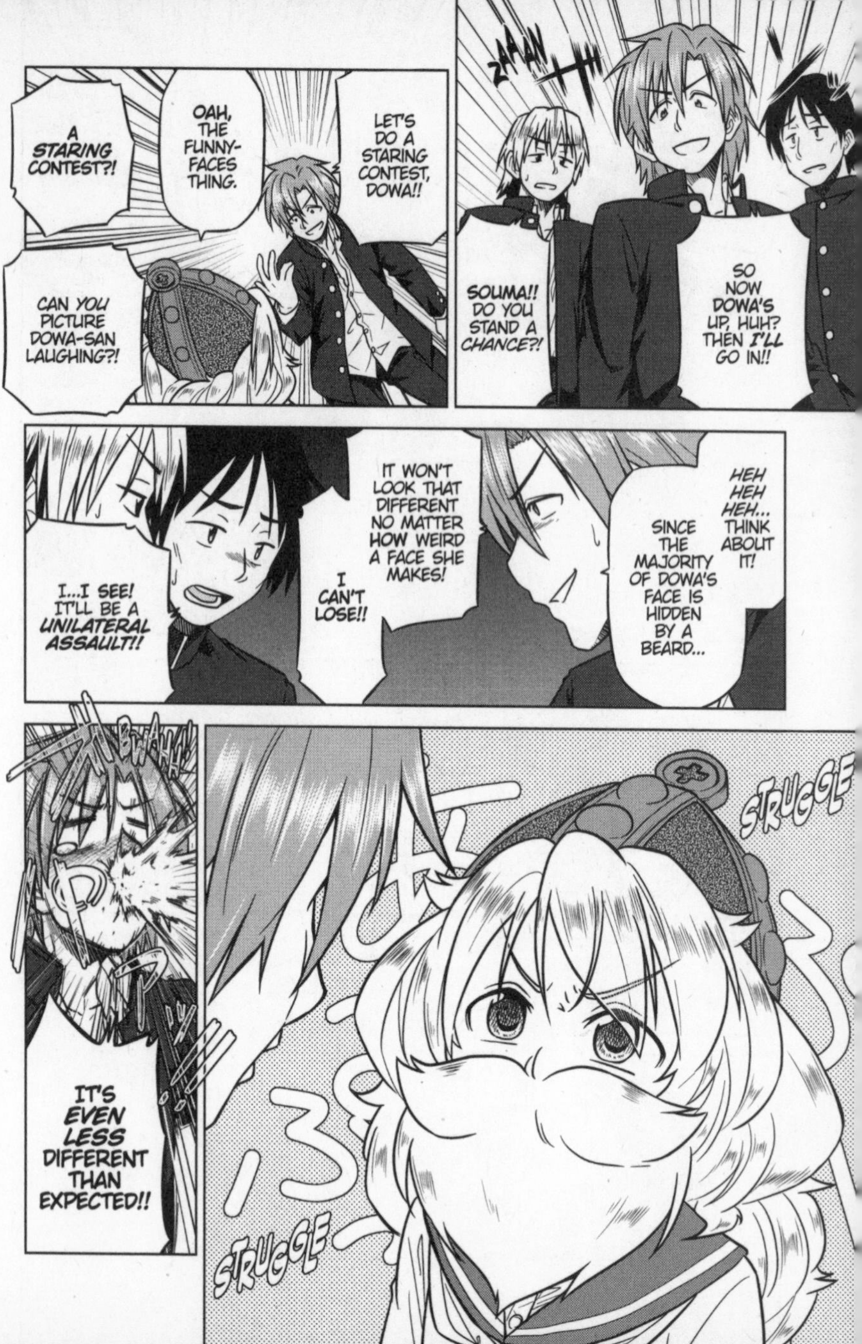
ZAAAN
SO NOW DOWA'S UP, HUH? THEN I'LL GO IN!!
SOUMA!! DO YOU STAND A CHANCE?!
LET'S DO A STARING CONTEST, DOWA!!
OAH, THE FUNNY-FACES THING.
A STARING CONTEST?!
CAN YOU PICTURE DOWA-SAN LAUGHING?!
HEH HEH HEH... THINK ABOUT IT!
SINCE THE MAJORITY OF DOWA'S FACE IS HIDDEN BY A BEARD...
IT WON'T LOOK THAT DIFFERENT NO MATTER HOW WEIRD A FACE SHE MAKES!
I CAN'T LOSE!!
I...I SEE! IT'LL BE A UNILATERAL ASSAULT!!
STRUGGLE
STRUGGLE
BWAHA!!
IT'S EVEN LESS DIFFERENT THAN EXPECTED!!

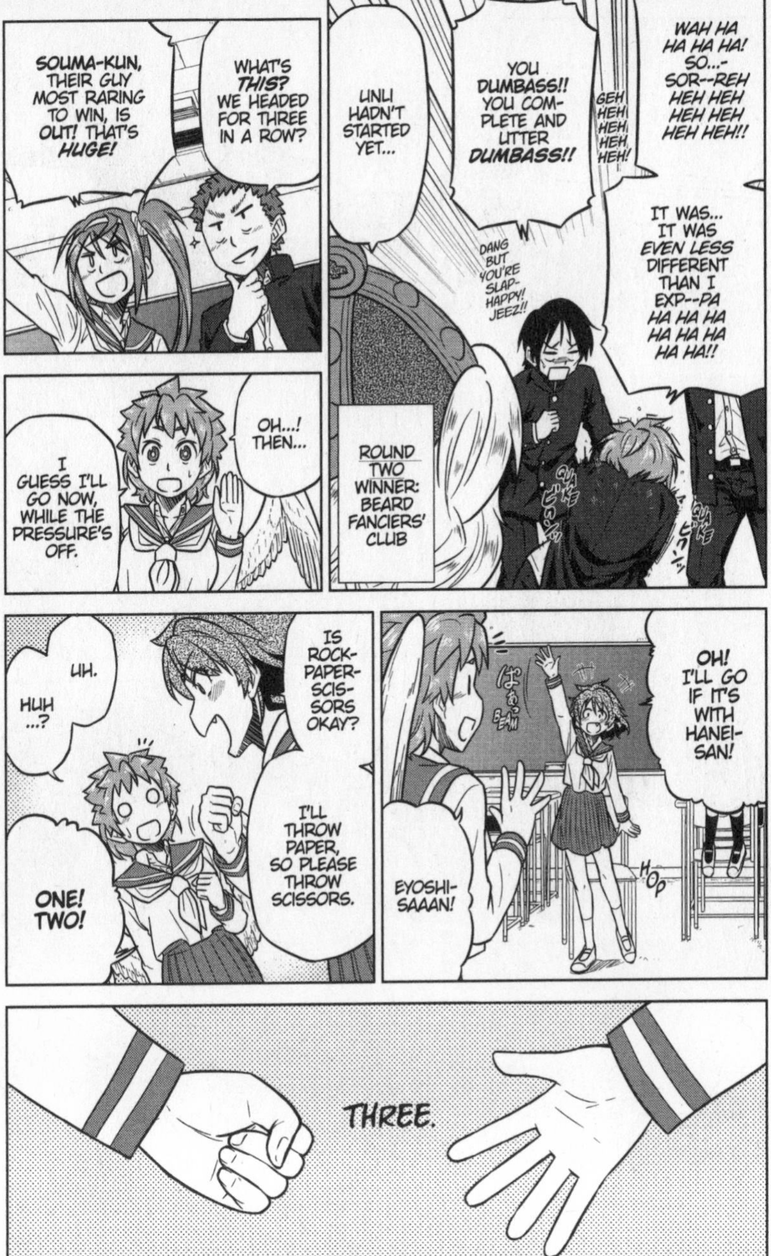
WAH HA HA HA! SO...- SOR--REH HEH HEH HEH HEH HEH HEH!!
GEH HEH HEH HEH HEH!
YOU DUMBASS!! YOU COMPLETE AND UTTER DUMBASS!!
UNLI HADN'T STARTED YET...
IT WAS... IT WAS EVEN LESS DIFFERENT THAN I EXP--PA HA HA HA HA HA HA HA HA!!
DANG BUT YOU'RE SLAP-HAPPY! JEEZ!!
QUAKE
QUAKE
ROUND TWO WINNER: BEARD FANCIERS' CLUB
WHAT'S THIS? WE HEADED FOR THREE IN A ROW?
SOUMA-KUN, THEIR GUY MOST RARING TO WIN, IS OUT! THAT'S HUGE!
OH...! THEN...
I GUESS I'LL GO NOW, WHILE THE PRESSURE'S OFF.
OH! I'LL GO IF IT'S WITH HANEI-SAN!
BEAM
HOP
EYOSHI-SAAAN!
IS ROCK-PAPER-SCISSORS OKAY?
UH.
HUH ...?
I'LL THROW PAPER, SO PLEASE THROW SCISSORS.
ONE! TWO!
THREE.

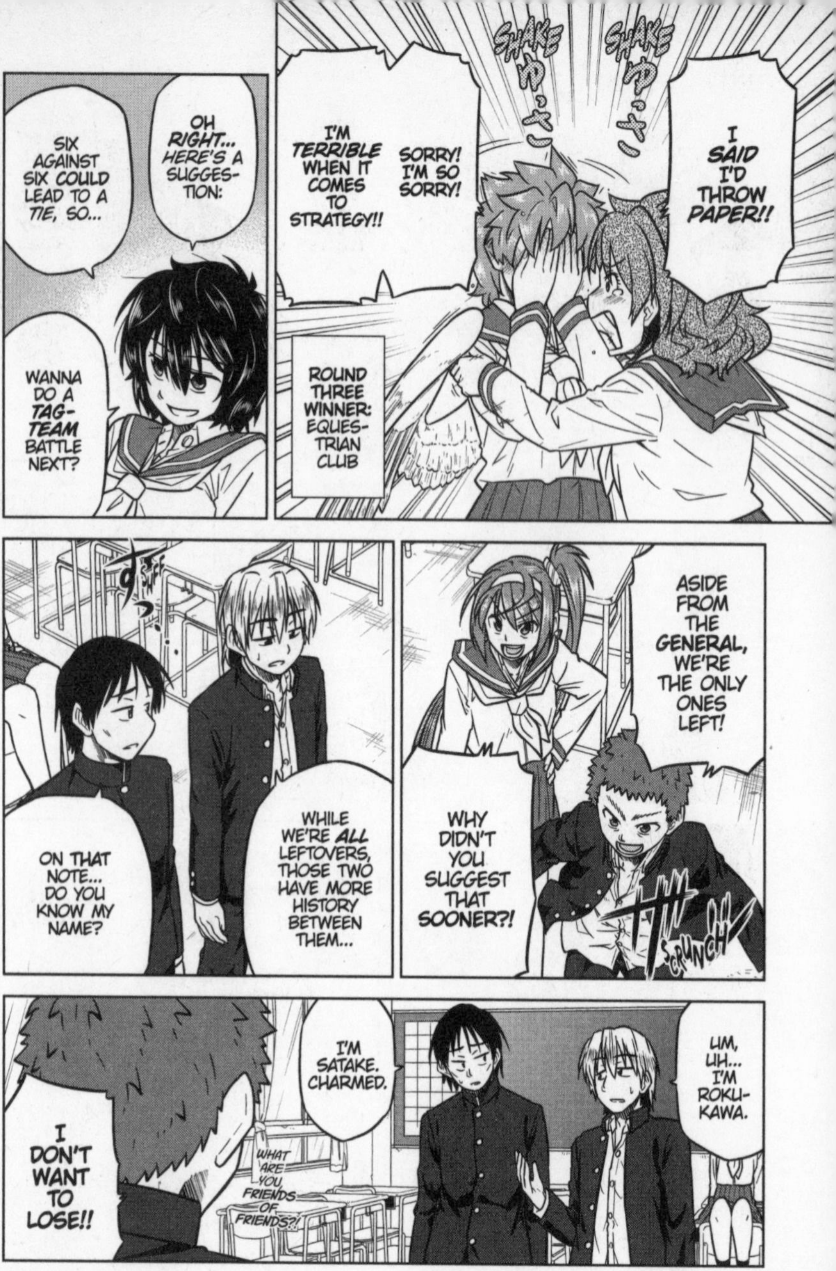
SHAKE
SHAKE
I SAID I'D THROW PAPER!!
SORRY! I'M SO SORRY!
I'M TERRIBLE WHEN IT COMES TO STRATEGY!!
ROUND THREE WINNER: EQUESTRIAN CLUB
OH RIGHT... HERE'S A SUGGESTION:
SIX AGAINST SIX COULD LEAD TO A TIE, SO...
WANNA DO A TAG-TEAM BATTLE NEXT?
ASIDE FROM THE GENERAL, WE'RE THE ONLY ONES LEFT!
WHY DIDN'T YOU SUGGEST THAT SOONER?!
SCRUNCH
STIFF
WHILE WE'RE ALL LEFTOVERS, THOSE TWO HAVE MORE HISTORY BETWEEN THEM...
ON THAT NOTE... DO YOU KNOW MY NAME?
UM, UH... I'M ROKUKAWA.
I'M SATAKE. CHARMED.
WHAT ARE YOU, FRIENDS OF FRIENDS?!
I DON'T WANT TO LOSE!!

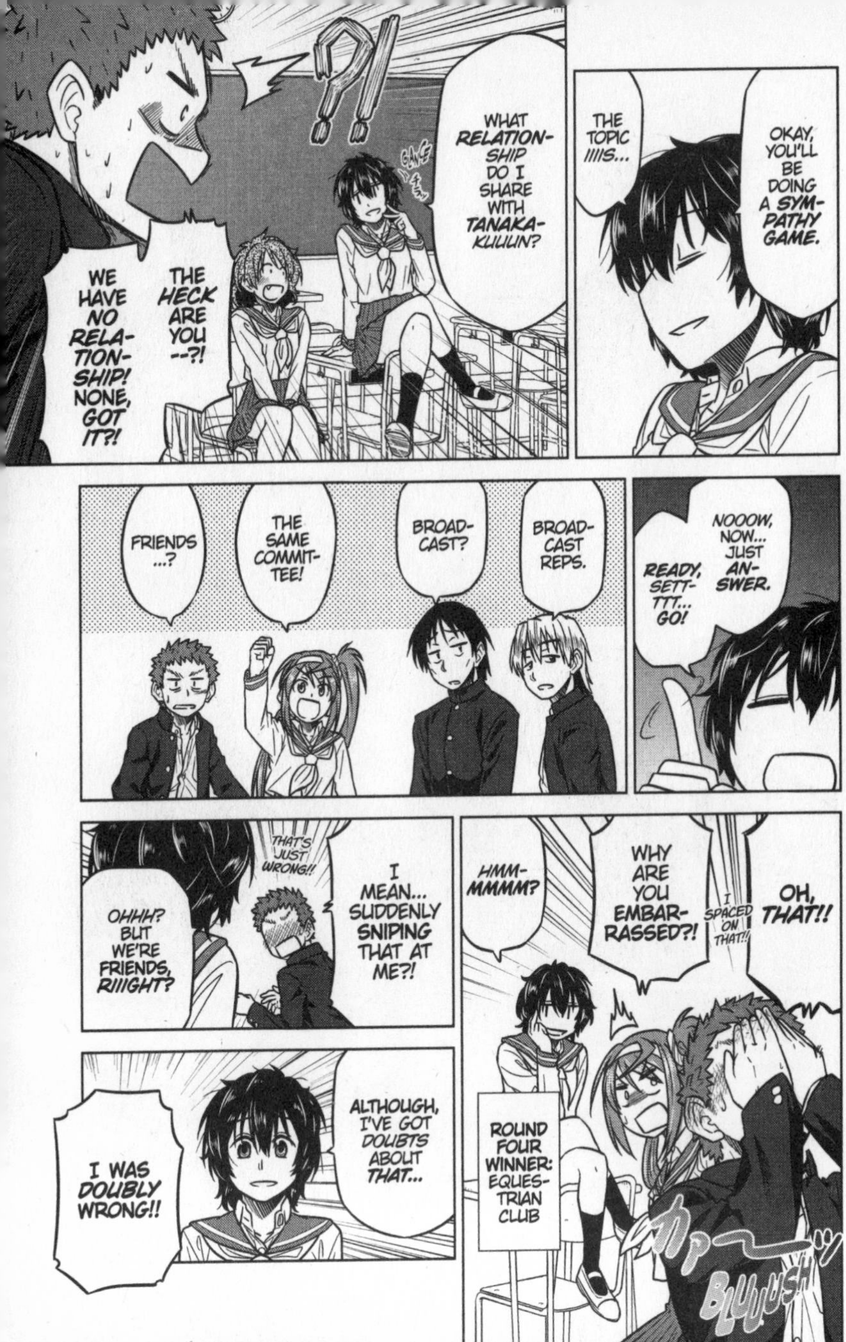
OKAY, YOU'LL BE DOING A SYMPATHY GAME.
THE TOPIC IIIIS...
WHAT RELATIONSHIP DO I SHARE WITH TANAKA-KUUUN?
?!
THE HECK ARE YOU--?!
WE HAVE NO RELATIONSHIP! NONE, GOT IT?!
NOOOW, NOW... JUST ANSWER.
READY, SETTTTT... GO!
BROADCAST REPS.
BROADCAST?
THE SAME COMMITTEE!
FRIENDS...?
OH, THAT!!
I SPACED ON THAT!!
WHY ARE YOU EMBARRASSED?!
HMM-MMMM?
ROUND FOUR WINNER: EQUESTRIAN CLUB
BLUUUSH
I MEAN... SUDDENLY SNIPING THAT AT ME?!
THAT'S JUST WRONG!!
OHHH? BUT WE'RE FRIENDS, RIIIGHT?
ALTHOUGH, I'VE GOT DOUBTS ABOUT THAT...
I WAS DOUBLY WRONG!!

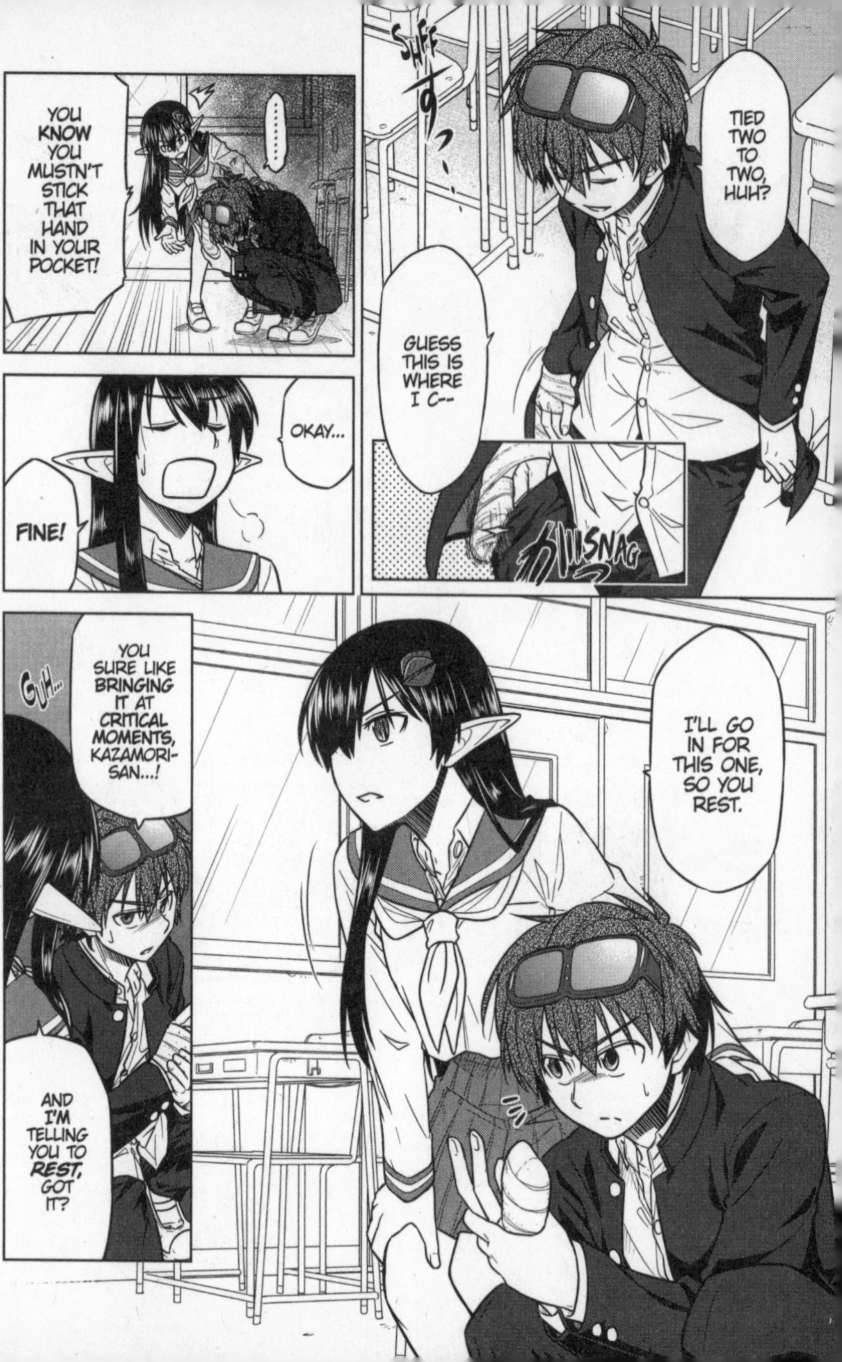
TIED TWO TO TWO, HUH?
SHFF
GUESS THIS IS WHERE I C--
SNAG
......
YOU KNOW YOU MUSTN'T STICK THAT HAND IN YOUR POCKET!
OKAY...
FINE!
I'LL GO IN FOR THIS ONE, SO YOU REST.
YOU SURE LIKE BRINGING IT AT CRITICAL MOMENTS, KAZAMORI-SAN...!
GUH...
AND I'M TELLING YOU TO *REST,* GOT IT?

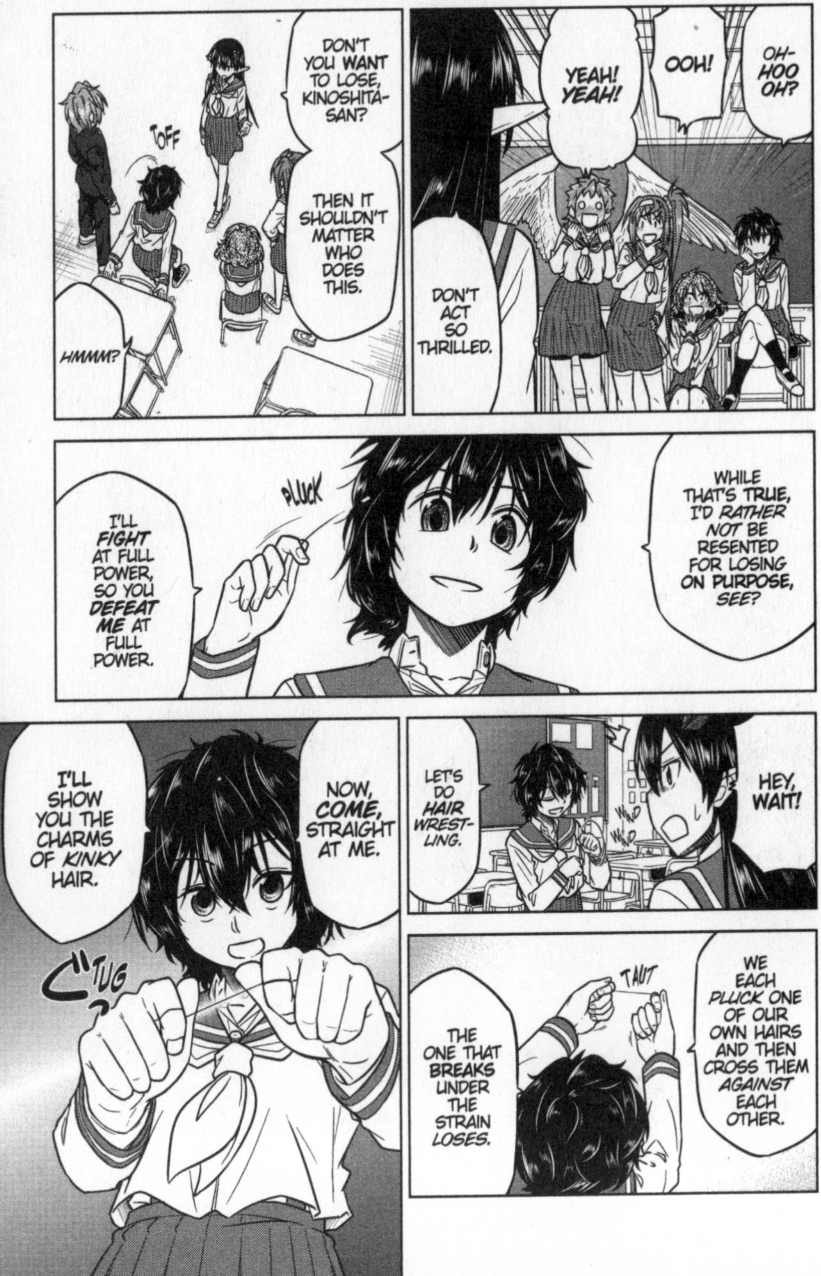
OH-HOO OH?
OOH!
YEAH! YEAH!
DON'T ACT SO THRILLED.
DON'T YOU WANT TO LOSE, KINOSHITA-SAN?
THEN IT SHOULDN'T MATTER WHO DOES THIS.
TOFF
HMMM?
WHILE THAT'S TRUE, I'D *RATHER NOT* BE RESENTED FOR LOSING **ON PURPOSE**, SEE?
PLUCK
I'LL ***FIGHT*** AT FULL POWER, SO YOU ***DEFEAT ME*** AT FULL POWER.
HEY, WAIT!
WIND WIND
LET'S DO *HAIR WRESTLING*.
WE EACH *PLUCK* ONE OF OUR OWN HAIRS AND THEN CROSS THEM *AGAINST* EACH OTHER.
TAUT
THE ONE THAT **BREAKS** UNDER THE STRAIN *LOSES*.
NOW, ***COME***, STRAIGHT AT ME.
I'LL SHOW YOU THE CHARMS OF *KINKY* HAIR.
TUG

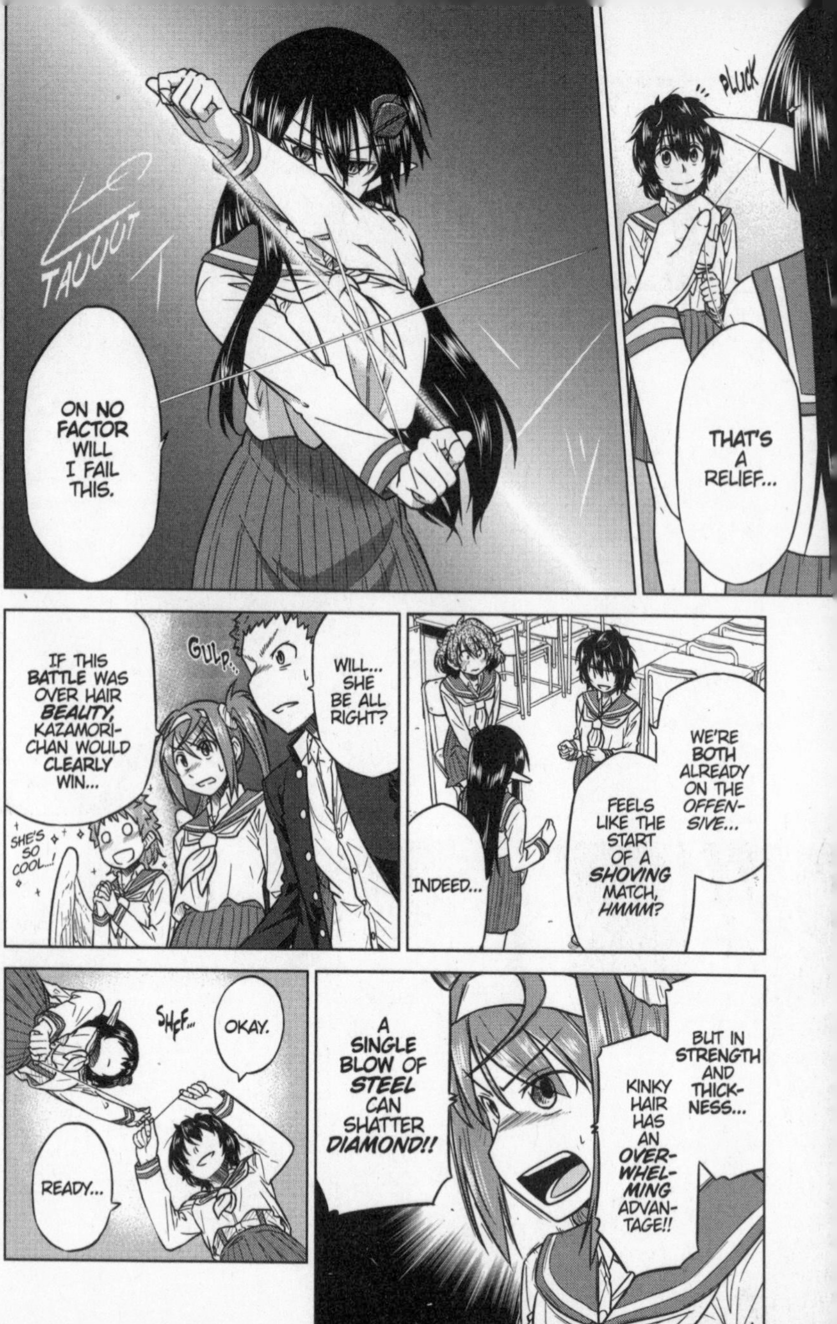
PLUCK
THAT'S A RELIEF...
TAUUUT
ON NO FACTOR WILL I FAIL THIS.
WE'RE BOTH ALREADY ON THE OFFEN-SIVE...
FEELS LIKE THE START OF A ***SHOVING*** MATCH, *HMMM?*
INDEED...
WILL... SHE BE ALL RIGHT?
GULP...
IF THIS BATTLE WAS OVER HAIR ***BEAUTY,*** KAZAMORI-CHAN WOULD CLEARLY WIN...
SHE'S SO COOL...!
BUT IN STRENGTH AND THICK-NESS...
KINKY HAIR HAS AN ***OVER-WHEL-MING*** ADVAN-TAGE!!
A SINGLE BLOW OF ***STEEL*** CAN SHATTER ***DIAMOND!!***
OKAY.
SHEF...
READY...

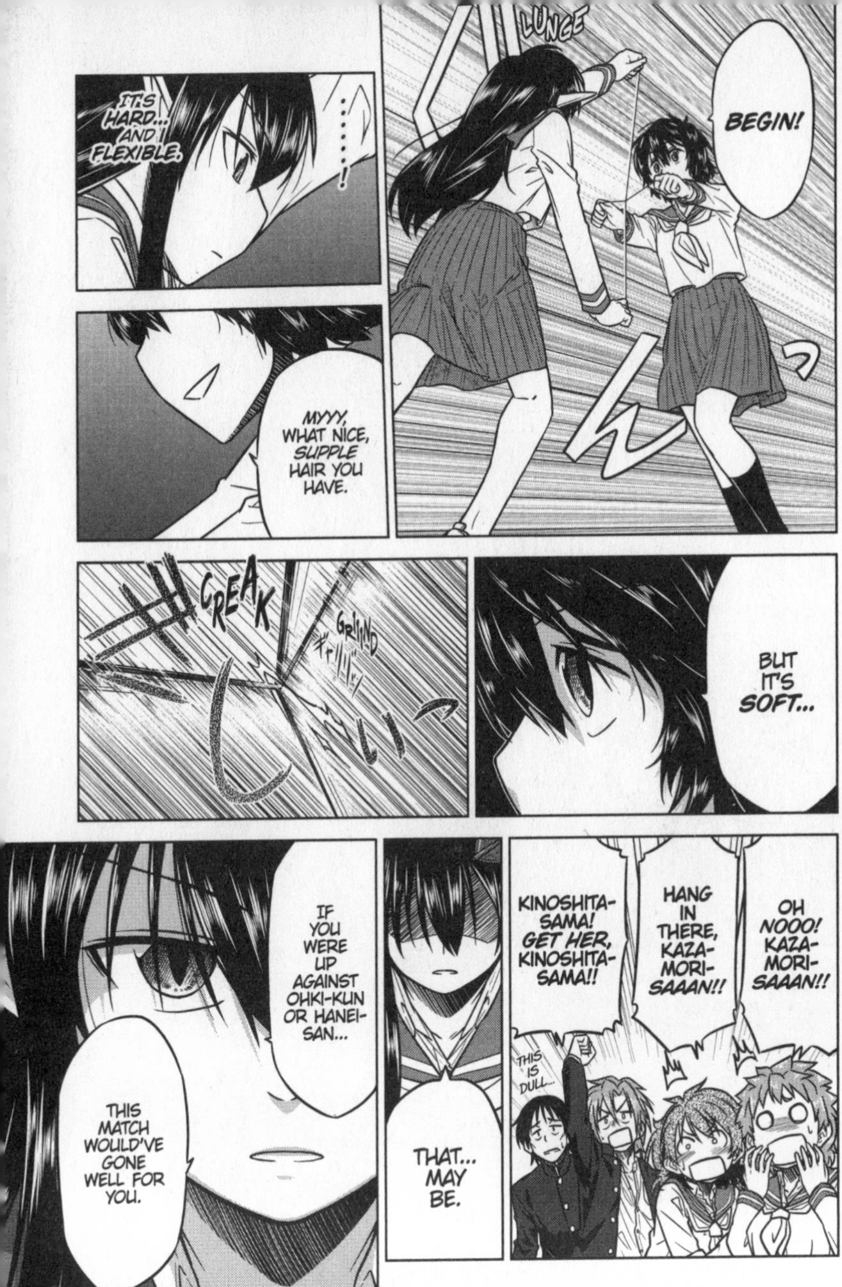
LUNGE
BEGIN!
IT'S HARD... AND FLEXIBLE.
......!
MYYY, WHAT NICE, SUPPLE HAIR YOU HAVE.
BUT IT'S SOFT...
CREAK
GRIIND
OH NOOO! KAZAMORI-SAAAN!!
HANG IN THERE, KAZAMORI-SAAAN!!
KINOSHITA-SAMA! GET HER, KINOSHITA-SAMA!!
THIS IS DULL...
THAT... MAY BE.
IF YOU WERE UP AGAINST OHKI-KUN OR HANEI-SAN...
THIS MATCH WOULD'VE GONE WELL FOR YOU.

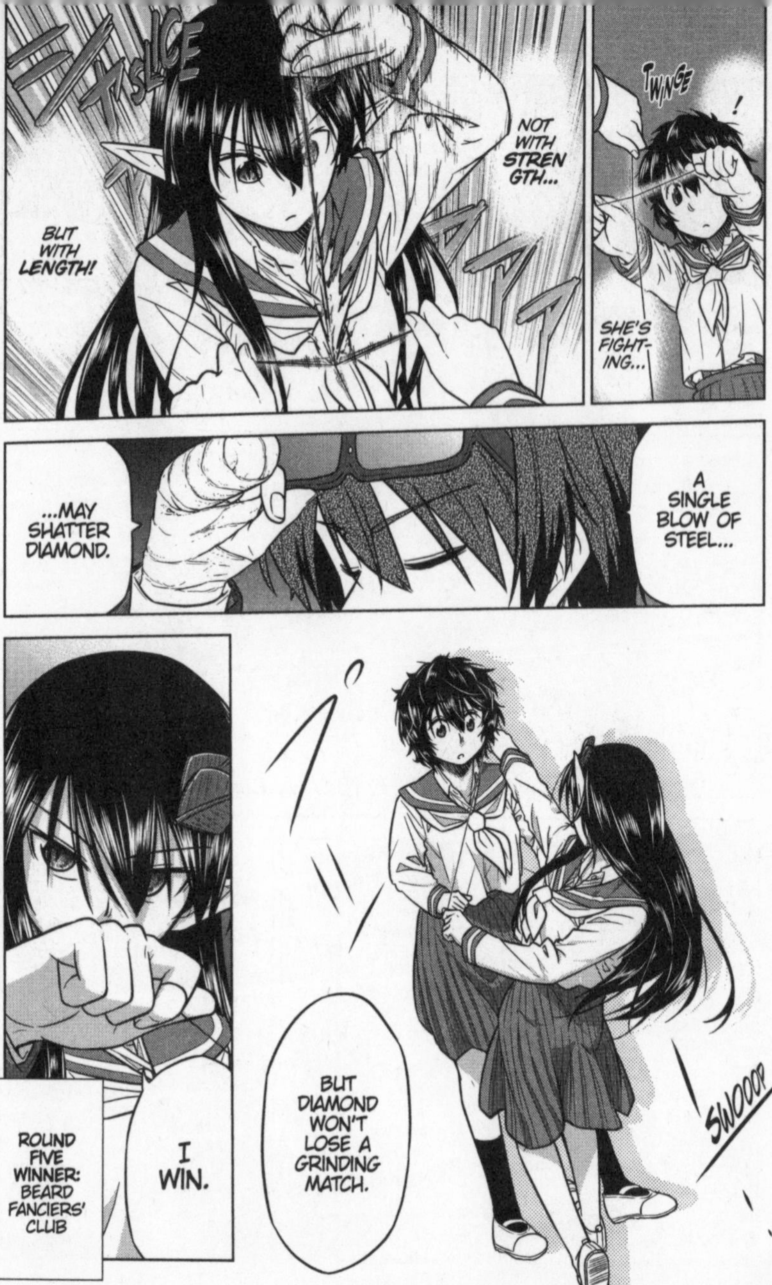
TWINGE
!
SHE'S FIGHTING...
SLICE
NOT WITH STRENGTH...
BUT WITH LENGTH!
A SINGLE BLOW OF STEEL...
...MAY SHATTER DIAMOND.
SWOOOP
BUT DIAMOND WON'T LOSE A GRINDING MATCH.
I WIN.
ROUND FIVE WINNER: BEARD FANCIERS' CLUB

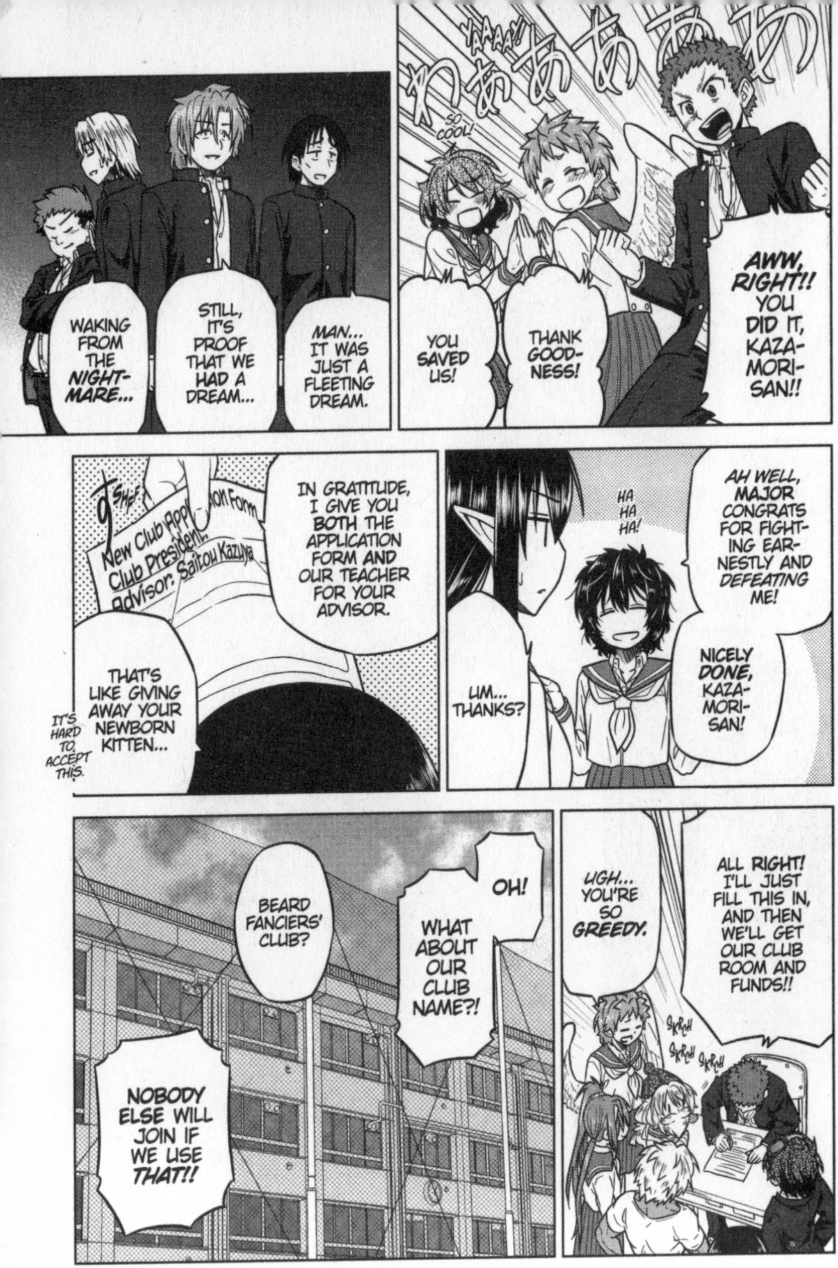

YAAAA!!
SO COOL!
AWW, RIGHT!! YOU DID IT, KAZAMORI-SAN!!
THANK GOODNESS!
YOU SAVED US!
MAN... IT WAS JUST A FLEETING DREAM.
STILL, IT'S PROOF THAT WE HAD A DREAM...
WAKING FROM THE NIGHTMARE...
AH WELL, MAJOR CONGRATS FOR FIGHTING EARNESTLY AND DEFEATING ME!
HA HA HA!
NICELY DONE, KAZAMORI-SAN!
UM... THANKS?
IN GRATITUDE, I GIVE YOU BOTH THE APPLICATION FORM AND OUR TEACHER FOR YOUR ADVISOR.
SHF
Club President:
Advisor: Saitou Kazuya
THAT'S LIKE GIVING AWAY YOUR NEWBORN KITTEN...
IT'S HARD TO ACCEPT THIS.
ALL RIGHT! I'LL JUST FILL THIS IN, AND THEN WE'LL GET OUR CLUB ROOM AND FUNDS!!
UGH... YOU'RE SO GREEDY.
SKRCH
SKRCH
SKRCH
OH!
WHAT ABOUT OUR CLUB NAME?!
BEARD FANCIERS' CLUB?
NOBODY ELSE WILL JOIN IF WE USE THAT!!

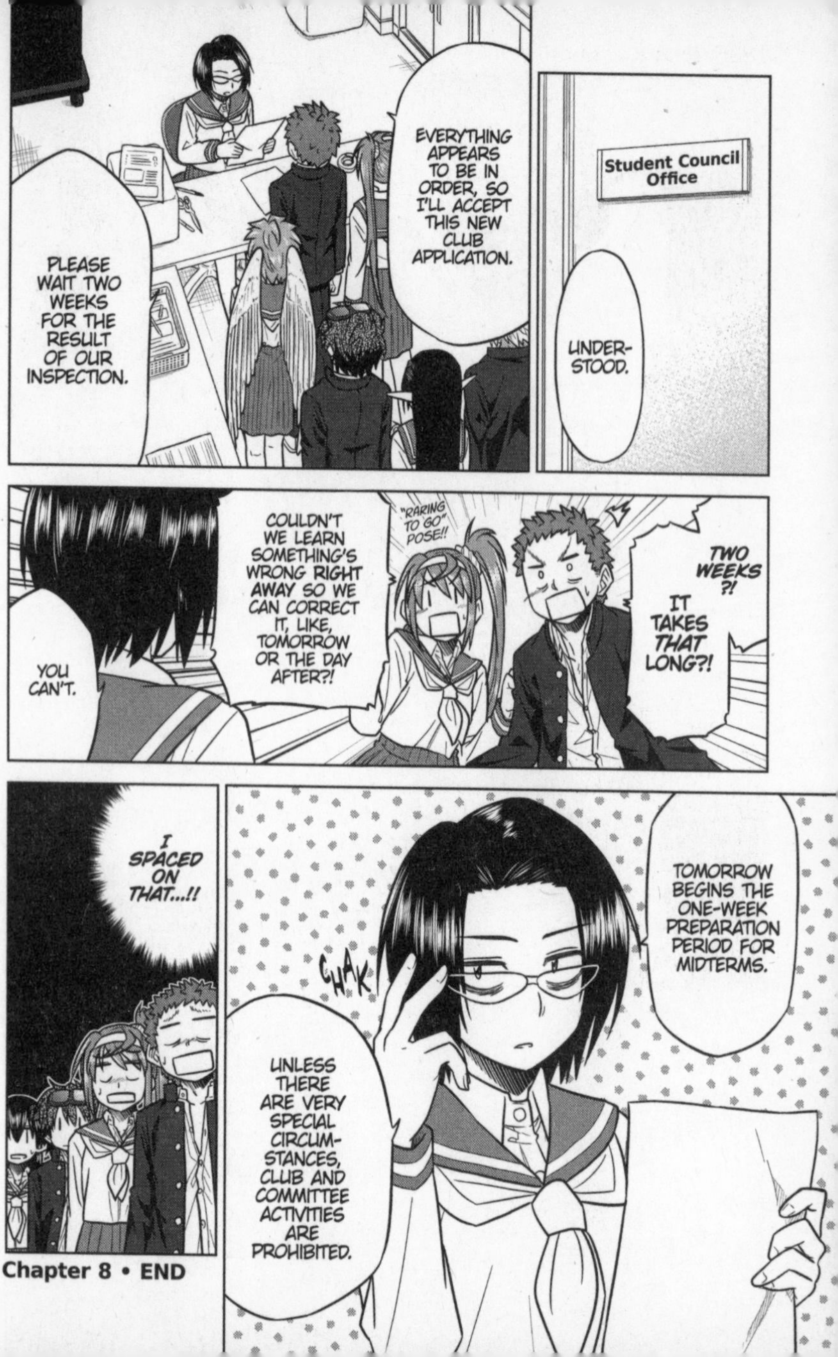
Student Council Office
UNDERSTOOD.
EVERYTHING APPEARS TO BE IN ORDER, SO I'LL ACCEPT THIS NEW CLUB APPLICATION.
PLEASE WAIT TWO WEEKS FOR THE RESULT OF OUR INSPECTION.
TWO WEEKS?!
IT TAKES THAT LONG?!
"RARING TO GO" POSE!!
COULDN'T WE LEARN SOMETHING'S WRONG RIGHT AWAY SO WE CAN CORRECT IT, LIKE, TOMORROW OR THE DAY AFTER?!
YOU CAN'T.
TOMORROW BEGINS THE ONE-WEEK PREPARATION PERIOD FOR MIDTERMS.
CHAK
UNLESS THERE ARE VERY SPECIAL CIRCUM-STANCES, CLUB AND COMMITTEE ACTIVITIES ARE PROHIBITED.
I SPACED ON THAT...!!

Chapter 8 • END

Chapter 9: Kazamori-san Learns

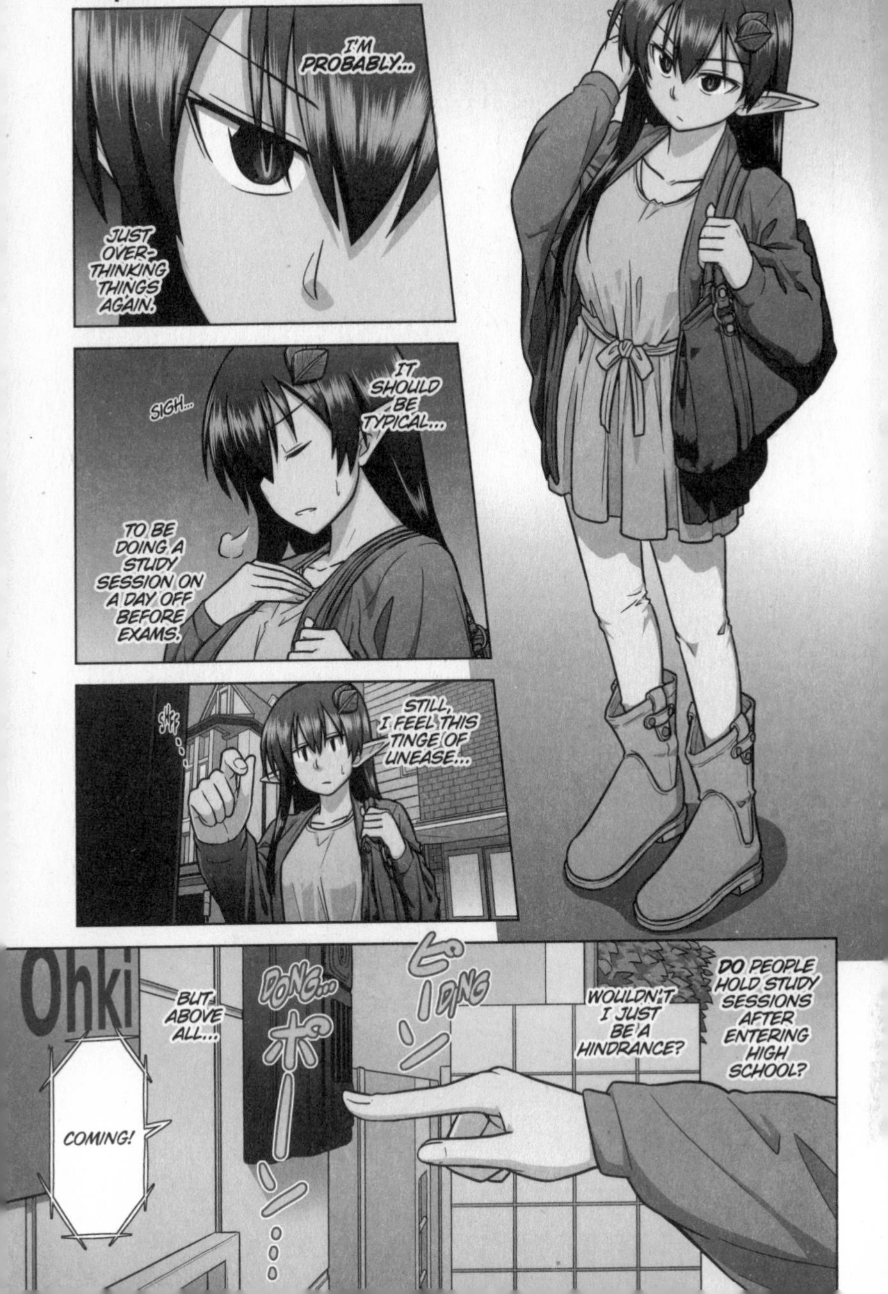
I'M PROBABLY...
JUST OVER-THINKING THINGS AGAIN.
IT SHOULD BE TYPICAL...
SIGH...
TO BE DOING A STUDY SESSION ON A DAY OFF BEFORE EXAMS.
STILL, I FEEL THIS TINGE OF UNEASE...
SNIFF
DO PEOPLE HOLD STUDY SESSIONS AFTER ENTERING HIGH SCHOOL?
WOULDN'T I JUST BE A HINDRANCE?
ピン
DING
DONG...
ポーン
BUT ABOVE ALL...
Ohki
COMING!

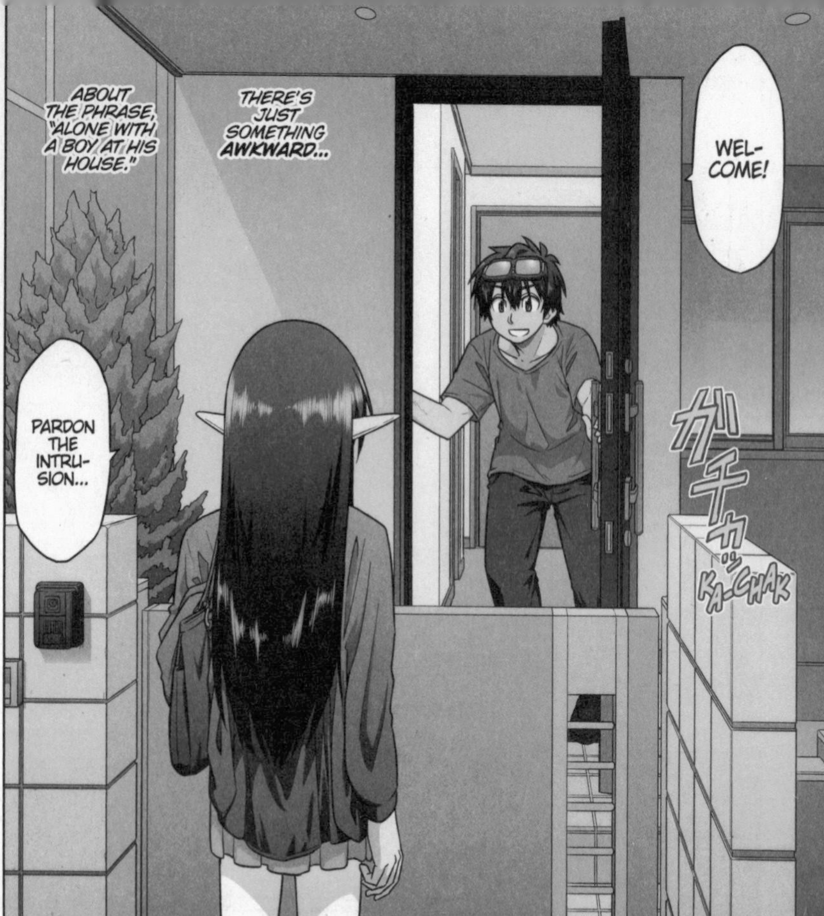
WEL-COME!
ガチャッ
KA-CHAK
THERE'S JUST SOMETHING AWKWARD...
ABOUT THE PHRASE, "ALONE WITH A BOY AT HIS HOUSE."
PARDON THE INTRU-SION...

Chapter 9: Kazamori-san Learns

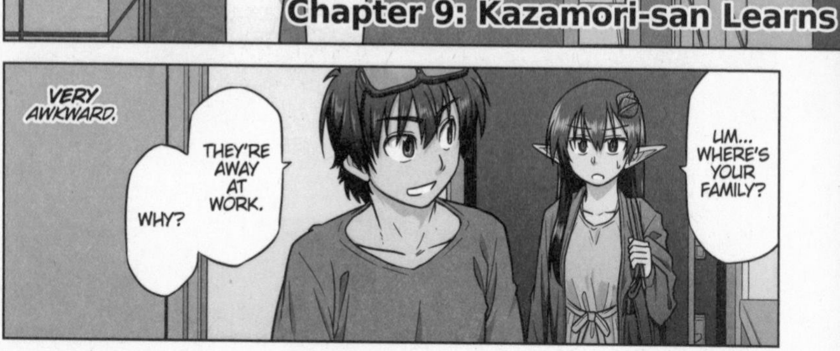
UM... WHERE'S YOUR FAMILY?
THEY'RE AWAY AT WORK.
WHY?
VERY AWKWARD.

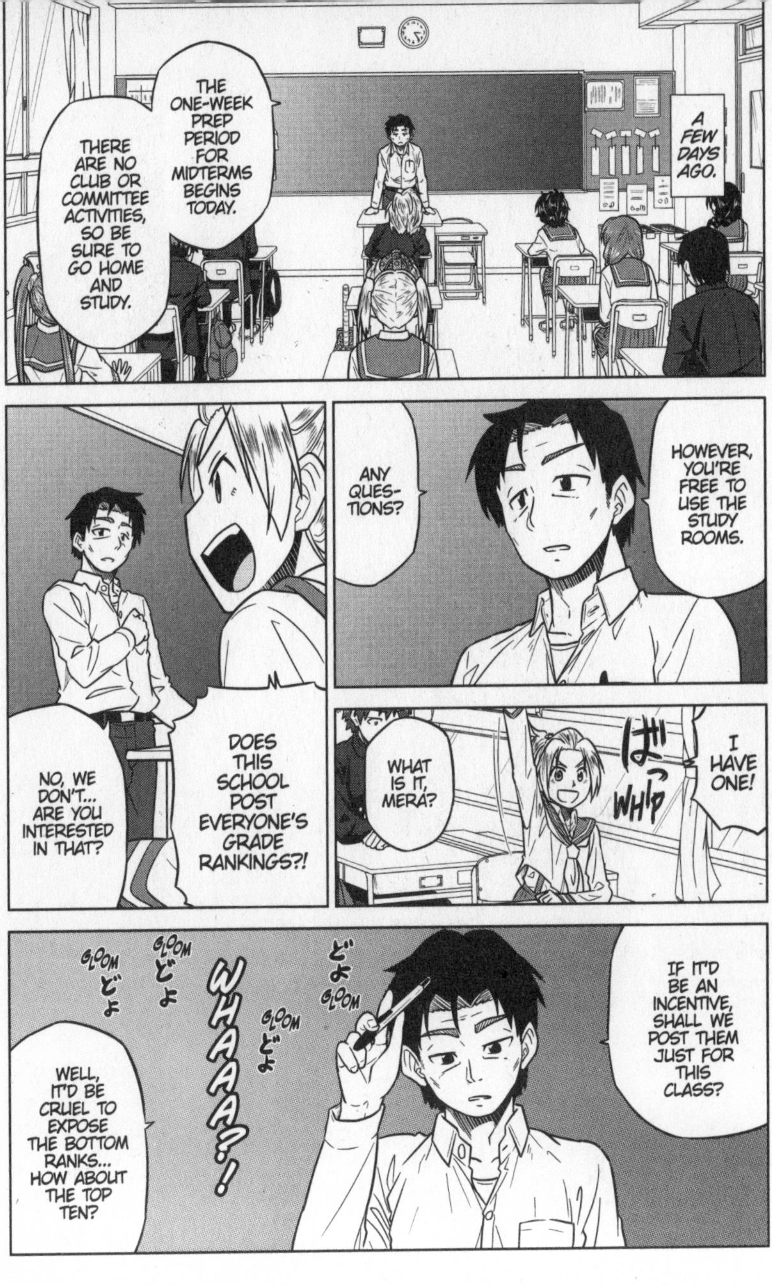

A FEW DAYS AGO.
THE ONE-WEEK PREP PERIOD FOR MIDTERMS BEGINS TODAY.
THERE ARE NO CLUB OR COMMITTEE ACTIVITIES, SO BE SURE TO GO HOME AND STUDY.
HOWEVER, YOU'RE FREE TO USE THE STUDY ROOMS.
ANY QUES-TIONS?
I HAVE ONE!
ばっ WHIP
WHAT IS IT, MERA?
DOES THIS SCHOOL POST EVERYONE'S GRADE RANKINGS?!
NO, WE DON'T... ARE YOU INTERESTED IN THAT?
IF IT'D BE AN INCENTIVE, SHALL WE POST THEM JUST FOR THIS CLASS?
どよ GLOOM
どよ GLOOM
WHAAAA?!
どよ GLOOM
どよ GLOOM
WELL, IT'D BE CRUEL TO EXPOSE THE BOTTOM RANKS... HOW ABOUT THE TOP TEN?

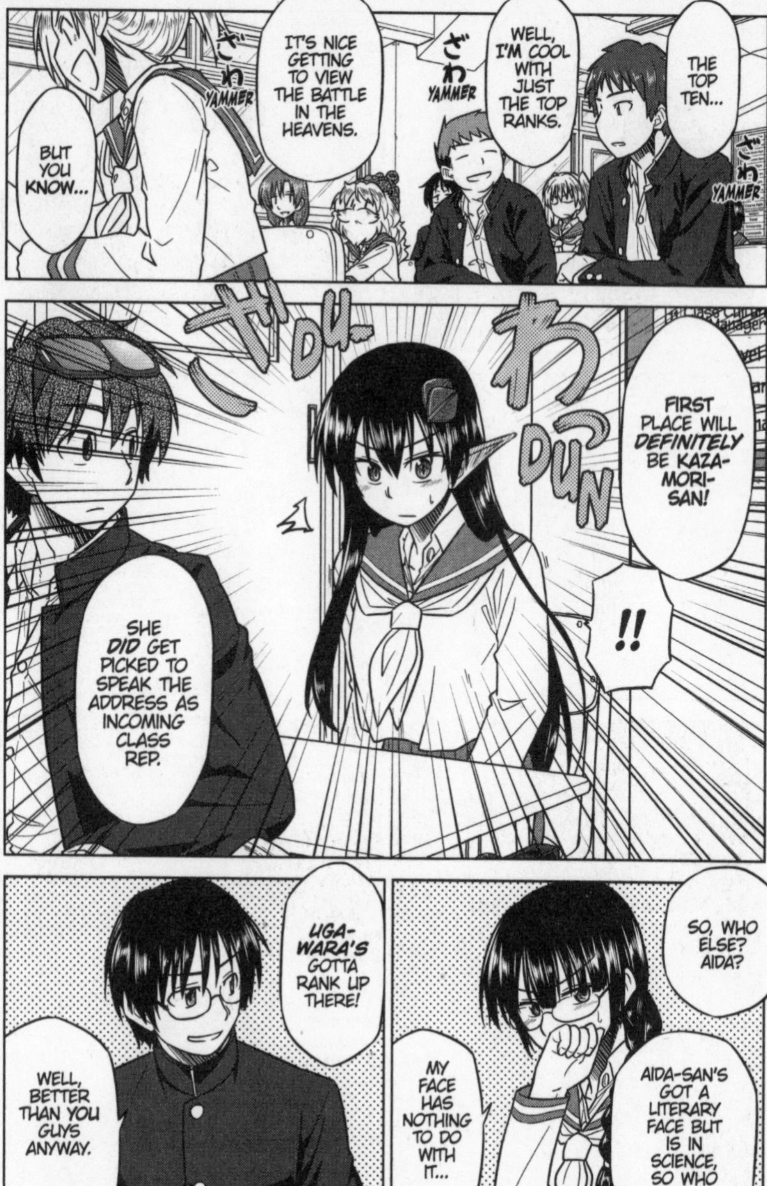
THE TOP TEN...
ざわ
YAMMER
WELL, I'M COOL WITH JUST THE TOP RANKS.
ざわ
YAMMER
IT'S NICE GETTING TO VIEW THE BATTLE IN THE HEAVENS.
ざわ
YAMMER
BUT YOU KNOW...
ざわ
DU-DUN
FIRST PLACE WILL *DEFINITELY* BE KAZAMORI-SAN!
!!
SHE *DID* GET PICKED TO SPEAK THE ADDRESS AS INCOMING CLASS REP.
SO, WHO ELSE? AIDA?
AIDA-SAN'S GOT A LITERARY FACE BUT IS IN SCIENCE, SO WHO KNOWS.
MY FACE HAS NOTHING TO DO WITH IT...
UGA-WARA'S GOTTA RANK UP THERE!
WELL, BETTER THAN YOU GUYS ANYWAY.

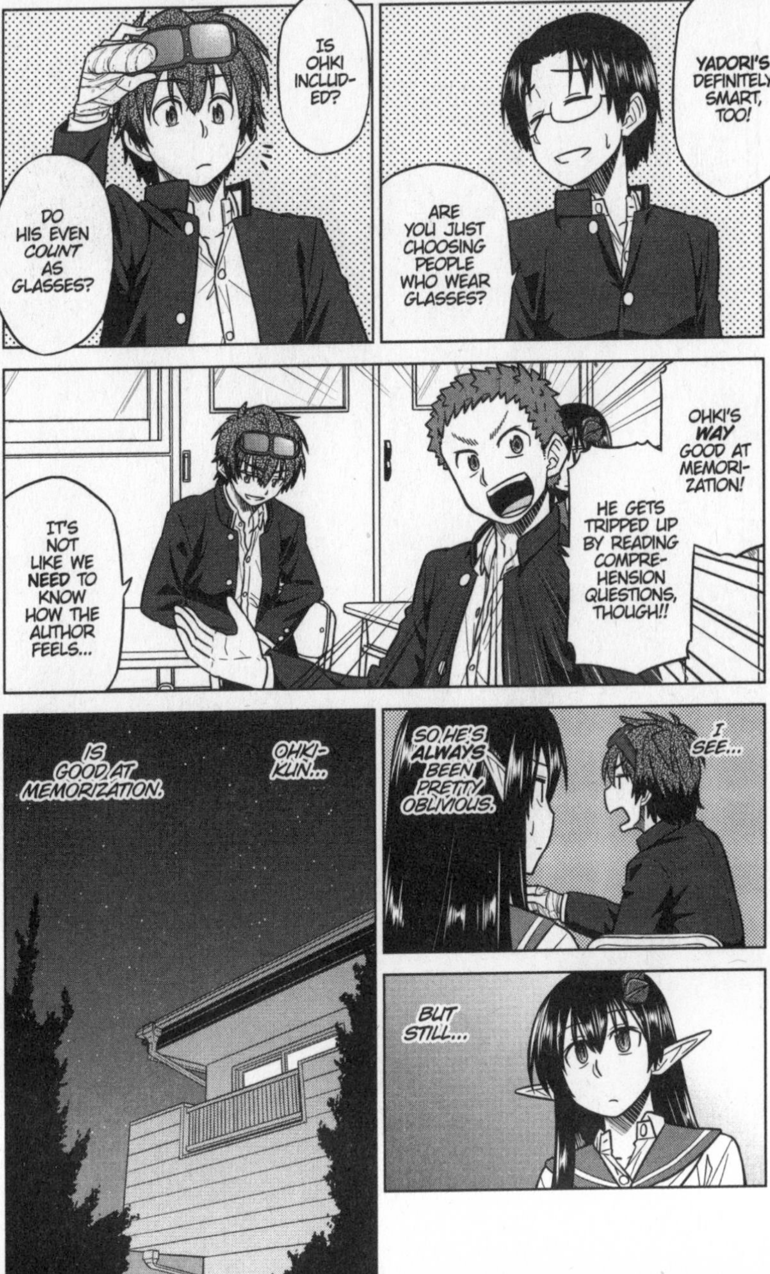
YADORI'S DEFINITELY SMART, TOO!
ARE YOU JUST CHOOSING PEOPLE WHO WEAR GLASSES?
IS OHKI INCLUDED?
DO HIS EVEN COUNT AS GLASSES?
OHKI'S WAY GOOD AT MEMORIZATION!
HE GETS TRIPPED UP BY READING COMPREHENSION QUESTIONS, THOUGH!!
IT'S NOT LIKE WE NEED TO KNOW HOW THE AUTHOR FEELS...
I SEE...
SO HE'S ALWAYS BEEN PRETTY OBLIVIOUS.
BUT STILL...
OHKI-KUN...
IS GOOD AT MEMORIZATION.

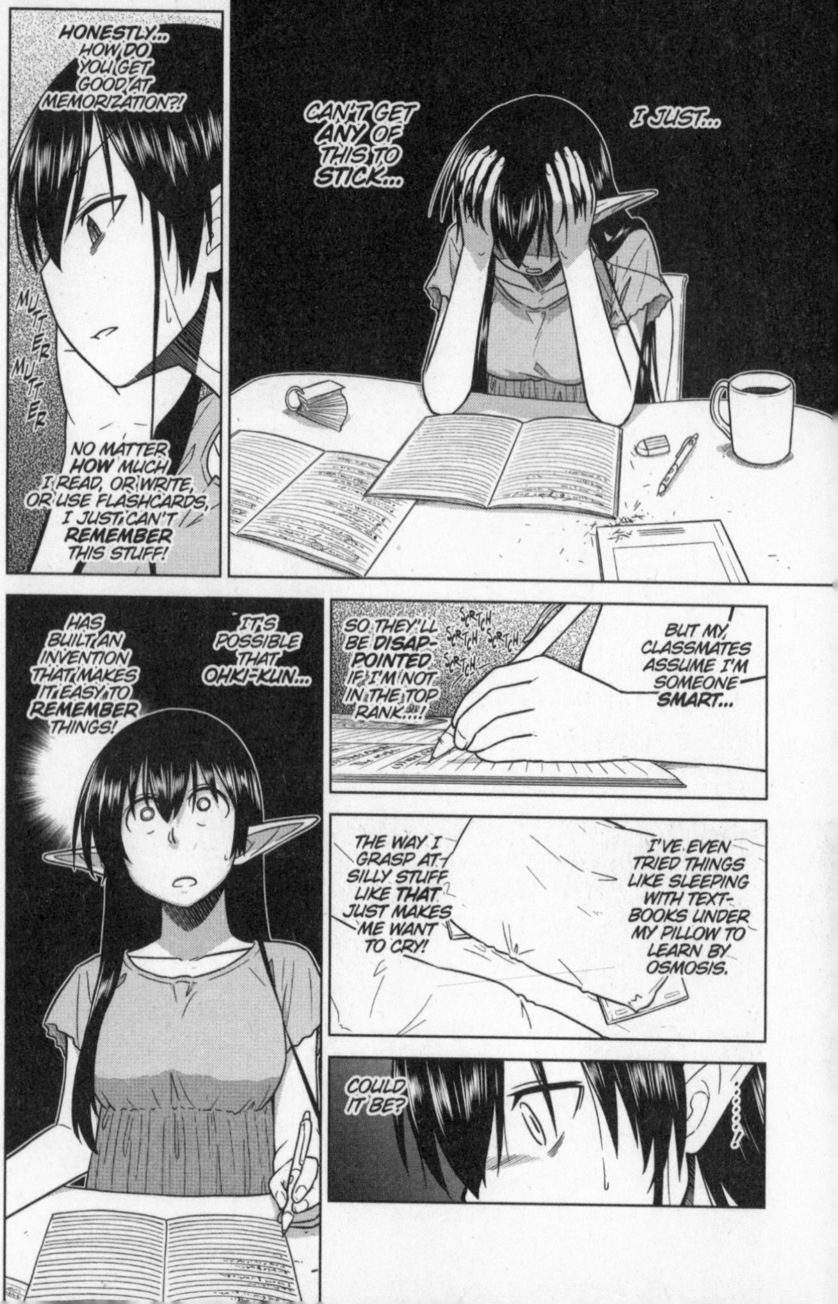
I JUST...
CAN'T GET ANY OF THIS TO STICK...
HONESTLY... HOW DO YOU GET GOOD AT MEMORIZATION?!
MUTTER MUTTER
NO MATTER HOW MUCH I READ, OR WRITE, OR USE FLASHCARDS, I JUST CAN'T REMEMBER THIS STUFF!
BUT MY CLASSMATES ASSUME I'M SOMEONE SMART...
SCRTCH SCRTCH SCRTCH SCRTCH
SO THEY'LL BE DISAPPOINTED IF I'M NOT IN THE TOP RANK...!
I'VE EVEN TRIED THINGS LIKE SLEEPING WITH TEXT-BOOKS UNDER MY PILLOW TO LEARN BY OSMOSIS.
THE WAY I GRASP AT SILLY STUFF LIKE THAT JUST MAKES ME WANT TO CRY!
COULD IT BE?
IT'S POSSIBLE THAT OHKI-KUN...
HAS BUILT AN INVENTION THAT MAKES IT EASY TO REMEMBER THINGS!

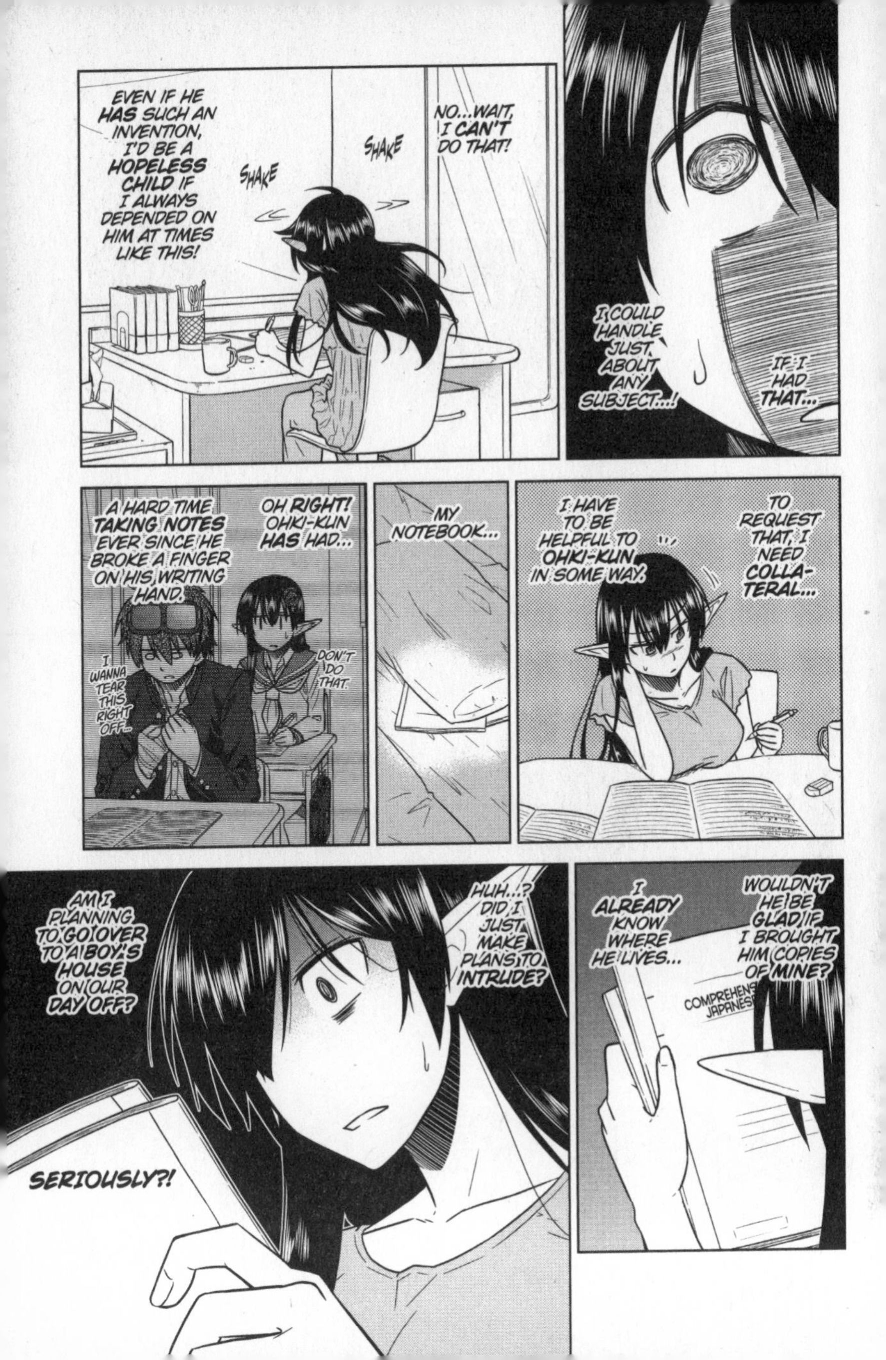
IF I HAD THAT...
I COULD HANDLE JUST ABOUT ANY SUBJECT...!
NO...WAIT, I CAN'T DO THAT!
SHAKE
SHAKE
EVEN IF HE HAS SUCH AN INVENTION, I'D BE A HOPELESS CHILD IF I ALWAYS DEPENDED ON HIM AT TIMES LIKE THIS!
TO REQUEST THAT, I NEED COLLA-TERAL...
I HAVE TO BE HELPFUL TO OHKI-KUN IN SOME WAY.
MY NOTEBOOK...
OH RIGHT! OHKI-KUN HAS HAD...
A HARD TIME TAKING NOTES EVER SINCE HE BROKE A FINGER ON HIS WRITING HAND.
DON'T DO THAT.
I WANNA TEAR THIS RIGHT OFF...
WOULDN'T HE BE GLAD IF I BROUGHT HIM COPIES OF MINE?
I ALREADY KNOW WHERE HE LIVES...
HUH...? DID I JUST MAKE PLANS TO INTRUDE?
AM I PLANNING TO GO OVER TO A BOY'S HOUSE ON OUR DAY OFF?
SERIOUSLY?!

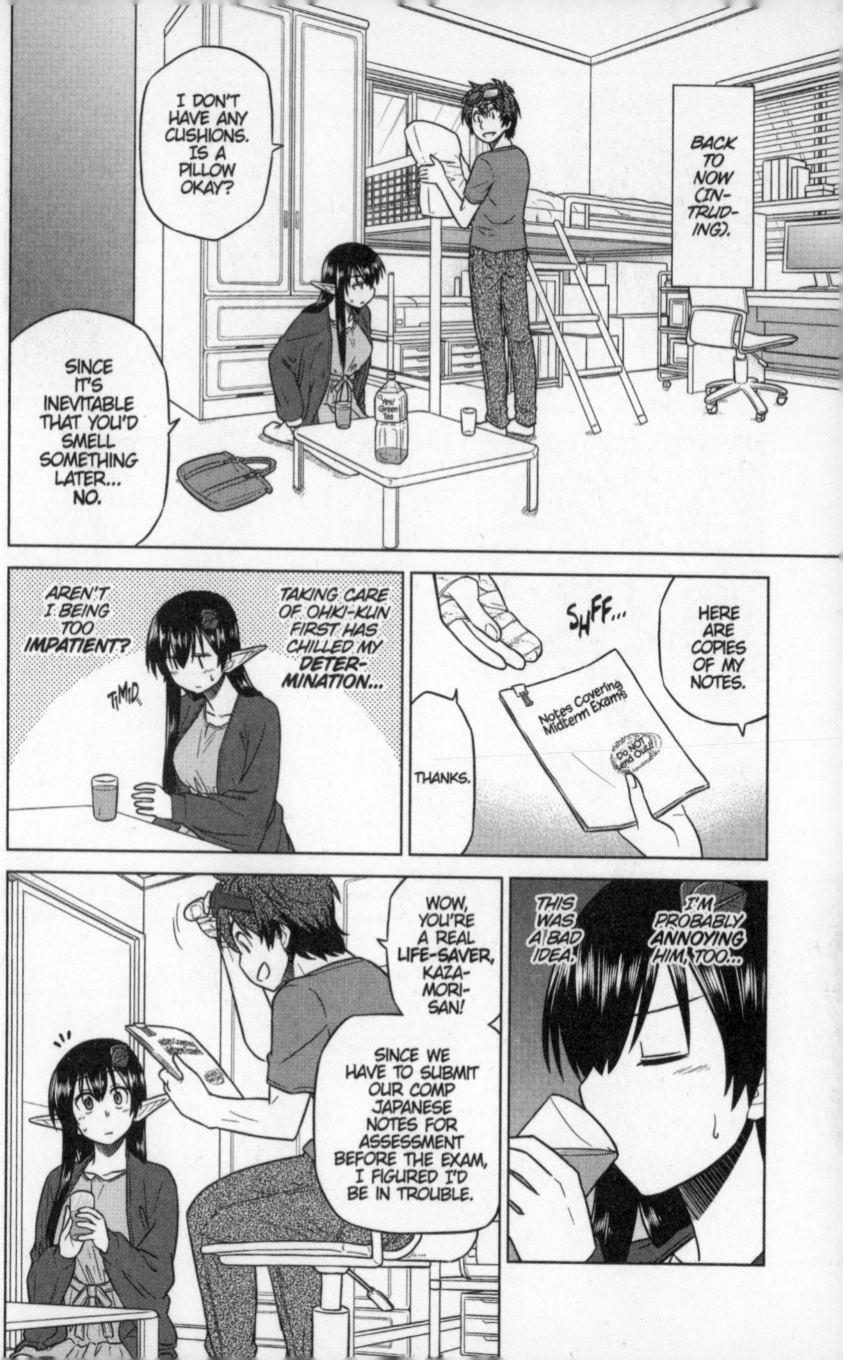
BACK TO NOW (IN-TRUDING).
I DON'T HAVE ANY CUSHIONS. IS A PILLOW OKAY?
Yes! Green Tea
SINCE IT'S INEVITABLE THAT YOU'D SMELL SOMETHING LATER... NO.
HERE ARE COPIES OF MY NOTES.
SHFF...
Notes Covering Midterm Exams
Do NOT Lend Out!!
THANKS.
TAKING CARE OF OHKI-KUN FIRST HAS CHILLED MY DETER-MINATION...
AREN'T I BEING TOO IMPATIENT?
TIMID...
I'M PROBABLY ANNOYING HIM, TOO...
THIS WAS A BAD IDEA.
WOW, YOU'RE A REAL LIFE-SAVER, KAZA-MORI-SAN!
SINCE WE HAVE TO SUBMIT OUR COMP JAPANESE NOTES FOR ASSESSMENT BEFORE THE EXAM, I FIGURED I'D BE IN TROUBLE.

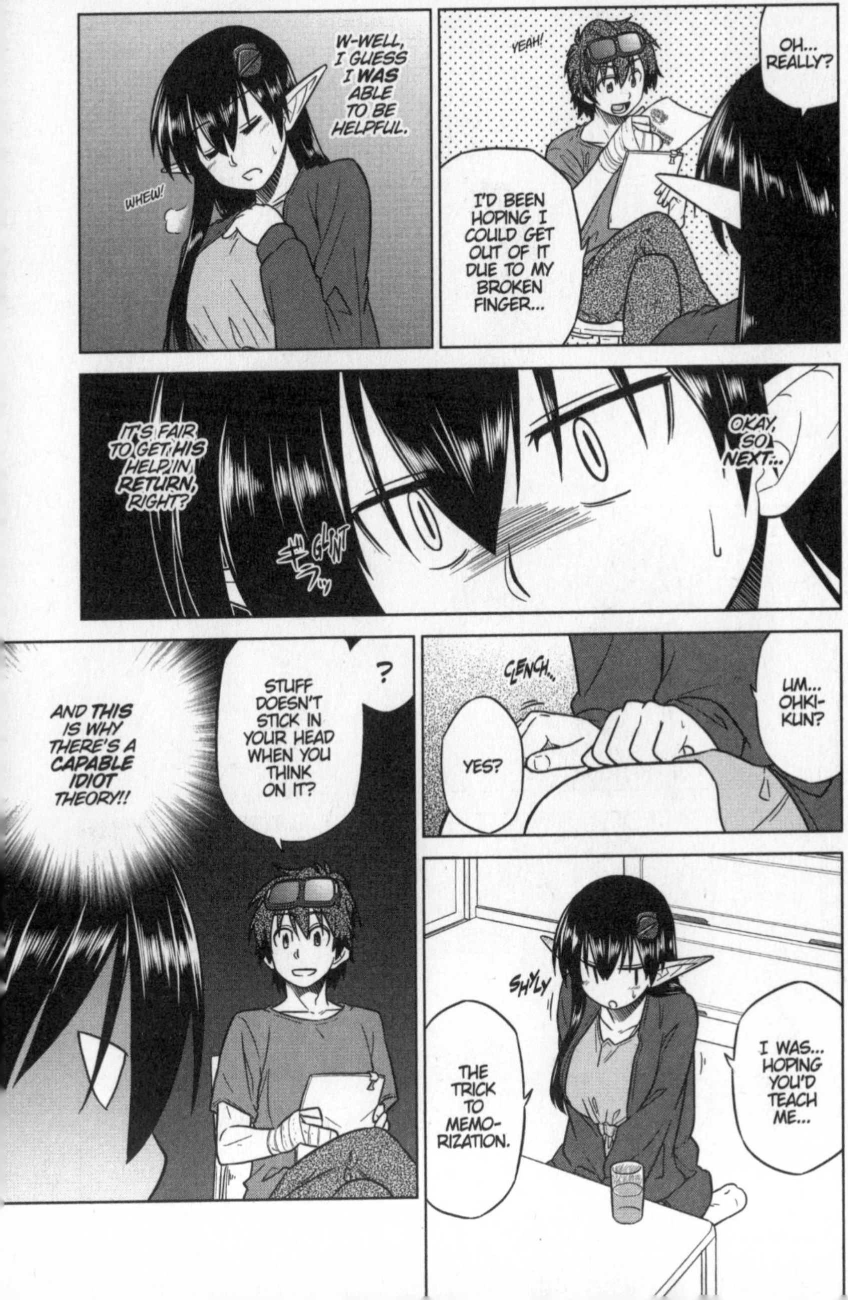
OH... REALLY?
YEAH!
I'D BEEN HOPING I COULD GET OUT OF IT DUE TO MY BROKEN FINGER...
W-WELL, I GUESS I WAS ABLE TO BE HELPFUL.
WHEW!
OKAY, SO NEXT...
IT'S FAIR TO GET HIS HELP IN RETURN, RIGHT?
ギラッ GLINT
UM... OHKI-KUN?
CLENCH...
YES?
I WAS... HOPING YOU'D TEACH ME...
SHYLY
THE TRICK TO MEMORIZATION.
?
STUFF DOESN'T STICK IN YOUR HEAD WHEN YOU THINK ON IT?
AND THIS IS WHY THERE'S A CAPABLE IDIOT THEORY!!

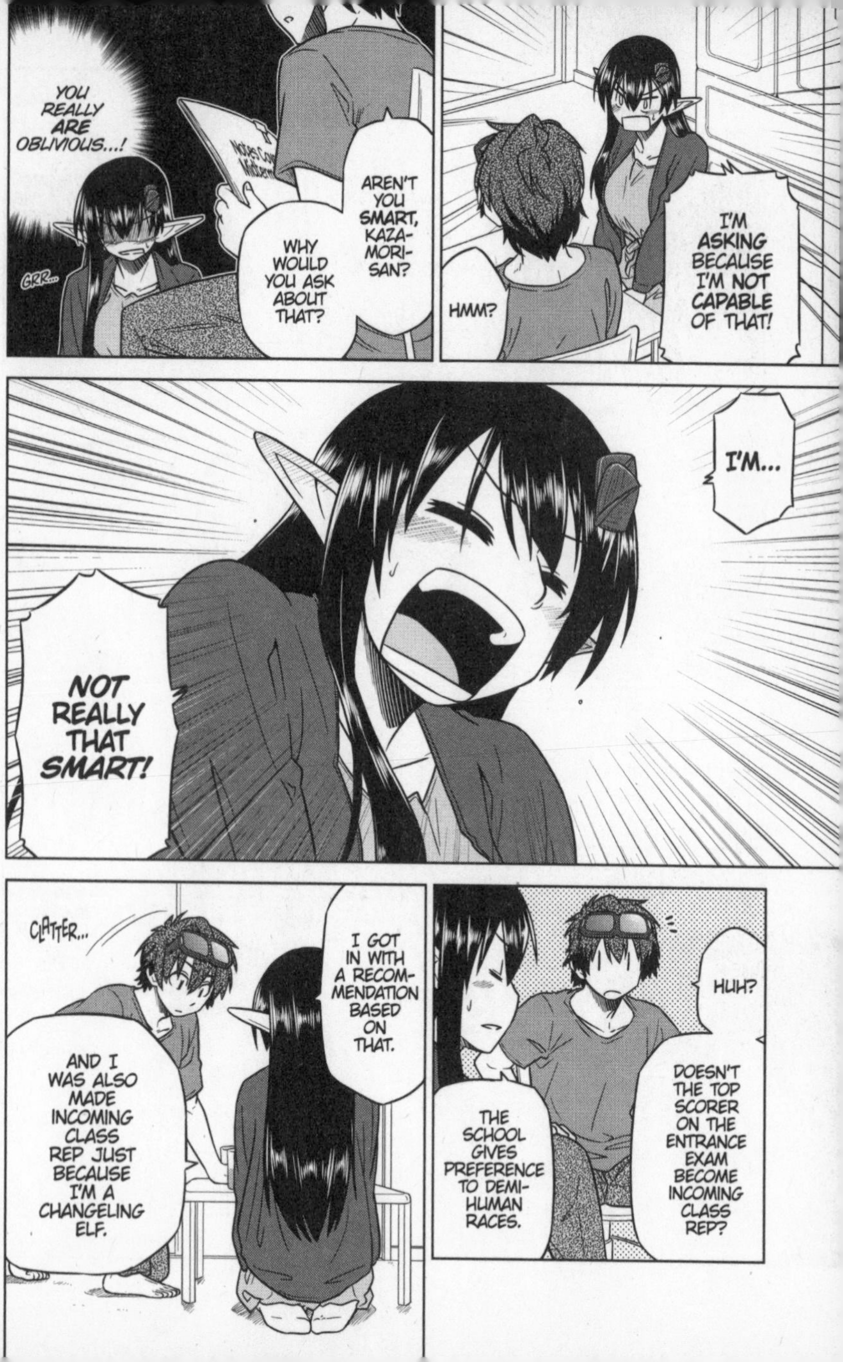

I'M ASKING BECAUSE I'M NOT CAPABLE OF THAT!
HMM?
AREN'T YOU SMART, KAZAMORI-SAN?
WHY WOULD YOU ASK ABOUT THAT?
YOU REALLY ARE OBLIVIOUS...!
GRR...
I'M...
NOT REALLY THAT SMART!
HUH?
DOESN'T THE TOP SCORER ON THE ENTRANCE EXAM BECOME INCOMING CLASS REP?
THE SCHOOL GIVES PREFERENCE TO DEMI-HUMAN RACES.
I GOT IN WITH A RECOMMENDATION BASED ON THAT.
CLATTER...
AND I WAS ALSO MADE INCOMING CLASS REP JUST BECAUSE I'M A CHANGELING ELF.

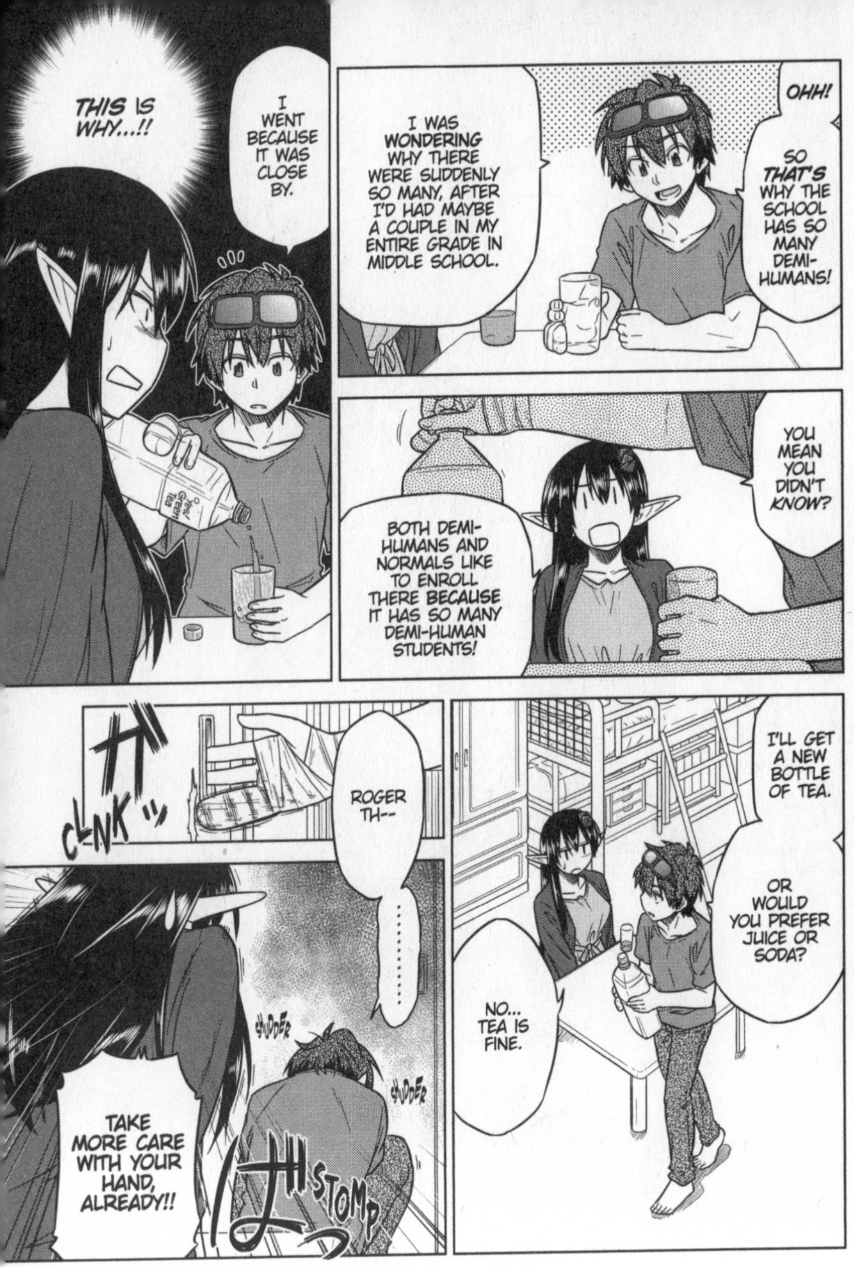
OHH!
SO THAT'S WHY THE SCHOOL HAS SO MANY DEMI-HUMANS!
I WAS WONDERING WHY THERE WERE SUDDENLY SO MANY, AFTER I'D HAD MAYBE A COUPLE IN MY ENTIRE GRADE IN MIDDLE SCHOOL.
YOU MEAN YOU DIDN'T KNOW?
BOTH DEMI-HUMANS AND NORMALS LIKE TO ENROLL THERE BECAUSE IT HAS SO MANY DEMI-HUMAN STUDENTS!
I WENT BECAUSE IT WAS CLOSE BY.
THIS IS WHY...!!
Yes! Green Tea
I'LL GET A NEW BOTTLE OF TEA.
OR WOULD YOU PREFER JUICE OR SODA?
NO... TEA IS FINE.
ROGER TH--
CLINK
....
SHUDDER
SHUDDER
TAKE MORE CARE WITH YOUR HAND, ALREADY!!
STOMP

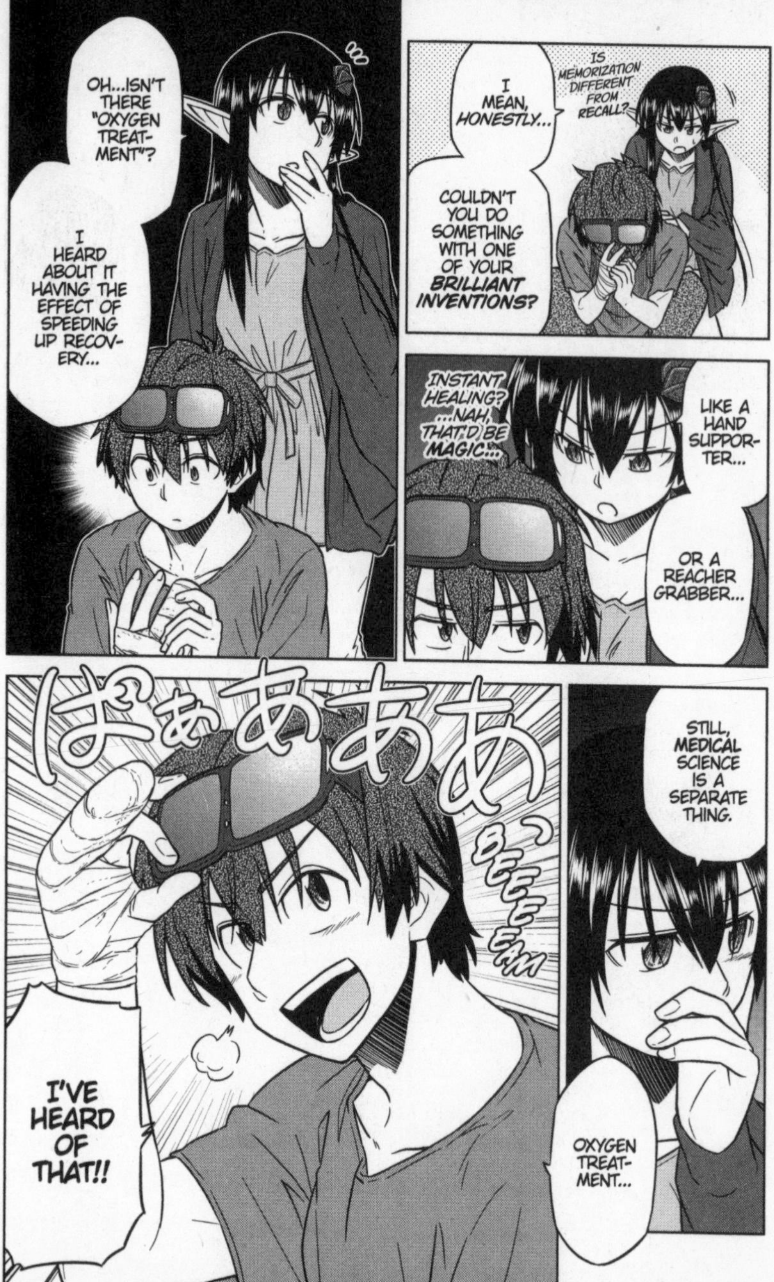
IS MEMORIZATION DIFFERENT FROM RECALL?
I MEAN, HONESTLY...
COULDN'T YOU DO SOMETHING WITH ONE OF YOUR BRILLIANT INVENTIONS?
LIKE A HAND SUPPORTER...
OR A REACHER GRABBER...
INSTANT HEALING? ...NAH, THAT'D BE MAGIC...
OH...ISN'T THERE "OXYGEN TREATMENT"?
I HEARD ABOUT IT HAVING THE EFFECT OF SPEEDING UP RECOVERY...
STILL, MEDICAL SCIENCE IS A SEPARATE THING.
OXYGEN TREATMENT...
ぱぁあああ
BEEEEAM
I'VE HEARD OF THAT!!

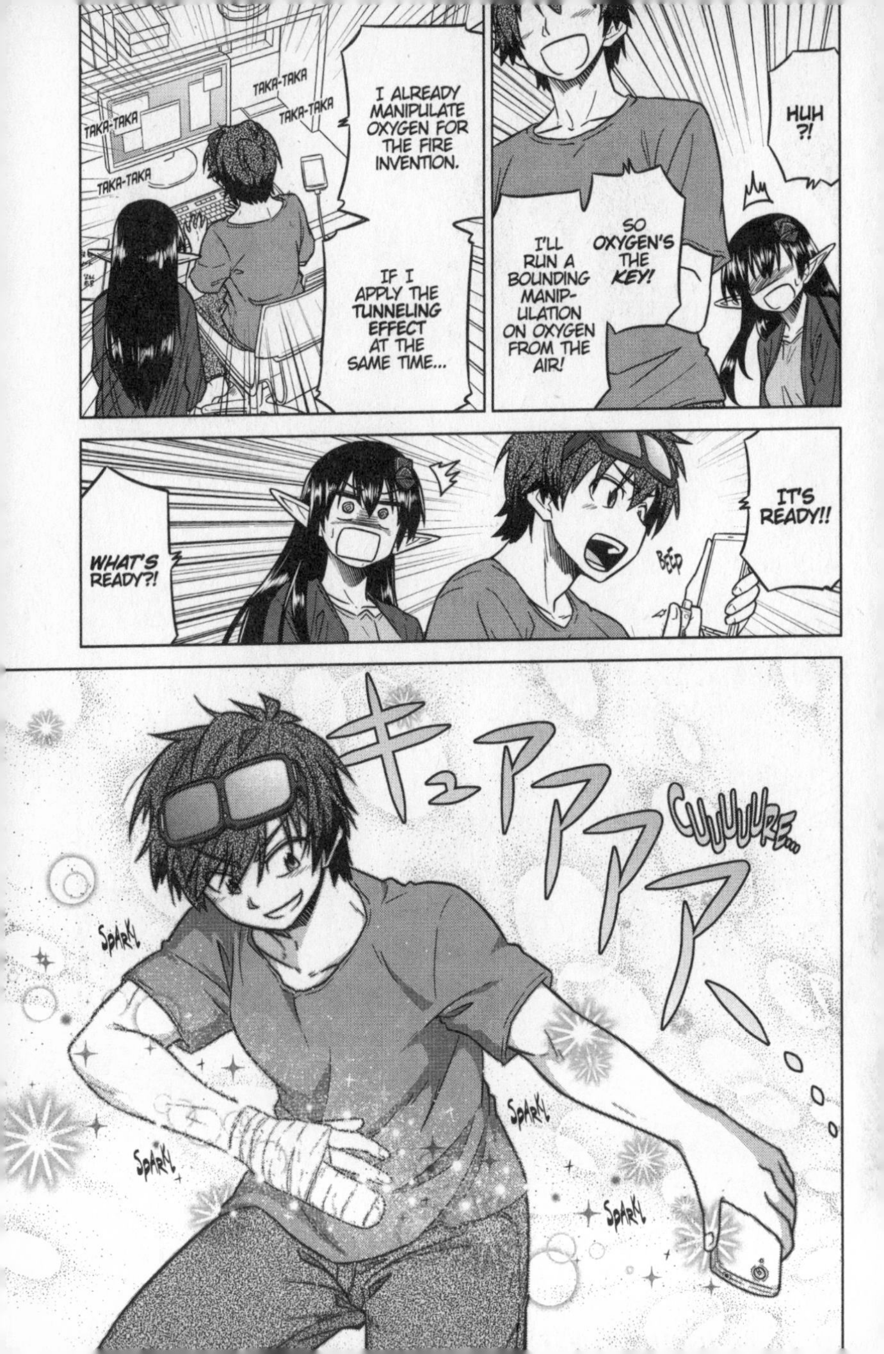
HUH?!
SO OXYGEN'S THE KEY!
I'LL RUN A BOUNDING MANIPULATION ON OXYGEN FROM THE AIR!
I ALREADY MANIPULATE OXYGEN FOR THE FIRE INVENTION.
TAKA-TAKA
TAKA-TAKA
TAKA-TAKA
TAKA-TAKA
IF I APPLY THE TUNNELING EFFECT AT THE SAME TIME...
IT'S READY!!
BEEP
WHAT'S READY?!
キュアアアア
CUUUUURE...
SPARKL
SPARKL
SPARKL
SPARKL

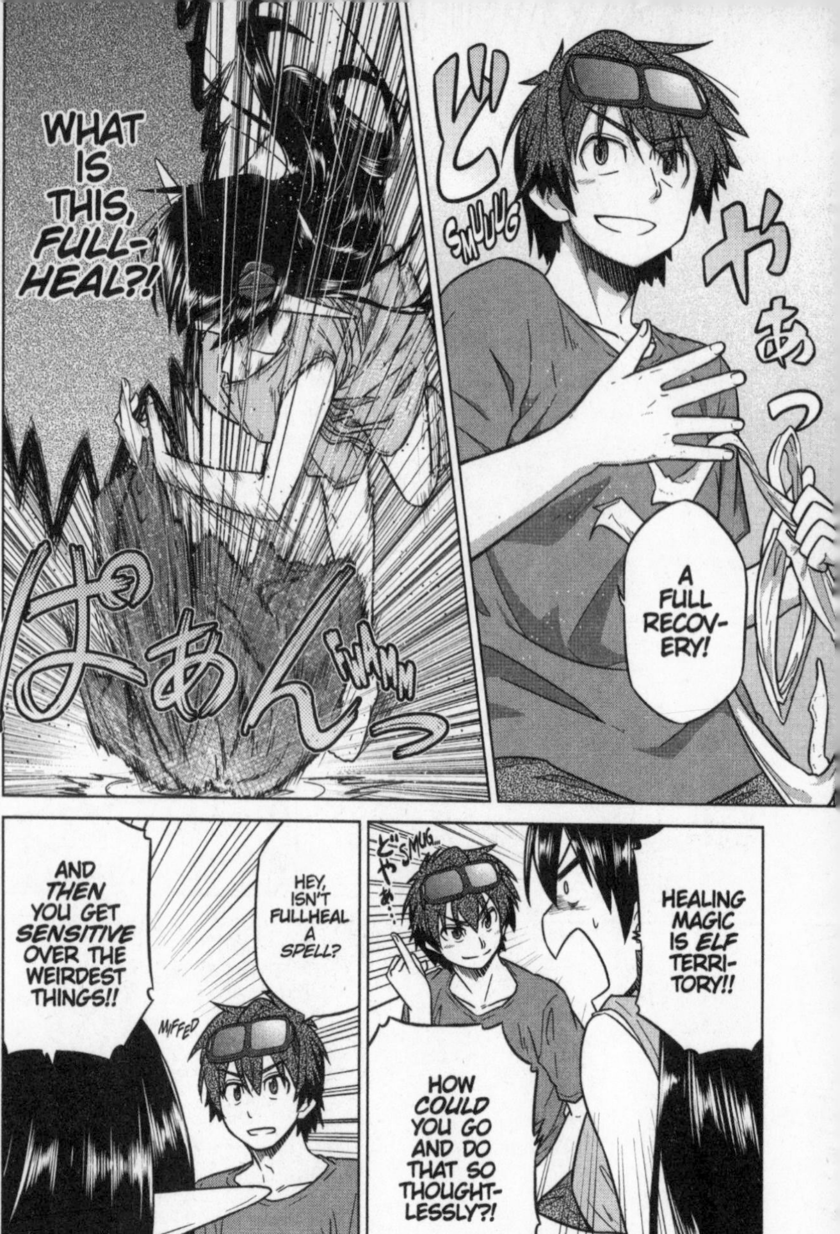
どやあっ
SMUUUG
A FULL RECOVERY!
WHAT IS THIS, FULL-HEAL?!
ぱあんっ
FWAMM
HEALING MAGIC IS ELF TERRITORY!!
どやぁ...
SMUG...
HOW COULD YOU GO AND DO THAT SO THOUGHTLESSLY?!
HEY, ISN'T FULLHEAL A SPELL?
AND THEN YOU GET SENSITIVE OVER THE WEIRDEST THINGS!!
MIFFED

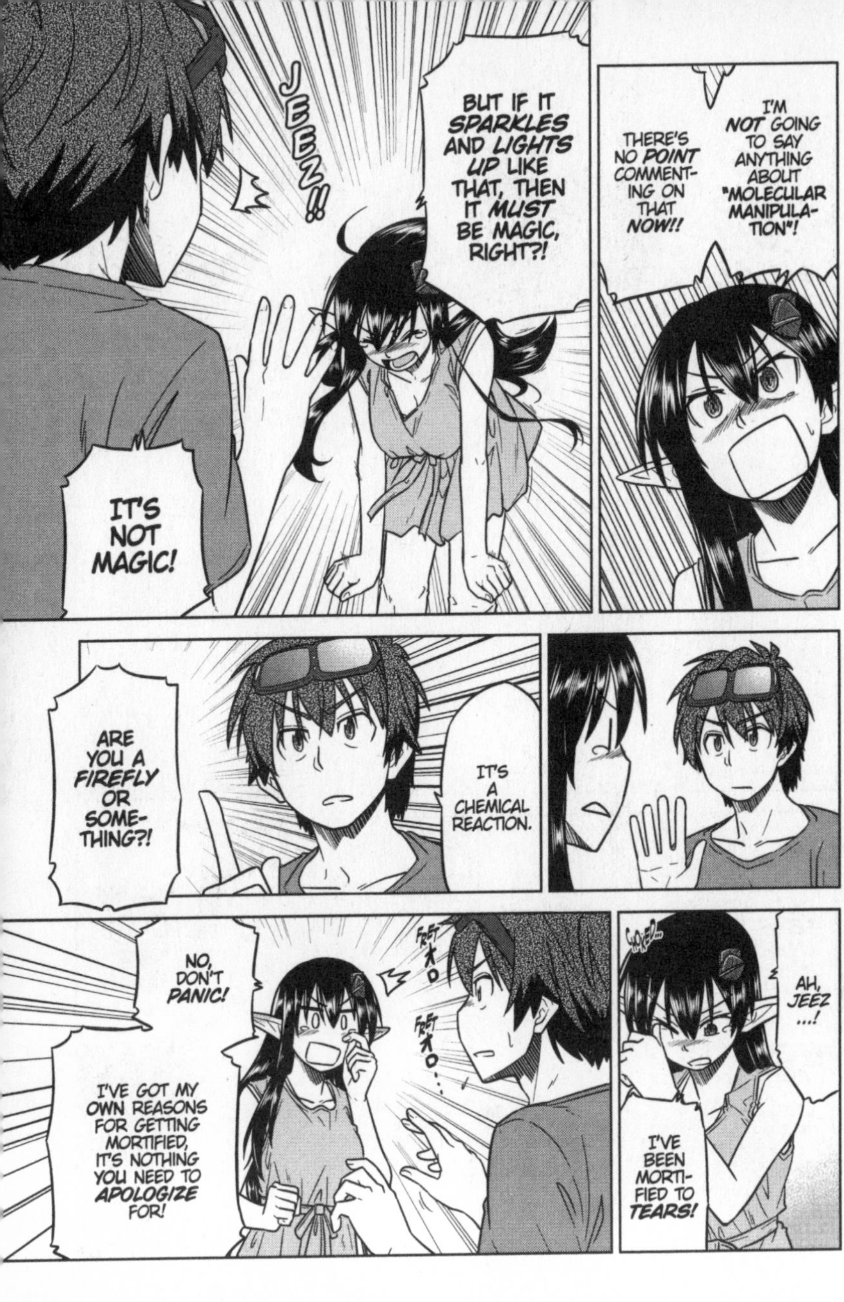
I'M NOT GOING TO SAY ANYTHING ABOUT "MOLECULAR MANIPULATION"!
THERE'S NO POINT COMMENTING ON THAT NOW!!
BUT IF IT SPARKLES AND LIGHTS UP LIKE THAT, THEN IT MUST BE MAGIC, RIGHT?!
JEEZ!!
IT'S NOT MAGIC!
IT'S A CHEMICAL REACTION.
ARE YOU A FIREFLY OR SOMETHING?!
AH, JEEZ...!
I'VE BEEN MORTIFIED TO TEARS!
FRET
FRET
NO, DON'T PANIC!
I'VE GOT MY OWN REASONS FOR GETTING MORTIFIED, IT'S NOTHING YOU NEED TO APOLOGIZE FOR!

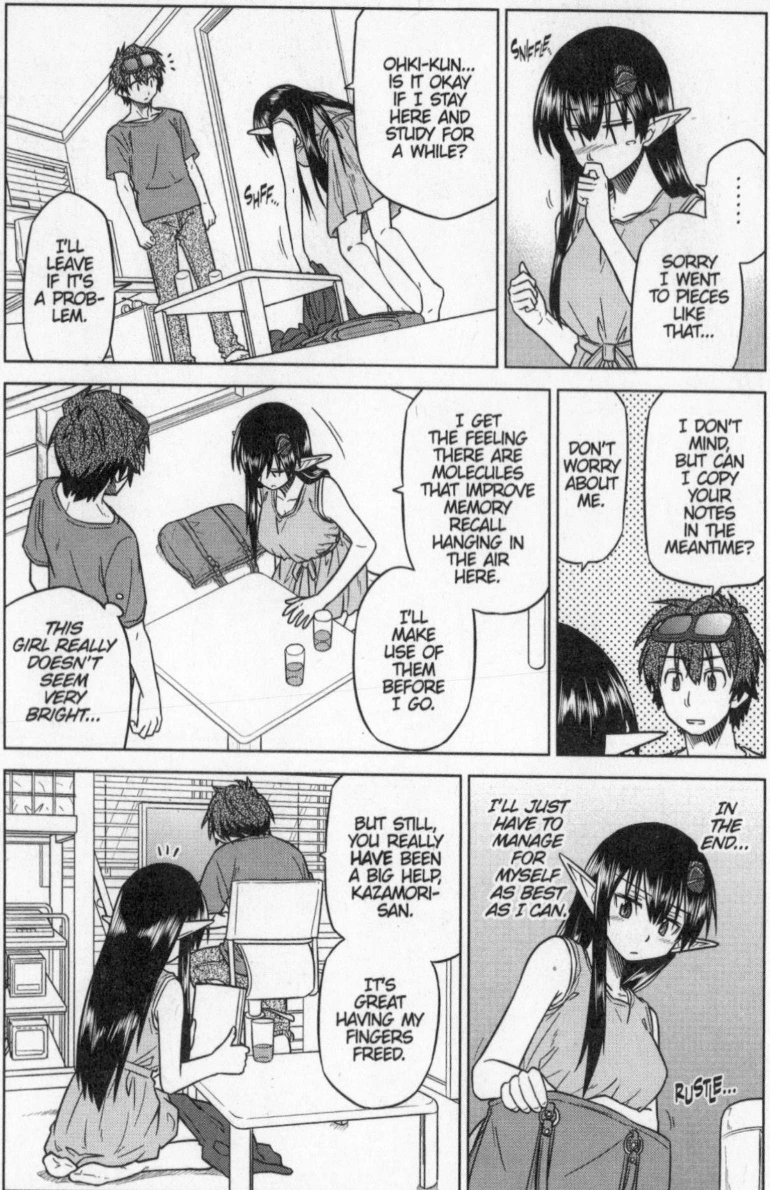
SNIFFLE
......
SORRY I WENT TO PIECES LIKE THAT...
OHKI-KUN... IS IT OKAY IF I STAY HERE AND STUDY FOR A WHILE?
SHFF...
I'LL LEAVE IF IT'S A PROB-LEM.
I DON'T MIND, BUT CAN I COPY YOUR NOTES IN THE MEANTIME?
DON'T WORRY ABOUT ME.
I GET THE FEELING THERE ARE MOLECULES THAT IMPROVE MEMORY RECALL HANGING IN THE AIR HERE.
I'LL MAKE USE OF THEM BEFORE I GO.
THIS GIRL REALLY DOESN'T SEEM VERY BRIGHT...
IN THE END...
I'LL JUST HAVE TO MANAGE FOR MYSELF AS BEST AS I CAN.
RUSTLE...
BUT STILL, YOU REALLY HAVE BEEN A BIG HELP, KAZAMORI-SAN.
IT'S GREAT HAVING MY FINGERS FREED.

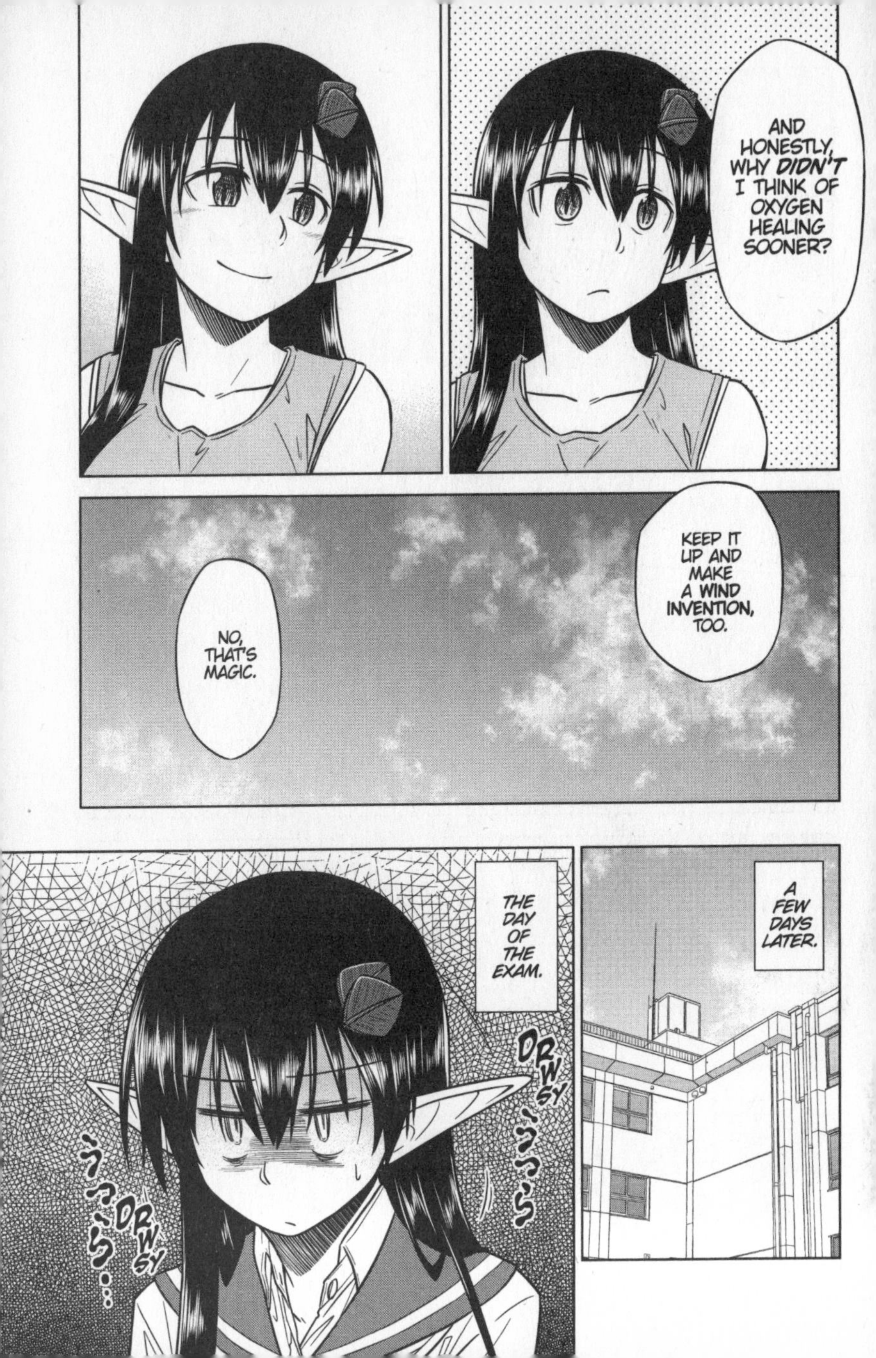
AND HONESTLY, WHY *DIDN'T* I THINK OF OXYGEN HEALING SOONER?
KEEP IT UP AND MAKE A WIND INVENTION, TOO.
NO, THAT'S MAGIC.
A FEW DAYS LATER.
THE DAY OF THE EXAM.
DRWSY
うつらうつら
DRWSY
うつらうつら…

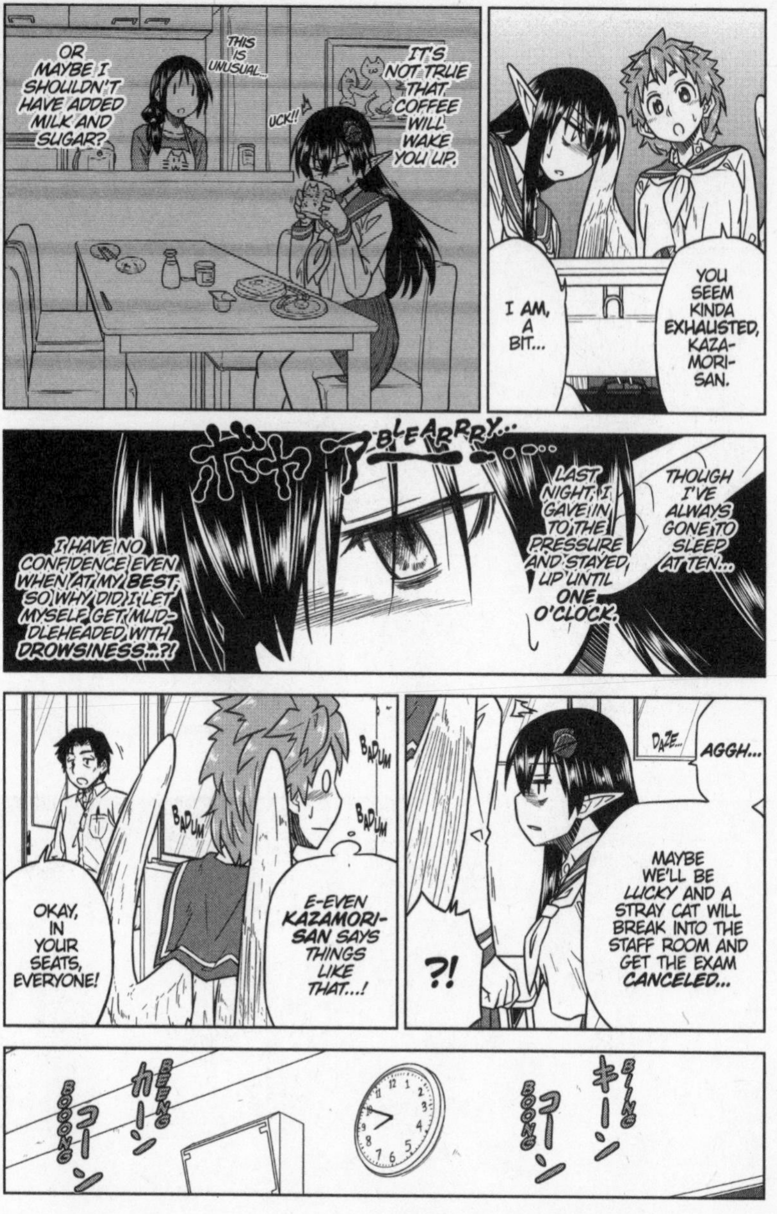

YOU SEEM KINDA EXHAUSTED, KAZAMORI-SAN.
I AM, A BIT...
IT'S NOT TRUE THAT COFFEE WILL WAKE YOU UP.
UCK!!
THIS IS UNUSUAL...
OR MAYBE I SHOULDN'T HAVE ADDED MILK AND SUGAR?
BLEARRRY...
THOUGH I'VE ALWAYS GONE TO SLEEP AT TEN...
LAST NIGHT, I GAVE IN TO THE PRESSURE AND STAYED UP UNTIL ONE O'CLOCK.
I HAVE NO CONFIDENCE EVEN WHEN AT MY BEST, SO WHY DID I LET MYSELF GET MUDDLEHEADED WITH DROWSINESS...?!
AGGH...
DAZE...
MAYBE WE'LL BE LUCKY AND A STRAY CAT WILL BREAK INTO THE STAFF ROOM AND GET THE EXAM CANCELED...
?!
BADUM
BADUM
BADUM
BADUM
E-EVEN KAZAMORI-SAN SAYS THINGS LIKE THAT...!
OKAY, IN YOUR SEATS, EVERYONE!
BING
BOONG
BEEING
BOOONG

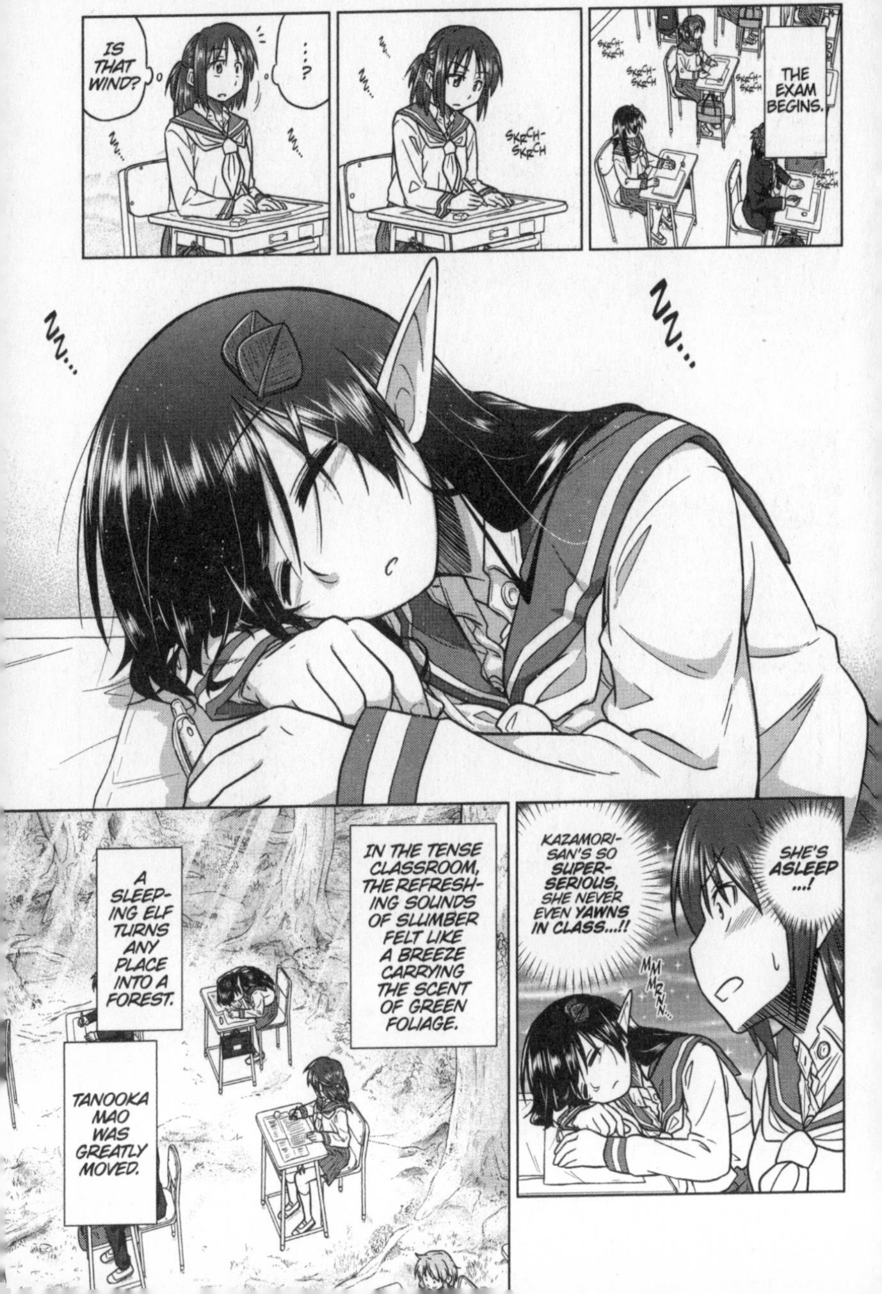
SKRCH-SKRCH
SKRCH-SKRCH
SKRCH-SKRCH
THE EXAM BEGINS.
SKRCH-SKRCH
ZZZ...
SKRCH-SKRCH
...?
IS THAT WIND?
ZZZ...
ZZZ...
SHE'S ASLEEP...!
KAZAMORI-SAN'S SO SUPER-SERIOUS, SHE NEVER EVEN YAWNS IN CLASS...!!
MMMRNN...
IN THE TENSE CLASSROOM, THE REFRESHING SOUNDS OF SLUMBER FELT LIKE A BREEZE CARRYING THE SCENT OF GREEN FOLIAGE.
A SLEEPING ELF TURNS ANY PLACE INTO A FOREST.
TANOOKA MAO WAS GREATLY MOVED.

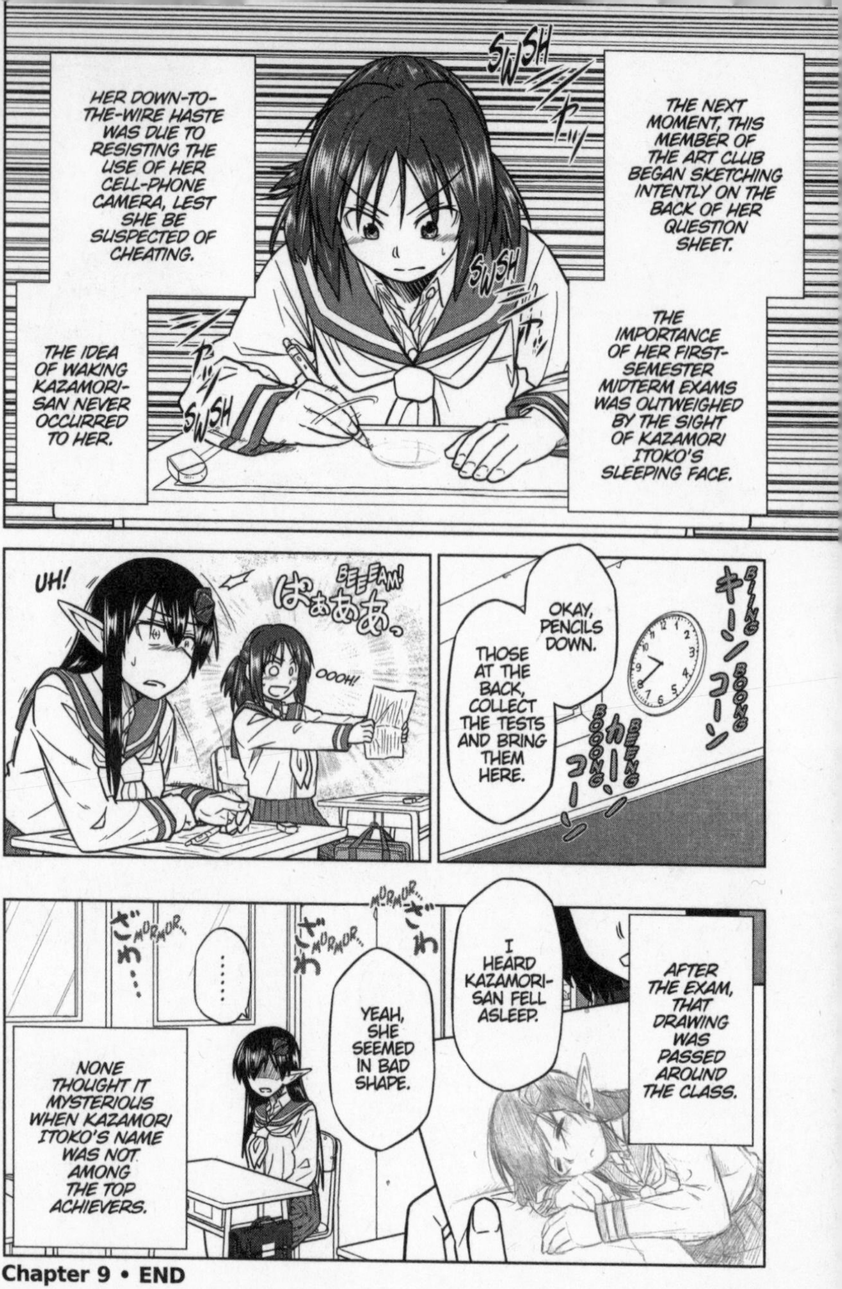
THE NEXT MOMENT, THIS MEMBER OF THE ART CLUB BEGAN SKETCHING INTENTLY ON THE BACK OF HER QUESTION SHEET.
SWSH
HER DOWN-TO-THE-WIRE HASTE WAS DUE TO RESISTING THE USE OF HER CELL-PHONE CAMERA, LEST SHE BE SUSPECTED OF CHEATING.
SWSH
THE IMPORTANCE OF HER FIRST-SEMESTER MIDTERM EXAMS WAS OUTWEIGHED BY THE SIGHT OF KAZAMORI ITOKO'S SLEEPING FACE.
SWSH
THE IDEA OF WAKING KAZAMORI-SAN NEVER OCCURRED TO HER.
BING
BOONG
OKAY, PENCILS DOWN.
THOSE AT THE BACK, COLLECT THE TESTS AND BRING THEM HERE.
BEEEN
BOOONG
BEEEAM!
OOOH!
UH!
AFTER THE EXAM, THAT DRAWING WAS PASSED AROUND THE CLASS.
I HEARD KAZAMORI-SAN FELL ASLEEP.
MURMUR...
YEAH, SHE SEEMED IN BAD SHAPE.
MURMUR...
......
MURMUR...
NONE THOUGHT IT MYSTERIOUS WHEN KAZAMORI ITOKO'S NAME WAS NOT AMONG THE TOP ACHIEVERS.

Chapter 9 • END

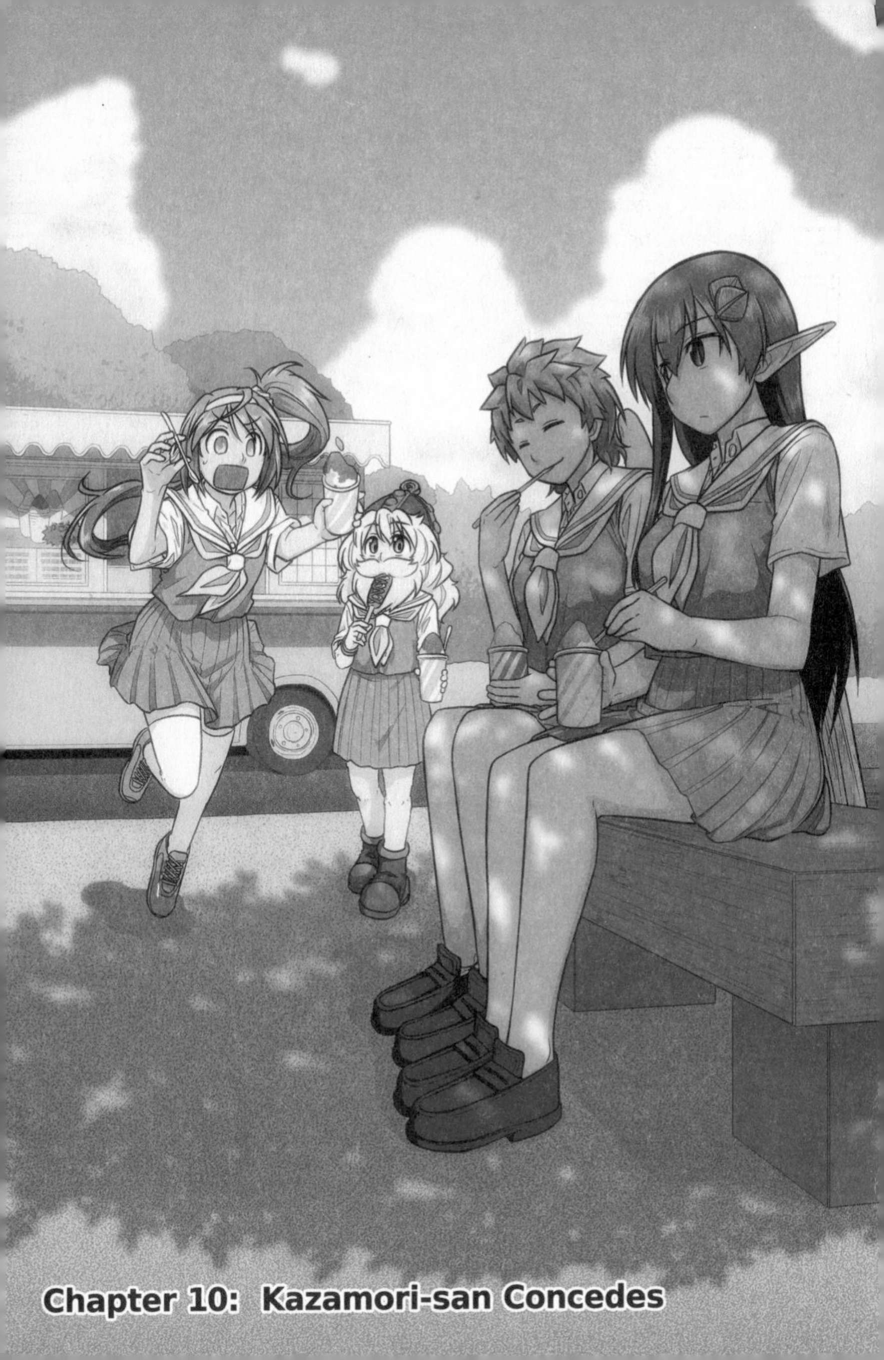

Chapter 10: Kazamori-san Concedes

KAZA-MORI-SAN, I HEARD YOU SLEPT THROUGH THE WHOLE EXAM?
YES... I WAS ASLEEP.
GO AHEAD AND LAUGH.
SULK
NO, I WASN'T GOING TO LAUGH AT YOU.
IF YOU'D ASKED, I'D HAVE CLEARED UP YOUR DROWSINESS.
YOU SHOULD'VE *TOLD* ME WHEN I LOOKED SLEEPY THAT MORNING!!
MY INVENTION, WHICH INDUCES SECRETION OF A STIMULATING SUBSTANCE THAT ACTIVATES THE BRAIN AND INHIBITS SLEEP-INDUCING CHEMICALS...
QUIT TINKERING WITH THE BRAIN LIKE A PRO-GRAMMER!!

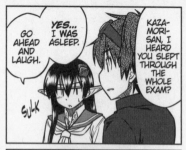

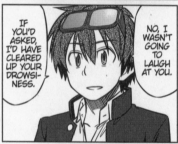

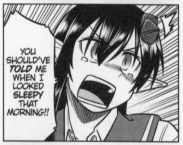

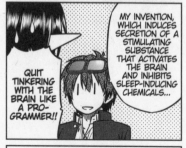

Aftereffects are Likely

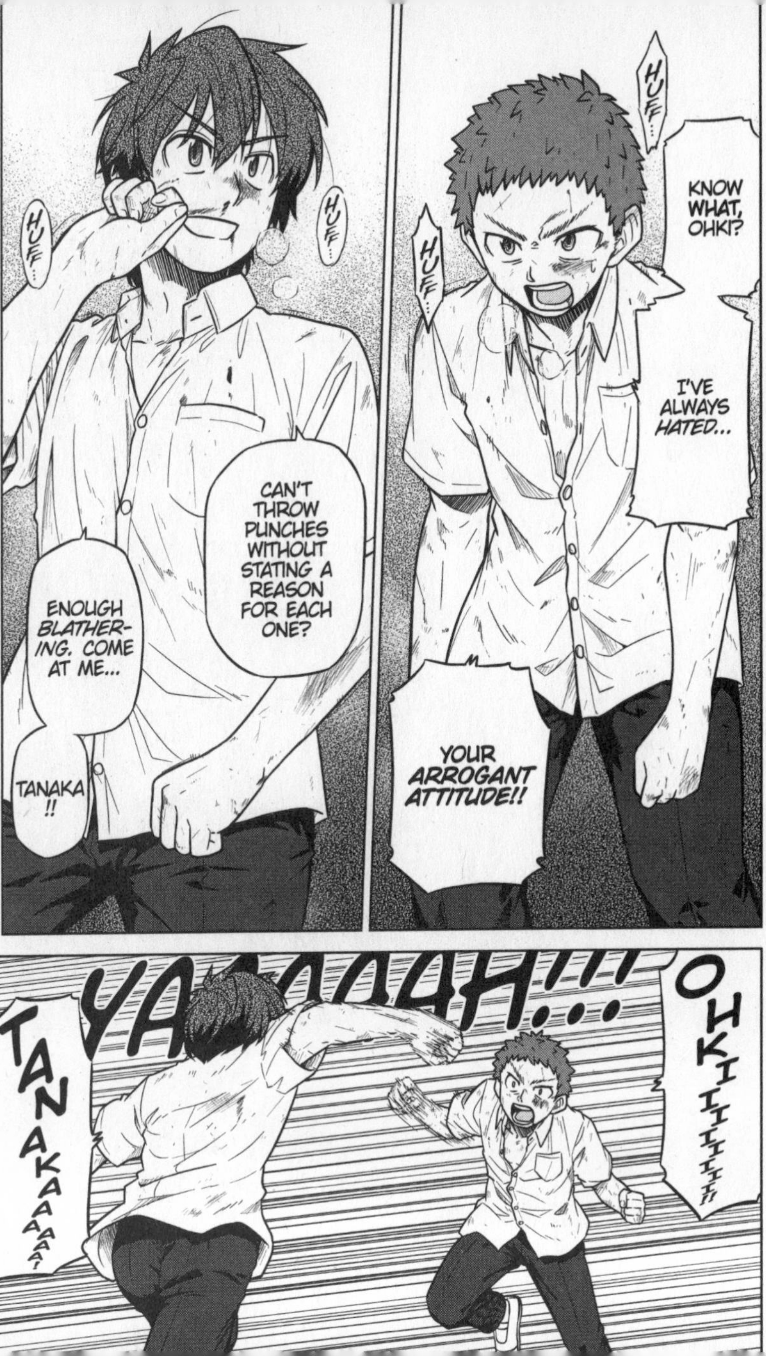
HUFF...
HUFF...
KNOW WHAT, OHKI?
I'VE ALWAYS HATED...
YOUR ARROGANT ATTITUDE!!
HUFF...
HUFF...
CAN'T THROW PUNCHES WITHOUT STATING A REASON FOR EACH ONE?
ENOUGH BLATHERING. COME AT ME...
TANAKA!!
OHKIIIIIII!!
YA
AAAH!!!
TANAKAAAAAAA!

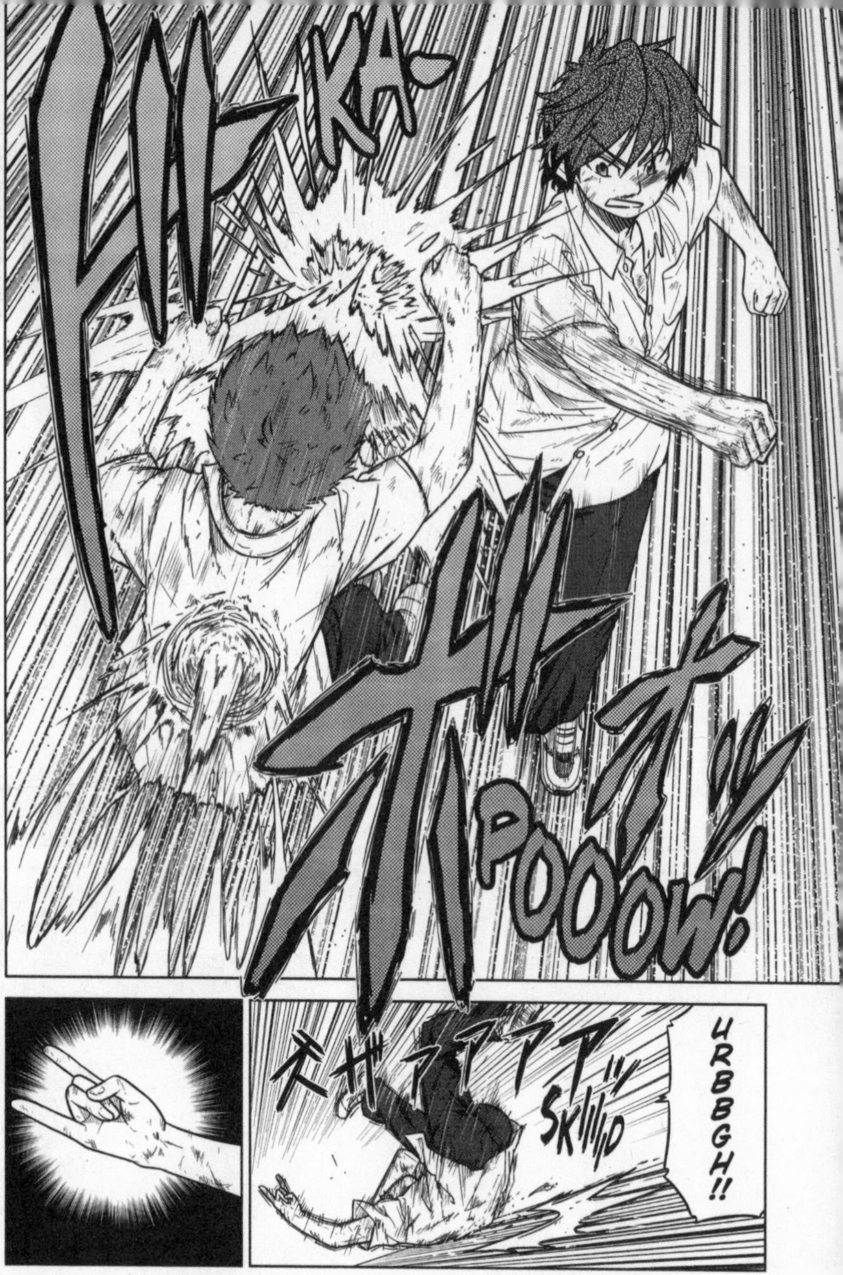
KA-
POOOW!
URBBGH!!
SKID

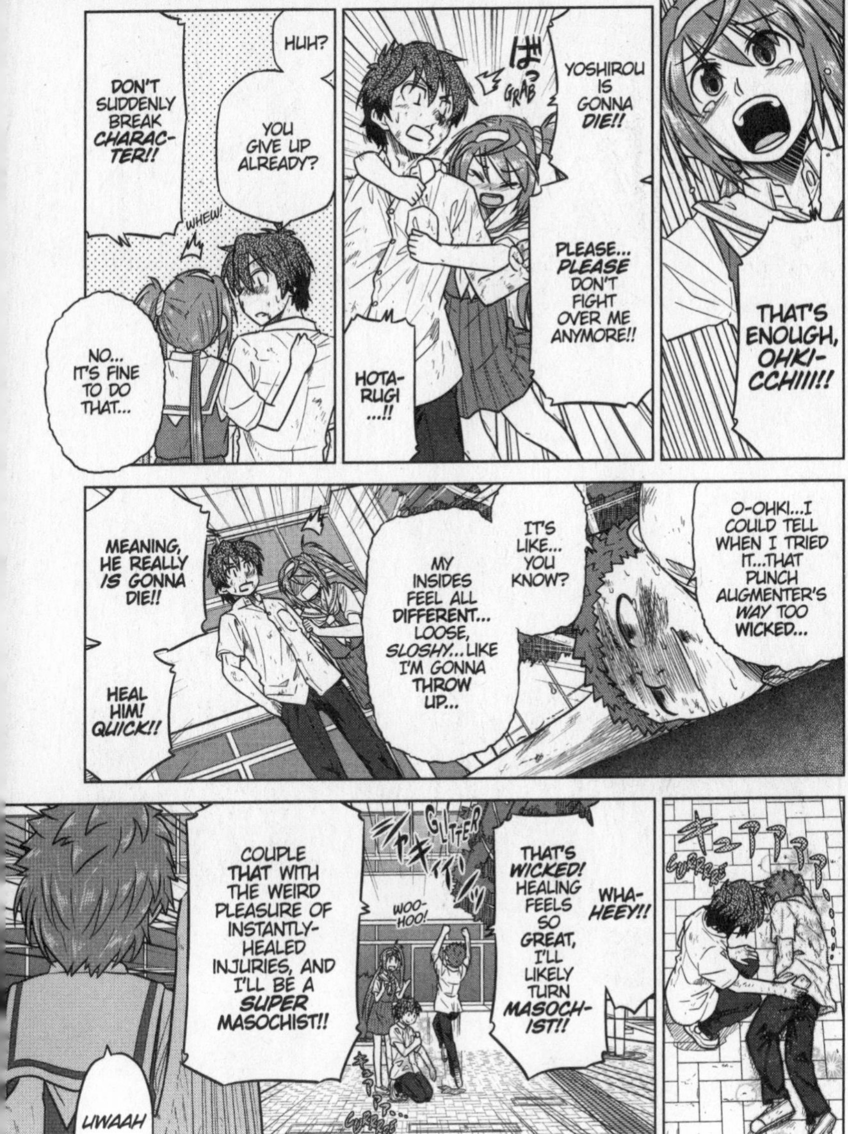

THAT'S ENOUGH, OHKI-CCHIIII!!
YOSHIROU IS GONNA DIE!!
ばっ
GRAB
PLEASE... PLEASE DON'T FIGHT OVER ME ANYMORE!!
HOTA-RUGI ...!!
HUH?
YOU GIVE UP ALREADY?
DON'T SUDDENLY BREAK CHARACTER!!
WHEW!
NO... IT'S FINE TO DO THAT...
O-OHKI...I COULD TELL WHEN I TRIED IT...THAT PUNCH AUGMENTER'S WAY TOO WICKED...
IT'S LIKE... YOU KNOW?
MY INSIDES FEEL ALL DIFFERENT... LOOSE, SLOSHY...LIKE I'M GONNA THROW UP...
MEANING, HE REALLY IS GONNA DIE!!
HEAL HIM! QUICK!!
WHA-HEEY!!
THAT'S WICKED! HEALING FEELS SO GREAT, I'LL LIKELY TURN MASOCH-IST!!
GLITTER
WOO-HOO!
COUPLE THAT WITH THE WEIRD PLEASURE OF INSTANTLY-HEALED INJURIES, AND I'LL BE A SUPER MASOCHIST!!
UWAAH ...

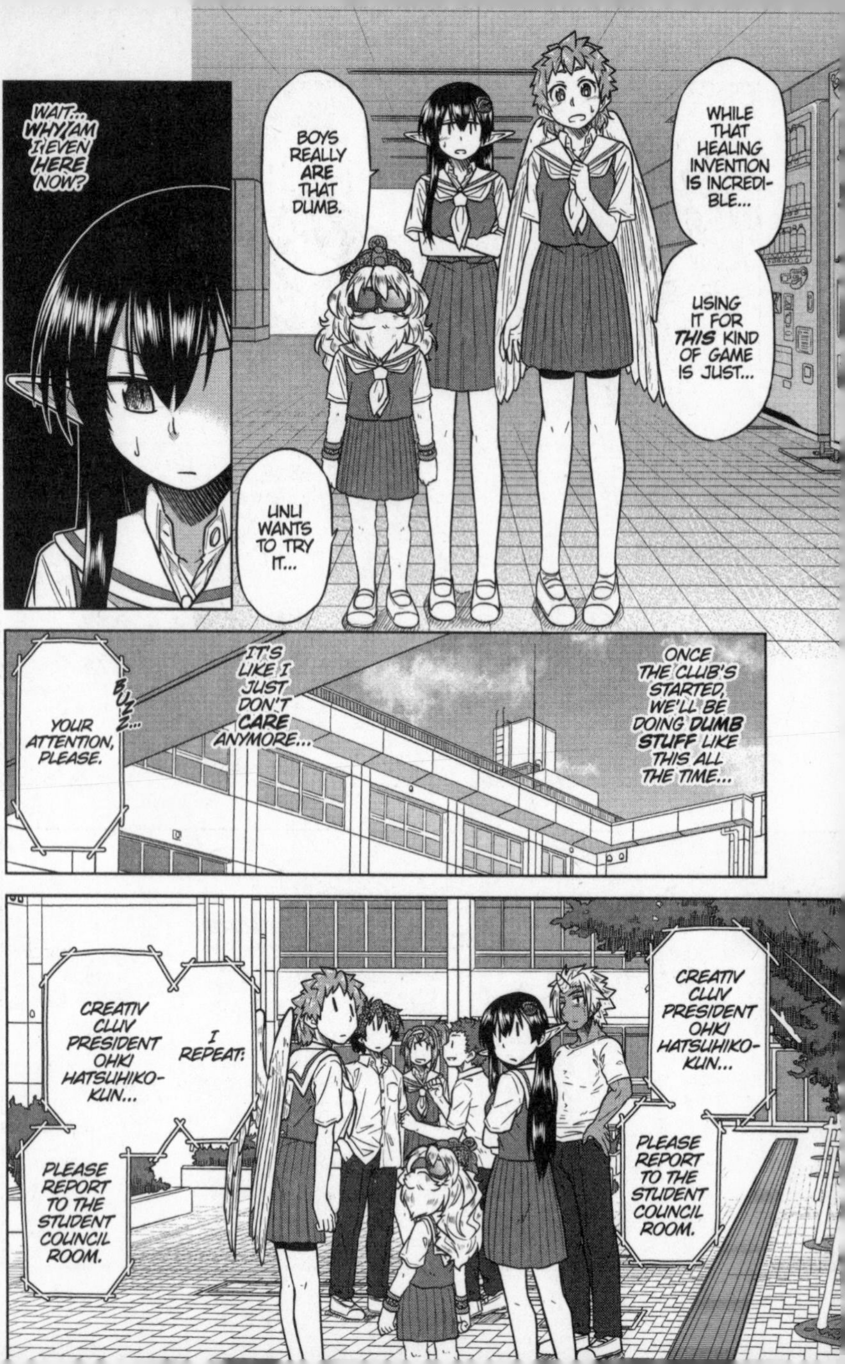
WHILE THAT HEALING INVENTION IS INCREDIBLE...
USING IT FOR THIS KIND OF GAME IS JUST...
BOYS REALLY ARE THAT DUMB.
UNLI WANTS TO TRY IT...
WAIT... WHY AM I EVEN HERE NOW?
ONCE THE CLUB'S STARTED, WE'LL BE DOING DUMB STUFF LIKE THIS ALL THE TIME...
IT'S LIKE I JUST DON'T CARE ANYMORE...
BZZZ...
YOUR ATTENTION, PLEASE.
CREATIV CLUV PRESIDENT OHKI HATSUHIKO-KUN...
PLEASE REPORT TO THE STUDENT COUNCIL ROOM.
I REPEAT:
CREATIV CLUV PRESIDENT OHKI HATSUHIKO-KUN...
PLEASE REPORT TO THE STUDENT COUNCIL ROOM.

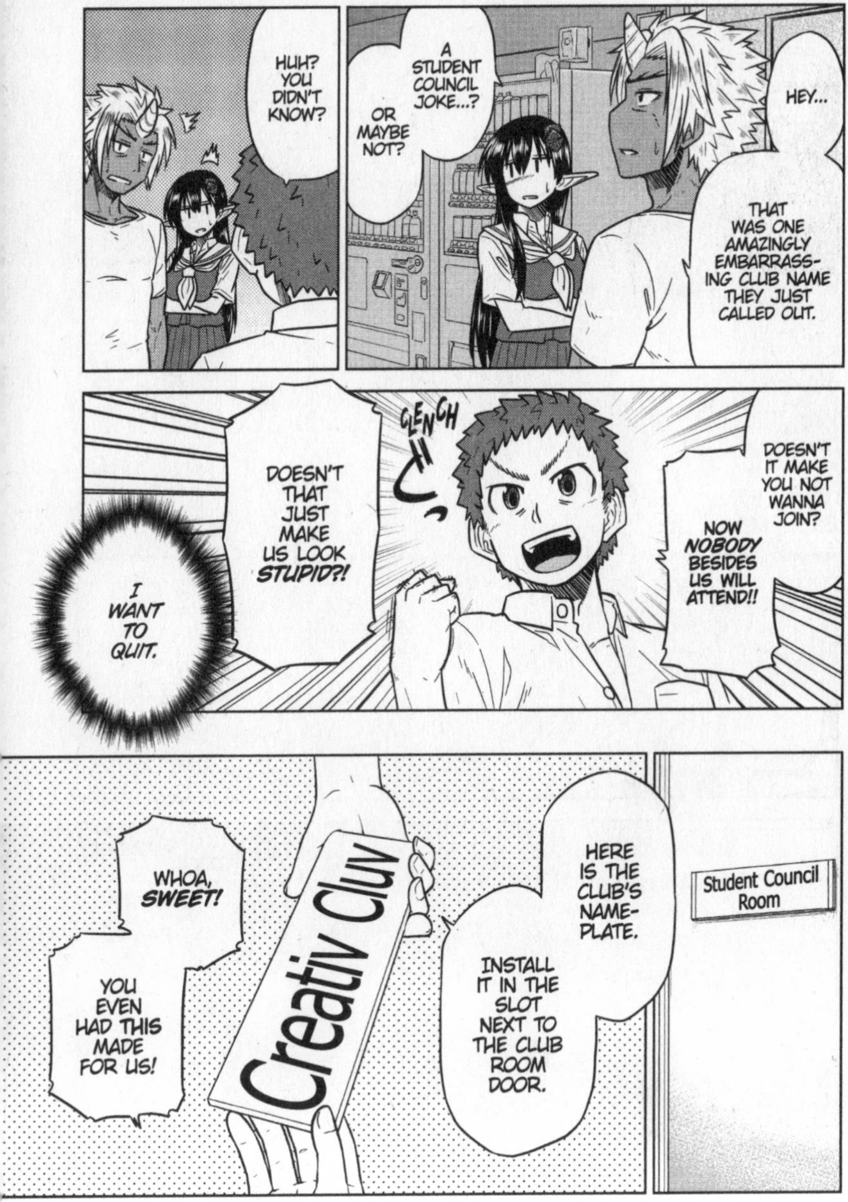
HEY...
THAT WAS ONE AMAZINGLY EMBARRASSING CLUB NAME THEY JUST CALLED OUT.
A STUDENT COUNCIL JOKE...?
OR MAYBE NOT?
HUH? YOU DIDN'T KNOW?
DOESN'T IT MAKE YOU NOT WANNA JOIN?
NOW NOBODY BESIDES US WILL ATTEND!!
CLENCH
DOESN'T THAT JUST MAKE US LOOK STUPID?!
I WANT TO QUIT.
Student Council Room
HERE IS THE CLUB'S NAMEPLATE.
INSTALL IT IN THE SLOT NEXT TO THE CLUB ROOM DOOR.
Creativ Cluv
WHOA, SWEET!
YOU EVEN HAD THIS MADE FOR US!

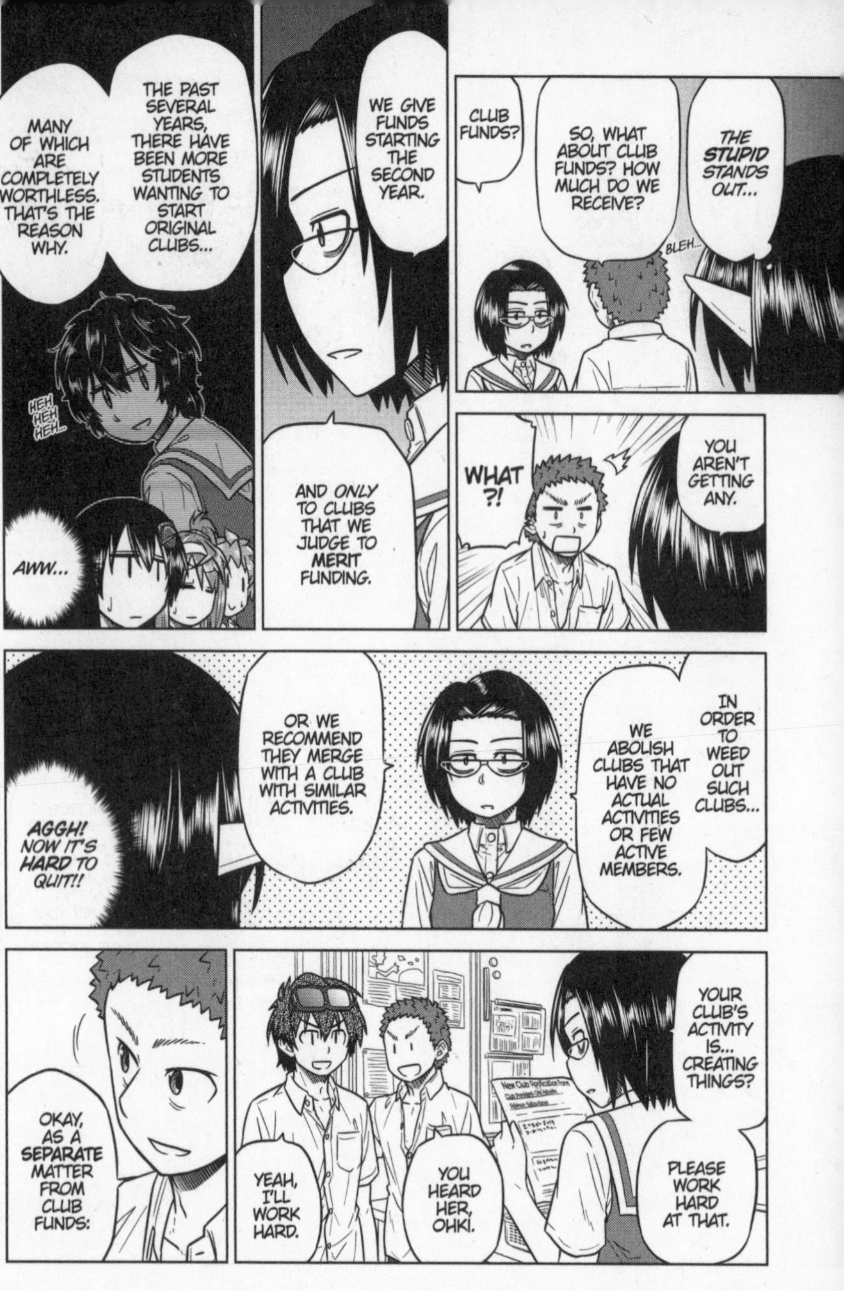
THE STUPID STANDS OUT...
SO, WHAT ABOUT CLUB FUNDS? HOW MUCH DO WE RECEIVE?
CLUB FUNDS?
BLEH...
YOU AREN'T GETTING ANY.
WHAT ?!
WE GIVE FUNDS STARTING THE SECOND YEAR.
AND ONLY TO CLUBS THAT WE JUDGE TO MERIT FUNDING.
THE PAST SEVERAL YEARS, THERE HAVE BEEN MORE STUDENTS WANTING TO START ORIGINAL CLUBS...
MANY OF WHICH ARE COMPLETELY WORTHLESS. THAT'S THE REASON WHY.
HEH HEH HEH...
AWW...
IN ORDER TO WEED OUT SUCH CLUBS...
WE ABOLISH CLUBS THAT HAVE NO ACTUAL ACTIVITIES OR FEW ACTIVE MEMBERS.
OR WE RECOMMEND THEY MERGE WITH A CLUB WITH SIMILAR ACTIVITIES.
AGGH! NOW IT'S HARD TO QUIT!!
YOUR CLUB'S ACTIVITY IS... CREATING THINGS?
PLEASE WORK HARD AT THAT.
YOU HEARD HER, OHKI.
YEAH, I'LL WORK HARD.
OKAY, AS A SEPARATE MATTER FROM CLUB FUNDS:

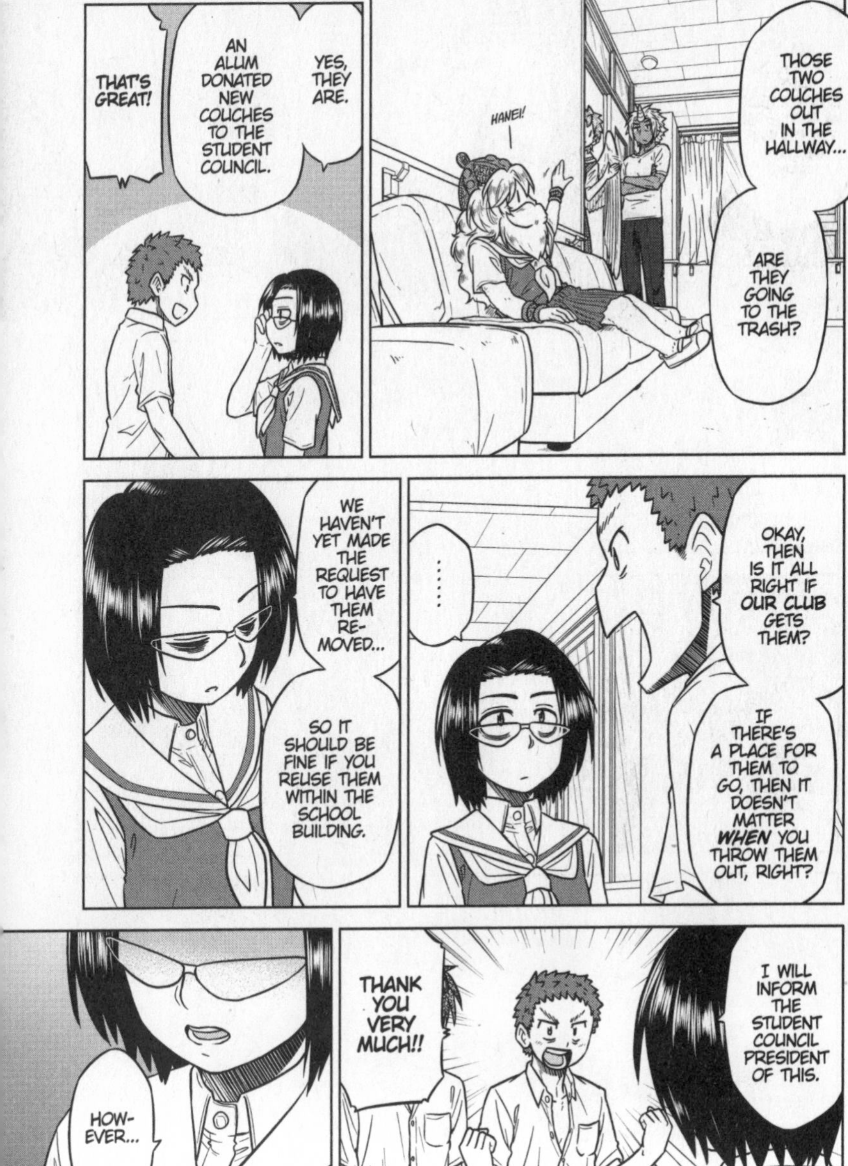
THOSE TWO COUCHES OUT IN THE HALLWAY...
HANEI!
ARE THEY GOING TO THE TRASH?
YES, THEY ARE.
AN ALUM DONATED NEW COUCHES TO THE STUDENT COUNCIL.
THAT'S GREAT!
OKAY, THEN IS IT ALL RIGHT IF OUR CLUB GETS THEM?
IF THERE'S A PLACE FOR THEM TO GO, THEN IT DOESN'T MATTER *WHEN* YOU THROW THEM OUT, RIGHT?
......
WE HAVEN'T YET MADE THE REQUEST TO HAVE THEM RE-MOVED...
SO IT SHOULD BE FINE IF YOU REUSE THEM WITHIN THE SCHOOL BUILDING.
I WILL INFORM THE STUDENT COUNCIL PRESIDENT OF THIS.
THANK YOU VERY MUCH!!
HOW-EVER...

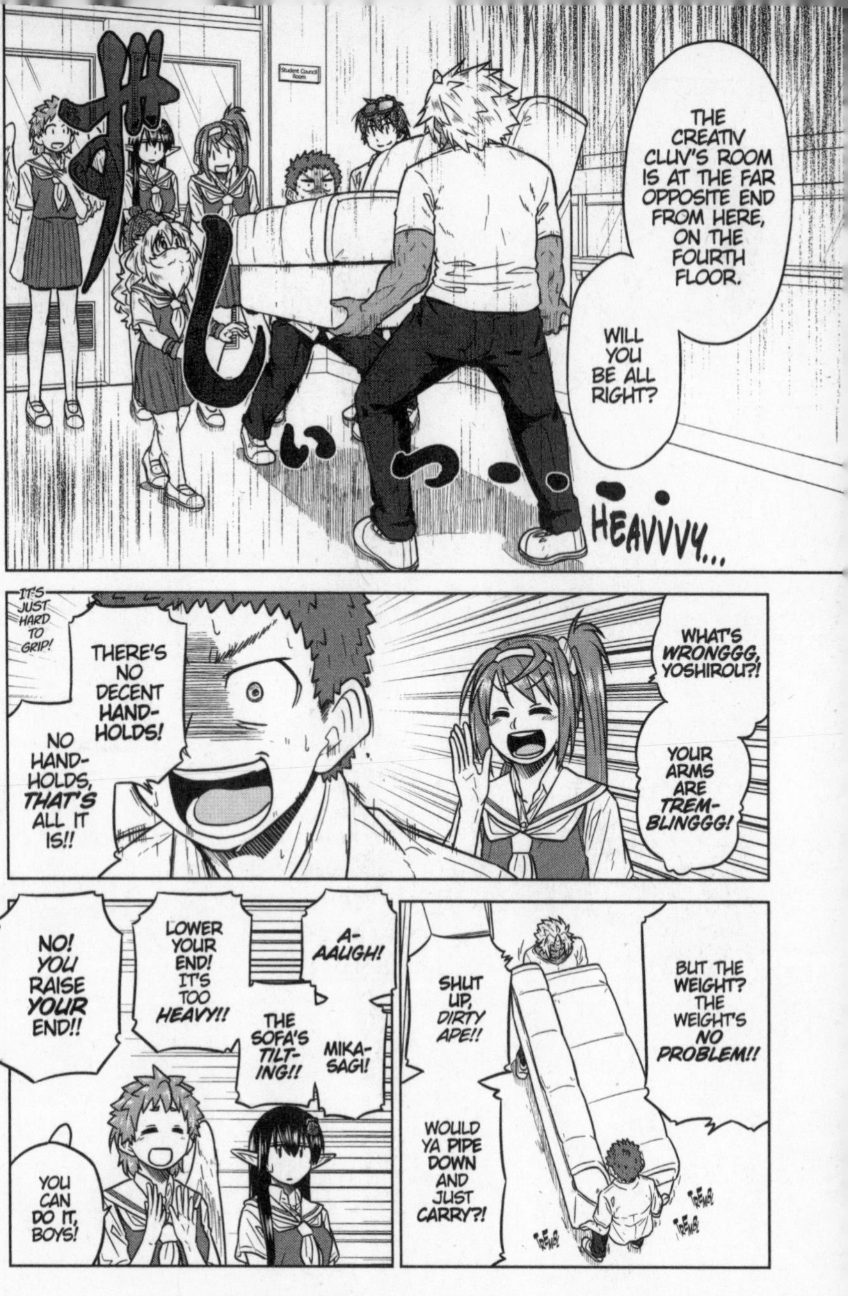
Student Council Room
THE CREATIV CLUV'S ROOM IS AT THE FAR OPPOSITE END FROM HERE, ON THE FOURTH FLOOR.
WILL YOU BE ALL RIGHT?
HEAVVVY...
WHAT'S WRONGGG, YOSHIROU?!
YOUR ARMS ARE TREM-BLINGGG!
THERE'S NO DECENT HAND-HOLDS!
IT'S JUST HARD TO GRIP!
NO HAND-HOLDS, THAT'S ALL IT IS!!
BUT THE WEIGHT? THE WEIGHT'S NO PROBLEM!!
SHUT UP, DIRTY APE!!
WOULD YA PIPE DOWN AND JUST CARRY?!
TREMB
TREMB
TREMB
A-AAUGH!
LOWER YOUR END! IT'S TOO HEAVY!!
NO! YOU RAISE YOUR END!!
MIKA-SAGI!
THE SOFA'S TILT-ING!!
YOU CAN DO IT, BOYS!

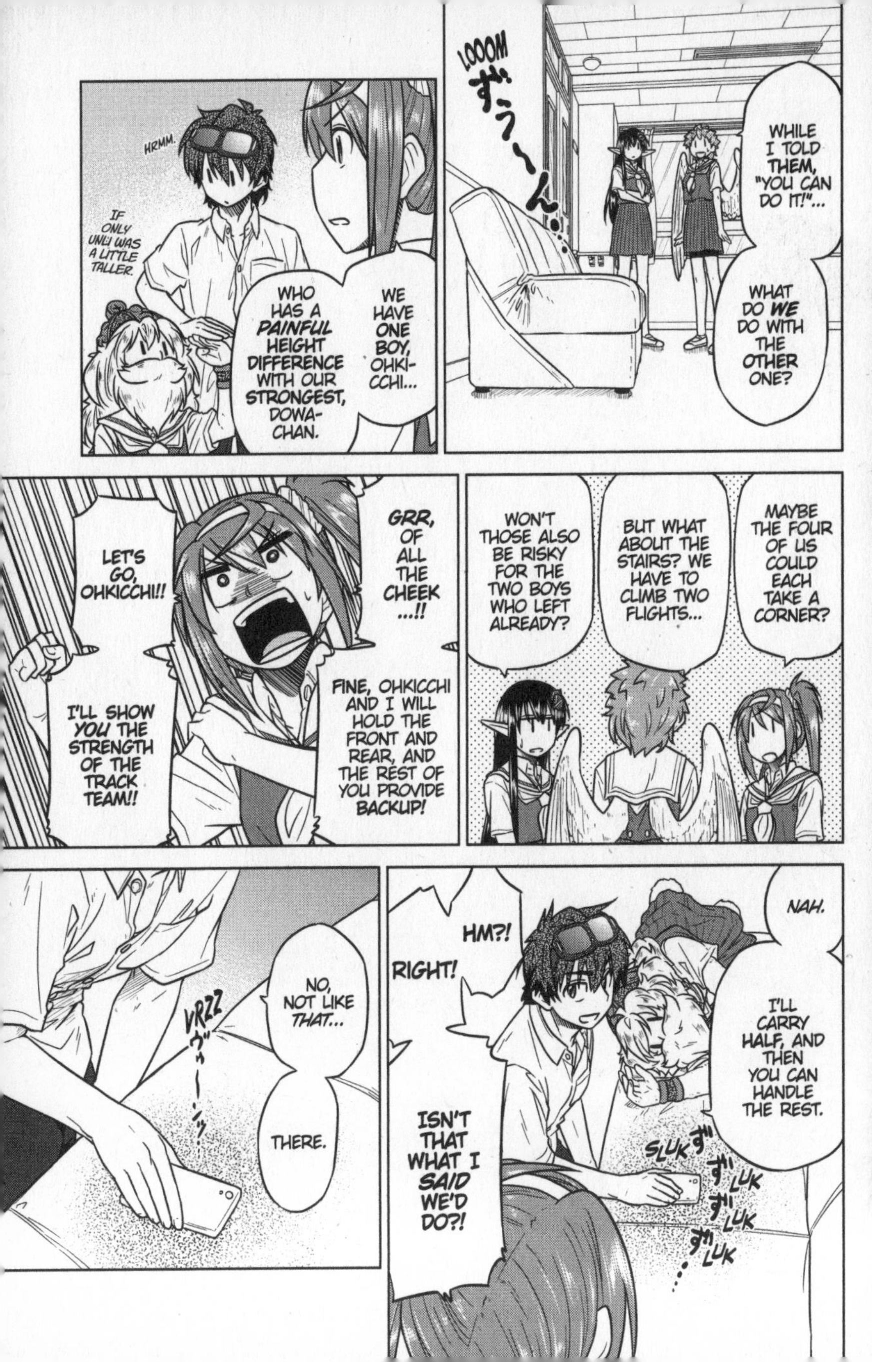
LOOOM
ずう～ん…
WHILE I TOLD THEM, "YOU CAN DO IT!"...
WHAT DO *WE* DO WITH THE OTHER ONE?
WE HAVE ONE BOY, OHKICCHI...
WHO HAS A *PAINFUL* HEIGHT DIFFERENCE WITH OUR STRONGEST, DOWA-CHAN.
HRMM.
IF ONLY UNLI WAS A LITTLE TALLER.
MAYBE THE FOUR OF US COULD EACH TAKE A CORNER?
BUT WHAT ABOUT THE STAIRS? WE HAVE TO CLIMB TWO FLIGHTS...
WON'T THOSE ALSO BE RISKY FOR THE TWO BOYS WHO LEFT ALREADY?
GRR, OF ALL THE CHEEK...!!
FINE, OHKICCHI AND I WILL HOLD THE FRONT AND REAR, AND THE REST OF YOU PROVIDE BACKUP!
LET'S GO, OHKICCHI!!
I'LL SHOW *YOU* THE STRENGTH OF THE TRACK TEAM!!
NAH.
I'LL CARRY HALF, AND THEN YOU CAN HANDLE THE REST.
HM?!
RIGHT!
ISN'T THAT WHAT I *SAID* WE'D DO?!
SLUK ず ず LUK ず LUK ず LUK...
NO, NOT LIKE *THAT*...
VRZZ ヴゥ～…ッ…
THERE.

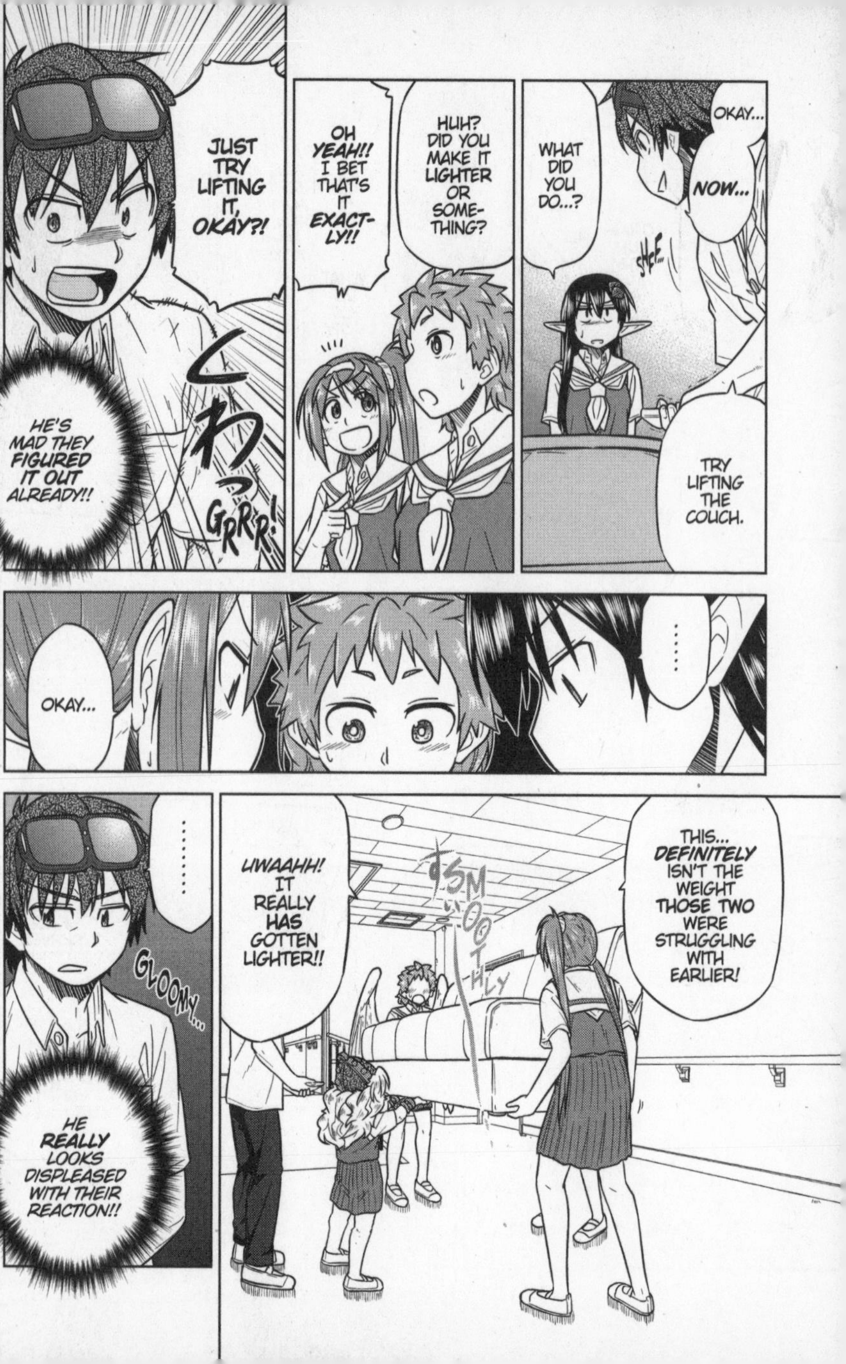
OKAY...
NOW...
TRY LIFTING THE COUCH.
WHAT DID YOU DO...?
HUH? DID YOU MAKE IT LIGHTER OR SOMETHING?
OH YEAH!! I BET THAT'S IT EXACTLY!!
JUST TRY LIFTING IT, OKAY?!
GRRR!
HE'S MAD THEY FIGURED IT OUT ALREADY!!
......
OKAY...
THIS... DEFINITELY ISN'T THE WEIGHT THOSE TWO WERE STRUGGLING WITH EARLIER!
SMOOTHLY
UWAAHH! IT REALLY HAS GOTTEN LIGHTER!!
......
GLOOMY...
HE REALLY LOOKS DISPLEASED WITH THEIR REACTION!!

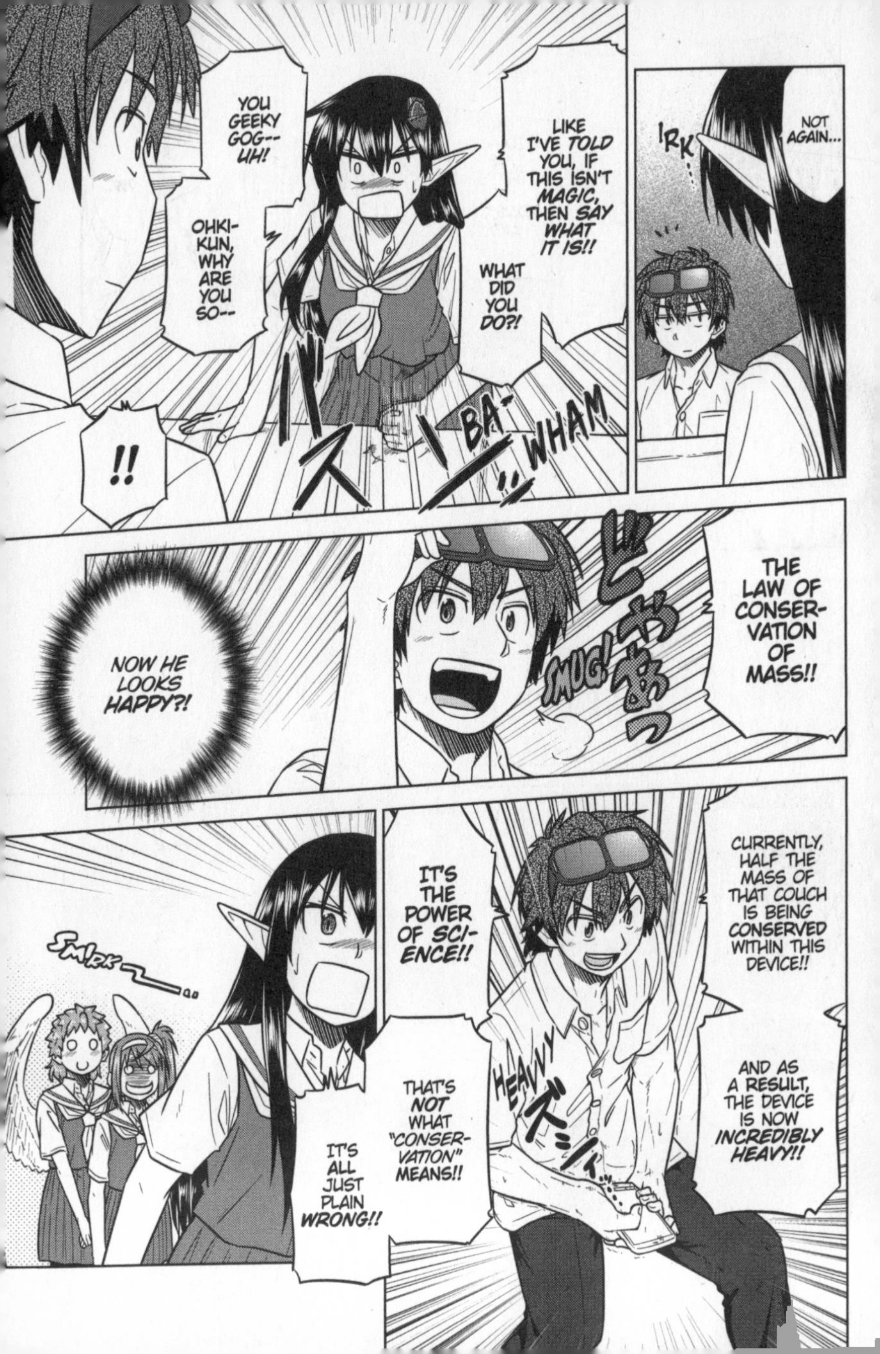
'RK
NOT AGAIN...
LIKE I'VE TOLD YOU, IF THIS ISN'T MAGIC, THEN SAY WHAT IT IS!!
WHAT DID YOU DO?!
YOU GEEKY GOG-- UH!
OHKI-KUN, WHY ARE YOU SO--
BA-WHAM
!!
THE LAW OF CONSERVATION OF MASS!!
SMUG!
NOW HE LOOKS HAPPY?!
CURRENTLY, HALF THE MASS OF THAT COUCH IS BEING CONSERVED WITHIN THIS DEVICE!!
IT'S THE POWER OF SCIENCE!!
AND AS A RESULT, THE DEVICE IS NOW INCREDIBLY HEAVY!!
HEAVY
THAT'S NOT WHAT "CONSERVATION" MEANS!!
IT'S ALL JUST PLAIN WRONG!!
SMIRK~..

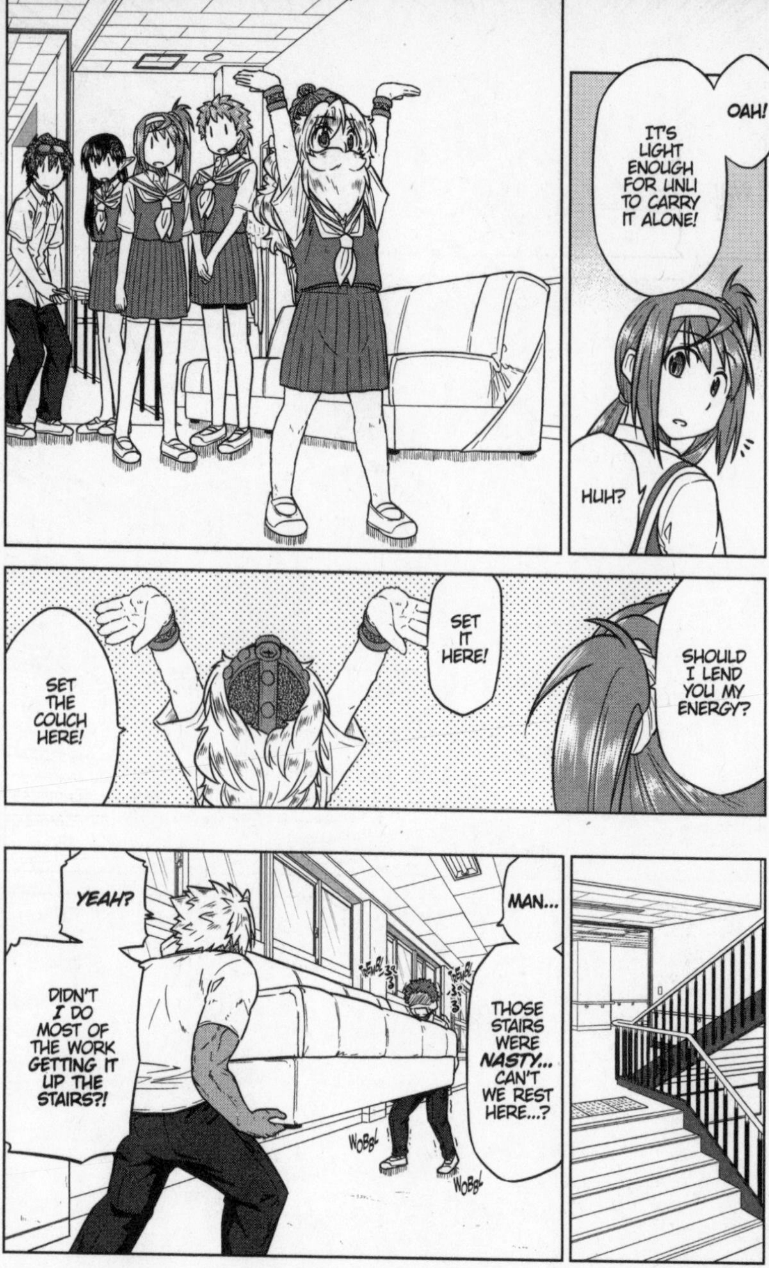
OAH!
IT'S LIGHT ENOUGH FOR UNLI TO CARRY IT ALONE!
HUH?
SHOULD I LEND YOU MY ENERGY?
SET IT HERE!
SET THE COUCH HERE!
MAN...
THOSE STAIRS WERE *NASTY*... CAN'T WE REST HERE...?
YEAH?
DIDN'T *I* DO MOST OF THE WORK GETTING IT UP THE STAIRS?!
WOBBL
WOBBL

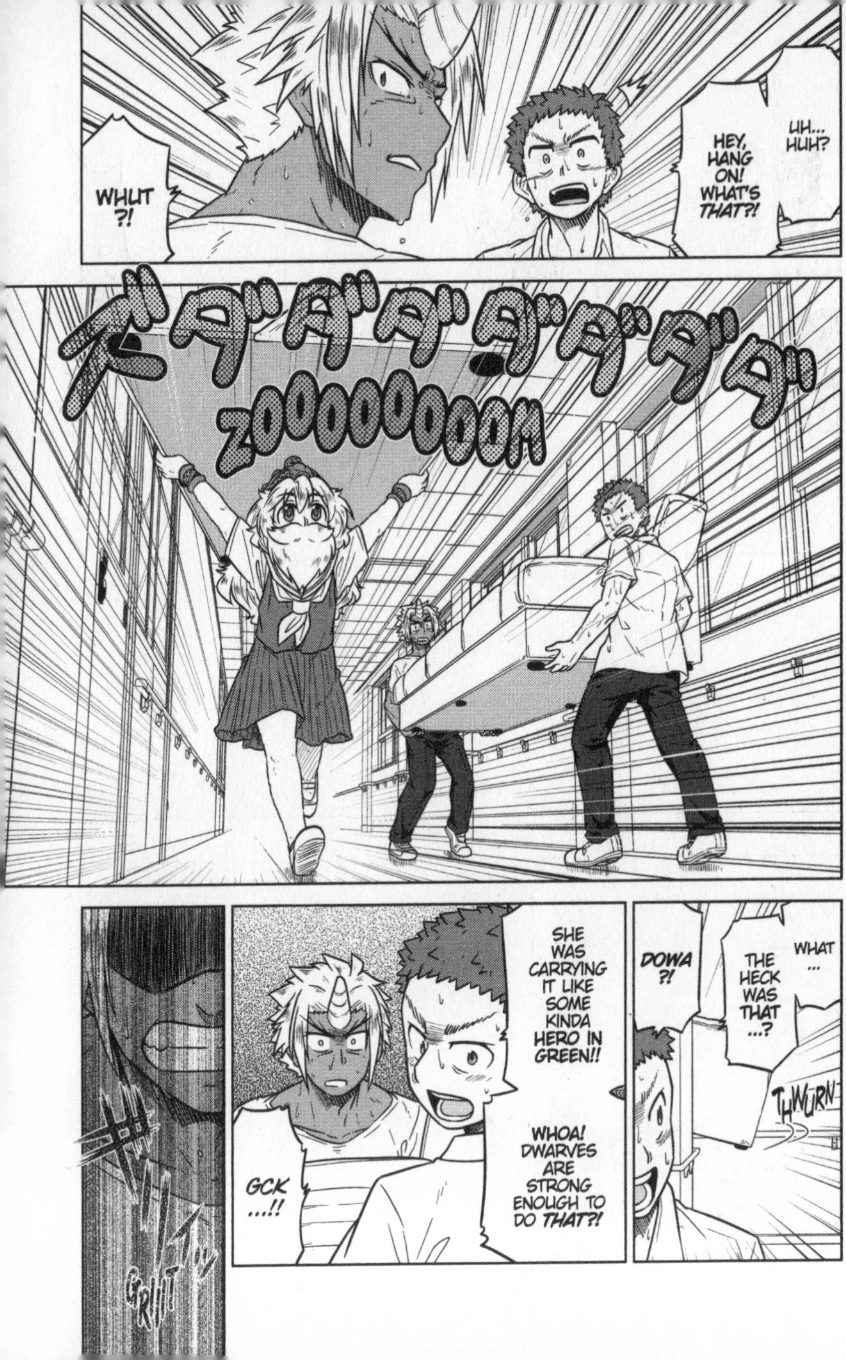
UH... HUH?
HEY, HANG ON! WHAT'S THAT?!
WHUT ?!
ズダダダダダダダ
ZOOOOOOOOOM
WHAT ...
THE HECK WAS THAT ...?
THWURN
DOWA ?!
SHE WAS CARRYING IT LIKE SOME KINDA HERO IN GREEN!!
WHOA! DWARVES ARE STRONG ENOUGH TO DO THAT?!
GCK ...!!
GRIT

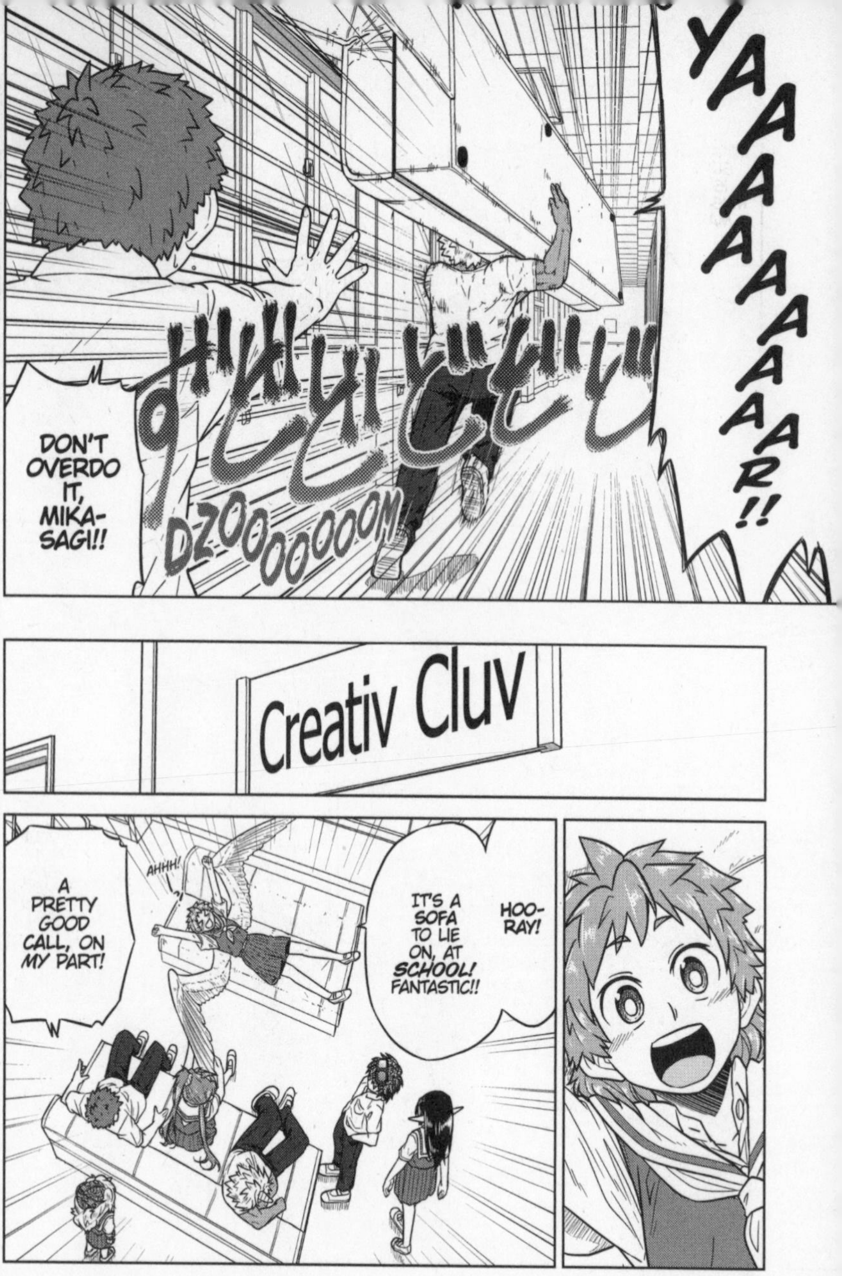
YAAAAAAAAAR!!
DZOOOOOOOM
DON'T OVERDO IT, MIKA-SAGI!!
Creativ Cluv
HOO-RAY!
IT'S A SOFA TO LIE ON, AT SCHOOL! FANTASTIC!!
AHHH!
A PRETTY GOOD CALL, ON MY PART!

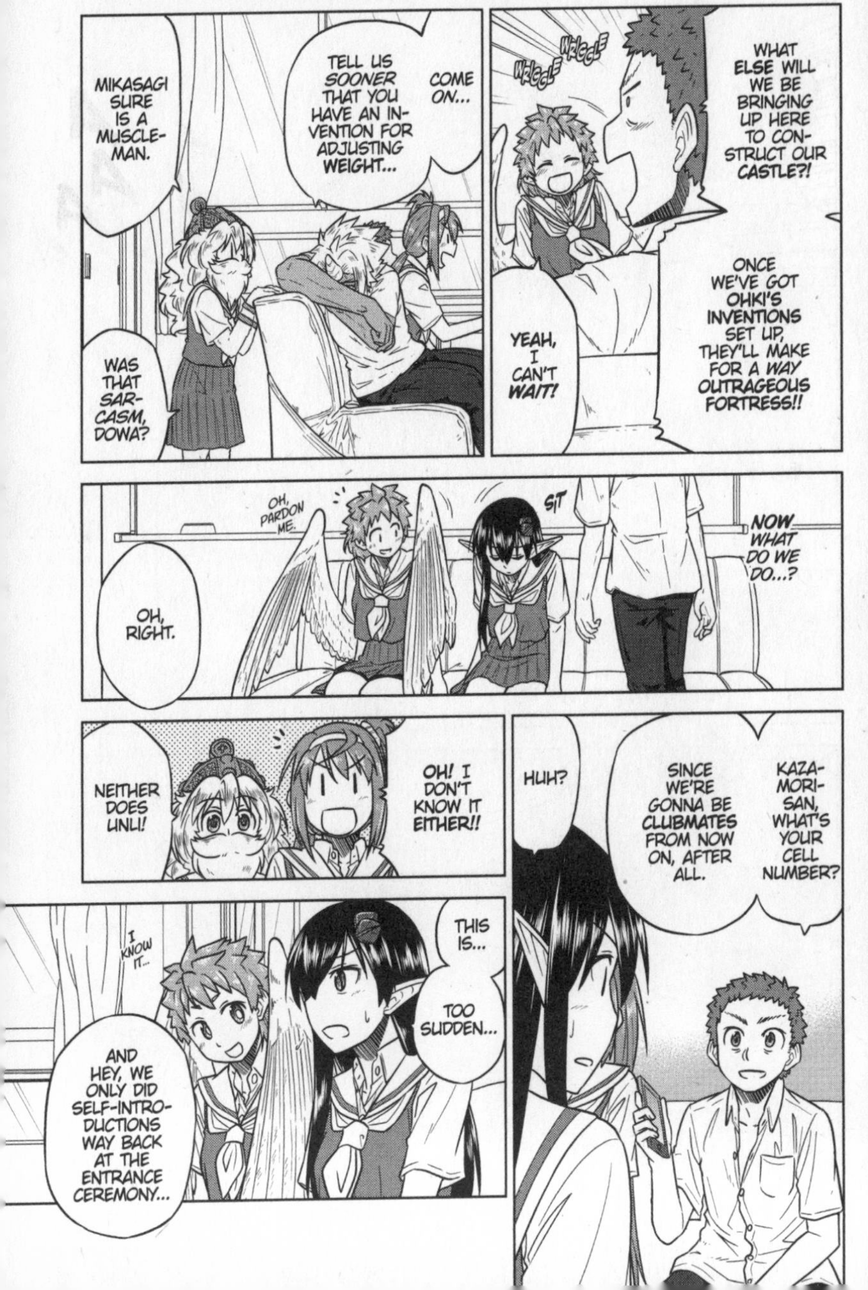
WRIGGLE WRIGGLE
WHAT ELSE WILL WE BE BRINGING UP HERE TO CONSTRUCT OUR CASTLE?!
ONCE WE'VE GOT OHKI'S INVENTIONS SET UP, THEY'LL MAKE FOR A *WAY* OUTRAGEOUS FORTRESS!!
YEAH, I CAN'T *WAIT!*
COME ON...
TELL US *SOONER* THAT YOU HAVE AN INVENTION FOR ADJUSTING WEIGHT...
MIKASAGI SURE IS A MUSCLEMAN.
WAS THAT *SARCASM,* DOWA?
NOW WHAT DO WE DO...?
SIT
OH, PARDON ME.
OH, RIGHT.
KAZAMORI-SAN, WHAT'S YOUR CELL NUMBER?
SINCE WE'RE GONNA BE CLUBMATES FROM NOW ON, AFTER ALL.
HUH?
OH! I DON'T KNOW IT EITHER!!
NEITHER DOES UNLI!
THIS IS...
TOO SUDDEN...
I KNOW IT...
AND HEY, WE ONLY DID SELF-INTRODUCTIONS WAY BACK AT THE ENTRANCE CEREMONY...

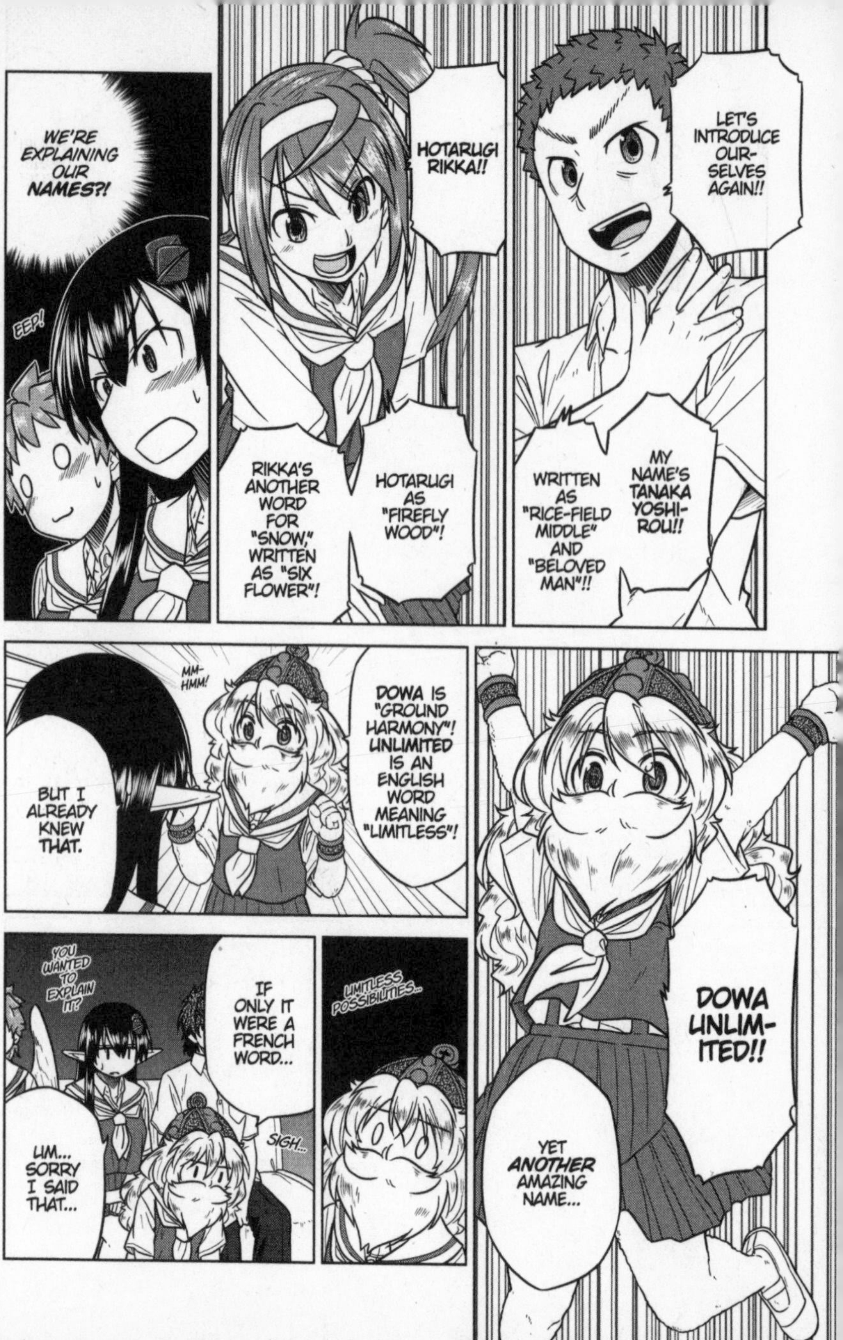
LET'S INTRODUCE OUR-SELVES AGAIN!!
MY NAME'S TANAKA YOSHI-ROU!!
WRITTEN AS "RICE-FIELD MIDDLE" AND "BELOVED MAN"!!
HOTARUGI RIKKA!!
HOTARUGI AS "FIREFLY WOOD"!
RIKKA'S ANOTHER WORD FOR "SNOW," WRITTEN AS "SIX FLOWER"!
WE'RE EXPLAINING OUR NAMES?!
EEP!
DOWA UNLIM-ITED!!
YET ANOTHER AMAZING NAME...
DOWA IS "GROUND HARMONY"! UNLIMITED IS AN ENGLISH WORD MEANING "LIMITLESS"!
MM-HMM!
BUT I ALREADY KNEW THAT.
LIMITLESS POSSIBILITIES...
SIGH...
IF ONLY IT WERE A FRENCH WORD...
YOU WANTED TO EXPLAIN IT?
UM... SORRY I SAID THAT...

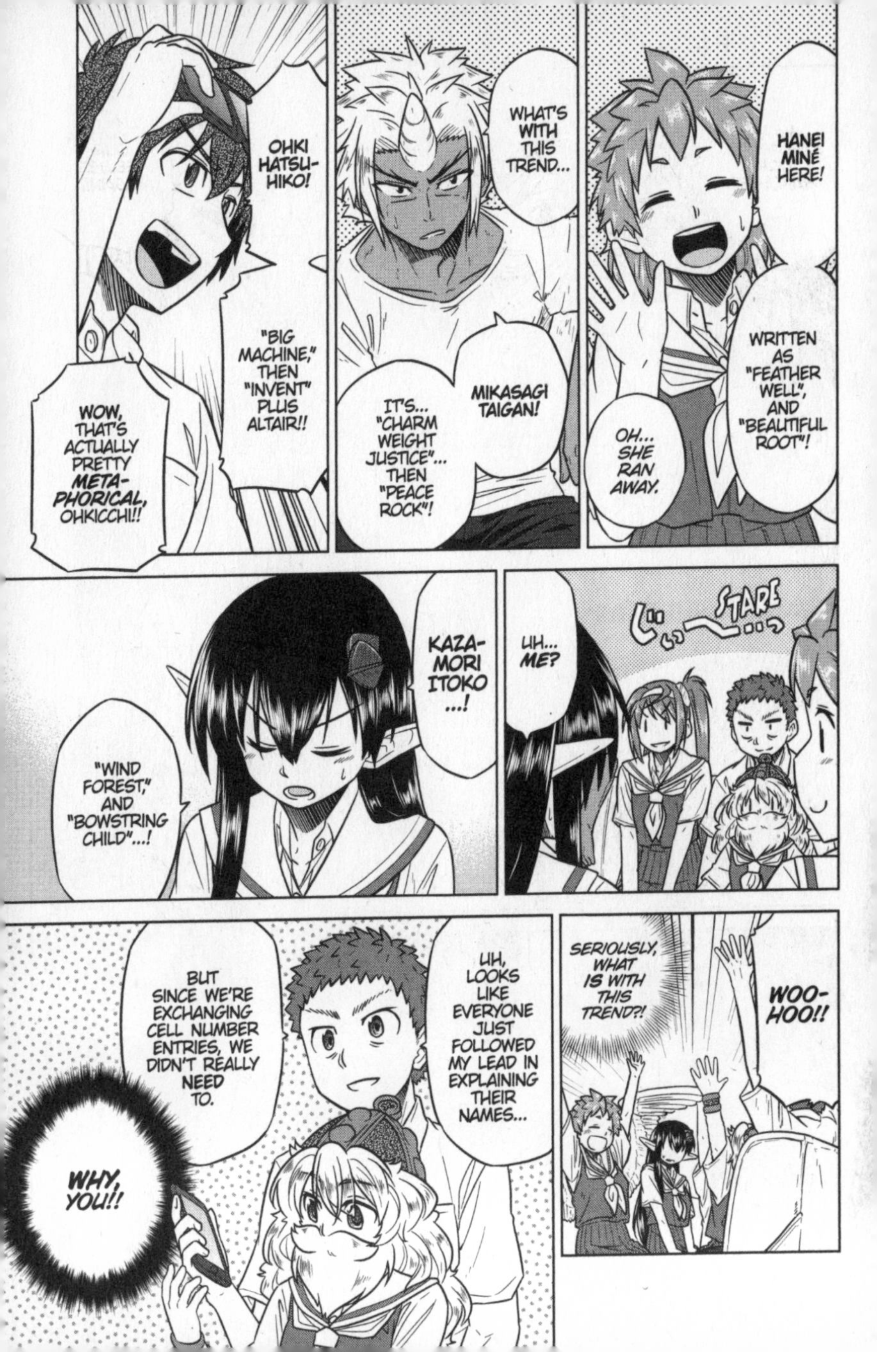
HANEI MINÉ HERE!
WRITTEN AS "FEATHER WELL", AND "BEAUTIFUL ROOT"!
OH... SHE RAN AWAY.
WHAT'S WITH THIS TREND...
MIKASAGI TAIGAN!
IT'S... "CHARM WEIGHT JUSTICE"... THEN "PEACE ROCK"!
OHKI HATSU-HIKO!
"BIG MACHINE," THEN "INVENT" PLUS ALTAIR!!
WOW, THAT'S ACTUALLY PRETTY **META-PHORICAL,** OHKICCHI!!
STARE
UH... **ME?**
KAZA-MORI ITOKO ...!
"WIND FOREST," AND "BOWSTRING CHILD"...!
WOO-HOO!!
SERIOUSLY, WHAT **IS** WITH THIS TREND?!
UH, LOOKS LIKE EVERYONE JUST FOLLOWED MY LEAD IN EXPLAINING THEIR NAMES...
BUT SINCE WE'RE EXCHANGING CELL NUMBER ENTRIES, WE DIDN'T REALLY NEED TO.
WHY, YOU!!

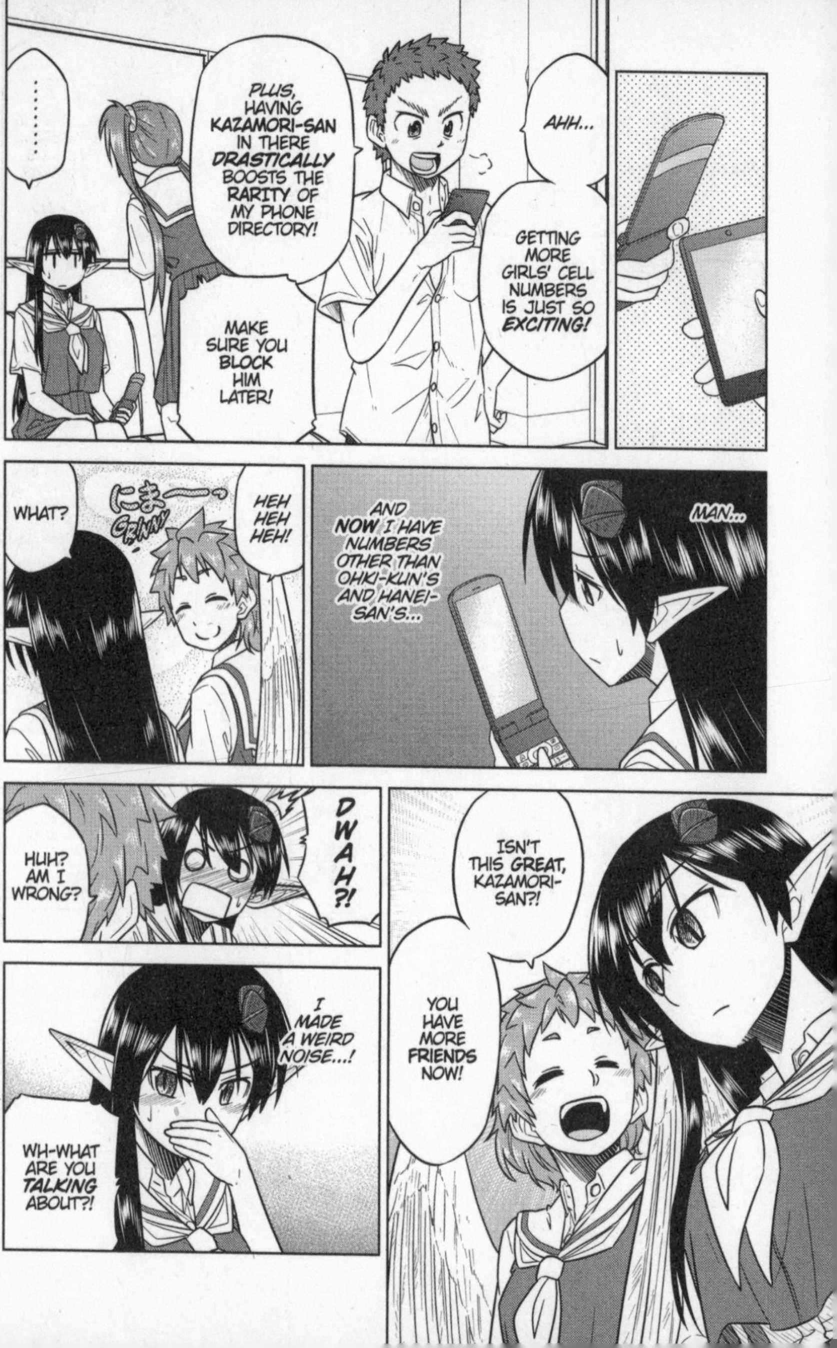
AHH...
GETTING MORE GIRLS' CELL NUMBERS IS JUST SO *EXCITING!*
PLUS, HAVING KAZAMORI-SAN IN THERE ***DRASTICALLY*** BOOSTS THE **RARITY** OF MY PHONE DIRECTORY!
MAKE SURE YOU BLOCK HIM LATER!
......
MAN...
AND **NOW** I HAVE NUMBERS OTHER THAN OHKI-KUN'S AND HANEI-SAN'S...
HEH HEH HEH!
にまーっ
GRINNY
WHAT?
ISN'T THIS **GREAT,** KAZAMORI-SAN?!
YOU HAVE MORE FRIENDS NOW!
DWAH?!
HUH? AM I WRONG?
I MADE A WEIRD NOISE...!
WH-WHAT ARE YOU ***TALKING*** ABOUT?!

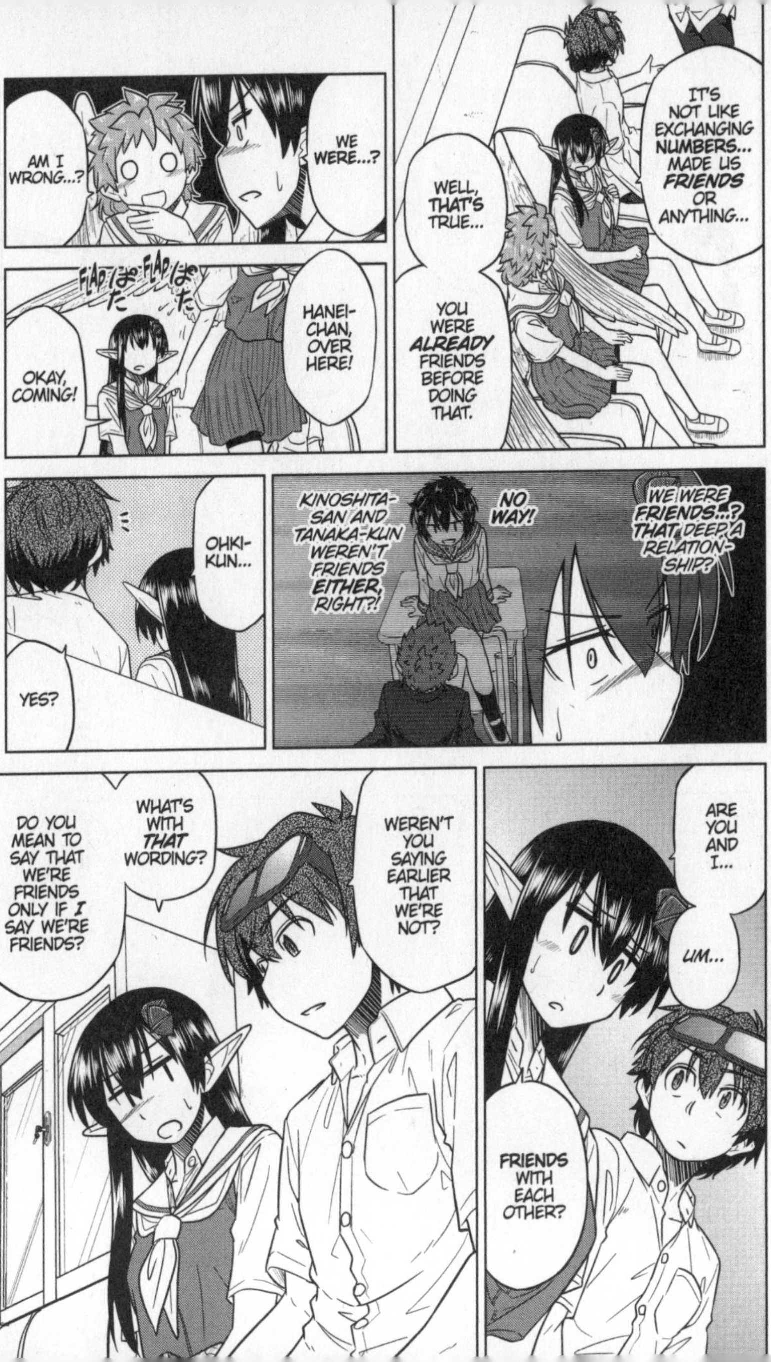
IT'S NOT LIKE EXCHANGING NUMBERS... MADE US FRIENDS OR ANYTHING...
WELL, THAT'S TRUE...
YOU WERE ALREADY FRIENDS BEFORE DOING THAT.
WE WERE...?
AM I WRONG...?
FLAP ぱた FLAP ぱた
HANEI-CHAN, OVER HERE!
OKAY, COMING!
WE WERE FRIENDS...? THAT DEEP A RELATIONSHIP?
NO WAY!
KINOSHITA-SAN AND TANAKA-KUN WEREN'T FRIENDS EITHER, RIGHT?!
OHKI-KUN...
YES?
ARE YOU AND I...
UM...
FRIENDS WITH EACH OTHER?
WEREN'T YOU SAYING EARLIER THAT WE'RE NOT?
WHAT'S WITH THAT WORDING?
DO YOU MEAN TO SAY THAT WE'RE FRIENDS ONLY IF I SAY WE'RE FRIENDS?

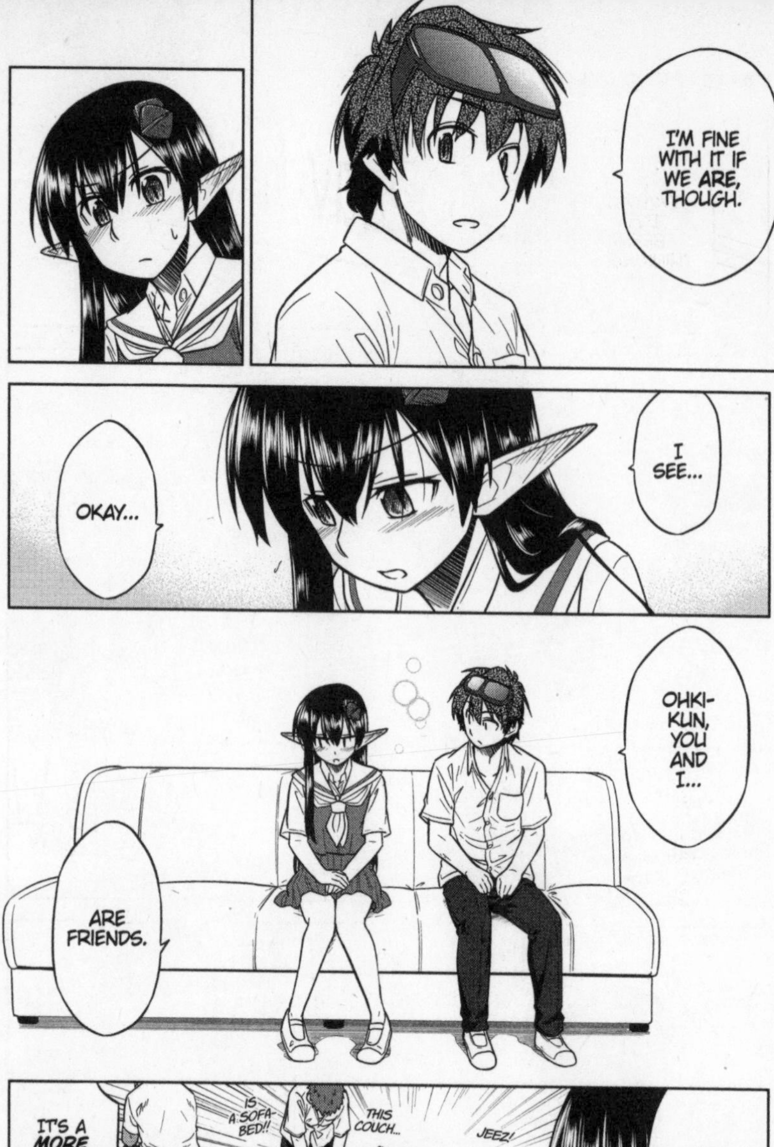
I'M FINE WITH IT IF WE ARE, THOUGH.
I SEE...
OKAY...
OHKI-KUN, YOU AND I...
ARE FRIENDS.
BUT AS FOR THEM...
JEEZ!
THIS COUCH...
IS A SOFA-BED!!
IT'S A MORE BLISSFUL BUNDLE THAN I IMAGINED!!

Chapter 10 • END

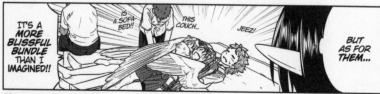

Chapter 11: Hotarugi-san Attacks

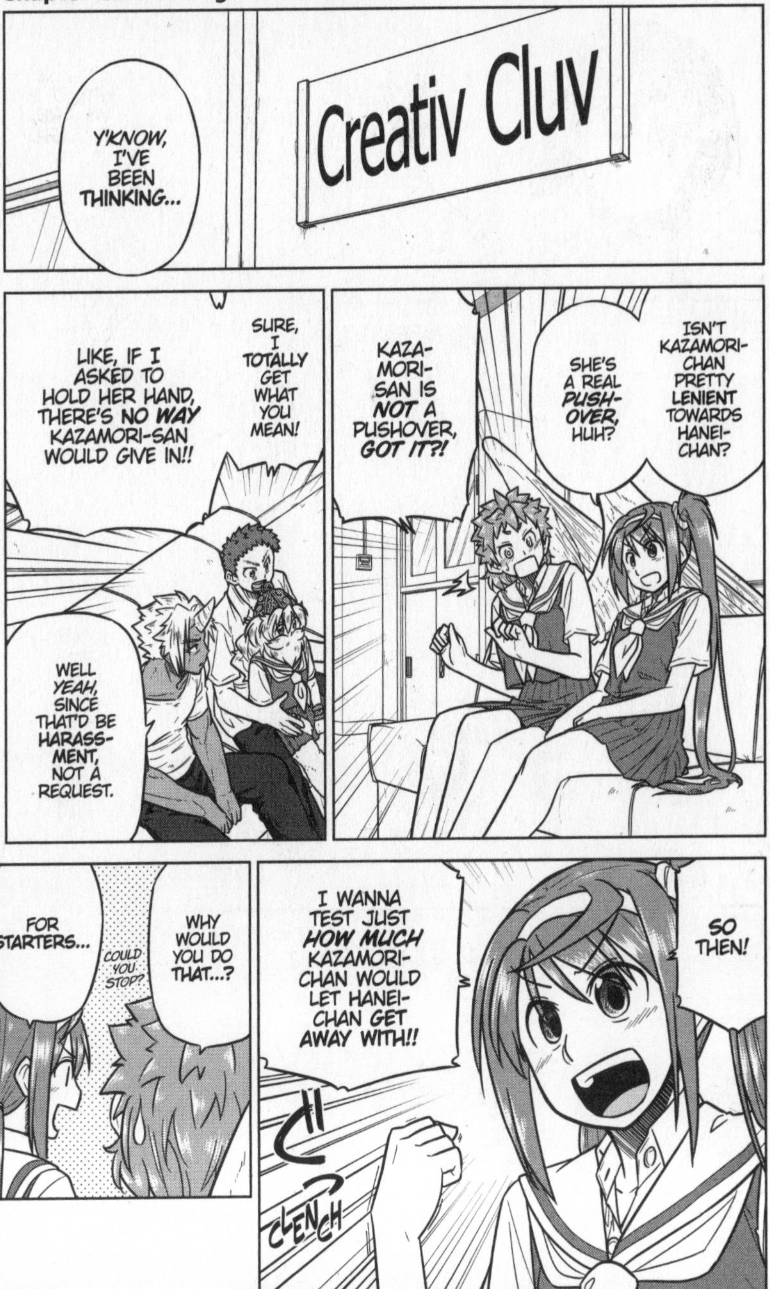

Creativ Cluv
Y'KNOW, I'VE BEEN THINKING...
ISN'T KAZAMORI-CHAN PRETTY LENIENT TOWARDS HANEI-CHAN?
SHE'S A REAL *PUSHOVER*, HUH?
KAZAMORI-SAN IS *NOT* A PUSHOVER, *GOT IT?!*
SURE, I TOTALLY GET WHAT YOU MEAN!
LIKE, IF I ASKED TO HOLD HER HAND, THERE'S **NO WAY** KAZAMORI-SAN WOULD GIVE IN!!
WELL *YEAH*, SINCE THAT'D BE HARASSMENT, NOT A REQUEST.
SO THEN!
I WANNA TEST JUST ***HOW MUCH*** KAZAMORI-CHAN WOULD LET HANEI-CHAN GET AWAY WITH!!
CLENCH
WHY WOULD YOU DO THAT...?
COULD YOU STOP?
FOR STARTERS...

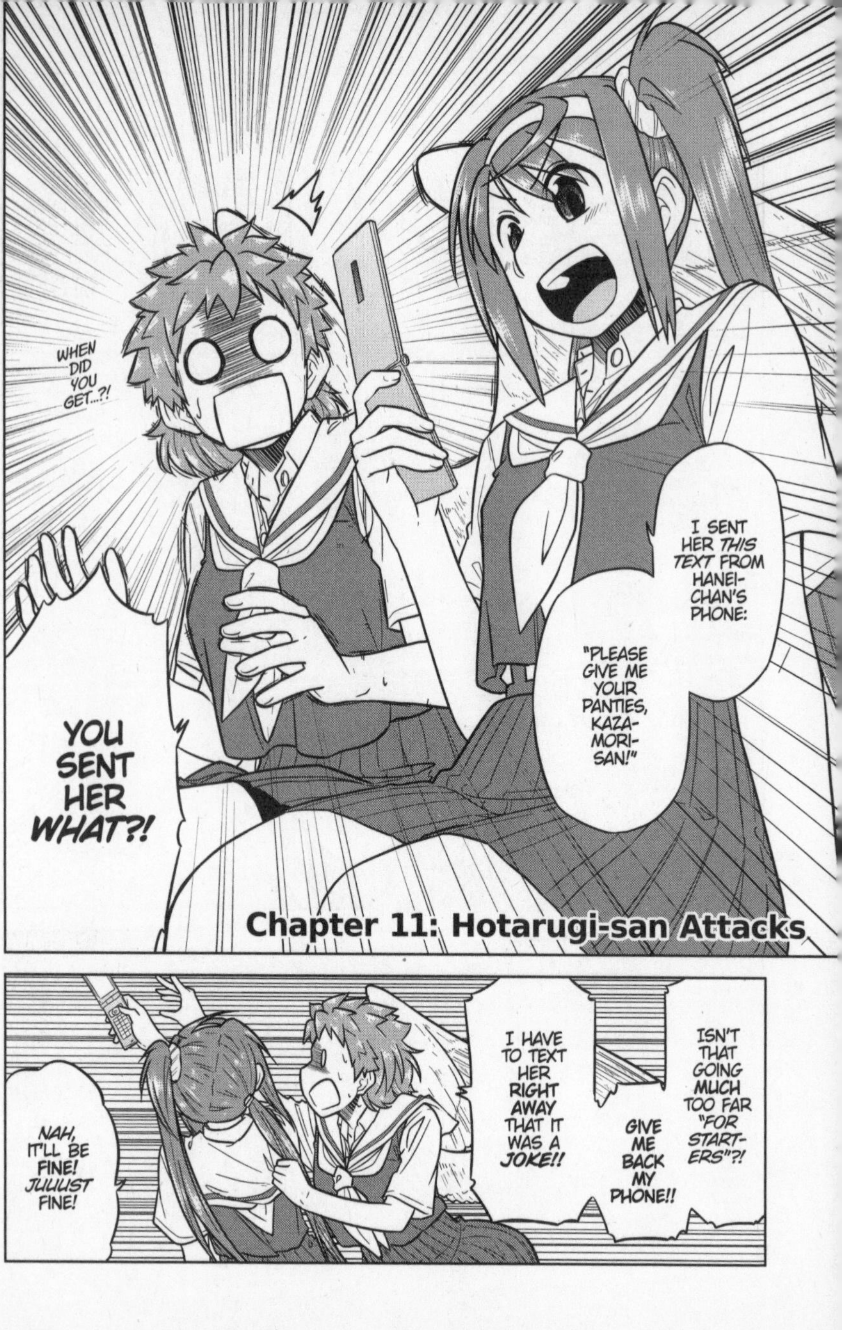
I SENT HER *THIS TEXT* FROM HANEI-CHAN'S PHONE: "PLEASE GIVE ME YOUR PANTIES, KAZAMORI-SAN!"
WHEN DID YOU GET...?!
YOU SENT HER *WHAT?!*
Chapter 11: Hotarugi-san Attacks
ISN'T THAT GOING MUCH TOO FAR *"FOR STARTERS"*?!
I HAVE TO TEXT HER RIGHT AWAY THAT IT WAS A *JOKE!!*
GIVE ME BACK MY PHONE!!
NAH, IT'LL BE FINE! JUUUST FINE!

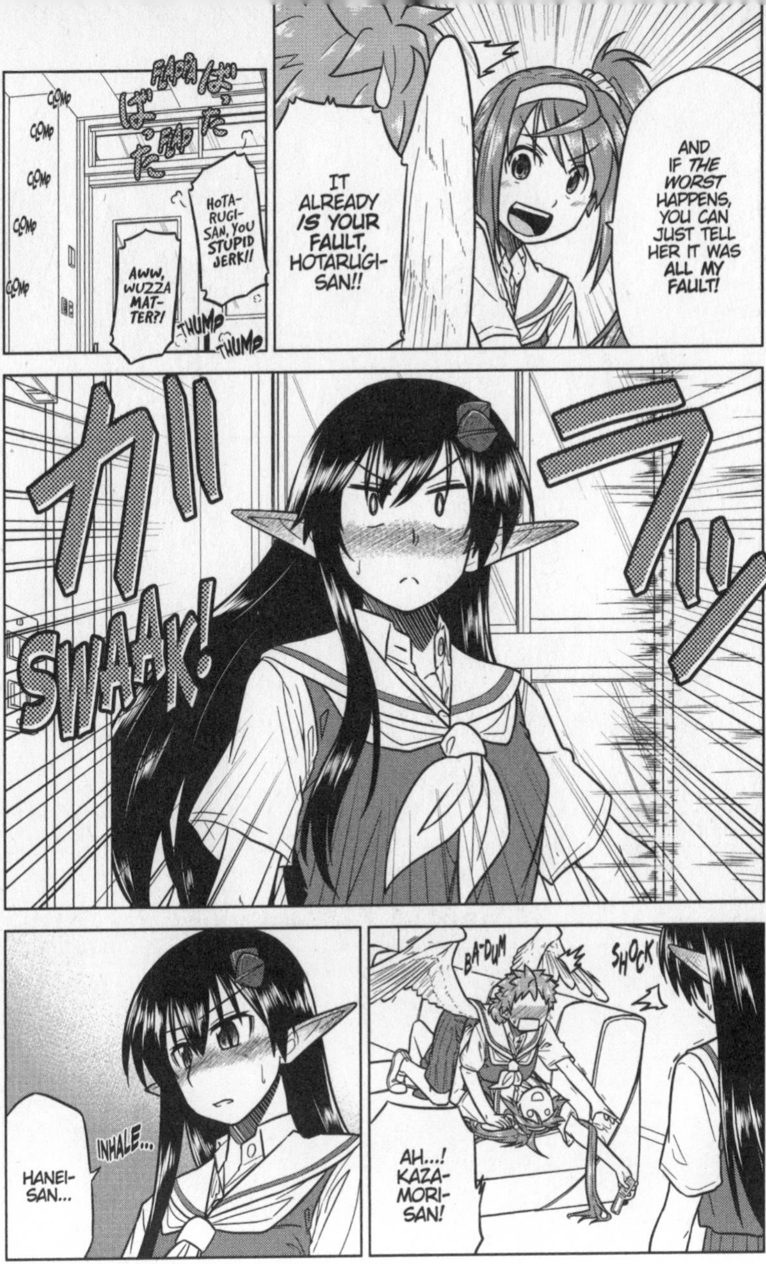

AND IF THE WORST HAPPENS, YOU CAN JUST TELL HER IT WAS ALL MY FAULT!
IT ALREADY IS YOUR FAULT, HOTARUGI-SAN!!
HOTA-RUGI-SAN, YOU STUPID JERK!!
AWW, WUZZA MAT-TER?!
THUMP
THUMP
CLOMP
CLOMP
CLOMP
CLOMP
CLOMP
SWAAK!
SHOCK
BA-DUM
AH...! KAZA-MORI-SAN!
INHALE...
HANEI-SAN...

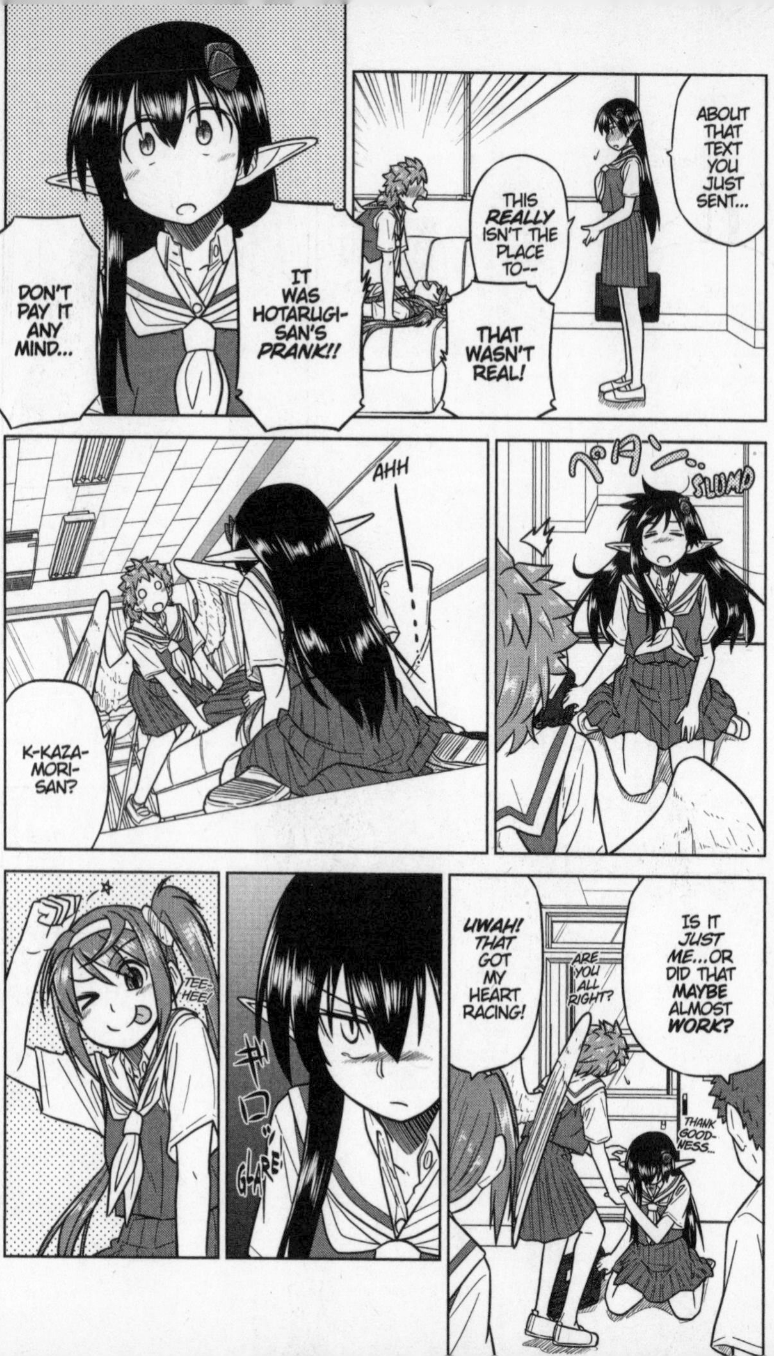
ABOUT THAT TEXT YOU JUST SENT...
THIS REALLY ISN'T THE PLACE TO--
THAT WASN'T REAL!
IT WAS HOTARUGI-SAN'S PRANK!!
DON'T PAY IT ANY MIND...
ペタン..
SLUMP
AHH
...
K-KAZAMORI-SAN?
IS IT JUST ME...OR DID THAT MAYBE ALMOST WORK?
ARE YOU ALL RIGHT?
UWAH! THAT GOT MY HEART RACING!
THANK GOODNESS...
ギロッ
GLARE!
TEE-HEE!

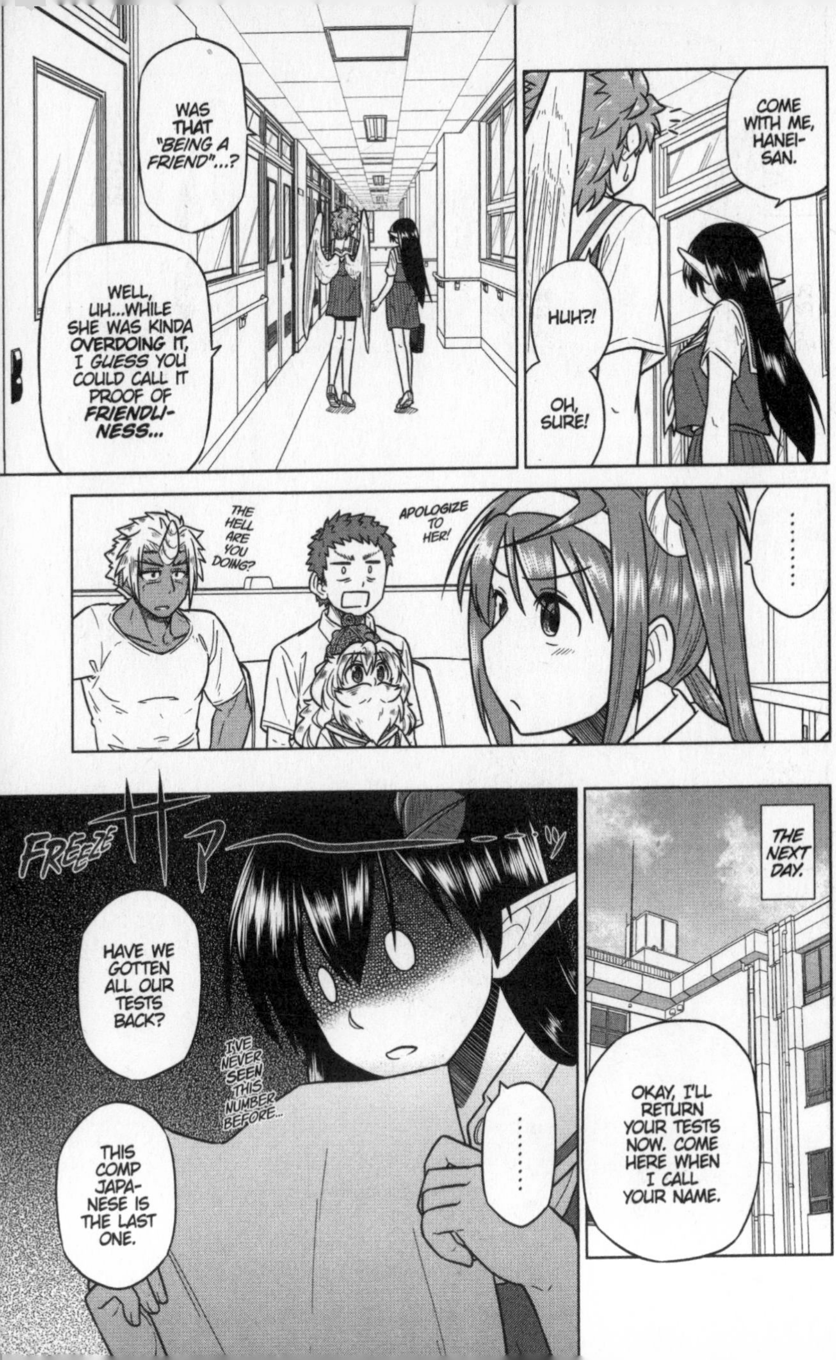
COME WITH ME, HANEI-SAN.
HUH?!
OH, SURE!
WAS THAT "BEING A FRIEND"...?
WELL, UH...WHILE SHE WAS KINDA OVERDOING IT, I GUESS YOU COULD CALL IT PROOF OF FRIENDLI-NESS...
......
APOLOGIZE TO HER!
THE HELL ARE YOU DOING?
THE NEXT DAY.
OKAY, I'LL RETURN YOUR TESTS NOW. COME HERE WHEN I CALL YOUR NAME.
FREEZE
......
I'VE NEVER SEEN THIS NUMBER BEFORE...
HAVE WE GOTTEN ALL OUR TESTS BACK?
THIS COMP JAPANESE IS THE LAST ONE.

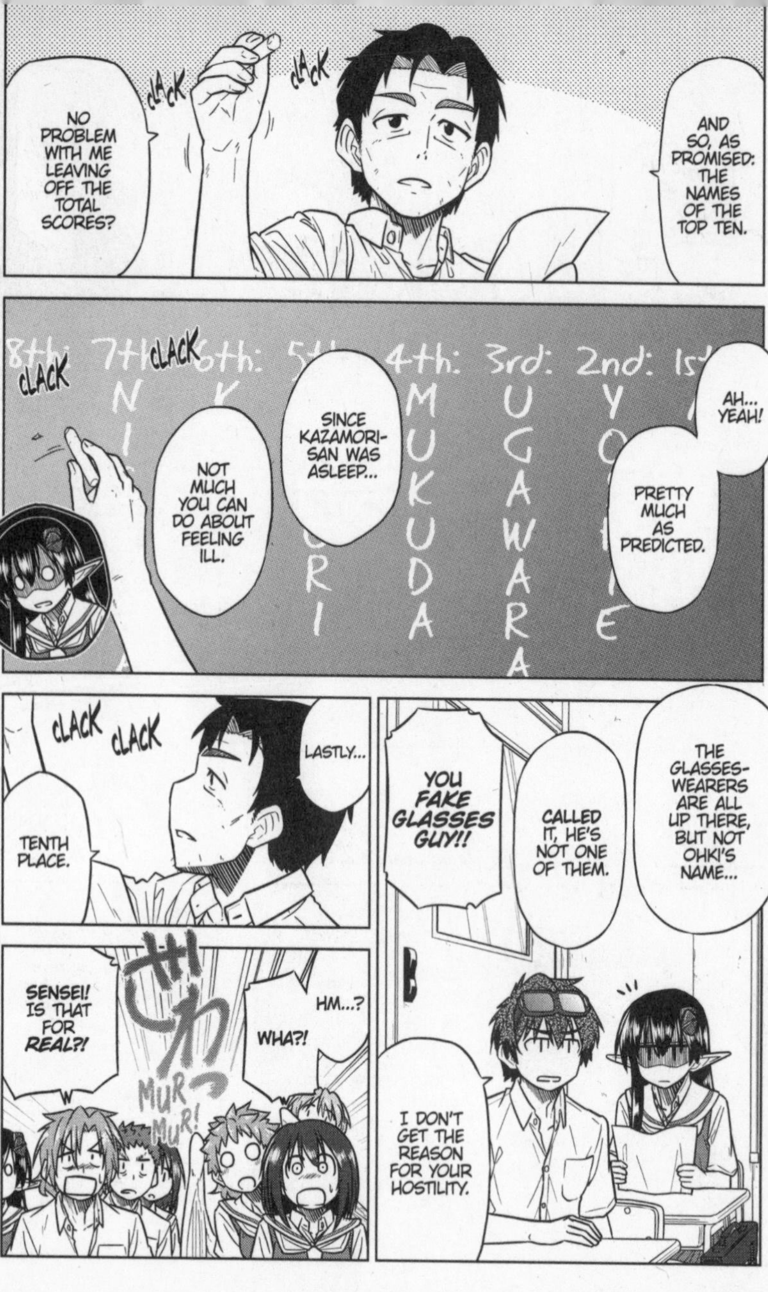
AND SO, AS PROMISED: THE NAMES OF THE TOP TEN.
CLACK
CLACK
NO PROBLEM WITH ME LEAVING OFF THE TOTAL SCORES?
AH... YEAH!
PRETTY MUCH AS PREDICTED.
6th: 4th: 3rd: 2nd:
MUKUDA
UGAWARA
SINCE KAZAMORI-SAN WAS ASLEEP...
NOT MUCH YOU CAN DO ABOUT FEELING ILL.
CLACK
CLACK
THE GLASSES-WEARERS ARE ALL UP THERE, BUT NOT OHKI'S NAME...
CALLED IT, HE'S NOT ONE OF THEM.
YOU *FAKE GLASSES* GUY!!
I DON'T GET THE REASON FOR YOUR HOSTILITY.
LASTLY...
TENTH PLACE.
CLACK
CLACK
HM...?
WHA?!
ざわ
MUR MUR!
SENSEI! IS THAT FOR *REAL*?!

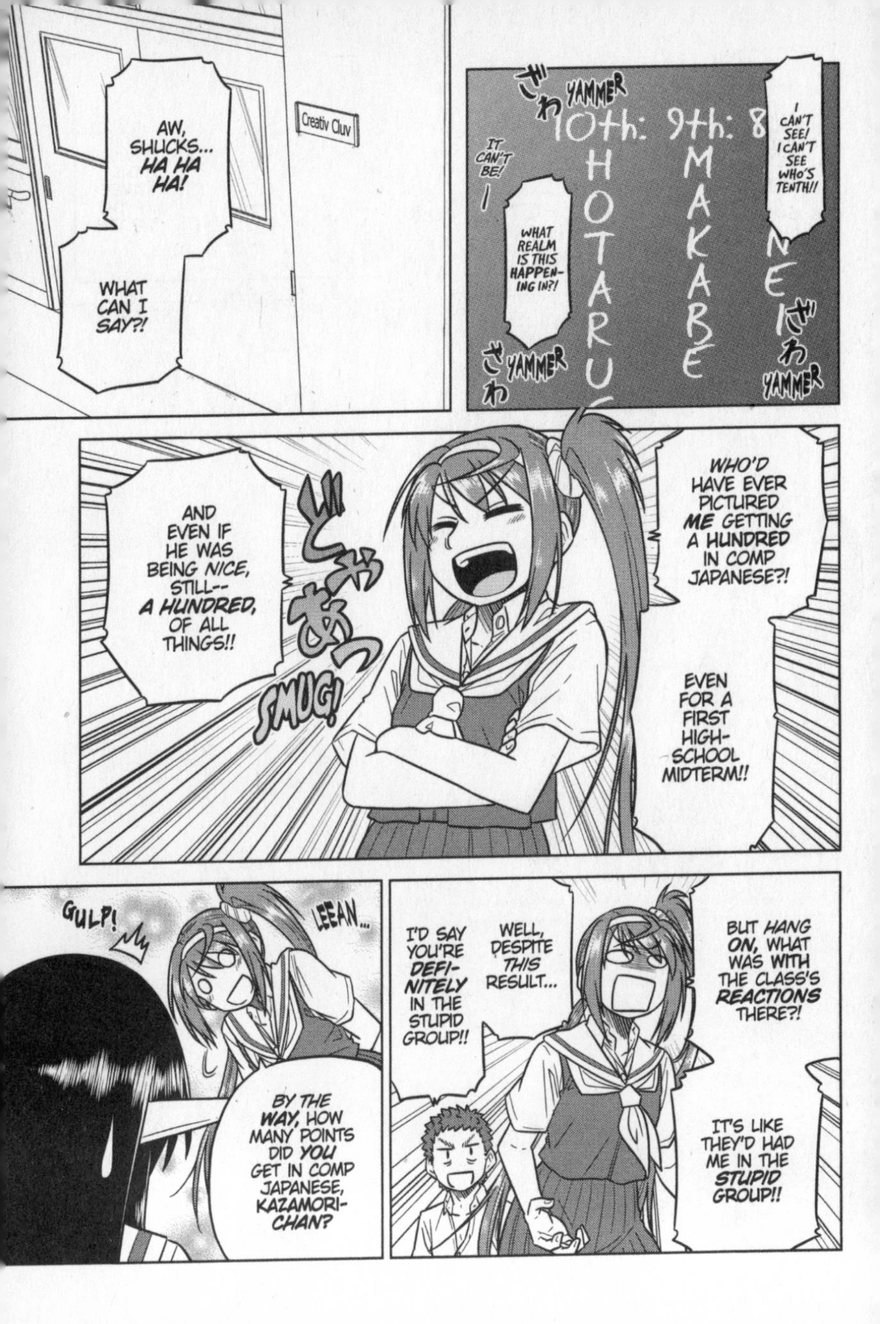

YAMMER
I CAN'T SEE! I CAN'T SEE WHO'S TENTH!!
10th: 9th: 8
NE
MAKABE
HOTARU
YAMMER
IT CAN'T BE!
WHAT REALM IS THIS HAPPENING IN?!
YAMMER
YAMMER
Creativ Cluv
AW, SHUCKS... HA HA HA!
WHAT CAN I SAY?!
WHO'D HAVE EVER PICTURED ME GETTING A HUNDRED IN COMP JAPANESE?!
EVEN FOR A FIRST HIGH-SCHOOL MIDTERM!!
SMUG!
AND EVEN IF HE WAS BEING NICE, STILL-- A HUNDRED, OF ALL THINGS!!
BUT HANG ON, WHAT WAS WITH THE CLASS'S REACTIONS THERE?!
IT'S LIKE THEY'D HAD ME IN THE STUPID GROUP!!
WELL, DESPITE THIS RESULT...
I'D SAY YOU'RE DEFINITELY IN THE STUPID GROUP!!
LEEAN...
GULP!
BY THE WAY, HOW MANY POINTS DID YOU GET IN COMP JAPANESE, KAZAMORI-CHAN?

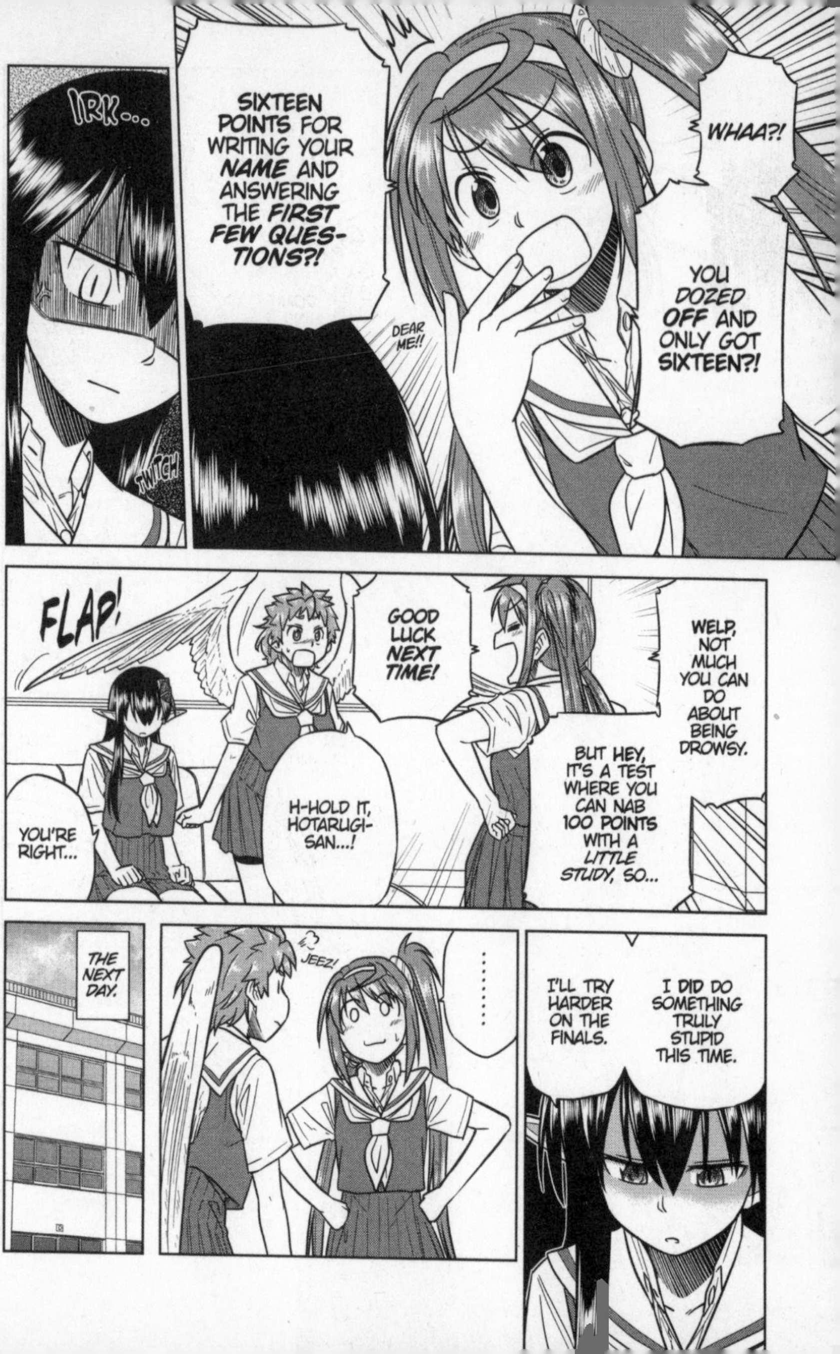
WHAA?!
YOU DOZED OFF AND ONLY GOT SIXTEEN?!
SIXTEEN POINTS FOR WRITING YOUR NAME AND ANSWERING THE FIRST FEW QUESTIONS?!
DEAR ME!!
TWITCH
IRK...
WELP, NOT MUCH YOU CAN DO ABOUT BEING DROWSY.
BUT HEY, IT'S A TEST WHERE YOU CAN NAB 100 POINTS WITH A LITTLE STUDY, SO...
GOOD LUCK NEXT TIME!
H-HOLD IT, HOTARUGI-SAN...!
FLAP!
YOU'RE RIGHT...
I DID DO SOMETHING TRULY STUPID THIS TIME.
I'LL TRY HARDER ON THE FINALS.
......
JEEZ!
THE NEXT DAY.

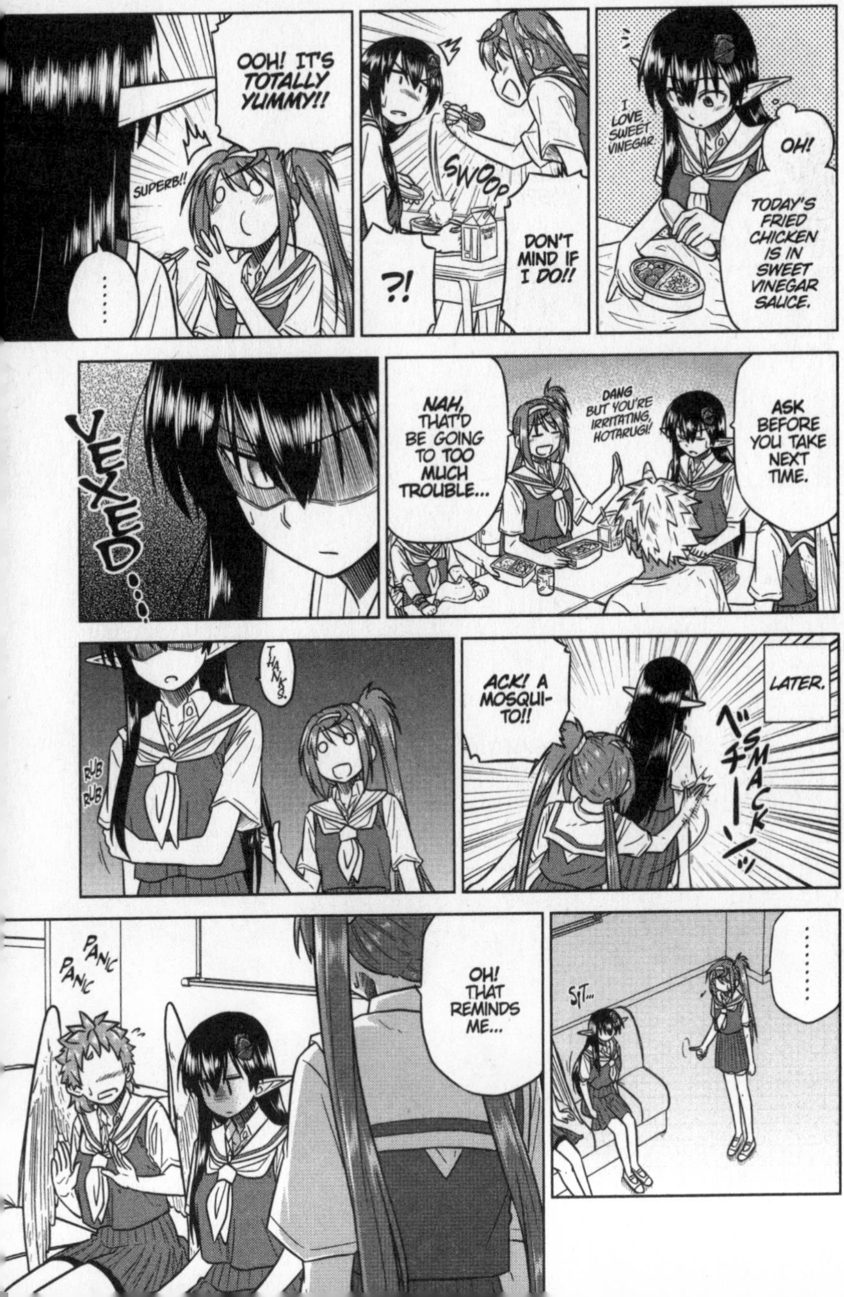
OH!
TODAY'S FRIED CHICKEN IS IN SWEET VINEGAR SAUCE.
I LOVE SWEET VINEGAR.
DON'T MIND IF I DO!!
SWOOP
?!
OOH! IT'S TOTALLY YUMMY!!
SUPERB!!
......
ASK BEFORE YOU TAKE NEXT TIME.
DANG BUT YOU'RE IRRITATING, HOTARUGI!
NAH, THAT'D BE GOING TO TOO MUCH TROUBLE...
VEXED...
LATER.
ACK! A MOSQUI-TO!!
ベチーン
SMACK
THANKS.
RUB RUB
......
SIT...
OH! THAT REMINDS ME...
PANIC PANIC

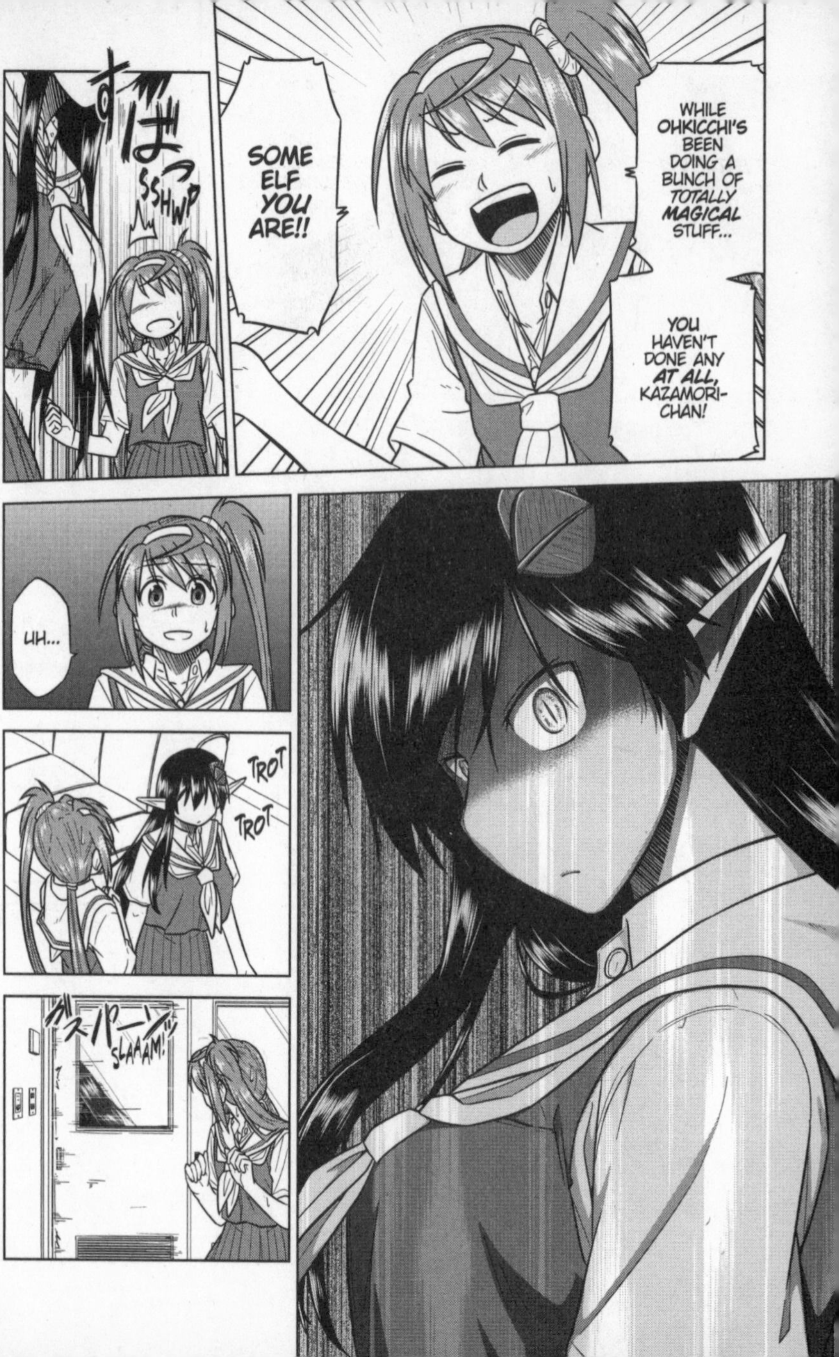
WHILE OHKICCHI'S BEEN DOING A BUNCH OF TOTALLY MAGICAL STUFF...
YOU HAVEN'T DONE ANY AT ALL, KAZAMORI-CHAN!
SOME ELF YOU ARE!!
すぼっ
SSHWP
UH...
TROT
TROT
ガスパーン
SLAAAM!

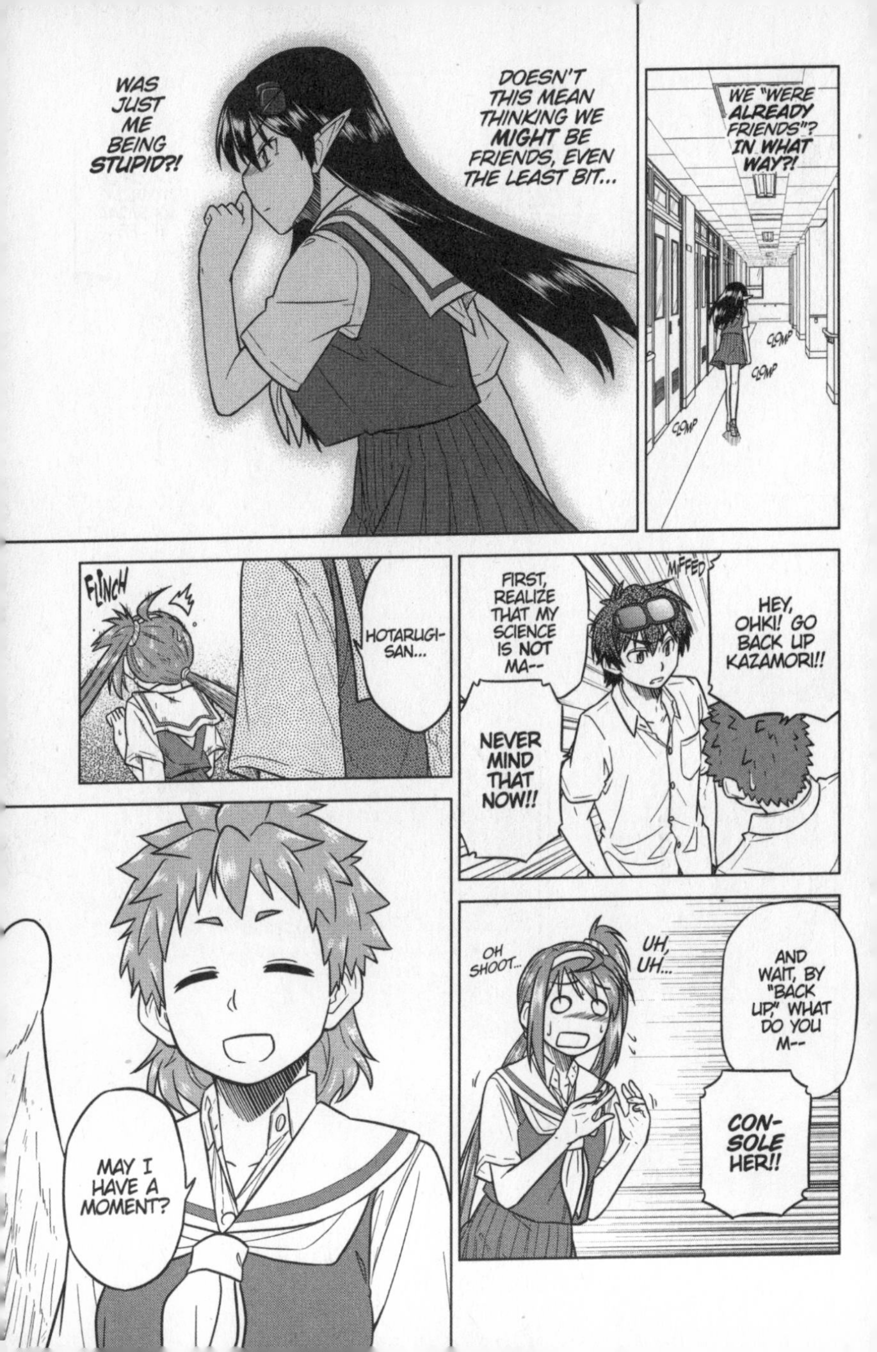
WE "WERE ALREADY FRIENDS"? IN WHAT WAY?!
CLOMP
CLOMP
CLOMP
DOESN'T THIS MEAN THINKING WE MIGHT BE FRIENDS, EVEN THE LEAST BIT...
WAS JUST ME BEING STUPID?!
MIFFED
HEY, OHKI! GO BACK UP KAZAMORI!!
FIRST, REALIZE THAT MY SCIENCE IS NOT MA--
NEVER MIND THAT NOW!!
FLINCH
HOTARUGI-SAN...
AND WAIT, BY "BACK UP," WHAT DO YOU M--
CONSOLE HER!!
UH, UH...
OH SHOOT...
MAY I HAVE A MOMENT?

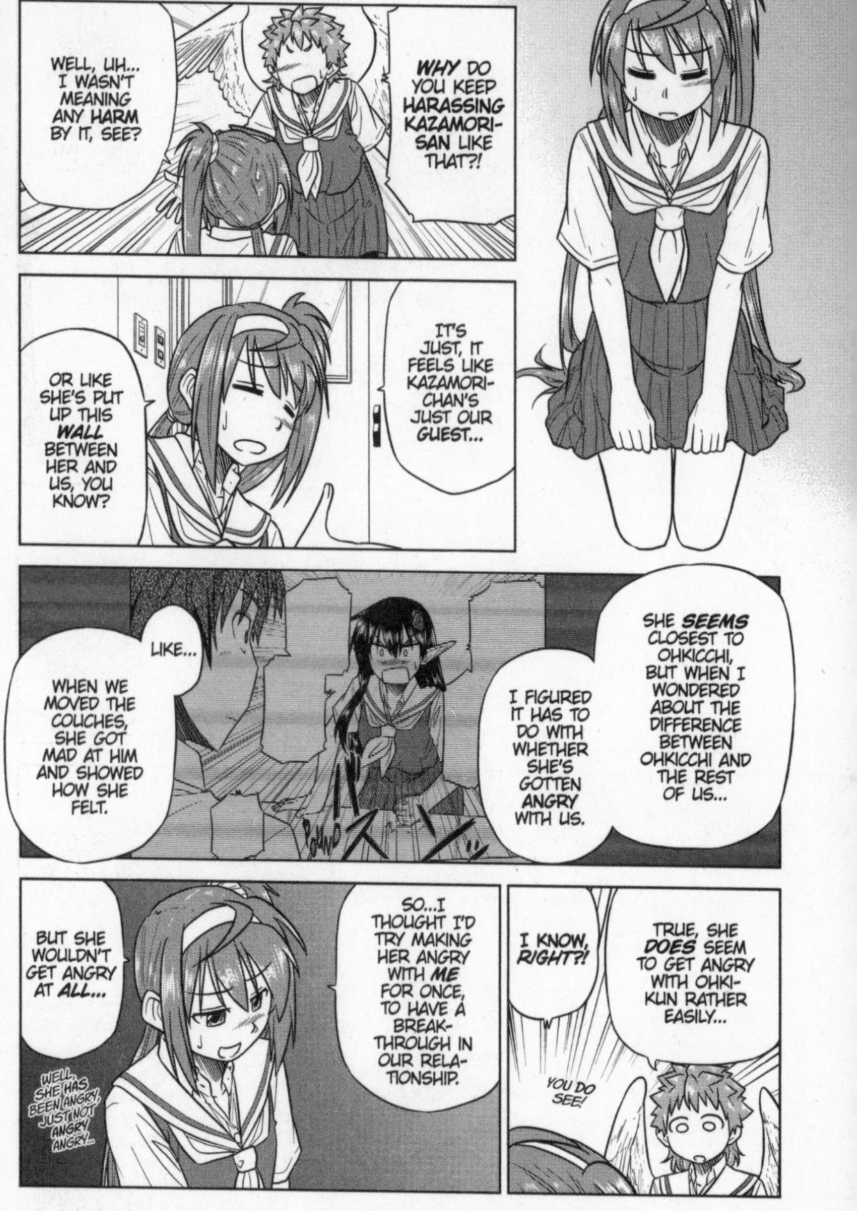
WHY DO YOU KEEP HARASSING KAZAMORI-SAN LIKE THAT?!
WELL, UH... I WASN'T MEANING ANY HARM BY IT, SEE?
IT'S JUST, IT FEELS LIKE KAZAMORI-CHAN'S JUST OUR GUEST...
OR LIKE SHE'S PUT UP THIS WALL BETWEEN HER AND US, YOU KNOW?
SHE SEEMS CLOSEST TO OHKICCHI, BUT WHEN I WONDERED ABOUT THE DIFFERENCE BETWEEN OHKICCHI AND THE REST OF US...
I FIGURED IT HAS TO DO WITH WHETHER SHE'S GOTTEN ANGRY WITH US.
LIKE...
WHEN WE MOVED THE COUCHES, SHE GOT MAD AT HIM AND SHOWED HOW SHE FELT.
POUND
TRUE, SHE DOES SEEM TO GET ANGRY WITH OHKI-KUN RATHER EASILY...
I KNOW, RIGHT?!
YOU DO SEE!
SO...I THOUGHT I'D TRY MAKING HER ANGRY WITH ME FOR ONCE, TO HAVE A BREAK-THROUGH IN OUR RELA-TIONSHIP.
BUT SHE WOULDN'T GET ANGRY AT ALL...
WELL, SHE HAS BEEN ANGRY, JUST NOT ANGRY ANGRY...

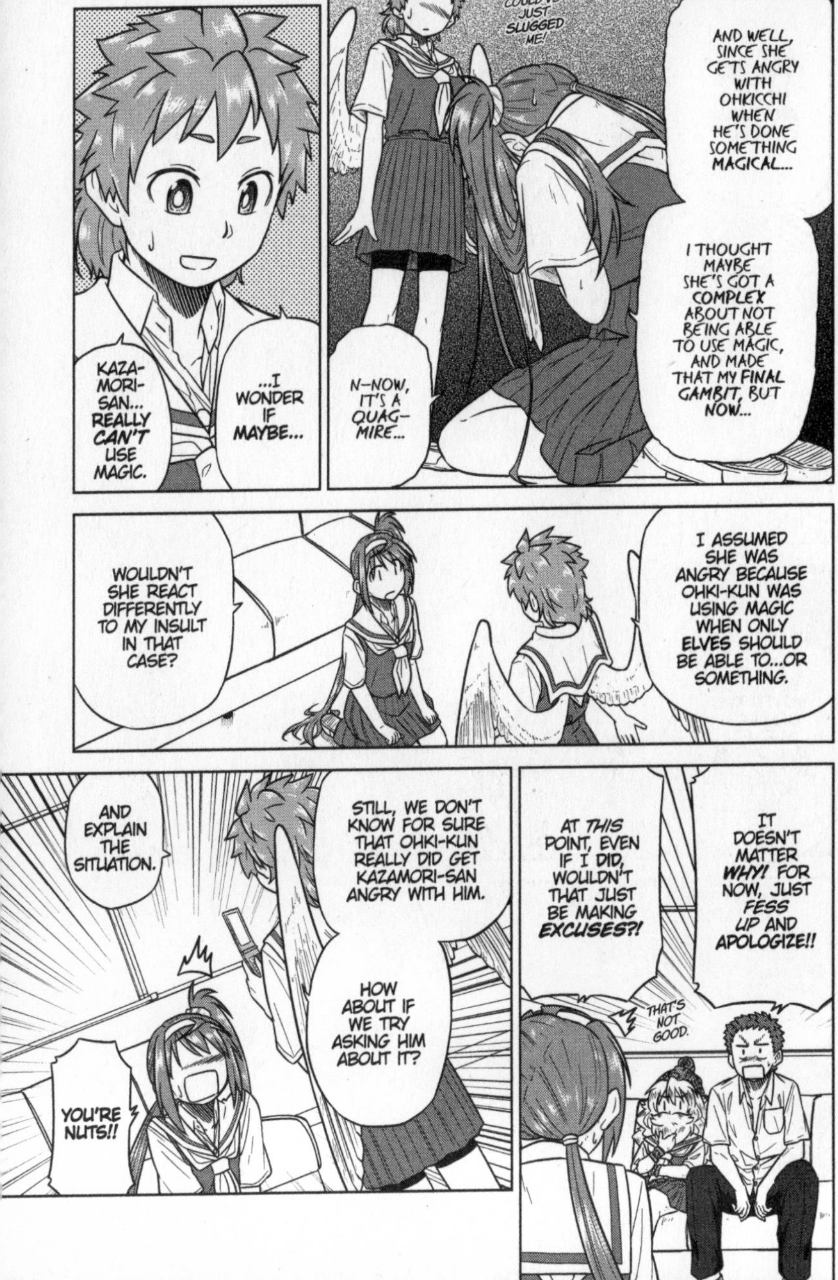
AND WELL, SINCE SHE GETS ANGRY WITH OHKICCHI WHEN HE'S DONE SOMETHING MAGICAL...
SHE COULD'VE JUST SLUGGED ME!
I THOUGHT MAYBE SHE'S GOT A COMPLEX ABOUT NOT BEING ABLE TO USE MAGIC, AND MADE THAT MY FINAL GAMBIT, BUT NOW...
N-NOW, IT'S A QUAGMIRE...
...I WONDER IF MAYBE...
KAZAMORI-SAN... REALLY CAN'T USE MAGIC.
I ASSUMED SHE WAS ANGRY BECAUSE OHKI-KUN WAS USING MAGIC WHEN ONLY ELVES SHOULD BE ABLE TO...OR SOMETHING.
WOULDN'T SHE REACT DIFFERENTLY TO MY INSULT IN THAT CASE?
IT DOESN'T MATTER WHY! FOR NOW, JUST FESS UP AND APOLOGIZE!!
AT THIS POINT, EVEN IF I DID, WOULDN'T THAT JUST BE MAKING EXCUSES?!
THAT'S NOT GOOD.
STILL, WE DON'T KNOW FOR SURE THAT OHKI-KUN REALLY DID GET KAZAMORI-SAN ANGRY WITH HIM.
HOW ABOUT IF WE TRY ASKING HIM ABOUT IT?
AND EXPLAIN THE SITUATION.
YOU'RE NUTS!!

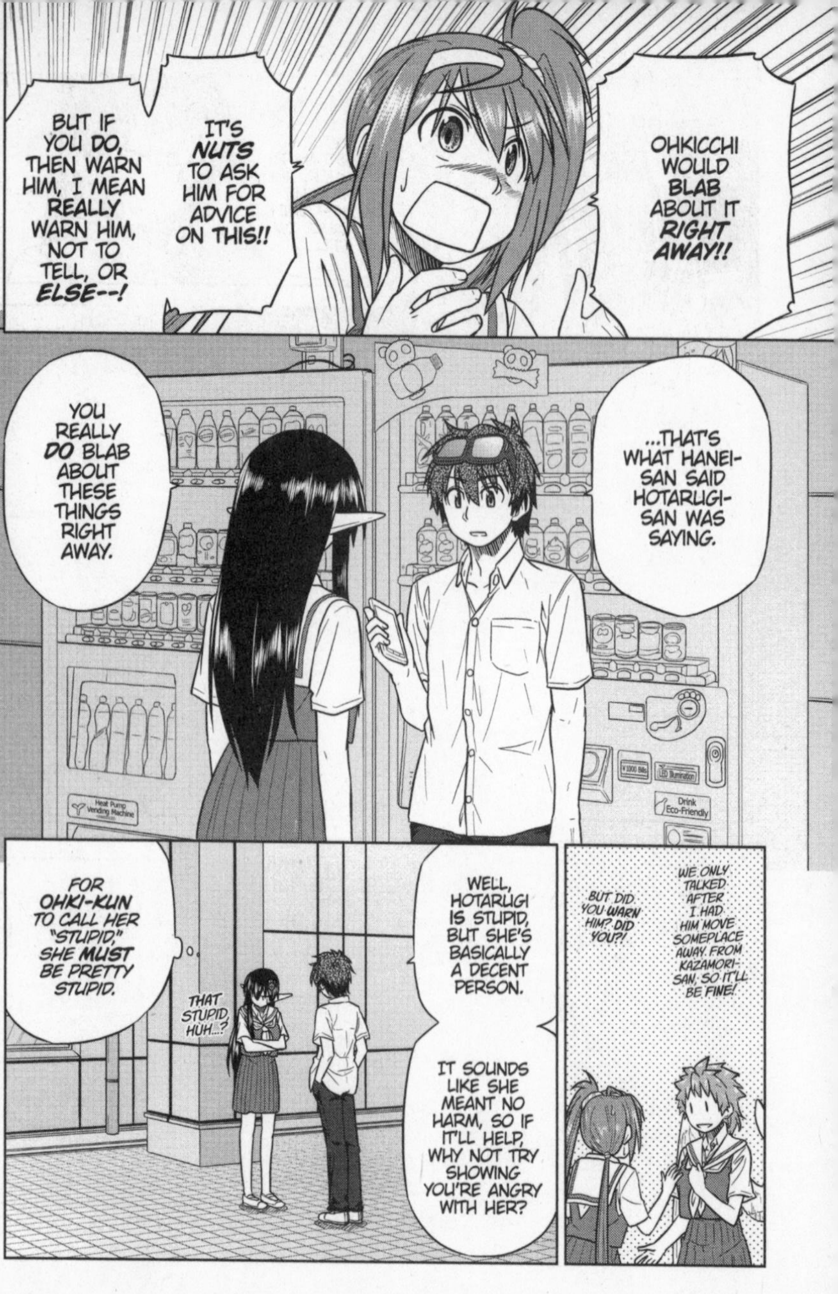
OHKICCHI WOULD BLAB ABOUT IT RIGHT AWAY!!
IT'S NUTS TO ASK HIM FOR ADVICE ON THIS!!
BUT IF YOU DO, THEN WARN HIM, I MEAN REALLY WARN HIM, NOT TO TELL, OR ELSE--!
...THAT'S WHAT HANEI-SAN SAID HOTARUGI-SAN WAS SAYING.
YOU REALLY DO BLAB ABOUT THESE THINGS RIGHT AWAY.
¥1000 Bills
LED Illumination
Drink Eco-Friendly
Heat Pump Vending Machine
WE ONLY TALKED AFTER I HAD HIM MOVE SOMEPLACE AWAY FROM KAZAMORI-SAN, SO IT'LL BE FINE!
BUT DID YOU WARN HIM? DID YOU?!
WELL, HOTARUGI IS STUPID, BUT SHE'S BASICALLY A DECENT PERSON.
IT SOUNDS LIKE SHE MEANT NO HARM, SO IF IT'LL HELP, WHY NOT TRY SHOWING YOU'RE ANGRY WITH HER?
FOR OHKI-KUN TO CALL HER "STUPID," SHE MUST BE PRETTY STUPID.
THAT STUPID, HUH...?

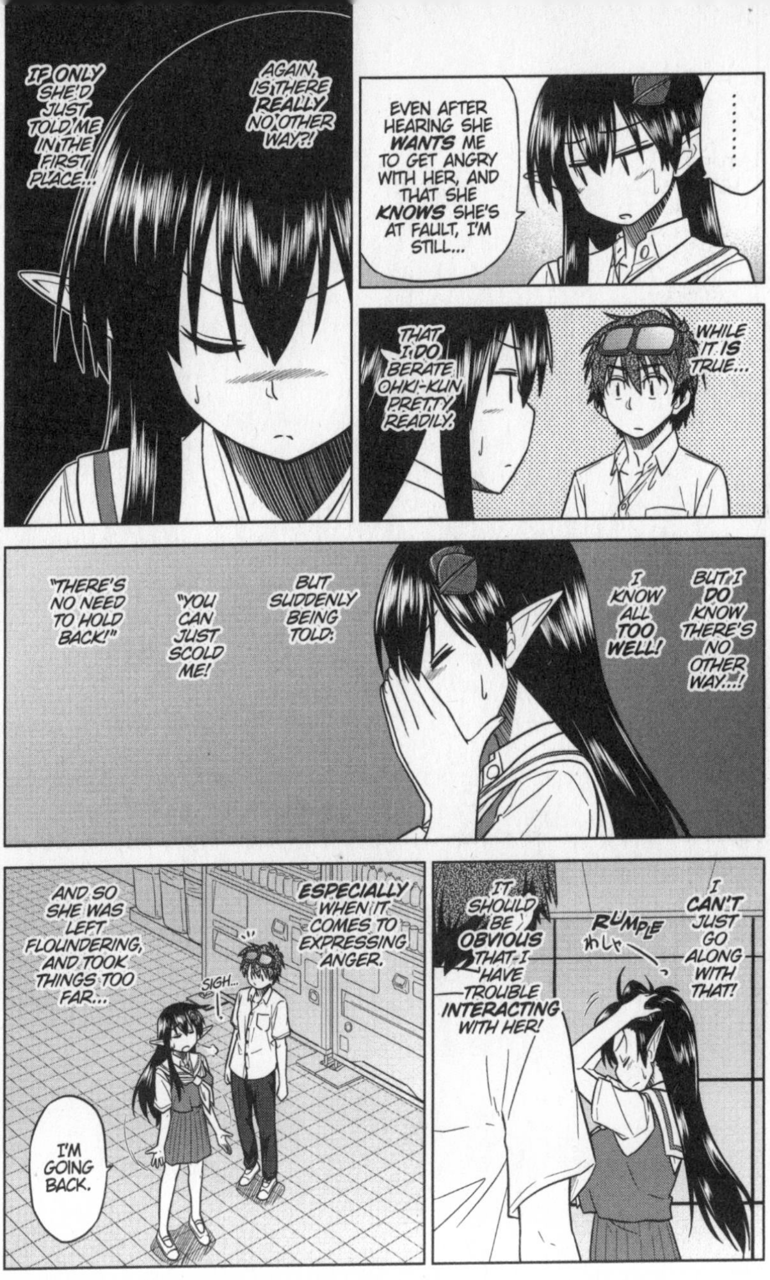
......
EVEN AFTER HEARING SHE WANTS ME TO GET ANGRY WITH HER, AND THAT SHE KNOWS SHE'S AT FAULT, I'M STILL...
WHILE IT IS TRUE...
THAT I DO BERATE OHKI-KUN PRETTY READILY.
AGAIN, IS THERE REALLY NO OTHER WAY?!
IF ONLY SHE'D JUST TOLD ME IN THE FIRST PLACE...
BUT I DO KNOW THERE'S NO OTHER WAY...!
I KNOW ALL TOO WELL!
BUT SUDDENLY BEING TOLD:
"YOU CAN JUST SCOLD ME!
"THERE'S NO NEED TO HOLD BACK!"
I CAN'T JUST GO ALONG WITH THAT!
RUMPLE
わしゃ
IT SHOULD BE OBVIOUS THAT I HAVE TROUBLE INTERACTING WITH HER!
ESPECIALLY WHEN IT COMES TO EXPRESSING ANGER.
AND SO SHE WAS LEFT FLOUNDERING, AND TOOK THINGS TOO FAR...
SIGH...
I'M GOING BACK.

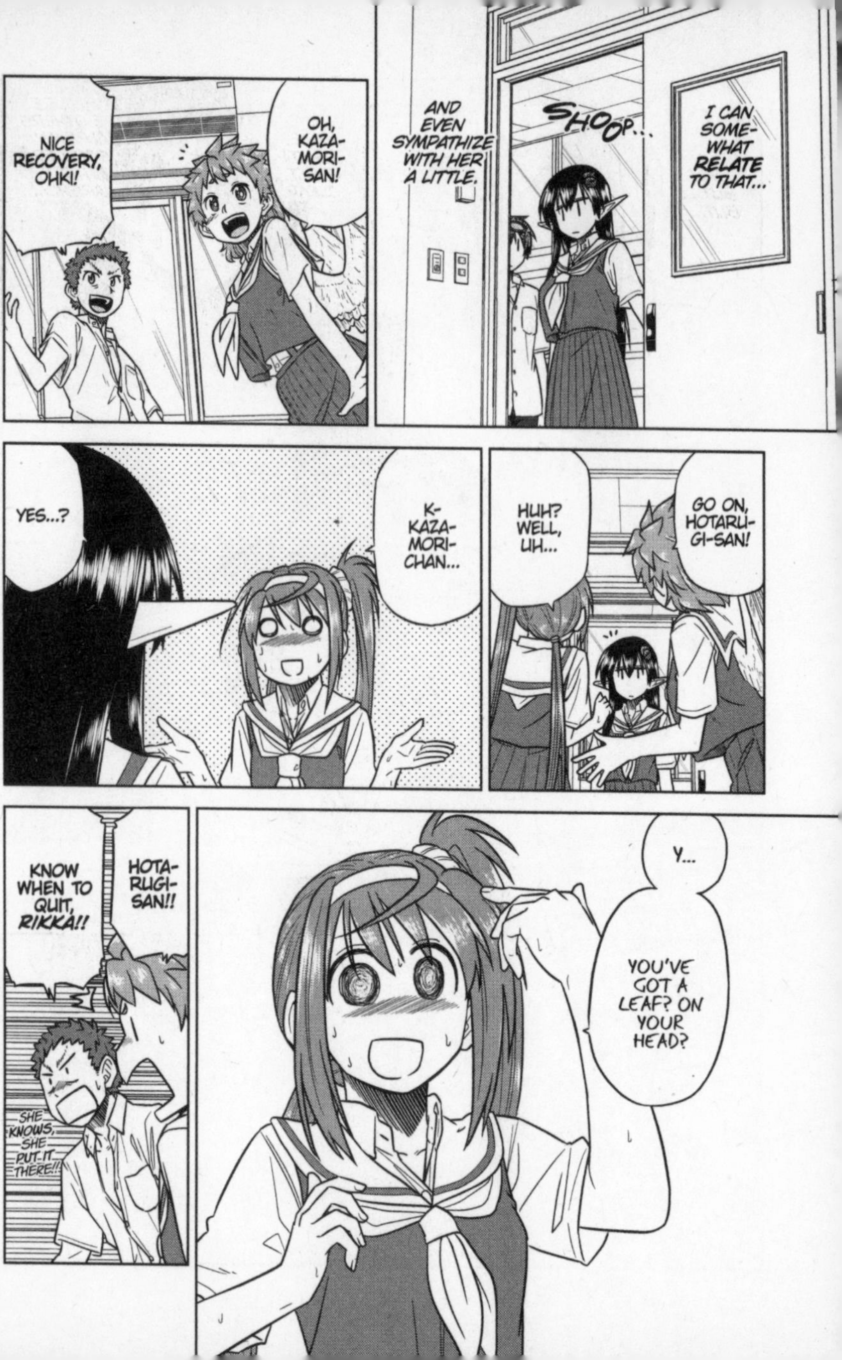
I CAN SOME-WHAT RELATE TO THAT...
SHOOP...
AND EVEN SYMPATHIZE WITH HER A LITTLE.
OH, KAZA-MORI-SAN!
NICE RECOVERY, OHKI!
GO ON, HOTARU-GI-SAN!
HUH? WELL, UH...
K-KAZA-MORI-CHAN...
YES...?
Y...
YOU'VE GOT A LEAF? ON YOUR HEAD?
HOTA-RUGI-SAN!!
KNOW WHEN TO QUIT, RIKKA!!
SHE KNOWS, SHE PUT IT THERE!!

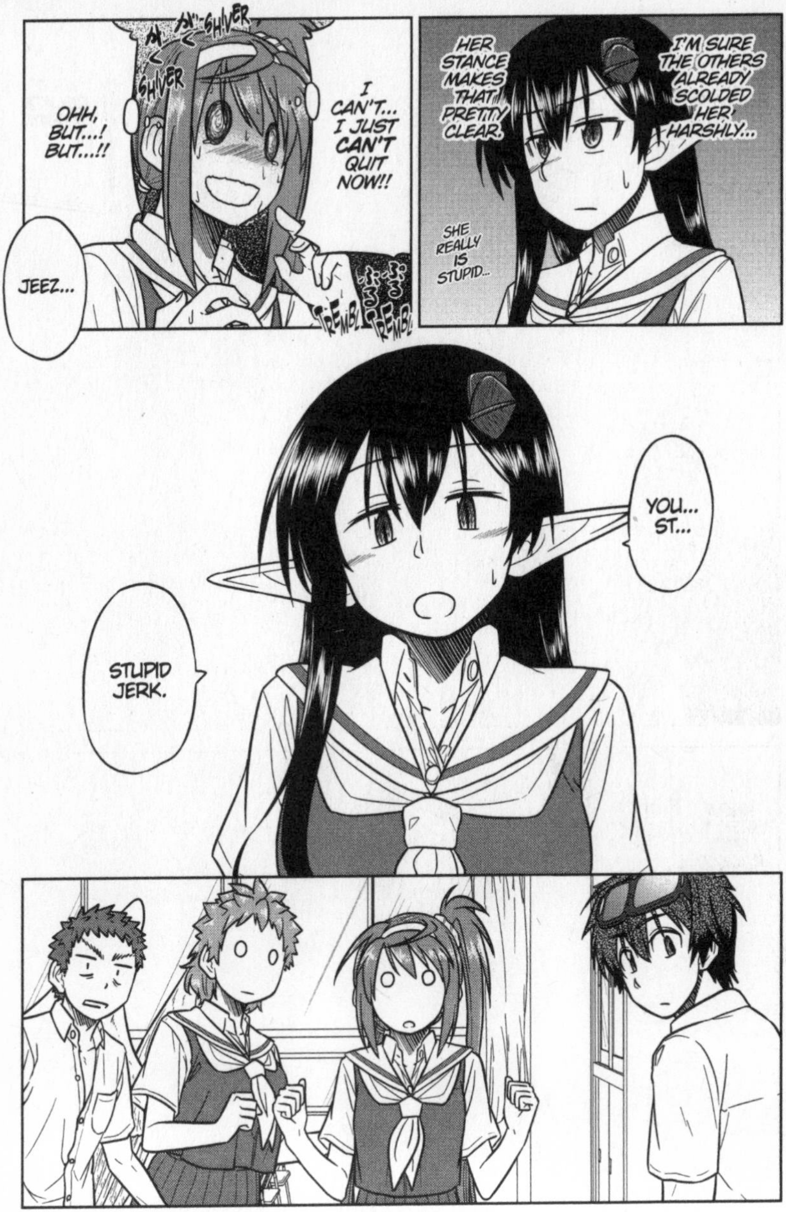

I'M SURE THE OTHERS ALREADY SCOLDED HER HARSHLY...
HER STANCE MAKES THAT PRETTY CLEAR.
SHE REALLY IS STUPID...
SHIVER
SHIVER
I CAN'T... I JUST CAN'T QUIT NOW!!
OHH, BUT...! BUT...!!
TREMBL
TREMBL
JEEZ...
YOU... ST...
STUPID JERK.

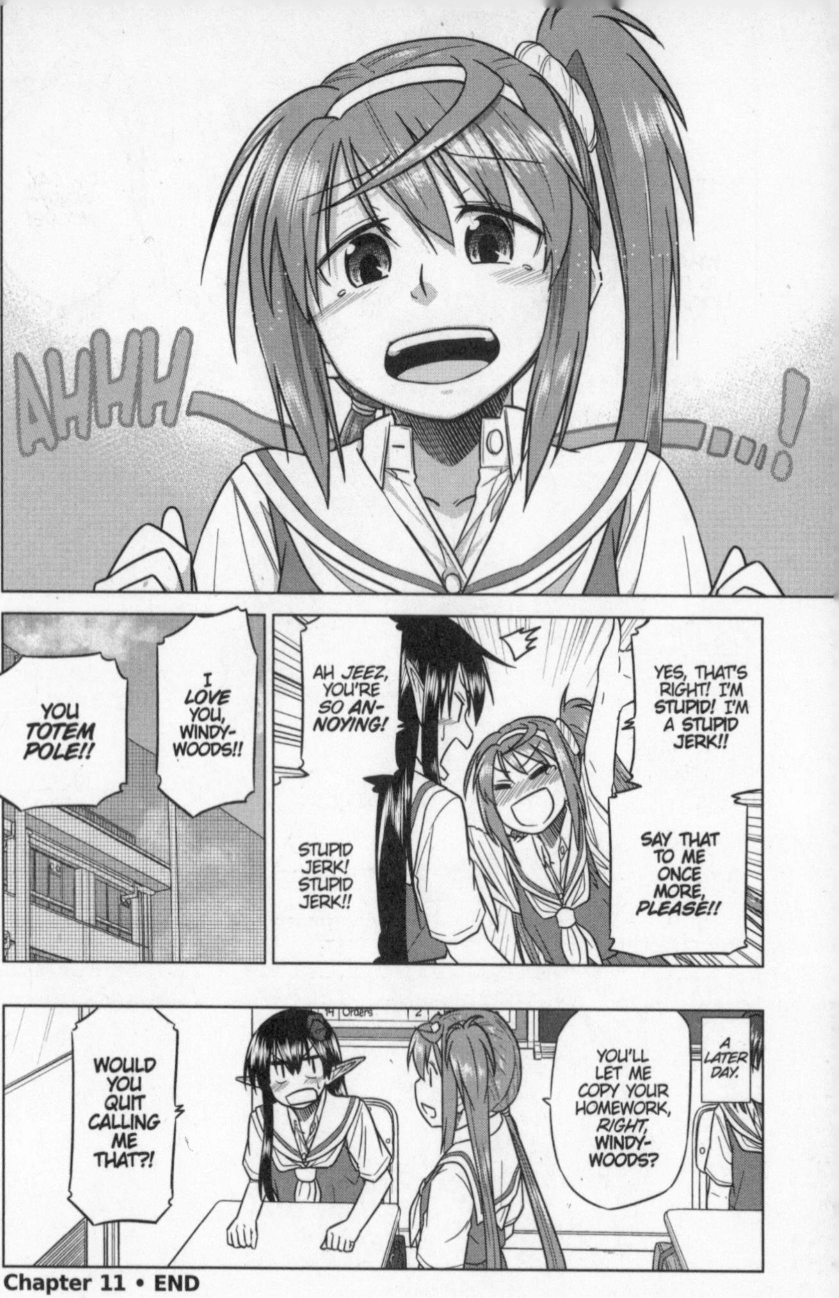
AHHH—...!
YES, THAT'S RIGHT! I'M STUPID! I'M A STUPID JERK!!
AH JEEZ, YOU'RE SO AN-NOYING!
SAY THAT TO ME ONCE MORE, PLEASE!!
STUPID JERK! STUPID JERK!!
I LOVE YOU, WINDY-WOODS!!
YOU TOTEM POLE!!
A LATER DAY.
YOU'LL LET ME COPY YOUR HOMEWORK, RIGHT, WINDY-WOODS?
WOULD YOU QUIT CALLING ME THAT?!

Chapter 11 • END

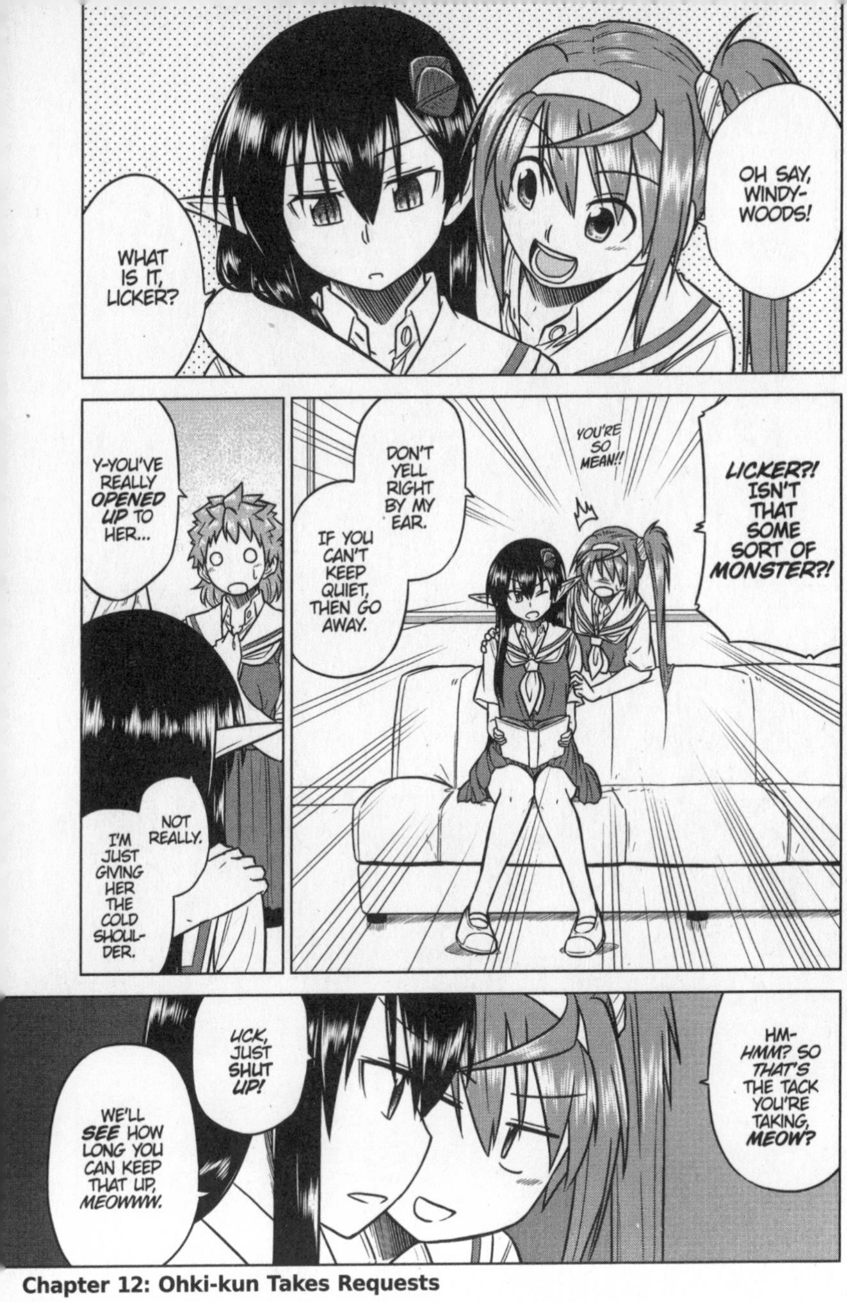
OH SAY, WINDY-WOODS!
WHAT IS IT, LICKER?
LICKER?! ISN'T THAT SOME SORT OF MONSTER?!
YOU'RE SO MEAN!!
DON'T YELL RIGHT BY MY EAR.
IF YOU CAN'T KEEP QUIET, THEN GO AWAY.
Y-YOU'VE REALLY OPENED UP TO HER...
NOT REALLY.
I'M JUST GIVING HER THE COLD SHOUL-DER.
HM-HMM? SO THAT'S THE TACK YOU'RE TAKING, MEOW?
UCK, JUST SHUT UP!
WE'LL SEE HOW LONG YOU CAN KEEP THAT UP, MEOWWW.

Chapter 12: Ohki-kun Takes Requests

Chapter 12: Ohki-kun Takes Requests

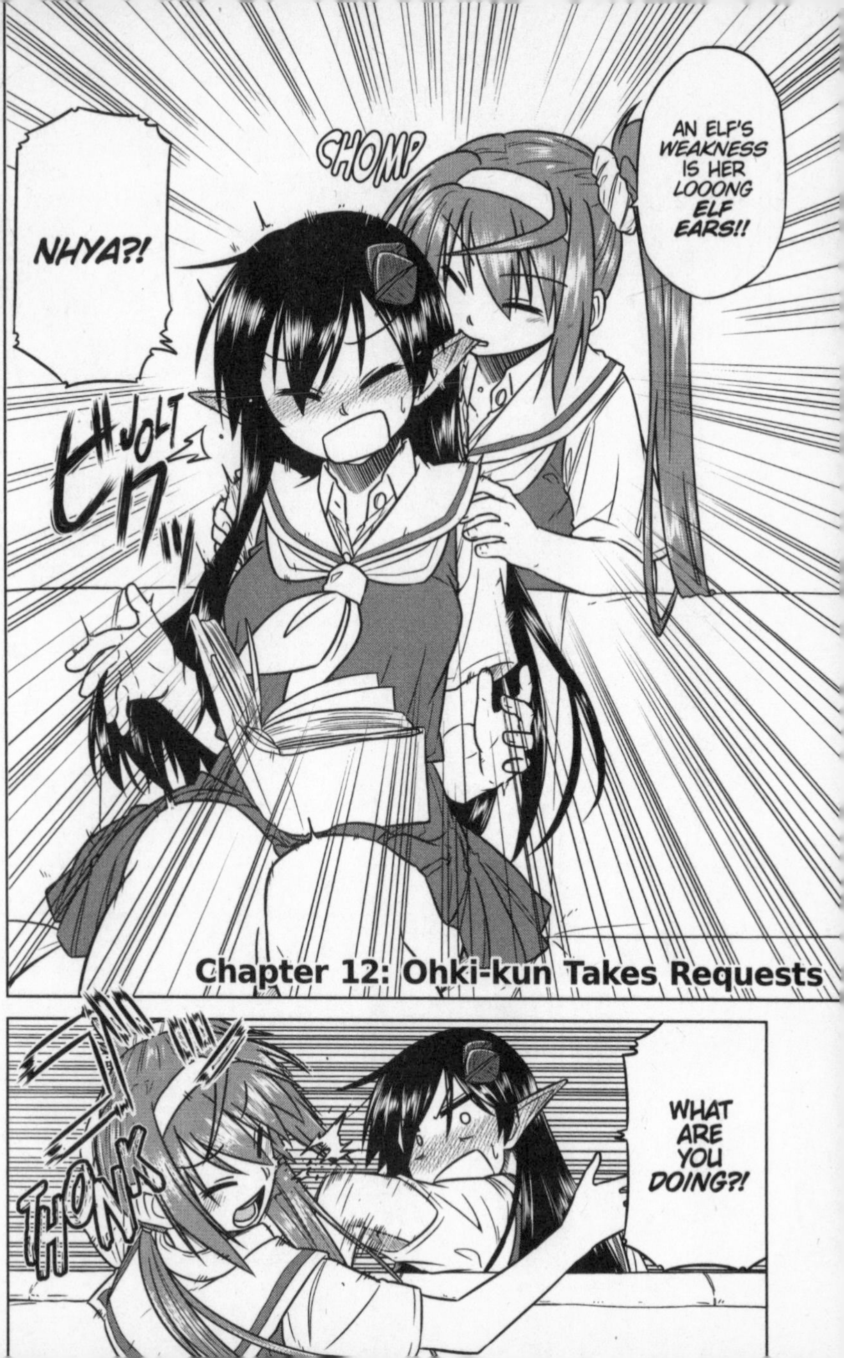
AN ELF'S WEAKNESS IS HER LOOONG ELF EARS!!
CHOMP
NHYA?!
JOLT
WHAT ARE YOU DOING?!
THONK

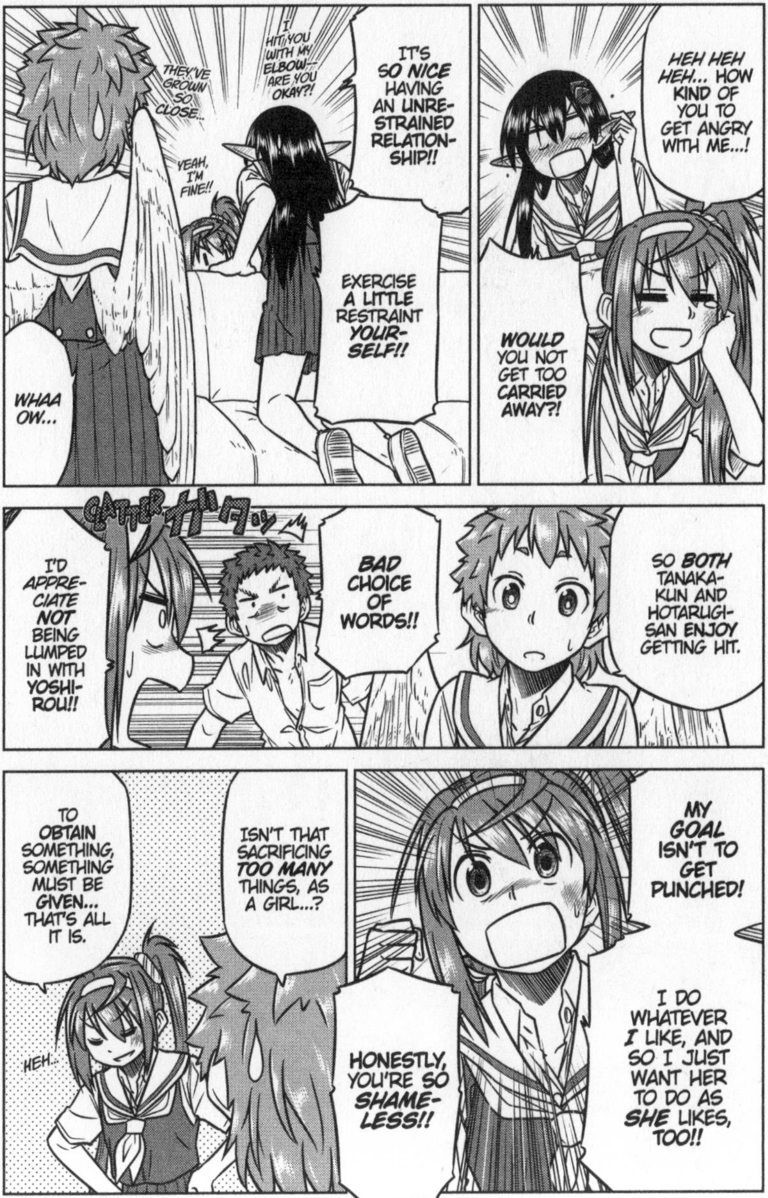
HEH HEH HEH... HOW KIND OF YOU TO GET ANGRY WITH ME...!
WOULD YOU NOT GET TOO CARRIED AWAY?!
IT'S SO NICE HAVING AN UNRESTRAINED RELATIONSHIP!!
I HIT YOU WITH MY ELBOW-- ARE YOU OKAY?!
THEY'VE GROWN SO CLOSE...
YEAH, I'M FINE!!
EXERCISE A LITTLE RESTRAINT YOURSELF!!
WHAAA OW...
SO BOTH TANAKA-KUN AND HOTARUGI-SAN ENJOY GETTING HIT.
BAD CHOICE OF WORDS!!
CLATTER
I'D APPRECIATE NOT BEING LUMPED IN WITH YOSHIROU!!
MY GOAL ISN'T TO GET PUNCHED!
I DO WHATEVER I LIKE, AND SO I JUST WANT HER TO DO AS SHE LIKES, TOO!!
ISN'T THAT SACRIFICING TOO MANY THINGS, AS A GIRL...?
TO OBTAIN SOMETHING, SOMETHING MUST BE GIVEN... THAT'S ALL IT IS.
HONESTLY, YOU'RE SO SHAMELESS!!
HEH...

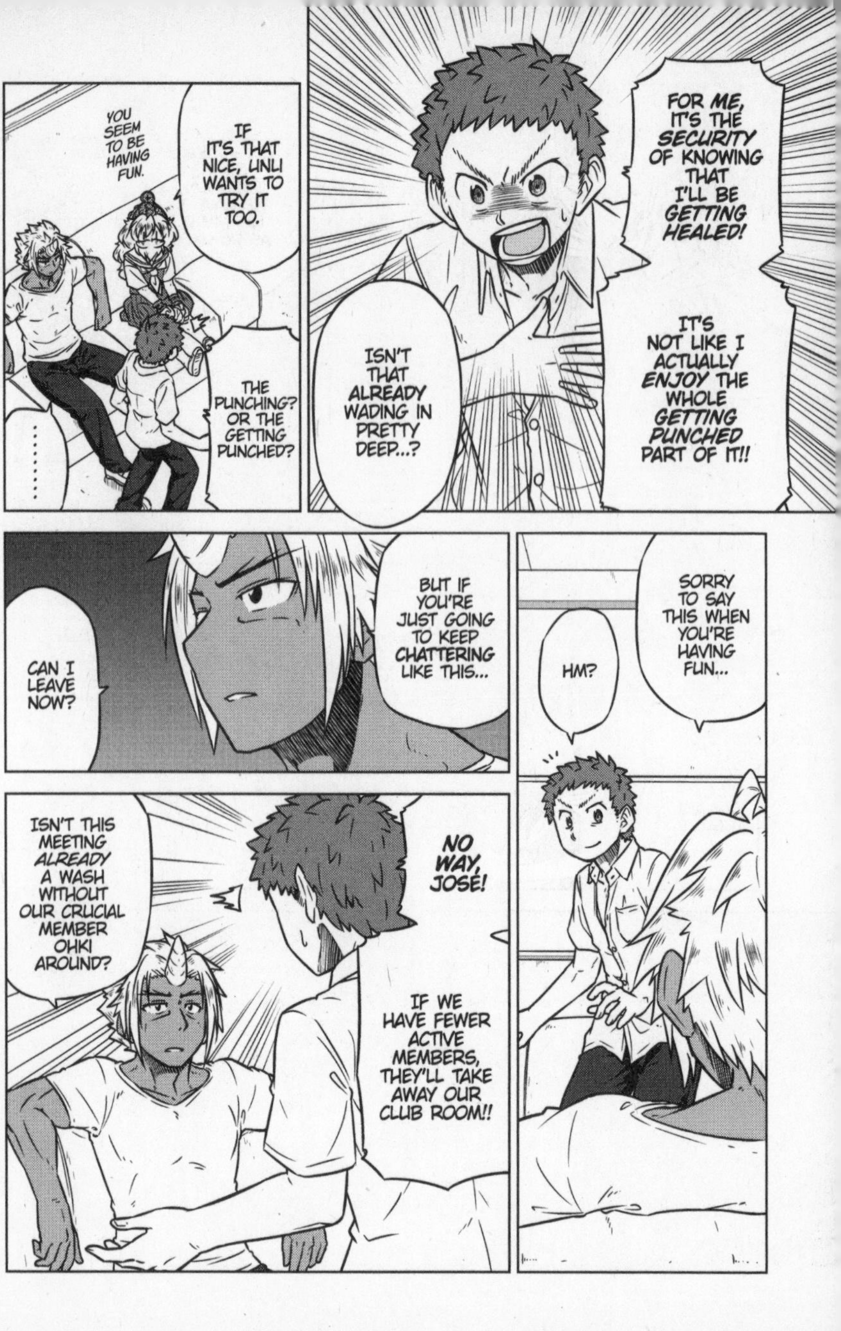
FOR ME, IT'S THE SECURITY OF KNOWING THAT I'LL BE GETTING HEALED!
IT'S NOT LIKE I ACTUALLY ENJOY THE WHOLE GETTING PUNCHED PART OF IT!!
ISN'T THAT ALREADY WADING IN PRETTY DEEP...?
IF IT'S THAT NICE, UNLI WANTS TO TRY IT TOO.
YOU SEEM TO BE HAVING FUN.
THE PUNCHING? OR THE GETTING PUNCHED?
......
SORRY TO SAY THIS WHEN YOU'RE HAVING FUN...
HM?
BUT IF YOU'RE JUST GOING TO KEEP CHATTERING LIKE THIS...
CAN I LEAVE NOW?
NO WAY, JOSÉ!
IF WE HAVE FEWER ACTIVE MEMBERS, THEY'LL TAKE AWAY OUR CLUB ROOM!!
ISN'T THIS MEETING ALREADY A WASH WITHOUT OUR CRUCIAL MEMBER OHKI AROUND?

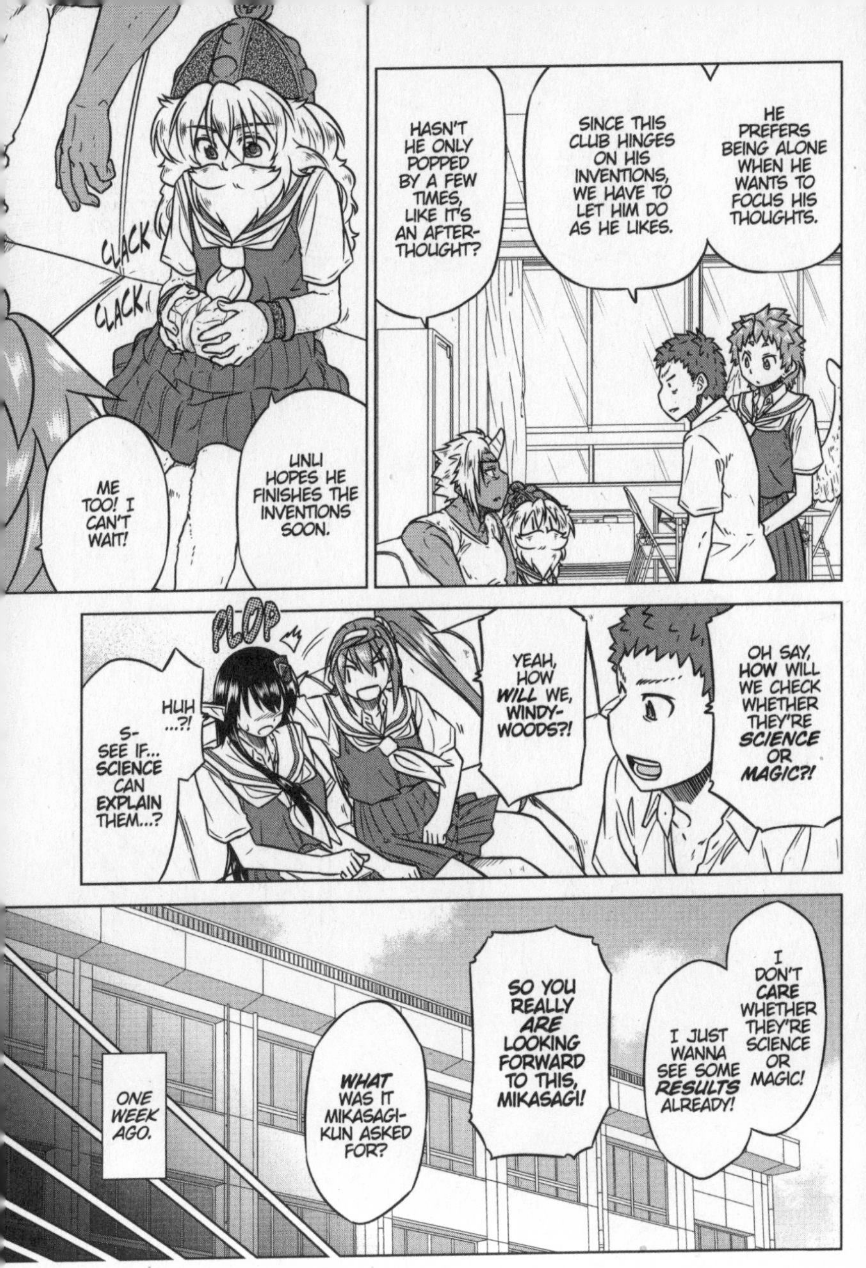
HE PREFERS BEING ALONE WHEN HE WANTS TO FOCUS HIS THOUGHTS.
SINCE THIS CLUB HINGES ON HIS INVENTIONS, WE HAVE TO LET HIM DO AS HE LIKES.
HASN'T HE ONLY POPPED BY A FEW TIMES, LIKE IT'S AN AFTER-THOUGHT?
CLACK
CLACK
UNLI HOPES HE FINISHES THE INVENTIONS SOON.
ME TOO! I CAN'T WAIT!
OH SAY, HOW WILL WE CHECK WHETHER THEY'RE *SCIENCE* OR *MAGIC?!*
YEAH, HOW *WILL* WE, WINDY-WOODS?!
PLOP
HUH ...?!
S-SEE IF... SCIENCE CAN EXPLAIN THEM...?
I DON'T *CARE* WHETHER THEY'RE SCIENCE OR MAGIC! I JUST WANNA SEE SOME *RESULTS* ALREADY!
SO YOU REALLY *ARE* LOOKING FORWARD TO THIS, MIKASAGI!
WHAT WAS IT MIKASAGI-KUN ASKED FOR?
ONE WEEK AGO.

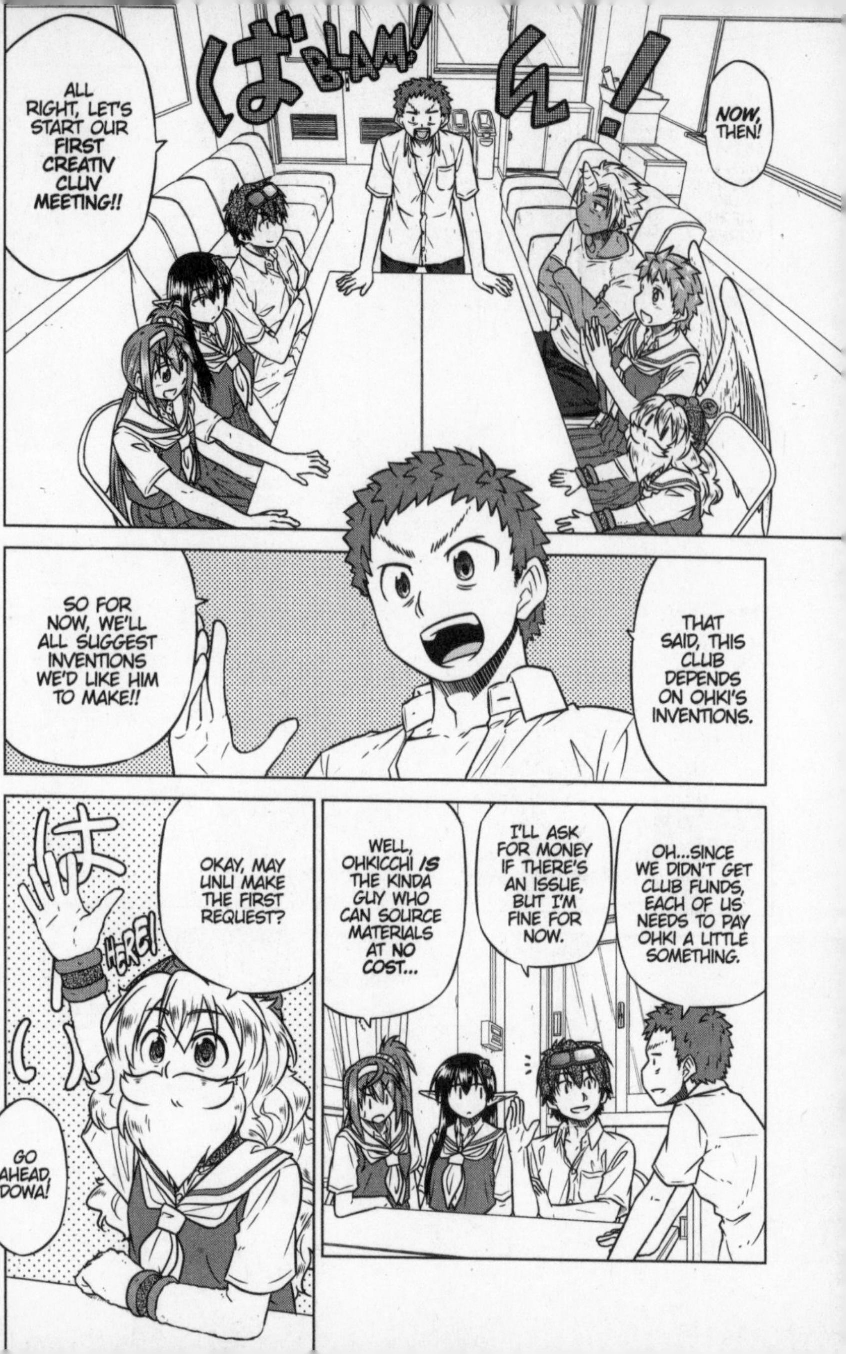
NOW, THEN!
くばん!
BLAM!
ALL RIGHT, LET'S START OUR FIRST CREATIV CLUV MEETING!!
THAT SAID, THIS CLUB DEPENDS ON OHKI'S INVENTIONS.
SO FOR NOW, WE'LL ALL SUGGEST INVENTIONS WE'D LIKE HIM TO MAKE!!
OH...SINCE WE DIDN'T GET CLUB FUNDS, EACH OF US NEEDS TO PAY OHKI A LITTLE SOMETHING.
I'LL ASK FOR MONEY IF THERE'S AN ISSUE, BUT I'M FINE FOR NOW.
WELL, OHKICCHI *IS* THE KINDA GUY WHO CAN SOURCE MATERIALS AT NO COST...
OKAY, MAY UNLI MAKE THE FIRST REQUEST?
はい
HERE!
GO AHEAD, DOWA!

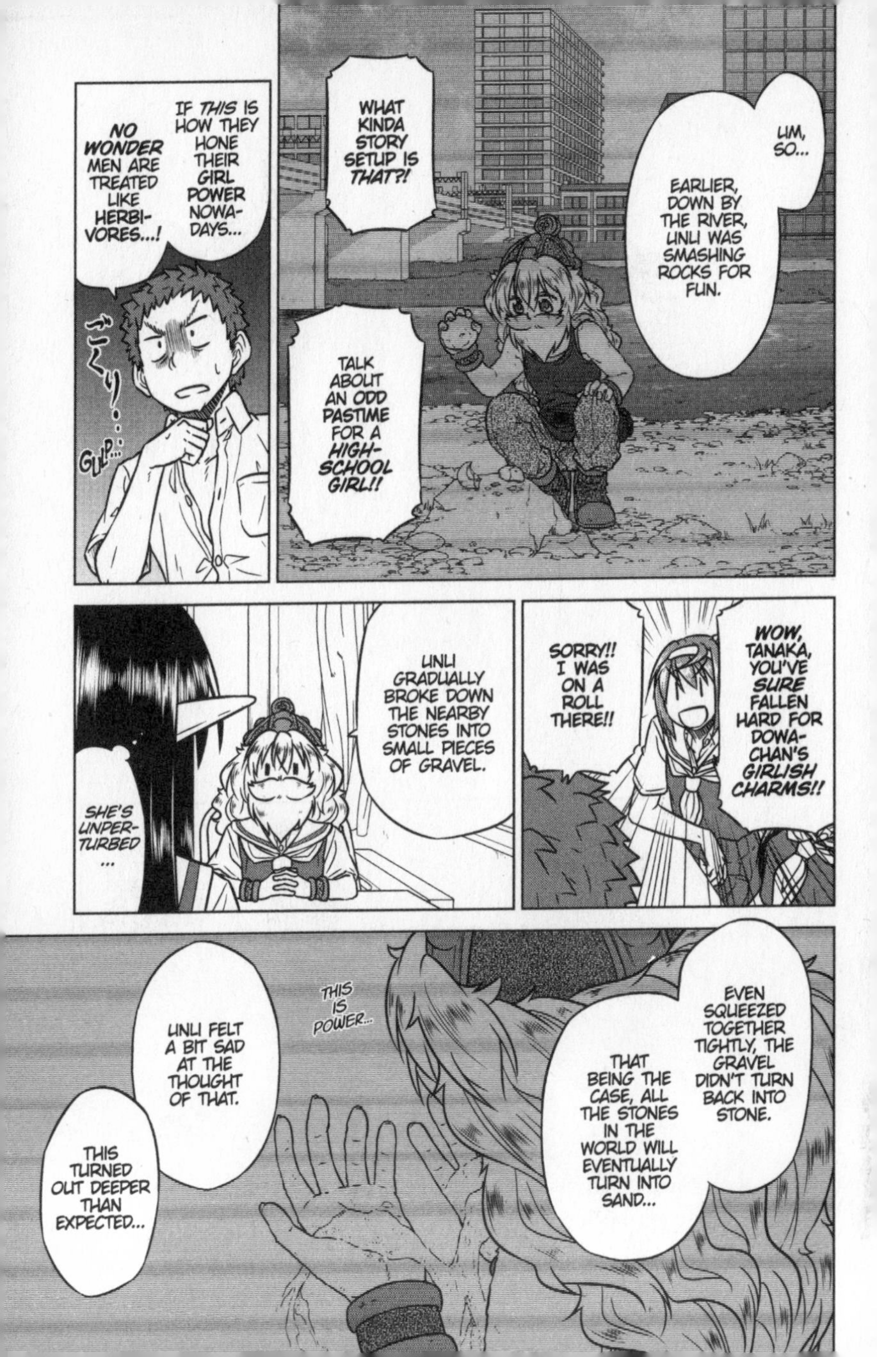
UM, SO...
EARLIER, DOWN BY THE RIVER, UNLI WAS SMASHING ROCKS FOR FUN.
WHAT KINDA STORY SETUP IS *THAT*?!
TALK ABOUT AN ODD PASTIME FOR A *HIGH-SCHOOL GIRL*!!
IF *THIS* IS HOW THEY HONE THEIR GIRL POWER NOWADAYS...
NO WONDER MEN ARE TREATED LIKE HERBIVORES...!
ごくり…
GULP...
WOW, **TANAKA, YOU'VE** ***SURE*** **FALLEN HARD FOR DOWA-CHAN'S** ***GIRLISH CHARMS!!***
SORRY!! I WAS ON A ROLL THERE!!
UNLI GRADUALLY BROKE DOWN THE NEARBY STONES INTO SMALL PIECES OF GRAVEL.
SHE'S UNPERTURBED...
EVEN SQUEEZED TOGETHER TIGHTLY, THE GRAVEL DIDN'T TURN BACK INTO STONE.
THAT BEING THE CASE, ALL THE STONES IN THE WORLD WILL EVENTUALLY TURN INTO SAND...
THIS IS POWER...
UNLI FELT A BIT SAD AT THE THOUGHT OF THAT.
THIS TURNED OUT DEEPER THAN EXPECTED...

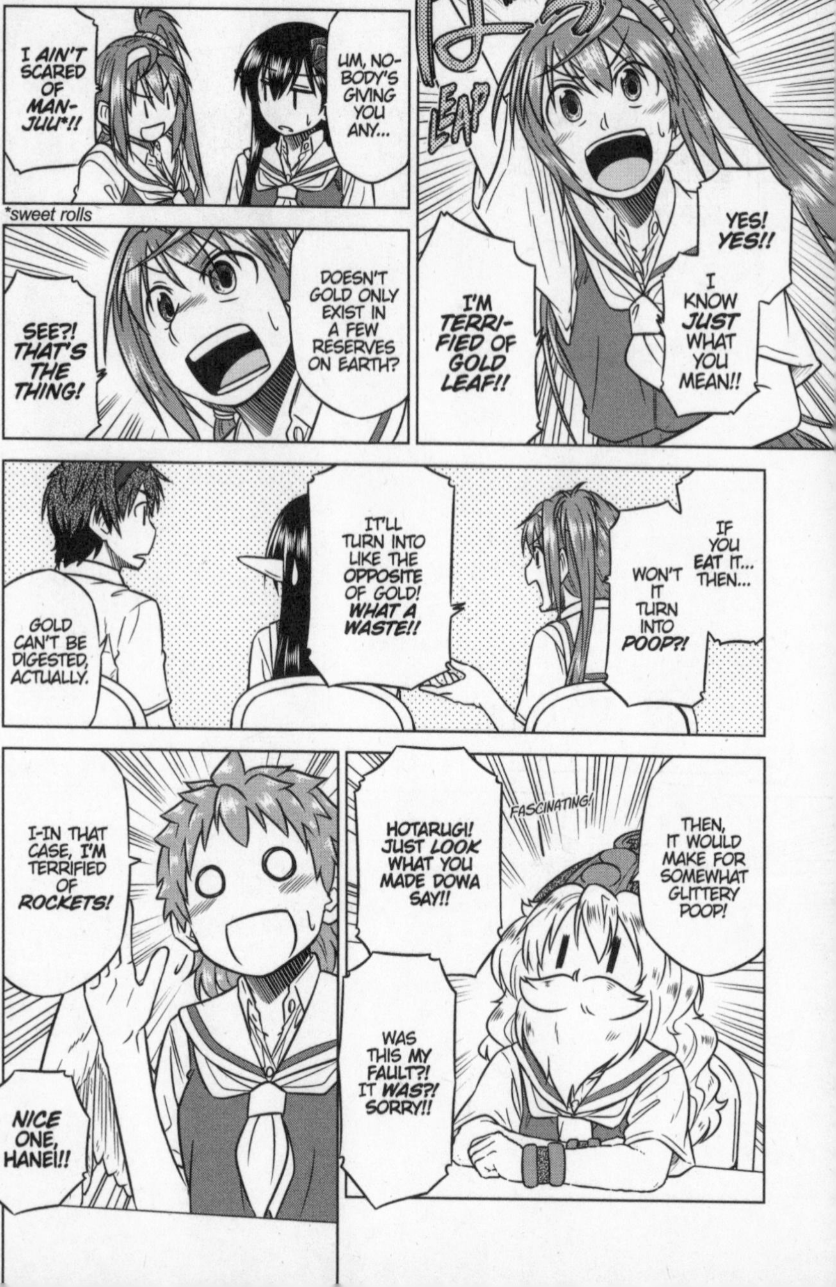
ぱっ
LEAP
YES! YES!!
I KNOW JUST WHAT YOU MEAN!!
I'M TERRIFIED OF GOLD LEAF!!
UM, NOBODY'S GIVING YOU ANY...
I AIN'T SCARED OF MANJUU*!!
*sweet rolls
DOESN'T GOLD ONLY EXIST IN A FEW RESERVES ON EARTH?
SEE?! THAT'S THE THING!
IF YOU EAT IT... THEN...
WON'T IT TURN INTO POOP?!
IT'LL TURN INTO LIKE THE OPPOSITE OF GOLD! WHAT A WASTE!!
GOLD CAN'T BE DIGESTED, ACTUALLY.
THEN, IT WOULD MAKE FOR SOMEWHAT GLITTERY POOP!
FASCINATING!
HOTARUGI! JUST LOOK WHAT YOU MADE DOWA SAY!!
WAS THIS MY FAULT?! IT WAS?! SORRY!!
I-IN THAT CASE, I'M TERRIFIED OF ROCKETS!
NICE ONE, HANE!!

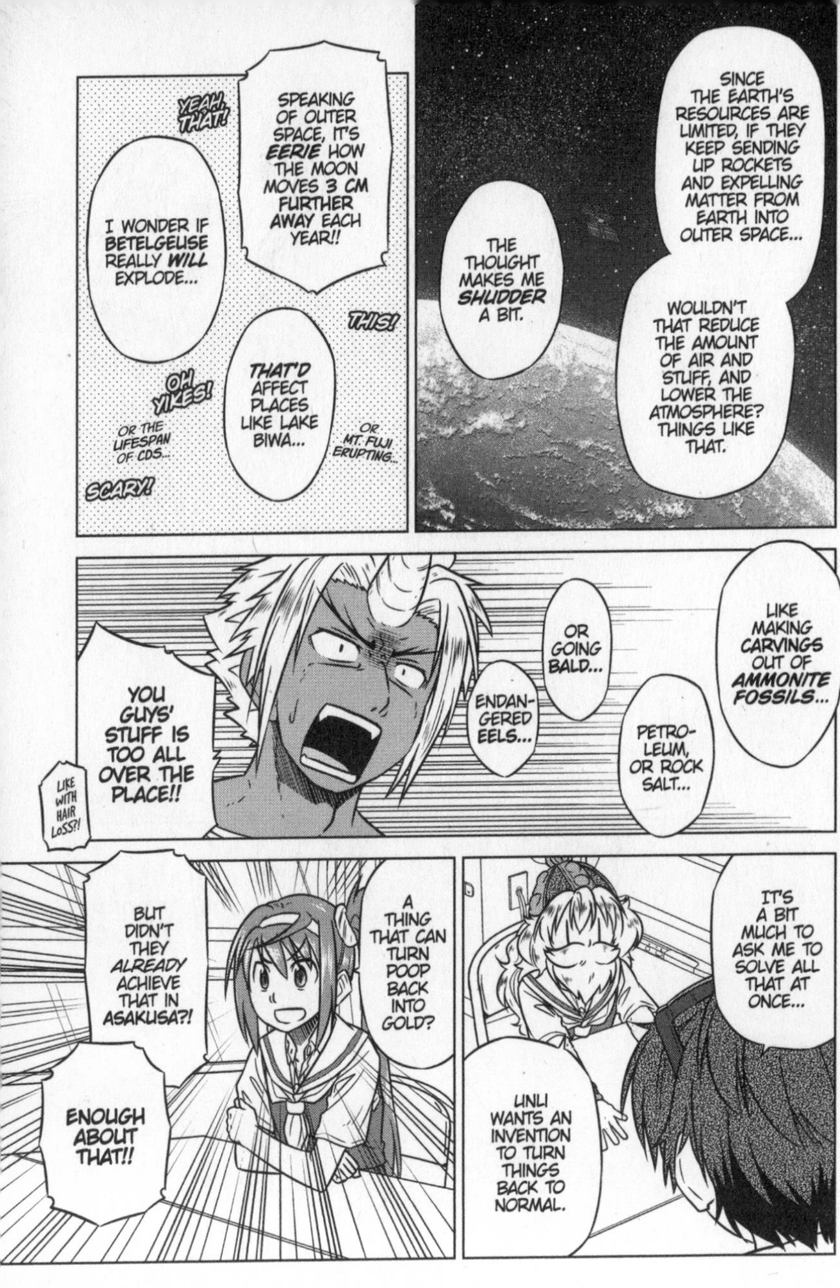
SINCE THE EARTH'S RESOURCES ARE LIMITED, IF THEY KEEP SENDING UP ROCKETS AND EXPELLING MATTER FROM EARTH INTO OUTER SPACE...
WOULDN'T THAT REDUCE THE AMOUNT OF AIR AND STUFF, AND LOWER THE ATMOSPHERE? THINGS LIKE THAT.
THE THOUGHT MAKES ME SHUDDER A BIT.
SPEAKING OF OUTER SPACE, IT'S EERIE HOW THE MOON MOVES 3 CM FURTHER AWAY EACH YEAR!!
YEAH, THAT!
I WONDER IF BETELGEUSE REALLY WILL EXPLODE...
THIS!
THAT'D AFFECT PLACES LIKE LAKE BIWA...
OR MT. FUJI ERUPTING...
OH YIKES!
OR THE LIFESPAN OF CDS...
SCARY!
LIKE MAKING CARVINGS OUT OF AMMONITE FOSSILS...
PETROLEUM, OR ROCK SALT...
OR GOING BALD...
ENDANGERED EELS...
YOU GUYS' STUFF IS TOO ALL OVER THE PLACE!!
LIKE WITH HAIR LOSS?!
IT'S A BIT MUCH TO ASK ME TO SOLVE ALL THAT AT ONCE...
UNLI WANTS AN INVENTION TO TURN THINGS BACK TO NORMAL.
A THING THAT CAN TURN POOP BACK INTO GOLD?
BUT DIDN'T THEY ALREADY ACHIEVE THAT IN ASAKUSA?!
ENOUGH ABOUT THAT!!

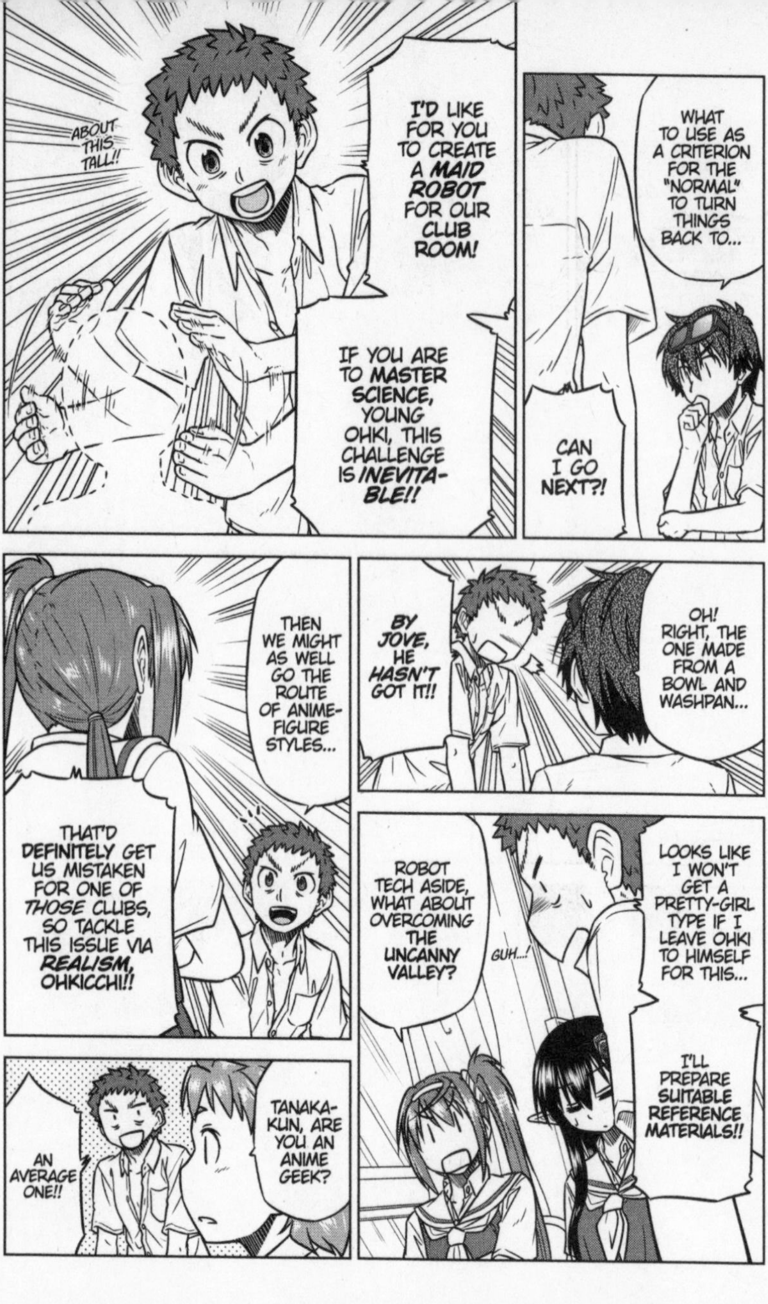
WHAT TO USE AS A CRITERION FOR THE "NORMAL" TO TURN THINGS BACK TO...
CAN I GO NEXT?!
I'D LIKE FOR YOU TO CREATE A MAID ROBOT FOR OUR CLUB ROOM!
ABOUT THIS TALL!!
IF YOU ARE TO MASTER SCIENCE, YOUNG OHKI, THIS CHALLENGE IS INEVITA-BLE!!
OH! RIGHT, THE ONE MADE FROM A BOWL AND WASHPAN...
BY JOVE, HE HASN'T GOT IT!!
THEN WE MIGHT AS WELL GO THE ROUTE OF ANIME-FIGURE STYLES...
THAT'D DEFINITELY GET US MISTAKEN FOR ONE OF THOSE CLUBS, SO TACKLE THIS ISSUE VIA REALISM, OHKICCHI!!
LOOKS LIKE I WON'T GET A PRETTY-GIRL TYPE IF I LEAVE OHKI TO HIMSELF FOR THIS...
ROBOT TECH ASIDE, WHAT ABOUT OVERCOMING THE UNCANNY VALLEY?
GUH...!
I'LL PREPARE SUITABLE REFERENCE MATERIALS!!
TANAKA-KUN, ARE YOU AN ANIME GEEK?
AN AVERAGE ONE!!

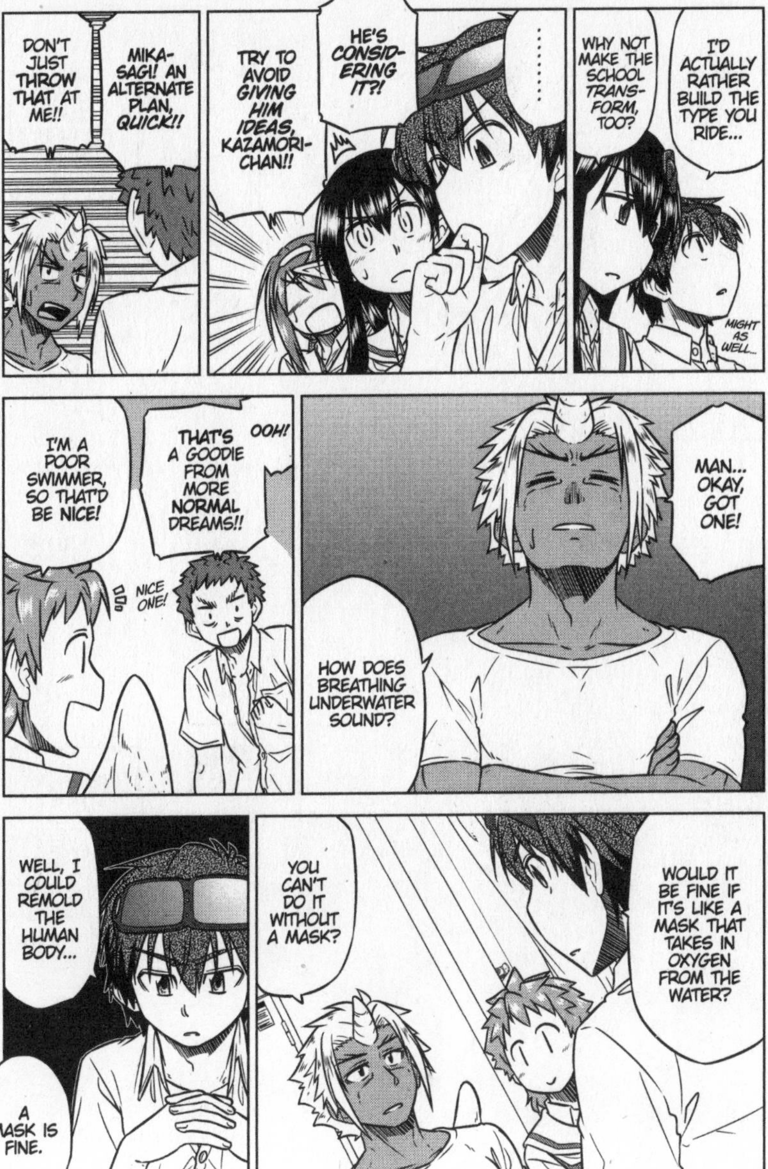
I'D ACTUALLY RATHER BUILD THE TYPE YOU RIDE...
WHY NOT MAKE THE SCHOOL TRANSFORM, TOO?
MIGHT AS WELL...
......
HE'S CONSIDERING IT?!
TRY TO AVOID GIVING HIM IDEAS, KAZAMORI-CHAN!!
MIKASAGI! AN ALTERNATE PLAN, QUICK!!
DON'T JUST THROW THAT AT ME!!
MAN... OKAY, GOT ONE!
HOW DOES BREATHING UNDERWATER SOUND?
OOH!
THAT'S A GOODIE FROM MORE NORMAL DREAMS!!
I'M A POOR SWIMMER, SO THAT'D BE NICE!
NICE ONE!
WOULD IT BE FINE IF IT'S LIKE A MASK THAT TAKES IN OXYGEN FROM THE WATER?
YOU CAN'T DO IT WITHOUT A MASK?
WELL, I COULD REMOLD THE HUMAN BODY...
A MASK IS FINE.

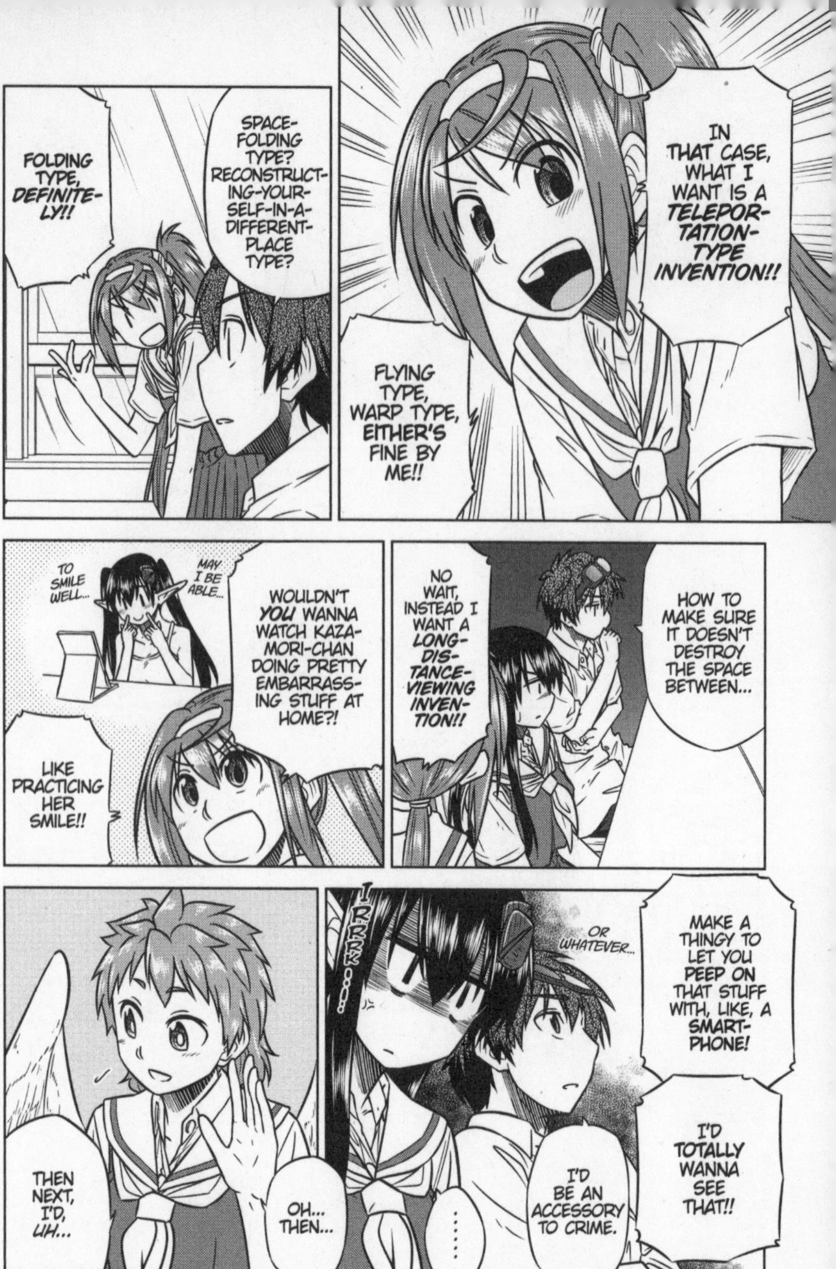
IN THAT CASE, WHAT I WANT IS A *TELEPORTATION-TYPE INVENTION!!*
FLYING TYPE, WARP TYPE, EITHER'S FINE BY ME!!
SPACE-FOLDING TYPE? RECONSTRUCTING-YOURSELF-IN-A-DIFFERENT-PLACE TYPE?
FOLDING TYPE, *DEFINITELY!!*
HOW TO MAKE SURE IT DOESN'T DESTROY THE SPACE BETWEEN...
NO WAIT, INSTEAD I WANT A *LONG-DISTANCE-VIEWING INVENTION!!*
WOULDN'T *YOU* WANNA WATCH KAZAMORI-CHAN DOING PRETTY EMBARRASSING STUFF AT HOME?!
MAY I BE ABLE...
TO SMILE WELL...
LIKE PRACTICING HER SMILE!!
MAKE A THINGY TO LET YOU PEEP ON THAT STUFF WITH, LIKE, A SMARTPHONE!
OR WHATEVER...
I'D TOTALLY WANNA SEE THAT!!
IRRRK...!!
I'D BE AN ACCESSORY TO CRIME.
......
OH... THEN...
THEN NEXT, I'D, *UH...*

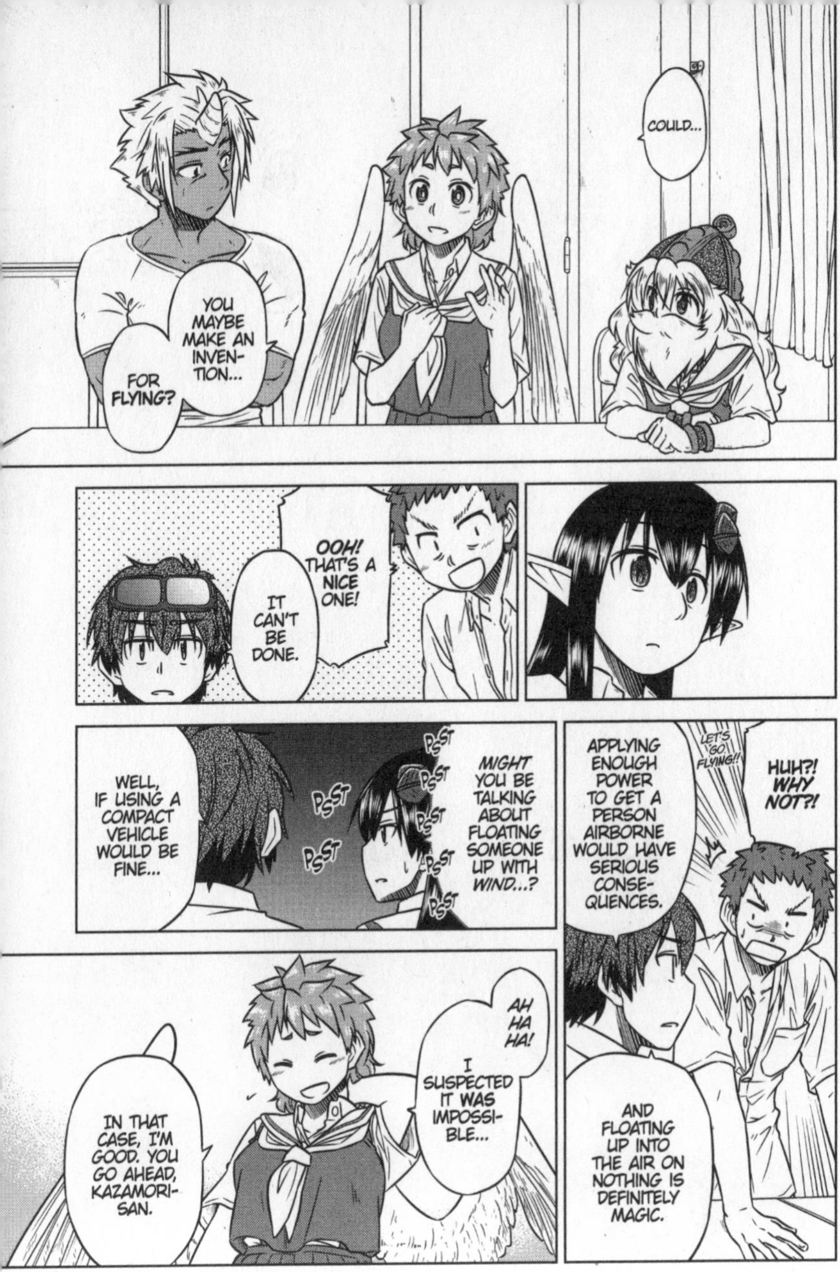
COULD...
YOU MAYBE MAKE AN INVENTION...
FOR FLYING?
OOH! THAT'S A NICE ONE!
IT CAN'T BE DONE.
HUH?! WHY NOT?!
LET'S GO FLYING!!
APPLYING ENOUGH POWER TO GET A PERSON AIRBORNE WOULD HAVE SERIOUS CONSE-QUENCES.
AND FLOATING UP INTO THE AIR ON NOTHING IS DEFINITELY MAGIC.
MIGHT YOU BE TALKING ABOUT FLOATING SOMEONE UP WITH WIND...?
PSST PSST PSST PSST PSST PSST
WELL, IF USING A COMPACT VEHICLE WOULD BE FINE...
AH HA HA!
I SUSPECTED IT WAS IMPOSSI-BLE...
IN THAT CASE, I'M GOOD. YOU GO AHEAD, KAZAMORI-SAN.

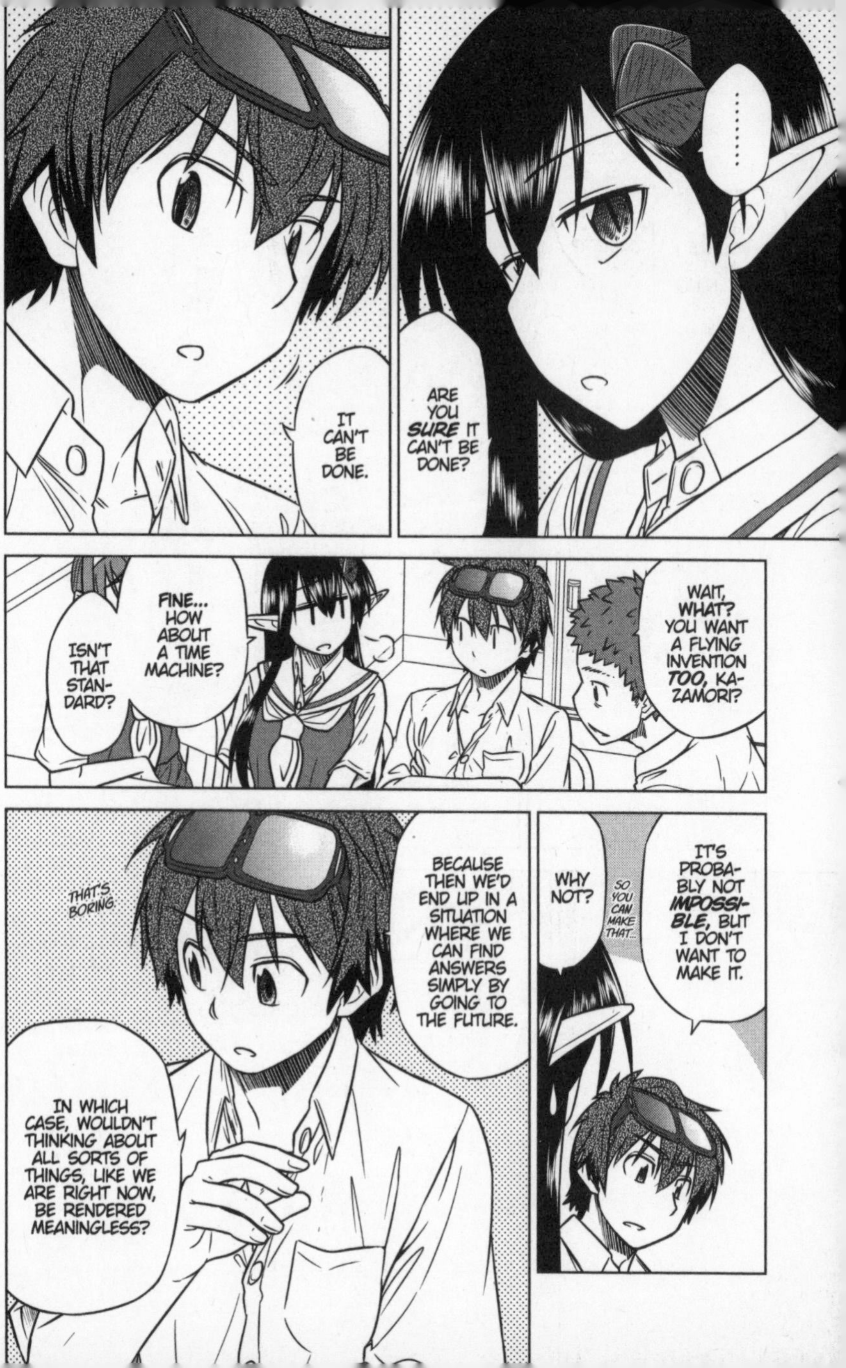
......
ARE YOU SURE IT CAN'T BE DONE?
IT CAN'T BE DONE.
WAIT, WHAT? YOU WANT A FLYING INVENTION TOO, KAZAMORI?
FINE... HOW ABOUT A TIME MACHINE?
ISN'T THAT STANDARD?
IT'S PROBABLY NOT IMPOSSIBLE, BUT I DON'T WANT TO MAKE IT.
SO YOU CAN MAKE THAT...
WHY NOT?
BECAUSE THEN WE'D END UP IN A SITUATION WHERE WE CAN FIND ANSWERS SIMPLY BY GOING TO THE FUTURE.
THAT'S BORING.
IN WHICH CASE, WOULDN'T THINKING ABOUT ALL SORTS OF THINGS, LIKE WE ARE RIGHT NOW, BE RENDERED MEANINGLESS?

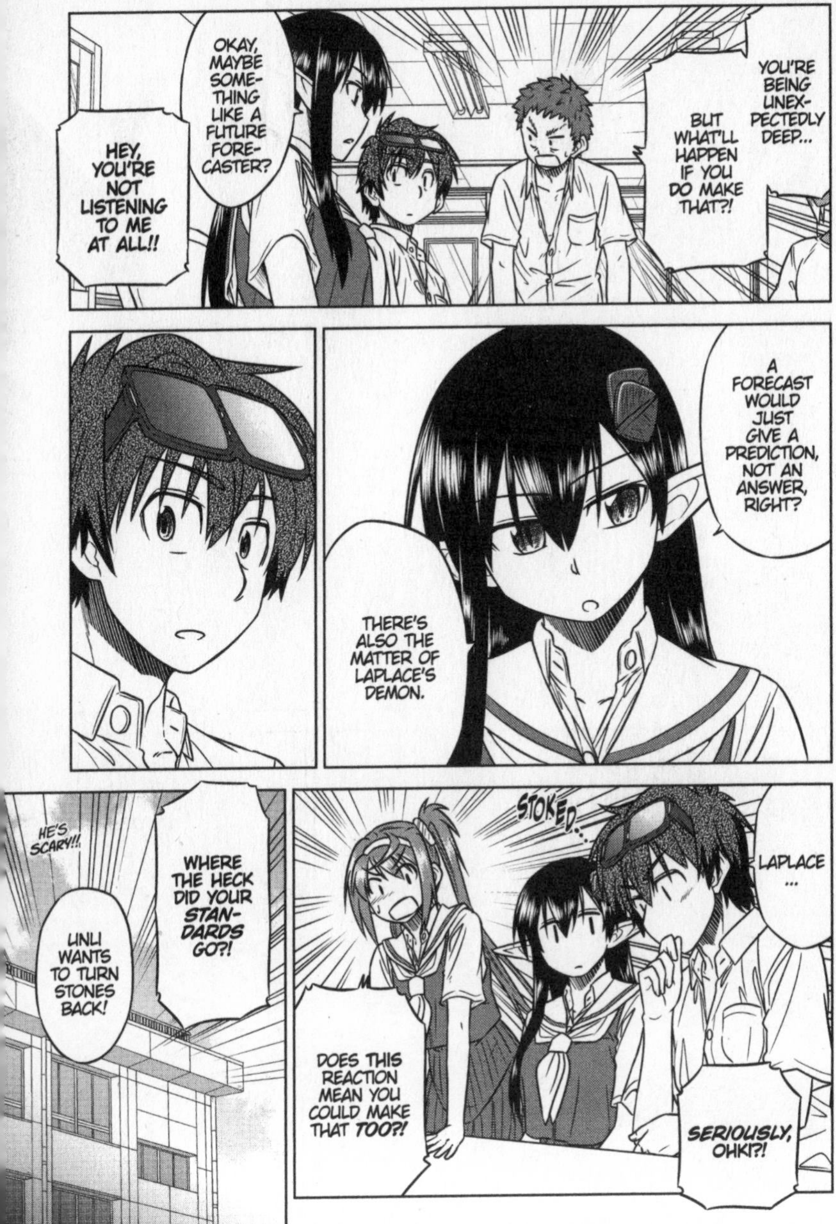
YOU'RE BEING UNEXPECTEDLY DEEP...
BUT WHAT'LL HAPPEN IF YOU DO MAKE THAT?!
OKAY, MAYBE SOMETHING LIKE A FUTURE FORECASTER?
HEY, YOU'RE NOT LISTENING TO ME AT ALL!!
A FORECAST WOULD JUST GIVE A PREDICTION, NOT AN ANSWER, RIGHT?
THERE'S ALSO THE MATTER OF LAPLACE'S DEMON.
STOKED...
LAPLACE...
SERIOUSLY, OHKI?!
DOES THIS REACTION MEAN YOU COULD MAKE THAT *TOO*?!
WHERE THE HECK DID YOUR *STANDARDS* GO?!
HE'S SCARY!!
UNLI WANTS TO TURN STONES BACK!

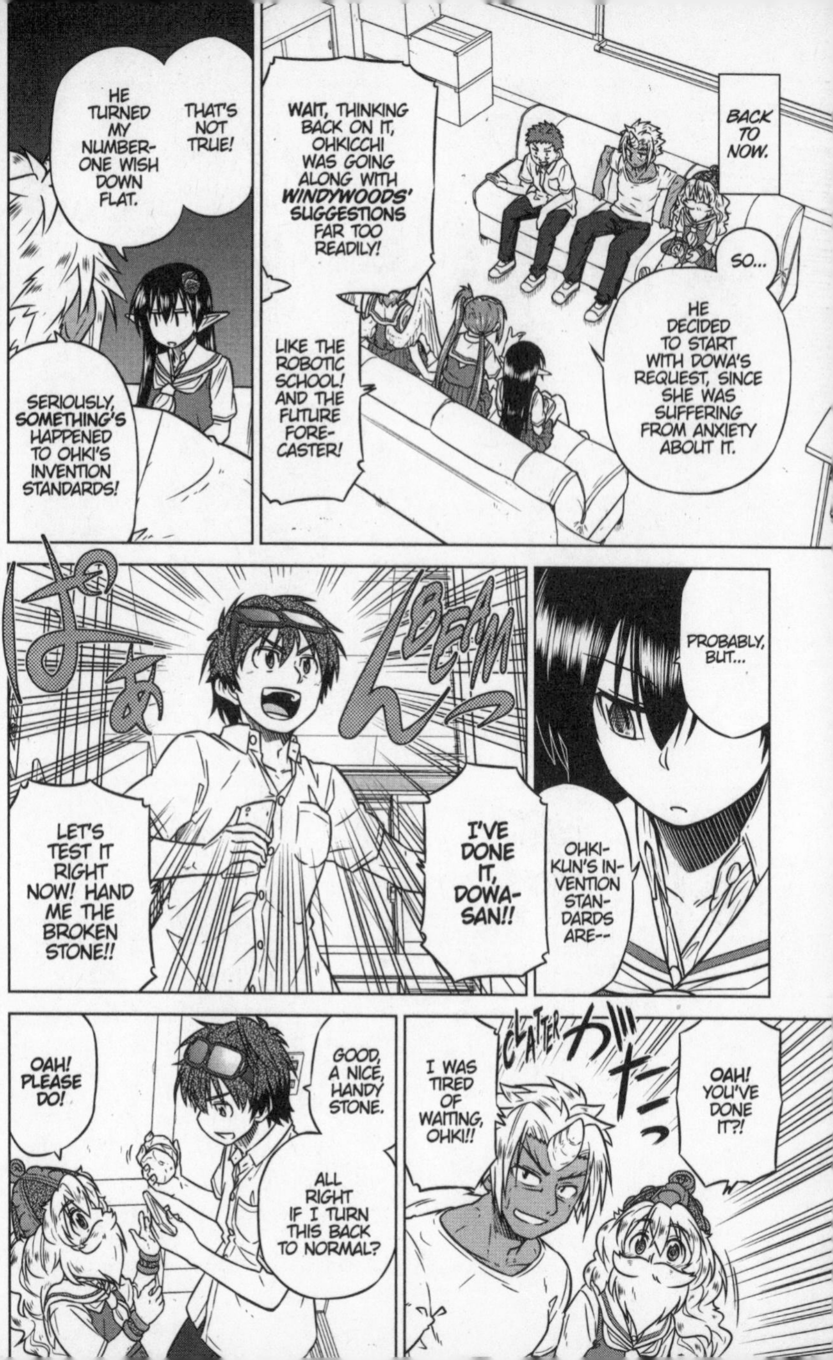
BACK TO NOW.
SO...
HE DECIDED TO START WITH DOWA'S REQUEST, SINCE SHE WAS SUFFERING FROM ANXIETY ABOUT IT.
WAIT, THINKING BACK ON IT, OHKICCHI WAS GOING ALONG WITH *WINDYWOODS'* SUGGESTIONS FAR TOO READILY!
LIKE THE ROBOTIC SCHOOL! AND THE FUTURE FORE-CASTER!
THAT'S NOT TRUE!
HE TURNED MY NUMBER-ONE WISH DOWN FLAT.
SERIOUSLY, SOMETHING'S HAPPENED TO OHKI'S INVENTION STANDARDS!
PROBABLY, BUT...
OHKI-KUN'S IN-VENTION STAN-DARDS ARE--
ぱぁんっ
BEAM
I'VE DONE IT, DOWA-SAN!!
LET'S TEST IT RIGHT NOW! HAND ME THE BROKEN STONE!!
OAH! YOU'VE DONE IT?!
がたっ
CLATTER
I WAS TIRED OF WAITING, OHKI!!
GOOD, A NICE, HANDY STONE.
ALL RIGHT IF I TURN THIS BACK TO NORMAL?
OAH! PLEASE DO!

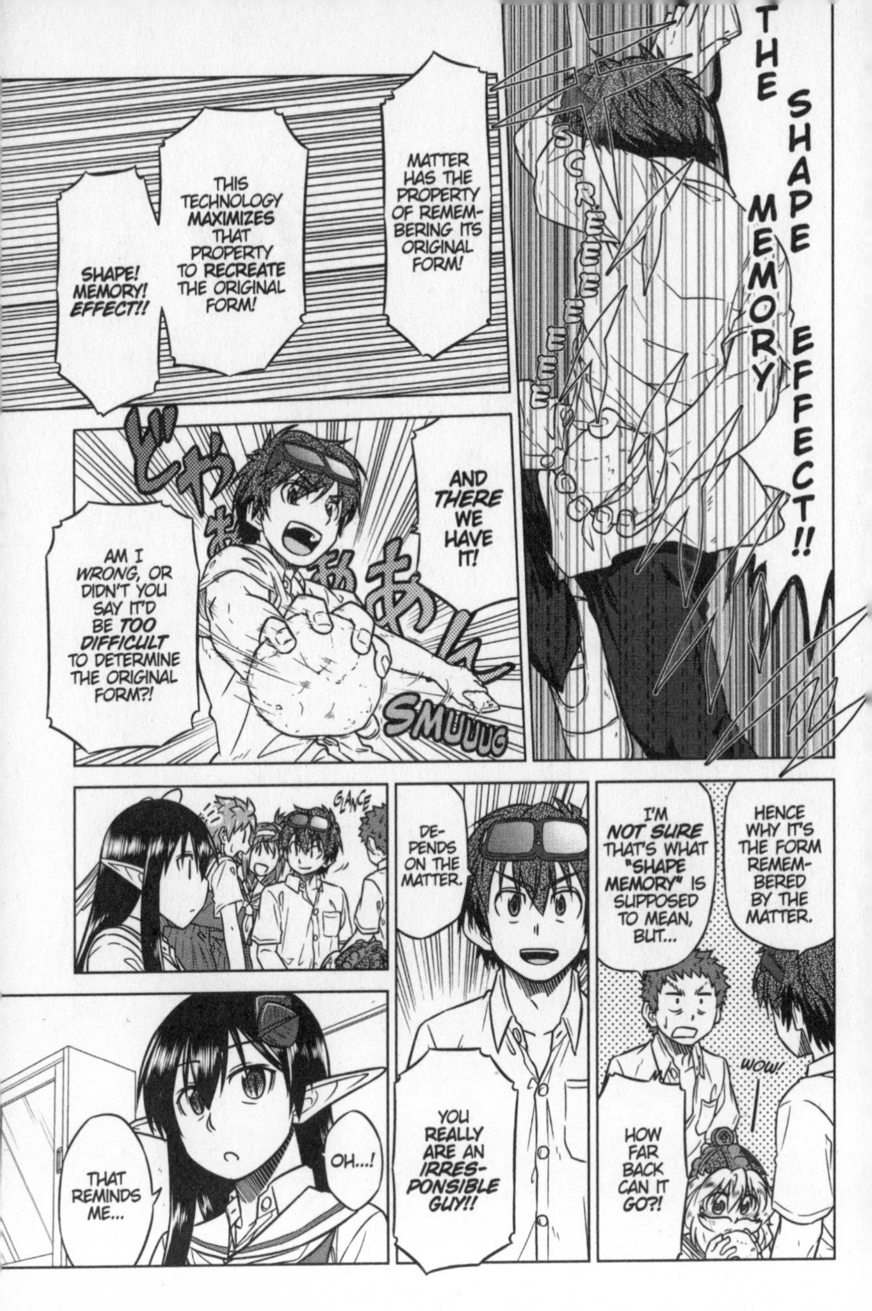
THE SHAPE MEMORY EFFECT!!
SCREEEEEEEE
MATTER HAS THE PROPERTY OF REMEM-BERING ITS ORIGINAL FORM!
THIS TECHNOLOGY MAXIMIZES THAT PROPERTY TO RECREATE THE ORIGINAL FORM!
SHAPE! MEMORY! EFFECT!!
AND THERE WE HAVE IT!
SMUUUG
AM I WRONG, OR DIDN'T YOU SAY IT'D BE TOO DIFFICULT TO DETERMINE THE ORIGINAL FORM?!
HENCE WHY IT'S THE FORM REMEM-BERED BY THE MATTER.
I'M NOT SURE THAT'S WHAT "SHAPE MEMORY" IS SUPPOSED TO MEAN, BUT...
WOW!
HOW FAR BACK CAN IT GO?!
DE-PENDS ON THE MATTER.
YOU REALLY ARE AN IRRES-PONSIBLE GUY!!
GLANCE
OH...!
THAT REMINDS ME...

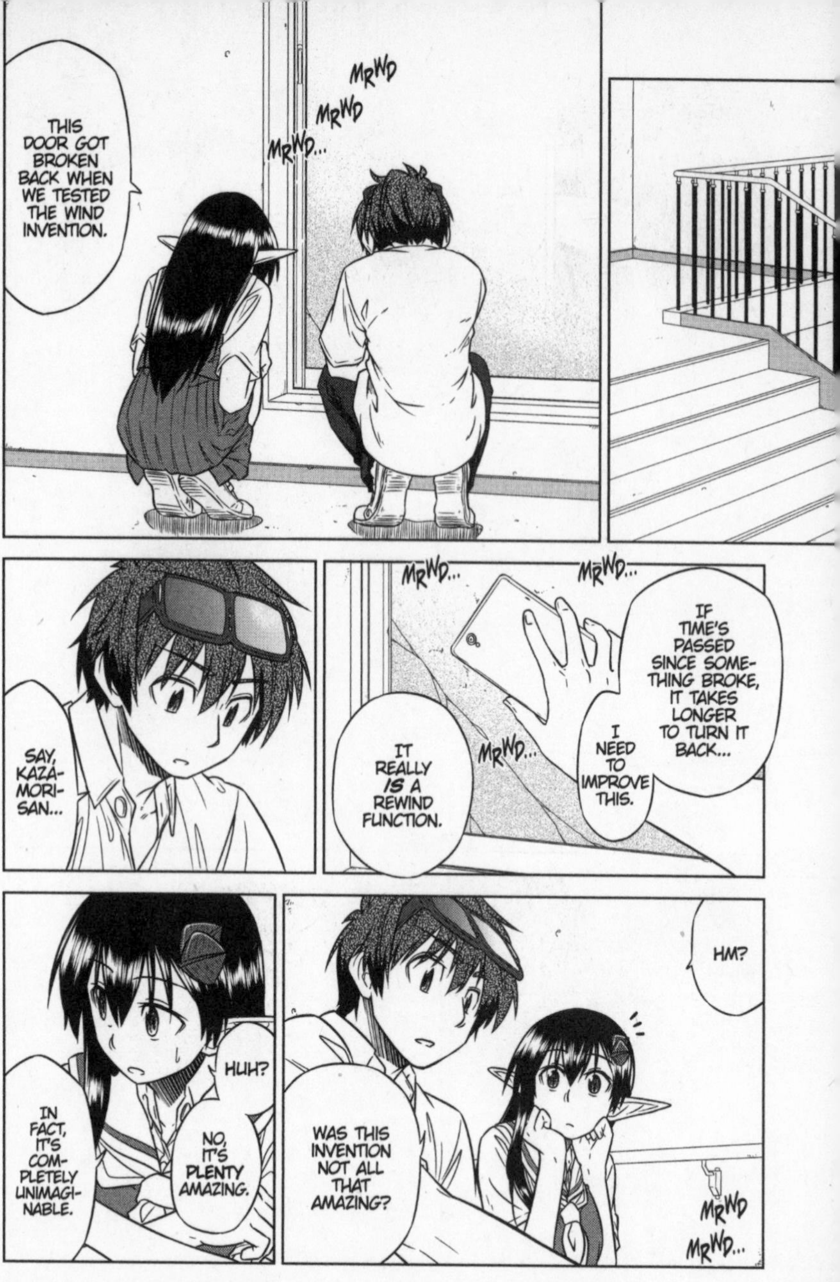
MRWD
MRWD
MRWD...
THIS DOOR GOT BROKEN BACK WHEN WE TESTED THE WIND INVENTION.
MRWD...
MRWD...
IF TIME'S PASSED SINCE SOMETHING BROKE, IT TAKES LONGER TO TURN IT BACK...
I NEED TO IMPROVE THIS.
MRWD...
IT REALLY *IS* A REWIND FUNCTION.
SAY, KAZAMORI-SAN...
HM?
WAS THIS INVENTION NOT ALL THAT AMAZING?
MRWD
MRWD...
HUH?
NO, IT'S PLENTY AMAZING.
IN FACT, IT'S COMPLETELY UNIMAGINABLE.

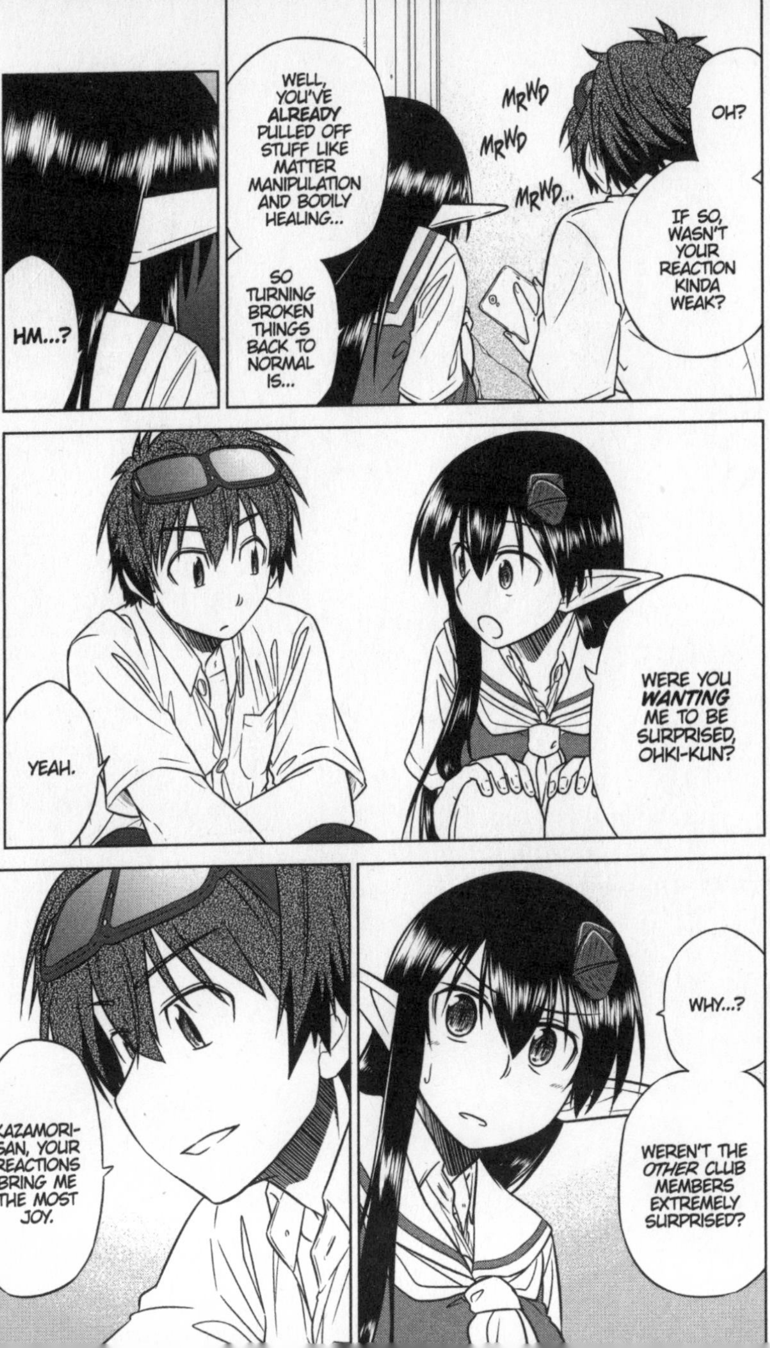
OH?
MRWD MRWD MRWD...
IF SO, WASN'T YOUR REACTION KINDA WEAK?
WELL, YOU'VE ALREADY PULLED OFF STUFF LIKE MATTER MANIPULATION AND BODILY HEALING...
SO TURNING BROKEN THINGS BACK TO NORMAL IS...
HM...?
WERE YOU *WANTING* ME TO BE SURPRISED, OHKI-KUN?
YEAH.
WHY...?
WEREN'T THE *OTHER* CLUB MEMBERS EXTREMELY SURPRISED?
KAZAMORI-SAN, YOUR REACTIONS BRING ME THE MOST JOY.

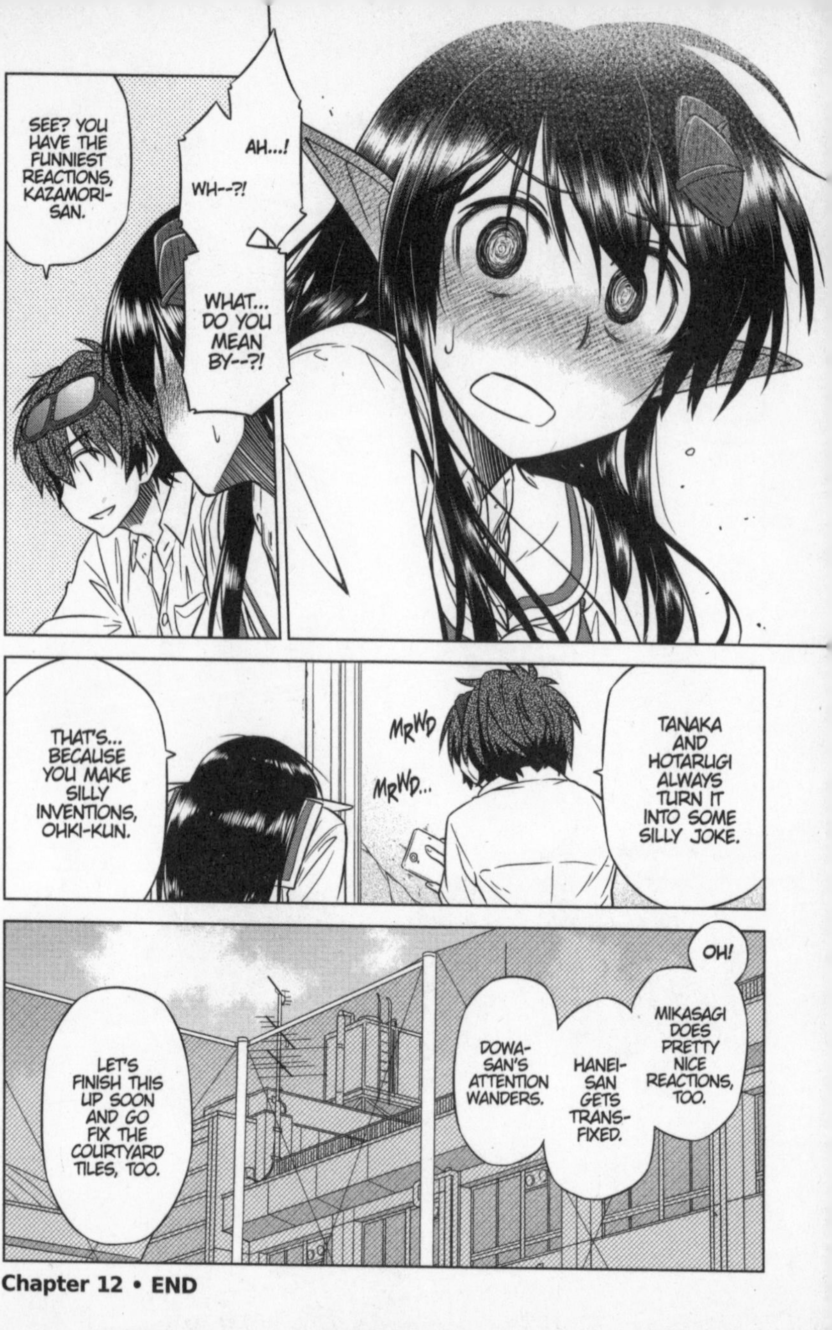
AH...!
WH--?!
WHAT... DO YOU MEAN BY--?!
SEE? YOU HAVE THE FUNNIEST REACTIONS, KAZAMORI-SAN.
TANAKA AND HOTARUGI ALWAYS TURN IT INTO SOME SILLY JOKE.
MRWD
MRWD...
THAT'S... BECAUSE YOU MAKE SILLY INVENTIONS, OHKI-KUN.
OH!
MIKASAGI DOES PRETTY NICE REACTIONS, TOO.
HANEI-SAN GETS TRANS-FIXED.
DOWA-SAN'S ATTENTION WANDERS.
LET'S FINISH THIS UP SOON AND GO FIX THE COURTYARD TILES, TOO.

Chapter 12 • END

Chapter 13: Hanei-san Reflects

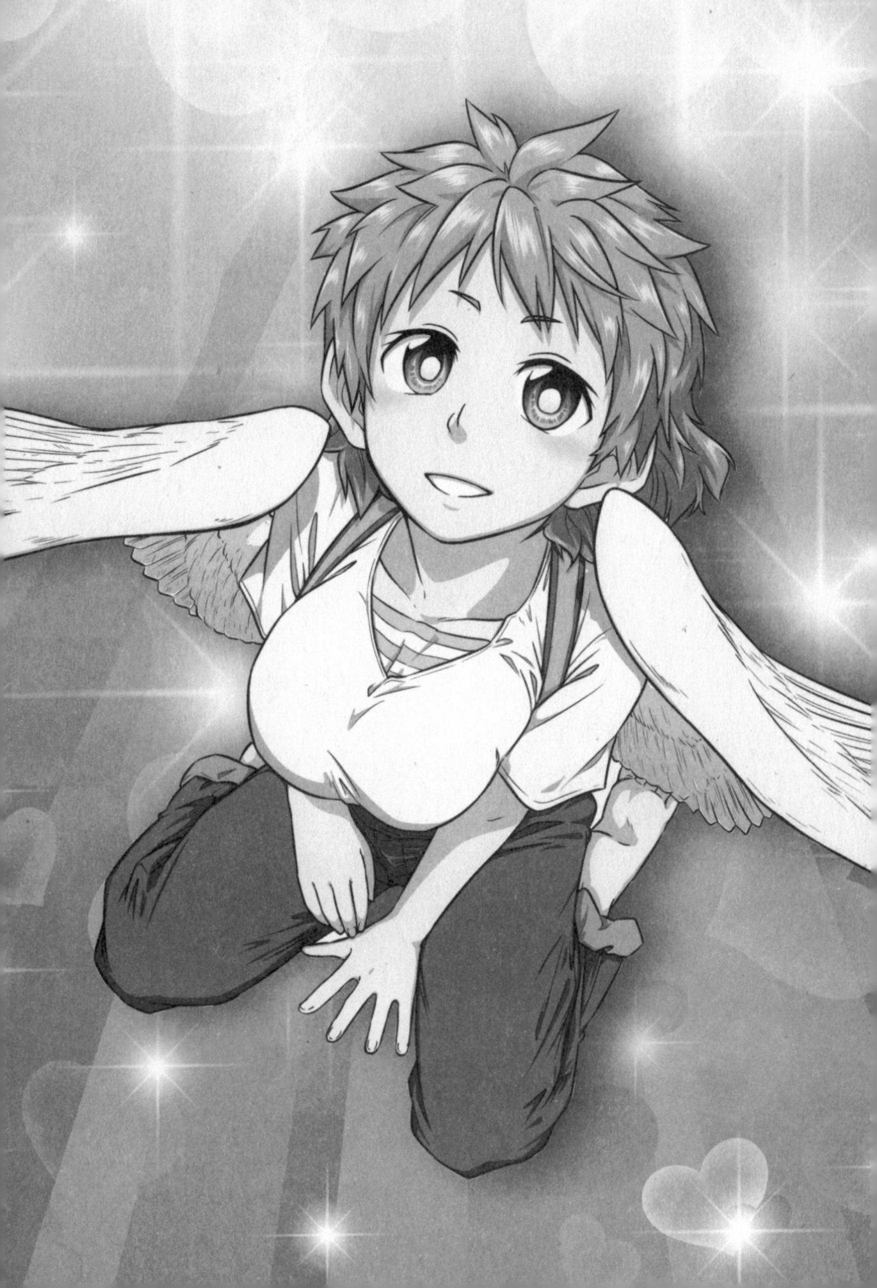

KAZAMORI-SAN, DO YOU LIKE SOUR FOODS?
I DO... WHY?
I HAVE AN INVENTION THAT CAN REPRODUCE ALL SORTS OF FLAVORS VIA ELECTRICAL SIGNALS ON THE TONGUE.
IT CAN ALSO MODIFY THE TEMPERATURE.
GIVE IT A TRY.
JUST FROM LICKING IT.
WHAA ...?
SOU-NDS UN-HEAL-THY...
GOMP...
SOUR-NESS: TWO HUN-DRED.
BLAGH!

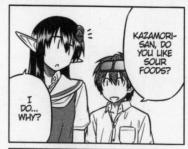

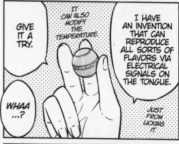

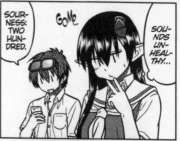

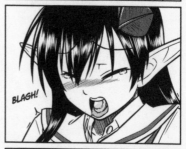

Sour!

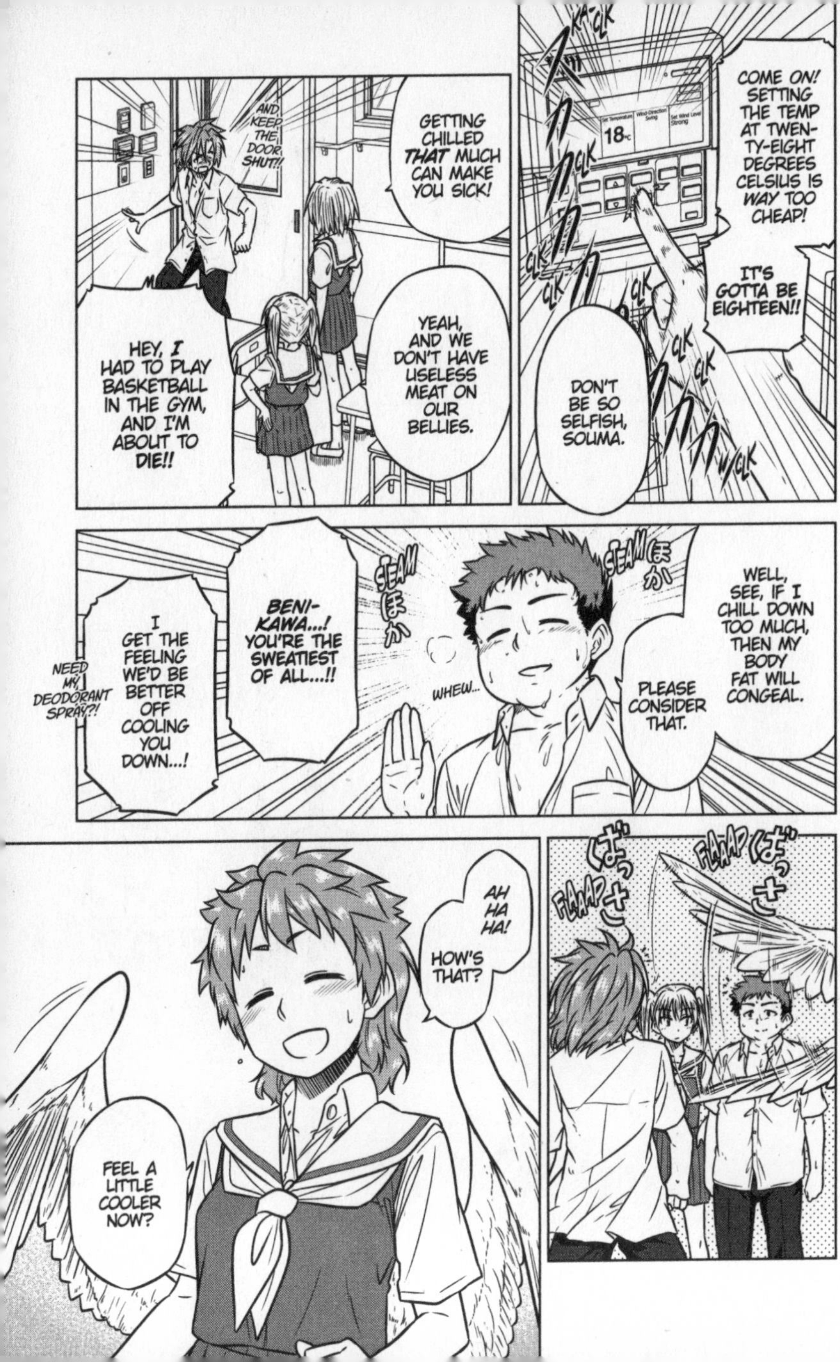
KA-CLK
COME ON! SETTING THE TEMP AT TWENTY-EIGHT DEGREES CELSIUS IS WAY TOO CHEAP!
IT'S GOTTA BE EIGHTEEN!!
CLK CLK CLK CLK CLK CLK CLK
DON'T BE SO SELFISH, SOUMA.
GETTING CHILLED THAT MUCH CAN MAKE YOU SICK!
AND KEEP THE DOOR SHUT!!
YEAH, AND WE DON'T HAVE USELESS MEAT ON OUR BELLIES.
HEY, I HAD TO PLAY BASKETBALL IN THE GYM, AND I'M ABOUT TO DIE!!
STEAM ほか
WELL, SEE, IF I CHILL DOWN TOO MUCH, THEN MY BODY FAT WILL CONGEAL.
PLEASE CONSIDER THAT.
WHEW...
STEAM ほか
BENI-KAWA...! YOU'RE THE SWEATIEST OF ALL...!!
I GET THE FEELING WE'D BE BETTER OFF COOLING YOU DOWN...!
NEED MY DEODORANT SPRAY?!
FLAAAP ばっさ
FLAAAP ばっさ
AH HA HA!
HOW'S THAT?
FEEL A LITTLE COOLER NOW?

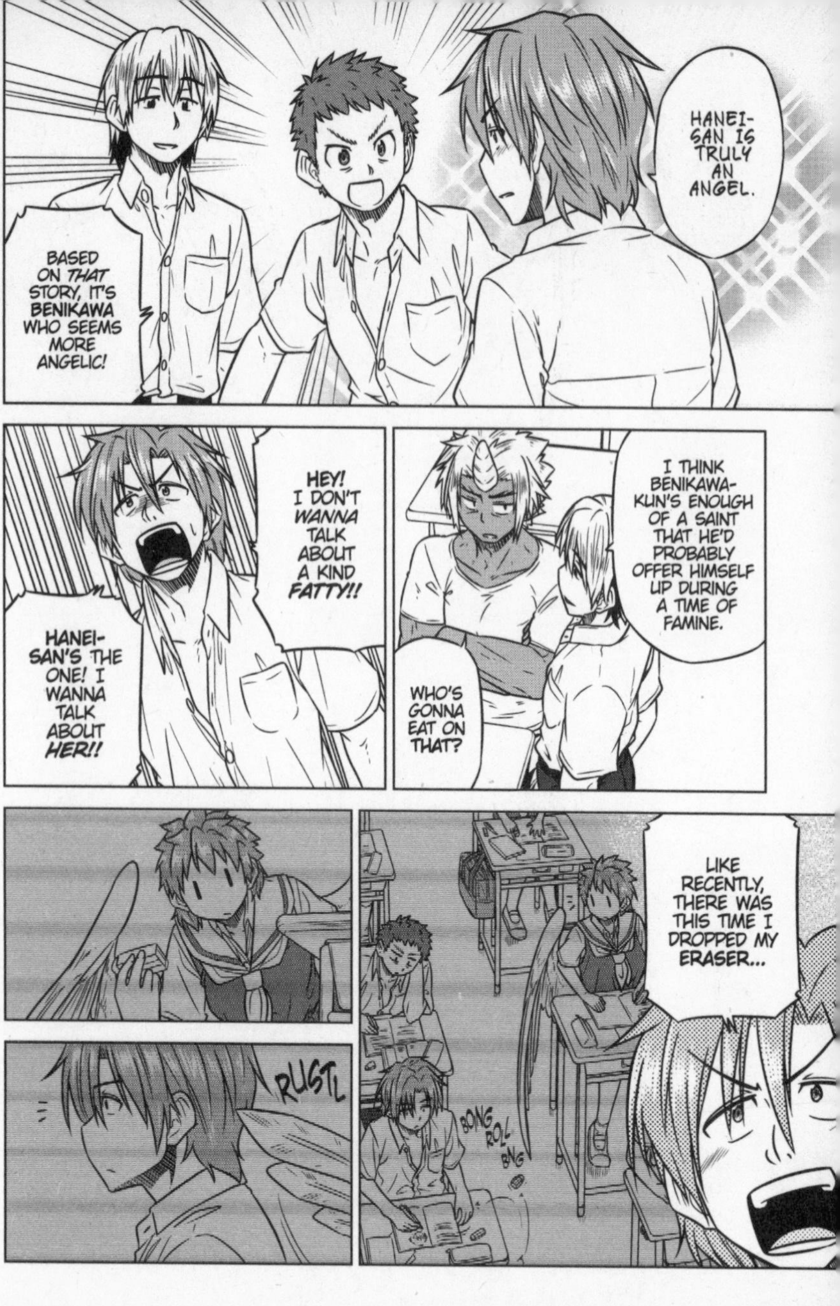
HANEI-SAN IS TRULY AN ANGEL.
BASED ON *THAT* STORY, IT'S BENIKAWA WHO SEEMS MORE ANGELIC!
I THINK BENIKAWA-KUN'S ENOUGH OF A SAINT THAT HE'D PROBABLY OFFER HIMSELF UP DURING A TIME OF FAMINE.
WHO'S GONNA EAT ON THAT?
HEY! I DON'T *WANNA* TALK ABOUT A KIND ***FATTY!!***
HANEI-SAN'S THE ONE! I WANNA TALK ABOUT ***HER!!***
LIKE RECENTLY, THERE WAS THIS TIME I DROPPED MY ERASER...
BONG
ROLL
BNG
RUSTL

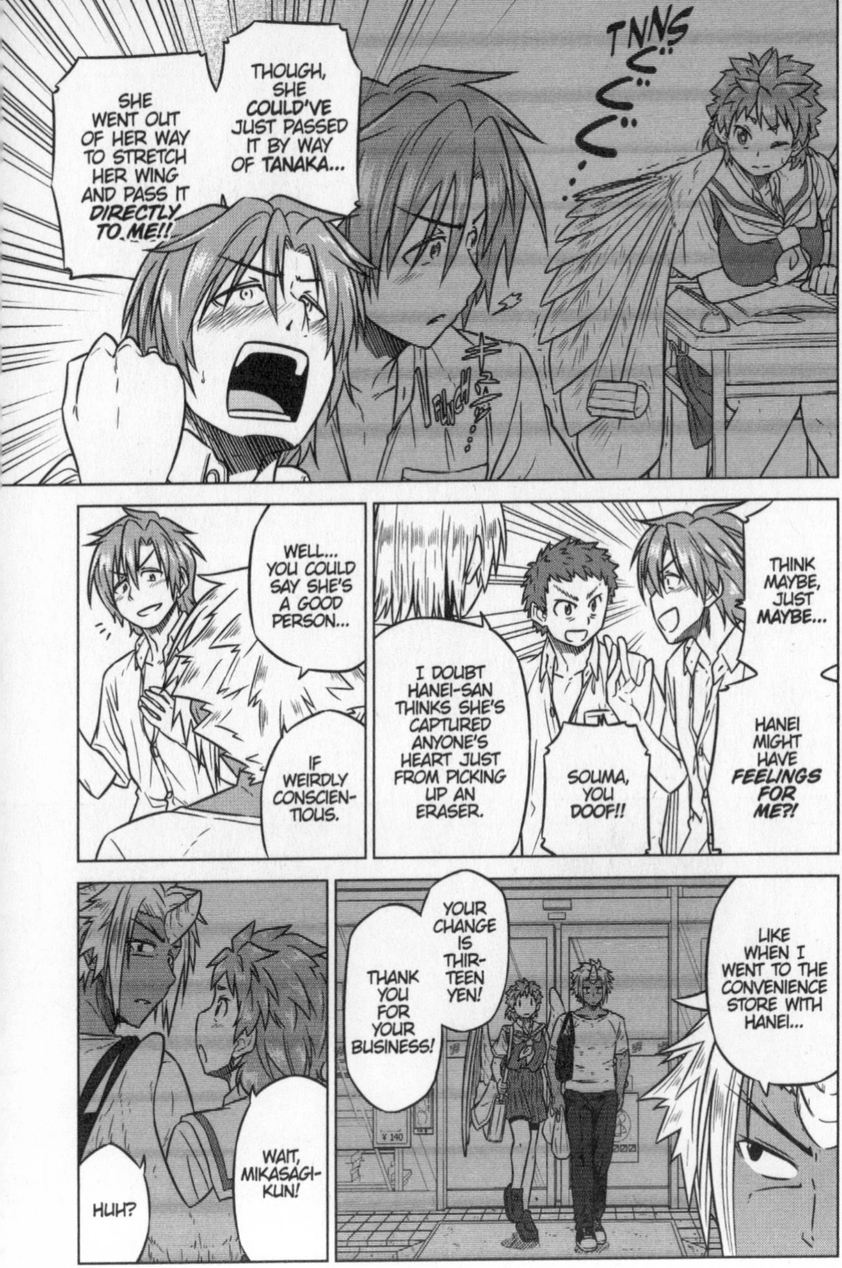
TNNS
ぐ ぐ ぐ
THOUGH, SHE COULD'VE JUST PASSED IT BY WAY OF TANAKA...
SHE WENT OUT OF HER WAY TO STRETCH HER WING AND PASS IT DIRECTLY TO ME!!
THINK MAYBE, JUST MAYBE...
HANEI MIGHT HAVE FEELINGS FOR ME?!
SOUMA, YOU DOOF!!
I DOUBT HANEI-SAN THINKS SHE'S CAPTURED ANYONE'S HEART JUST FROM PICKING UP AN ERASER.
WELL... YOU COULD SAY SHE'S A GOOD PERSON...
IF WEIRDLY CONSCIEN-TIOUS.
LIKE WHEN I WENT TO THE CONVENIENCE STORE WITH HANEI...
YOUR CHANGE IS THIR-TEEN YEN!
THANK YOU FOR YOUR BUSINESS!
WAIT, MIKASAGI-KUN!
HUH?

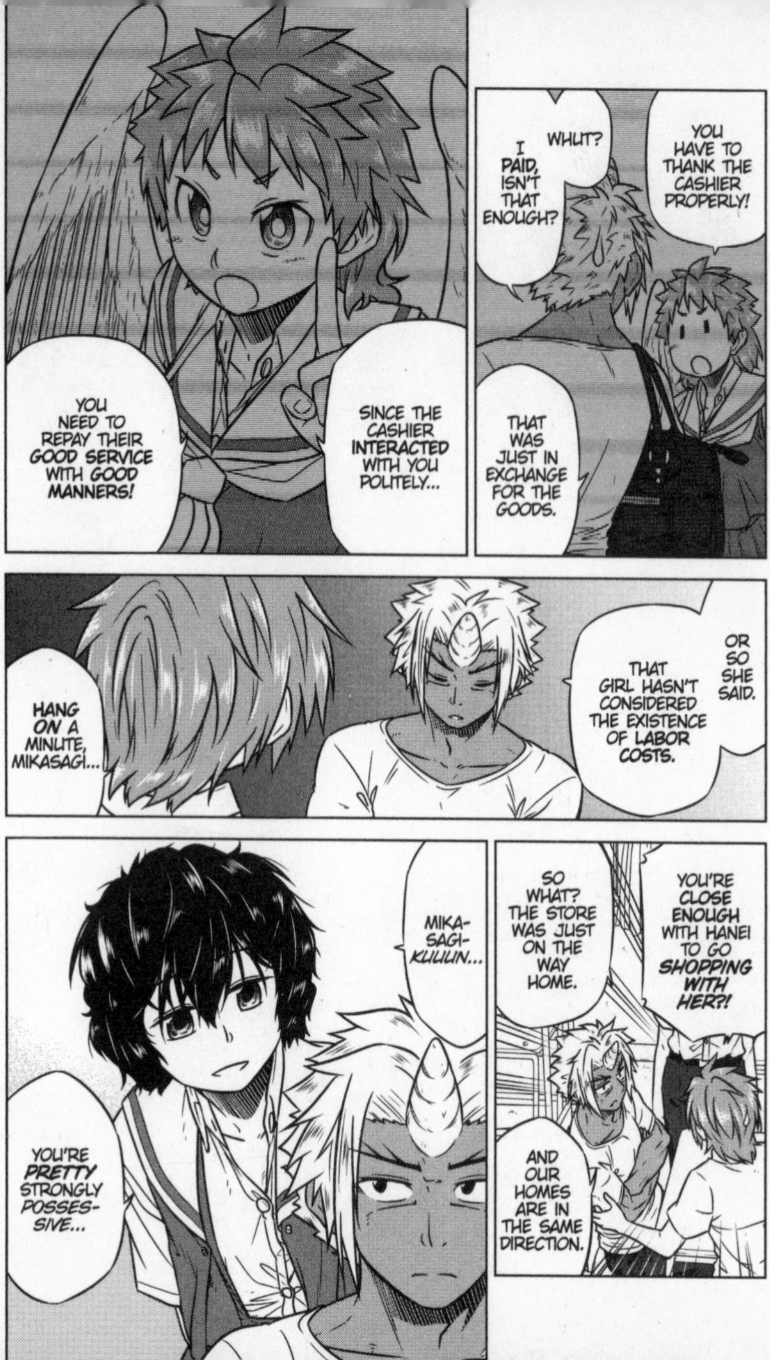
YOU HAVE TO THANK THE CASHIER PROPERLY!
WHUT?
I PAID, ISN'T THAT ENOUGH?
THAT WAS JUST IN EXCHANGE FOR THE GOODS.
SINCE THE CASHIER INTERACTED WITH YOU POLITELY...
YOU NEED TO REPAY THEIR GOOD SERVICE WITH GOOD MANNERS!
OR SO SHE SAID.
THAT GIRL HASN'T CONSIDERED THE EXISTENCE OF LABOR COSTS.
HANG ON A MINUTE, MIKASAGI...
YOU'RE CLOSE ENOUGH WITH HANEI TO GO SHOPPING WITH HER?!
SO WHAT? THE STORE WAS JUST ON THE WAY HOME.
AND OUR HOMES ARE IN THE SAME DIRECTION.
MIKA-SAGI-KUUUN...
YOU'RE PRETTY STRONGLY POSSES-SIVE...

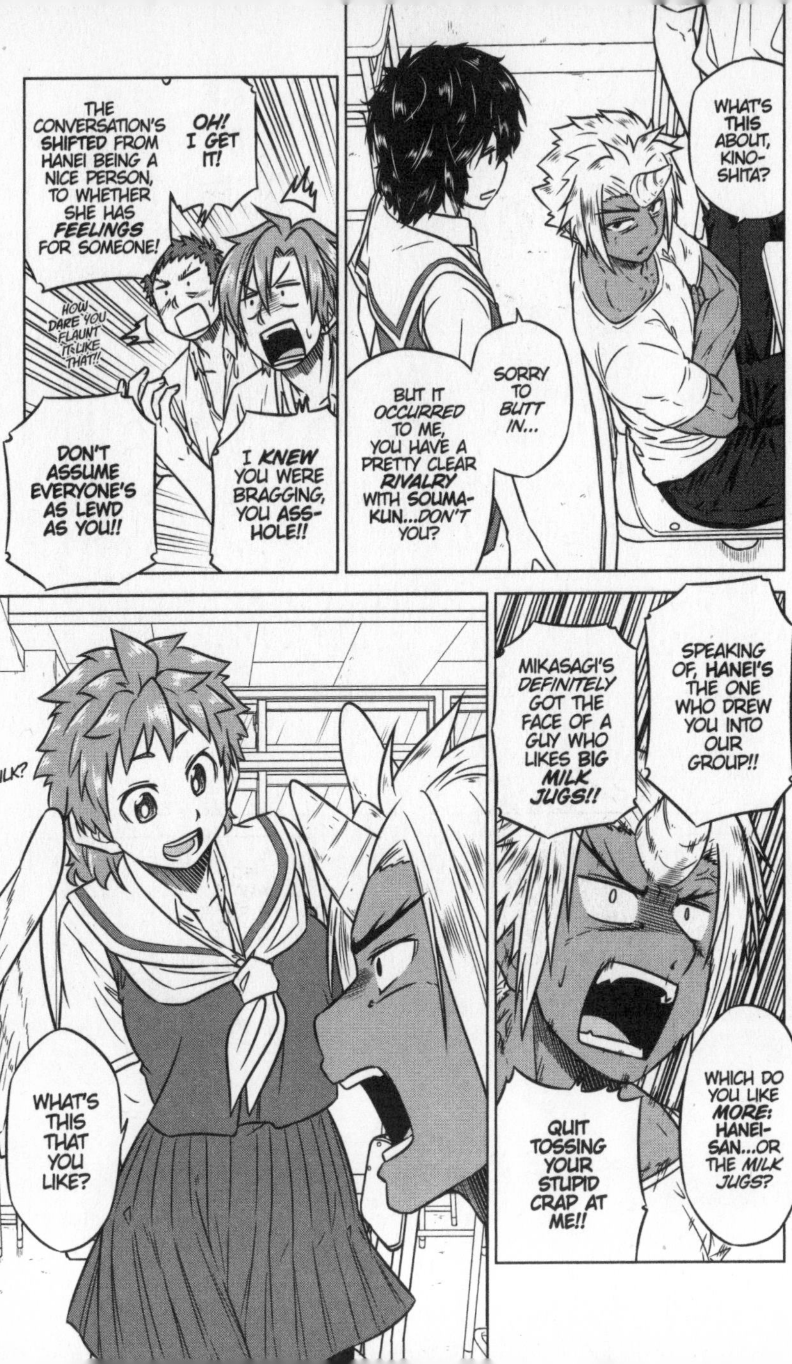
WHAT'S THIS ABOUT, KINO-SHITA?
SORRY TO BUTT IN...
BUT IT OCCURRED TO ME, YOU HAVE A PRETTY CLEAR RIVALRY WITH SOUMA-KUN...DON'T YOU?
OH! I GET IT!
THE CONVERSATION'S SHIFTED FROM HANEI BEING A NICE PERSON, TO WHETHER SHE HAS FEELINGS FOR SOMEONE!
HOW DARE YOU FLAUNT IT LIKE THAT!!
I KNEW YOU WERE BRAGGING, YOU ASS-HOLE!!
DON'T ASSUME EVERYONE'S AS LEWD AS YOU!!
SPEAKING OF, HANEI'S THE ONE WHO DREW YOU INTO OUR GROUP!!
MIKASAGI'S DEFINITELY GOT THE FACE OF A GUY WHO LIKES BIG MILK JUGS!!
WHICH DO YOU LIKE MORE: HANEI-SAN...OR THE MILK JUGS?
QUIT TOSSING YOUR STUPID CRAP AT ME!!
MILK?
WHAT'S THIS THAT YOU LIKE?

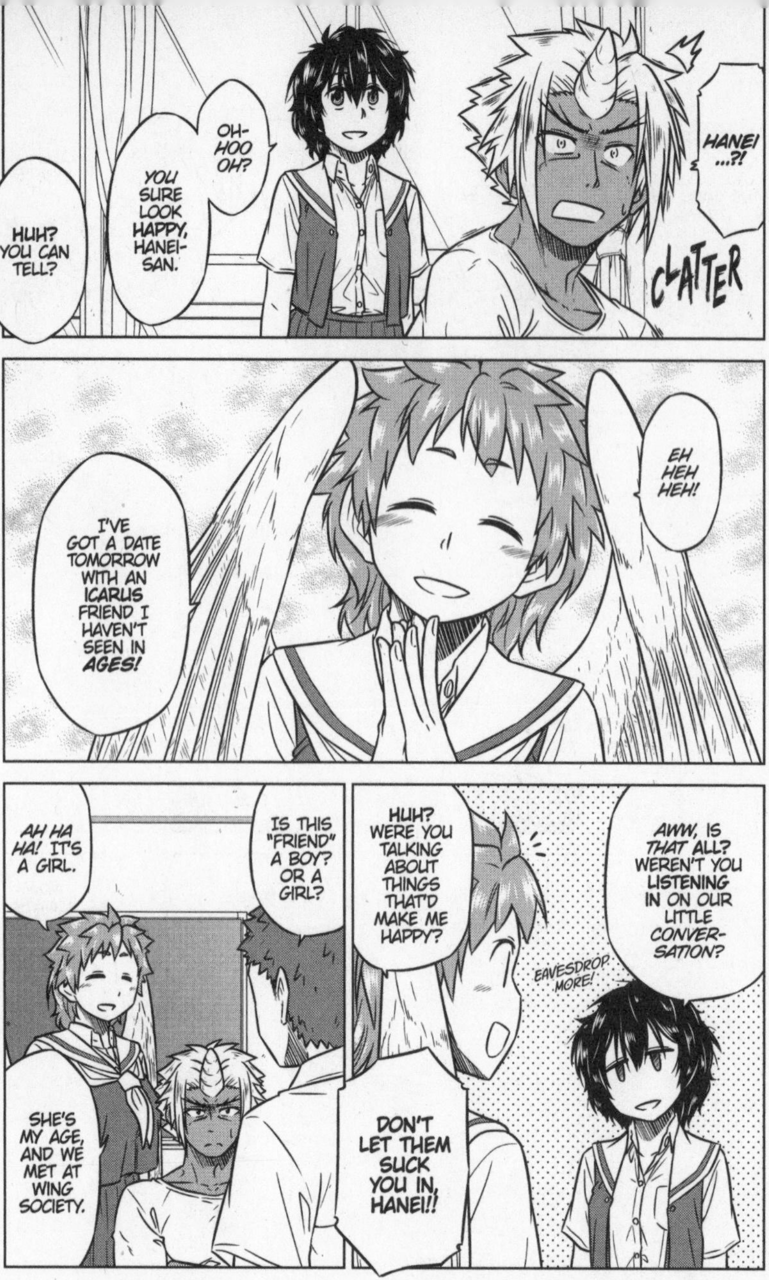
HANEI ...?!
CLATTER
OH-HOO OH?
YOU SURE LOOK HAPPY, HANEI-SAN.
HUH? YOU CAN TELL?
EH HEH HEH!
I'VE GOT A DATE TOMORROW WITH AN ICARUS FRIEND I HAVEN'T SEEN IN AGES!
AWW, IS THAT ALL? WEREN'T YOU LISTENING IN ON OUR LITTLE CONVERSATION?
HUH? WERE YOU TALKING ABOUT THINGS THAT'D MAKE ME HAPPY?
EAVESDROP MORE!
DON'T LET THEM SUCK YOU IN, HANEI!!
IS THIS "FRIEND" A BOY? OR A GIRL?
AH HA HA! IT'S A GIRL.
SHE'S MY AGE, AND WE MET AT WING SOCIETY.

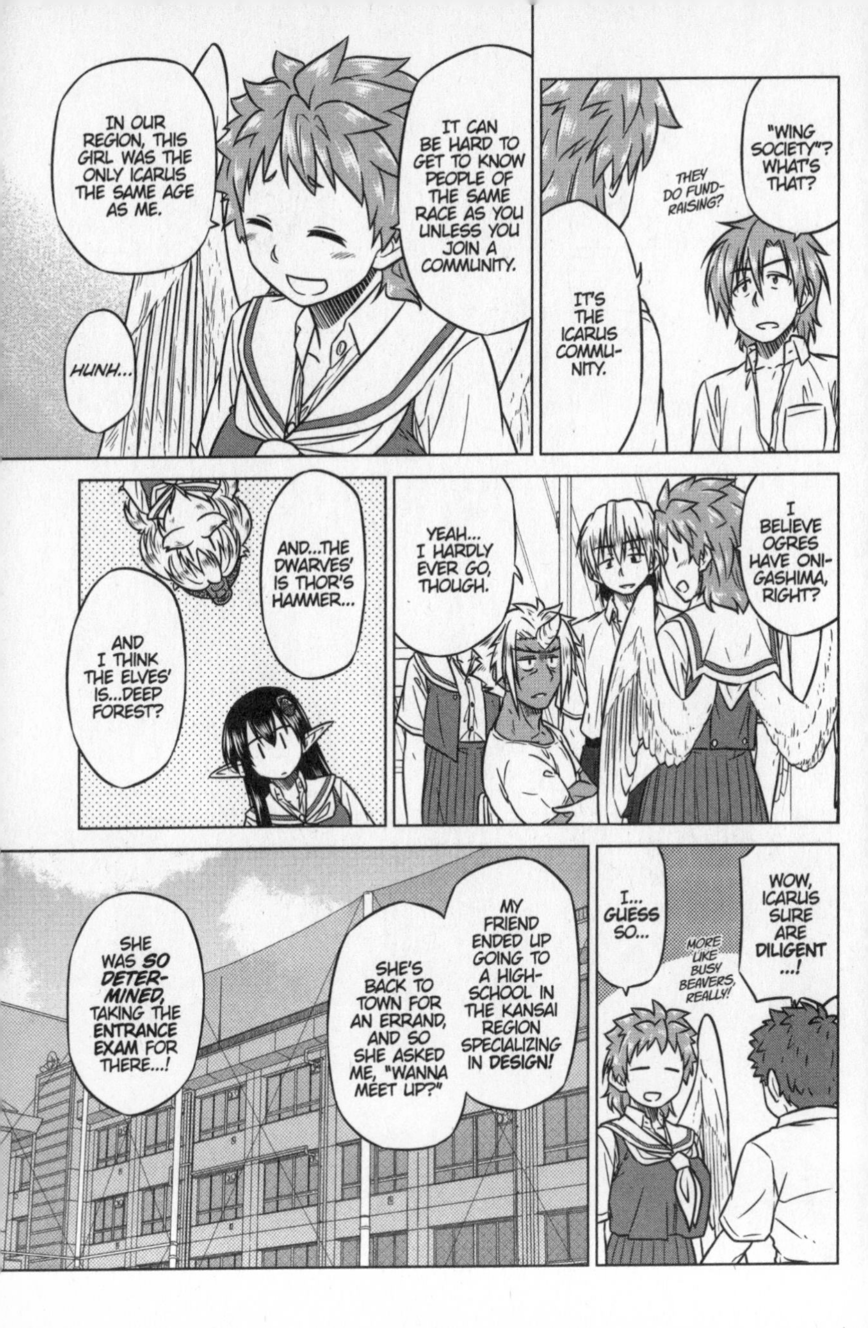
"WING SOCIETY"? WHAT'S THAT?
THEY DO FUND-RAISING?
IT'S THE ICARUS COMMUNITY.
IT CAN BE HARD TO GET TO KNOW PEOPLE OF THE SAME RACE AS YOU UNLESS YOU JOIN A COMMUNITY.
IN OUR REGION, THIS GIRL WAS THE ONLY ICARUS THE SAME AGE AS ME.
HUNH...
I BELIEVE OGRES HAVE ONI-GASHIMA, RIGHT?
YEAH... I HARDLY EVER GO, THOUGH.
AND...THE DWARVES' IS THOR'S HAMMER...
AND I THINK THE ELVES' IS...DEEP FOREST?
WOW, ICARUS SURE ARE DILIGENT...!
MORE LIKE BUSY BEAVERS, REALLY!
I... GUESS SO...
MY FRIEND ENDED UP GOING TO A HIGH-SCHOOL IN THE KANSAI REGION SPECIALIZING IN DESIGN!
SHE'S BACK TO TOWN FOR AN ERRAND, AND SO SHE ASKED ME, "WANNA MEET UP?"
SHE WAS SO DETERMINED, TAKING THE ENTRANCE EXAM FOR THERE...!

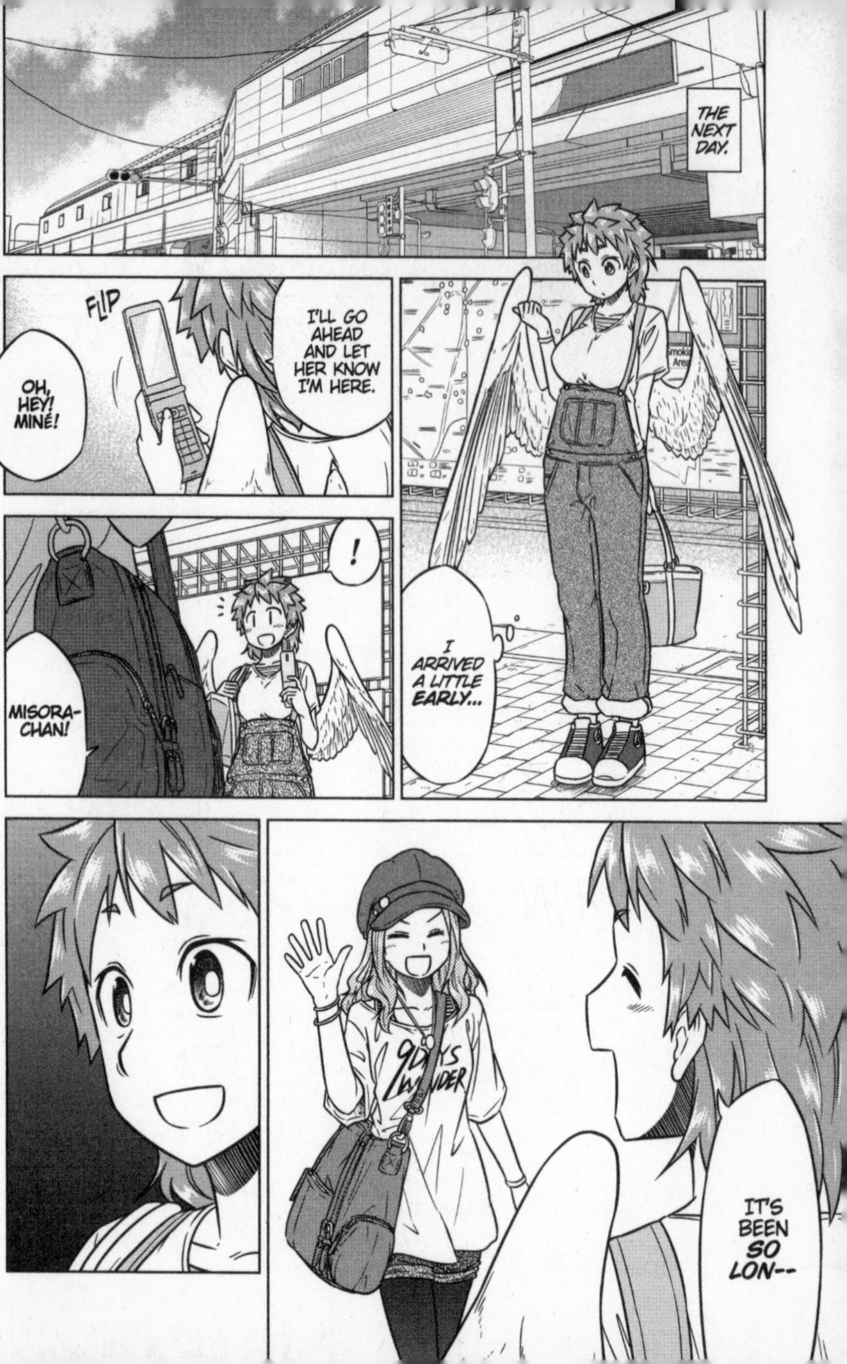
THE NEXT DAY.
I ARRIVED A LITTLE EARLY...
I'LL GO AHEAD AND LET HER KNOW I'M HERE.
FLIP
OH, HEY! MINÉ!
!
MISORA-CHAN!
IT'S BEEN SO LON--

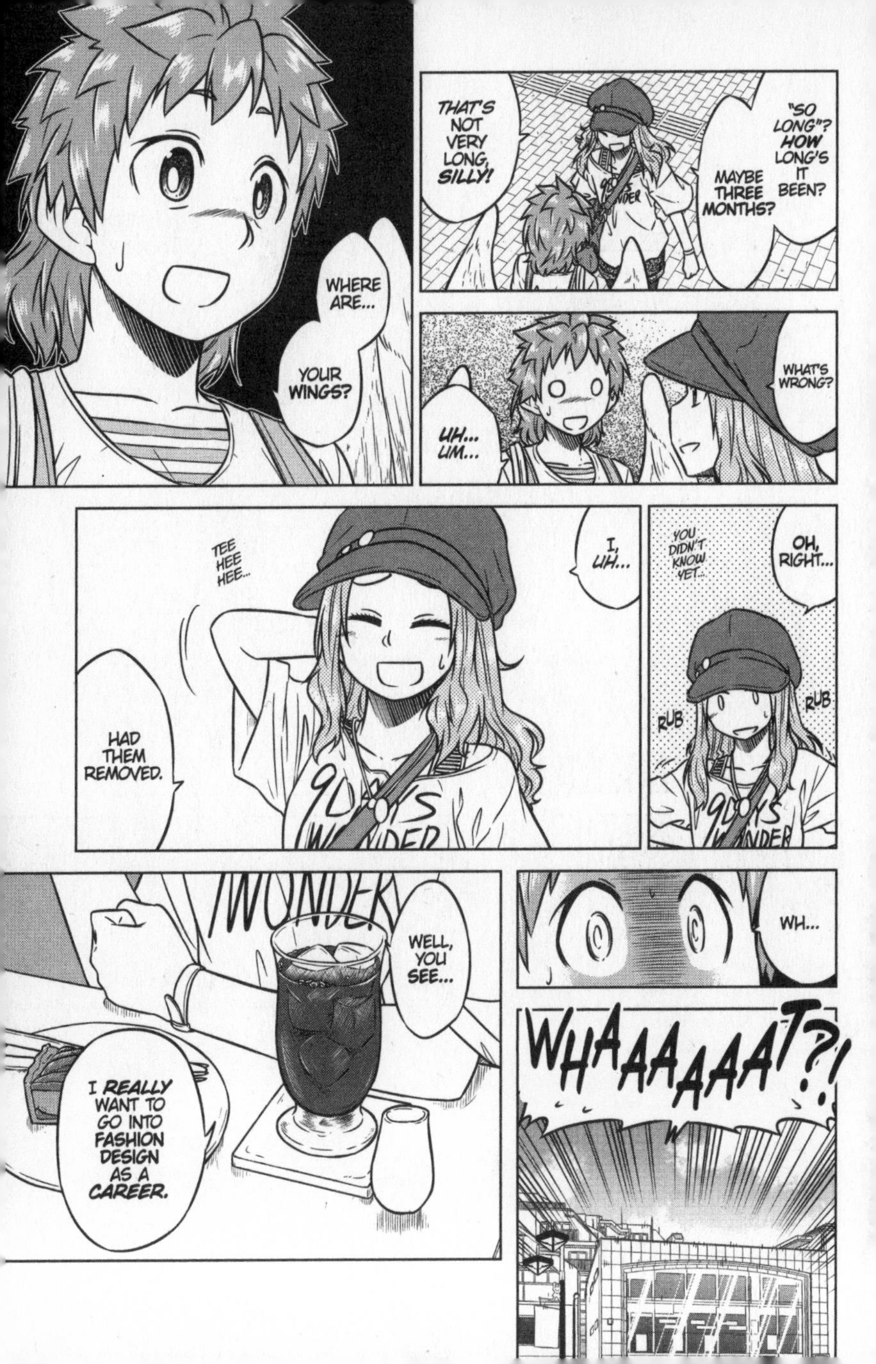
"SO LONG"? HOW LONG'S IT BEEN?
MAYBE THREE MONTHS?
THAT'S NOT VERY LONG, SILLY!
WHAT'S WRONG?
UH... UM...
WHERE ARE...
YOUR WINGS?
OH, RIGHT...
YOU DIDN'T KNOW YET...
RUB
RUB
I, UH...
TEE HEE HEE...
HAD THEM REMOVED.
WH...
WHAAAAAAT?!
WELL, YOU SEE...
I REALLY WANT TO GO INTO FASHION DESIGN AS A CAREER.

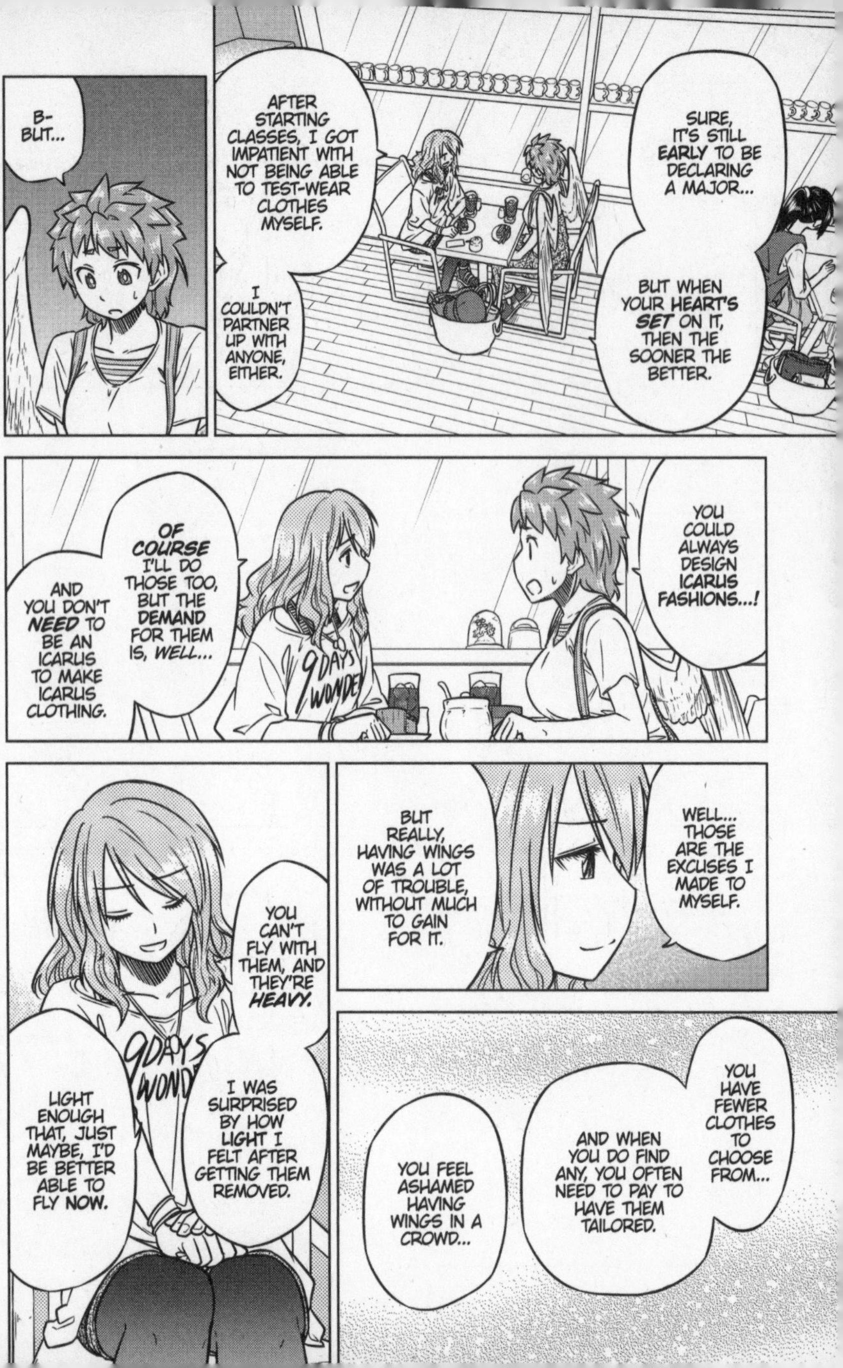
SURE, IT'S STILL EARLY TO BE DECLARING A MAJOR...
BUT WHEN YOUR HEART'S SET ON IT, THEN THE SOONER THE BETTER.
AFTER STARTING CLASSES, I GOT IMPATIENT WITH NOT BEING ABLE TO TEST-WEAR CLOTHES MYSELF.
I COULDN'T PARTNER UP WITH ANYONE, EITHER.
B-BUT...
YOU COULD ALWAYS DESIGN ICARUS FASHIONS...!
OF COURSE I'LL DO THOSE TOO, BUT THE DEMAND FOR THEM IS, WELL...
AND YOU DON'T NEED TO BE AN ICARUS TO MAKE ICARUS CLOTHING.
WELL... THOSE ARE THE EXCUSES I MADE TO MYSELF.
BUT REALLY, HAVING WINGS WAS A LOT OF TROUBLE, WITHOUT MUCH TO GAIN FOR IT.
YOU HAVE FEWER CLOTHES TO CHOOSE FROM...
AND WHEN YOU DO FIND ANY, YOU OFTEN NEED TO PAY TO HAVE THEM TAILORED.
YOU FEEL ASHAMED HAVING WINGS IN A CROWD...
YOU CAN'T FLY WITH THEM, AND THEY'RE HEAVY.
I WAS SURPRISED BY HOW LIGHT I FELT AFTER GETTING THEM REMOVED.
LIGHT ENOUGH THAT, JUST MAYBE, I'D BE BETTER ABLE TO FLY NOW.

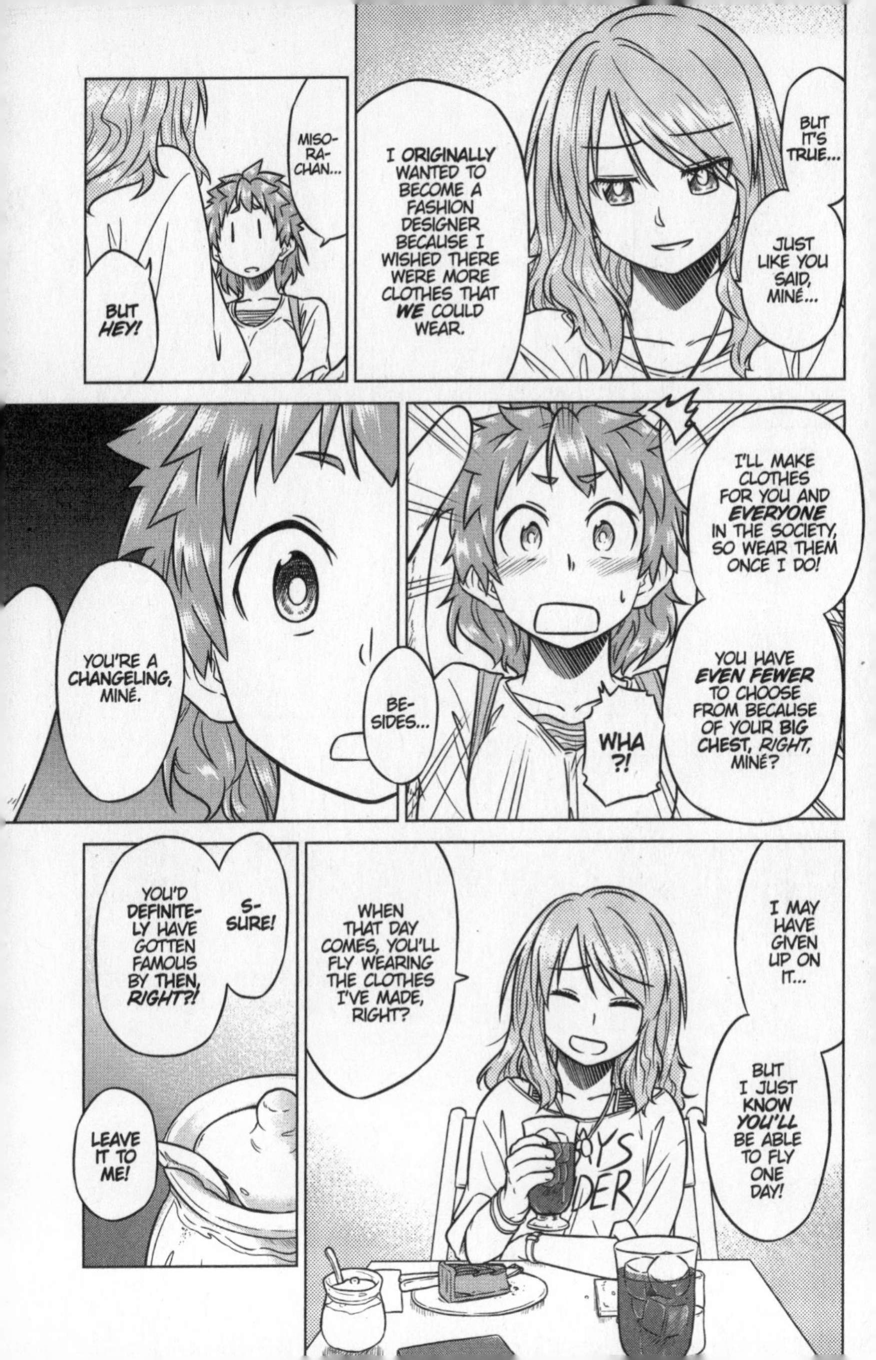
BUT IT'S TRUE...
JUST LIKE YOU SAID, MINÉ...
I ORIGINALLY WANTED TO BECOME A FASHION DESIGNER BECAUSE I WISHED THERE WERE MORE CLOTHES THAT WE COULD WEAR.
MISO-RA-CHAN...
BUT HEY!
I'LL MAKE CLOTHES FOR YOU AND EVERYONE IN THE SOCIETY, SO WEAR THEM ONCE I DO!
YOU HAVE EVEN FEWER TO CHOOSE FROM BECAUSE OF YOUR BIG CHEST, RIGHT, MINÉ?
WHA?!
BE-SIDES...
YOU'RE A CHANGELING, MINÉ.
I MAY HAVE GIVEN UP ON IT...
BUT I JUST KNOW YOU'LL BE ABLE TO FLY ONE DAY!
WHEN THAT DAY COMES, YOU'LL FLY WEARING THE CLOTHES I'VE MADE, RIGHT?
S-SURE!
YOU'D DEFINITELY HAVE GOTTEN FAMOUS BY THEN, RIGHT?!
LEAVE IT TO ME!

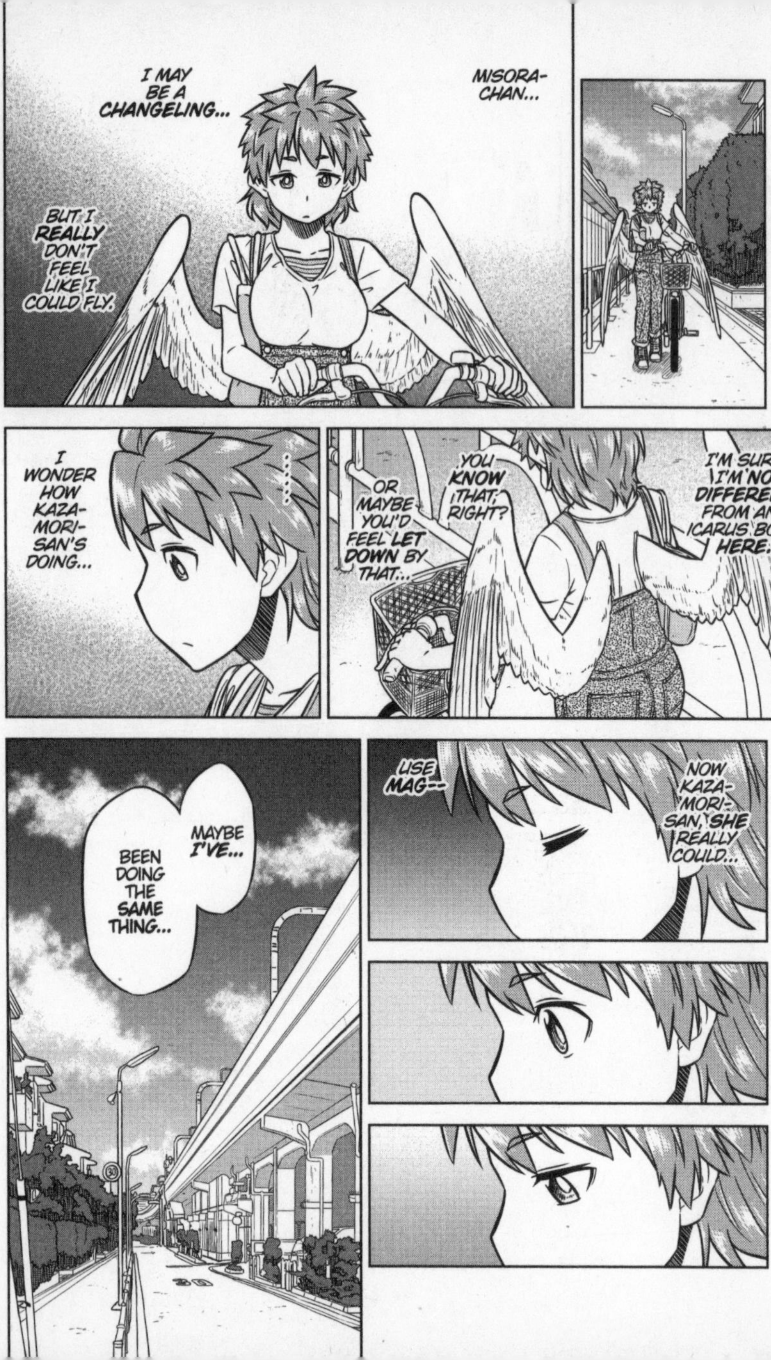
MISORA-CHAN...
I MAY BE A CHANGELING...
BUT I REALLY DON'T FEEL LIKE I COULD FLY.
I'M SURE I'M NO DIFFERENT FROM ANY ICARUS BORN HERE.
YOU KNOW THAT, RIGHT?
OR MAYBE YOU'D FEEL LET DOWN BY THAT...
......
I WONDER HOW KAZA-MORI-SAN'S DOING...
NOW KAZA-MORI-SAN, SHE REALLY COULD...
USE MAG--
MAYBE I'VE...
BEEN DOING THE SAME THING...

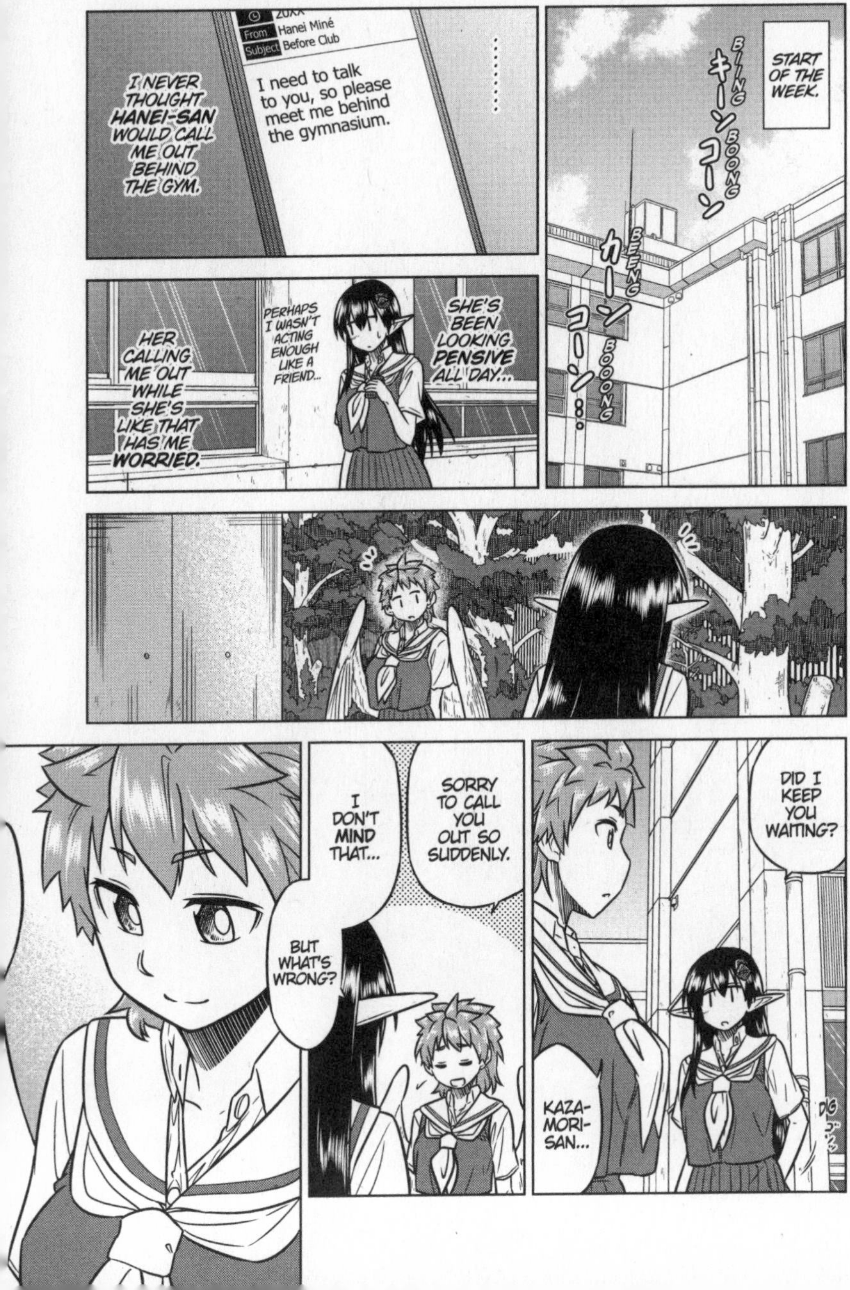
START OF THE WEEK.
BIING キーンコーン BOONG
BEENG カーンコーン BOOONG
......
20XX
From: Hanei Miné
Subject: Before Club
I need to talk to you, so please meet me behind the gymnasium.
I NEVER THOUGHT HANEI-SAN WOULD CALL ME OUT BEHIND THE GYM.
SHE'S BEEN LOOKING PENSIVE ALL DAY...
PERHAPS I WASN'T ACTING ENOUGH LIKE A FRIEND...
HER CALLING ME OUT WHILE SHE'S LIKE THAT HAS ME WORRIED.
DID I KEEP YOU WAITING?
DIG
KAZAMORI-SAN...
SORRY TO CALL YOU OUT SO SUDDENLY.
I DON'T MIND THAT...
BUT WHAT'S WRONG?

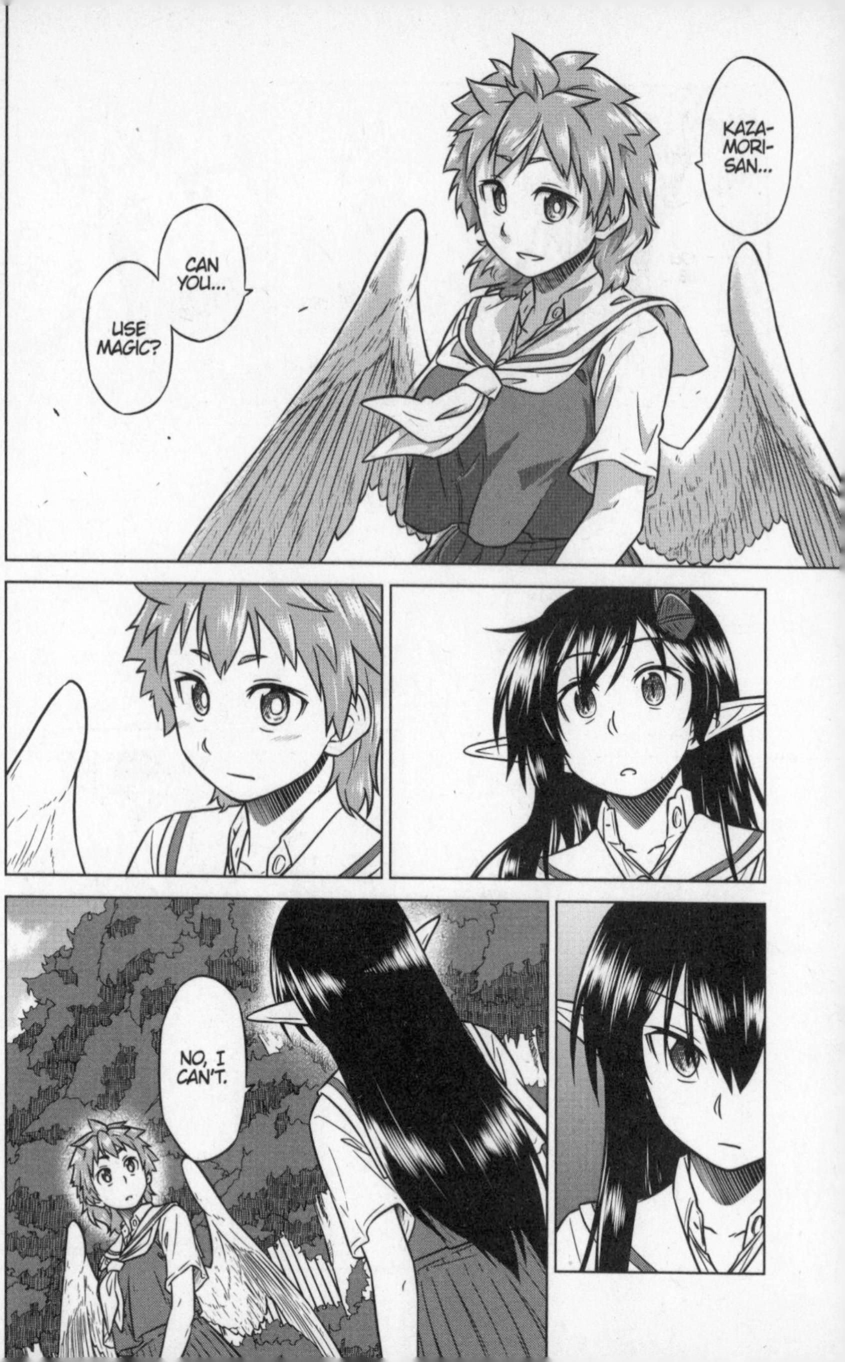
KAZA-MORI-SAN...
CAN YOU...
USE MAGIC?
NO, I CAN'T.

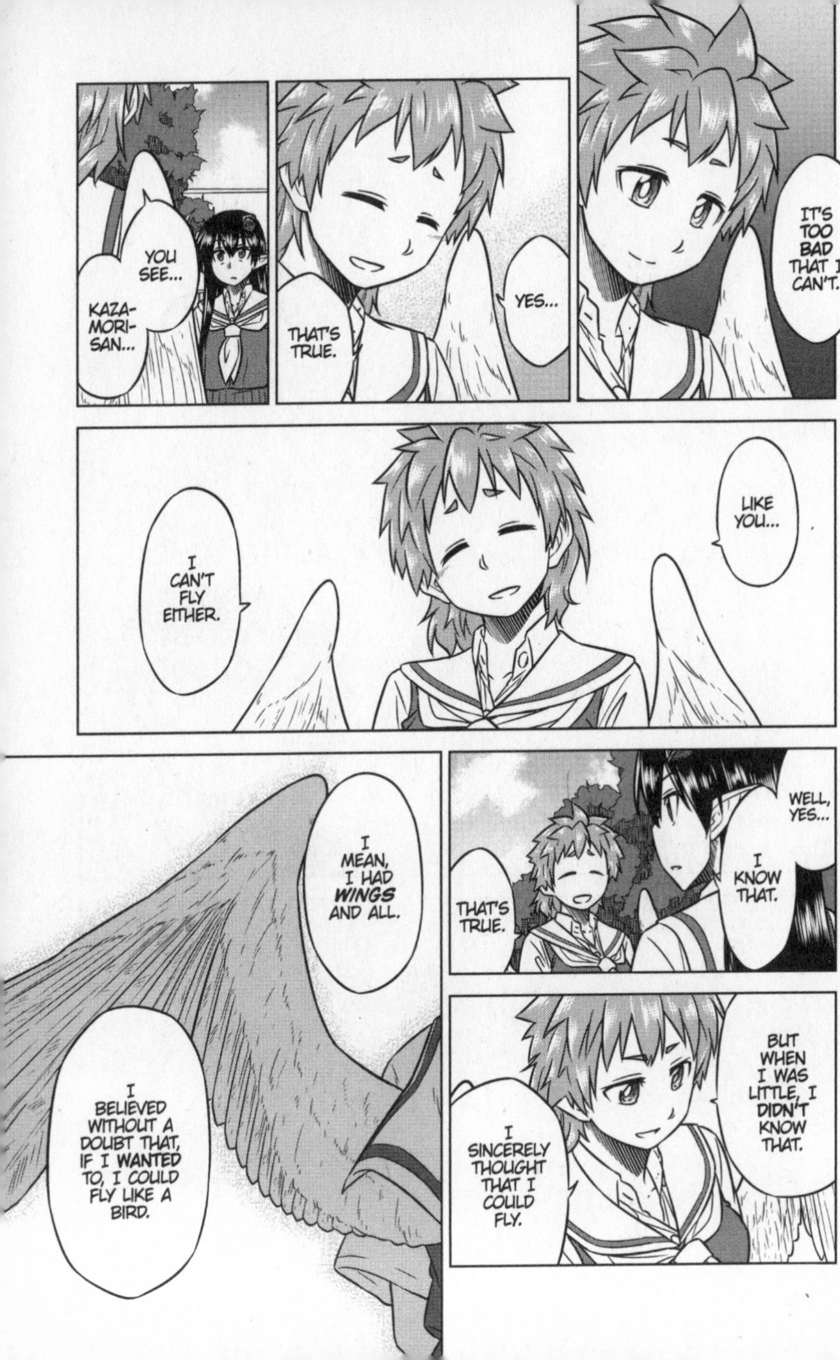
IT'S TOO BAD THAT I CAN'T.
YES...
THAT'S TRUE.
YOU SEE...
KAZAMORI-SAN...
LIKE YOU...
I CAN'T FLY EITHER.
WELL, YES...
I KNOW THAT.
THAT'S TRUE.
BUT WHEN I WAS LITTLE, I DIDN'T KNOW THAT.
I SINCERELY THOUGHT THAT I COULD FLY.
I MEAN, I HAD ***WINGS*** AND ALL.
I BELIEVED WITHOUT A DOUBT THAT, IF I WANTED TO, I COULD FLY LIKE A BIRD.

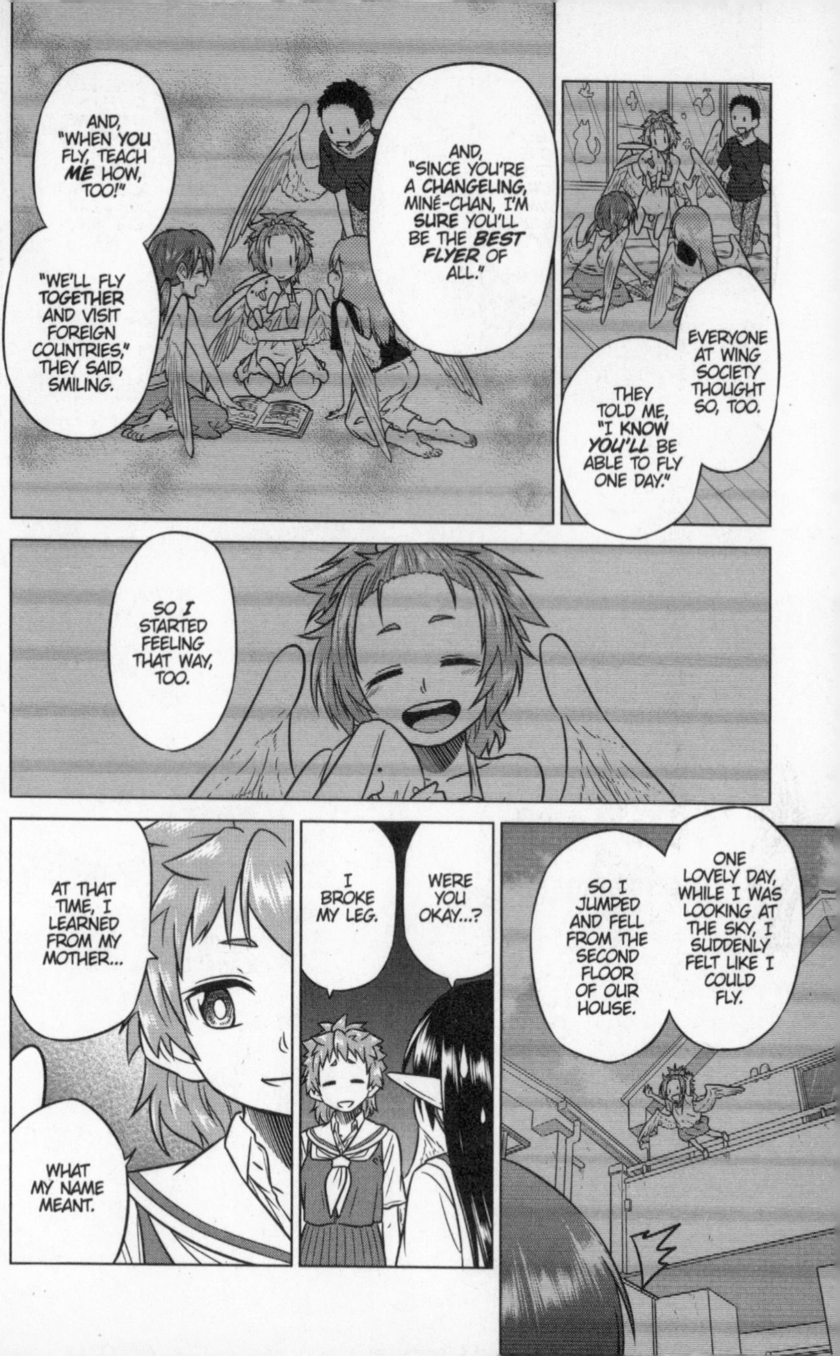
EVERYONE AT WING SOCIETY THOUGHT SO, TOO.
THEY TOLD ME, "I KNOW YOU'LL BE ABLE TO FLY ONE DAY."
AND, "SINCE YOU'RE A CHANGELING, MINÉ-CHAN, I'M SURE YOU'LL BE THE BEST FLYER OF ALL."
AND, "WHEN YOU FLY, TEACH ME HOW, TOO!"
"WE'LL FLY TOGETHER AND VISIT FOREIGN COUNTRIES," THEY SAID, SMILING.
SO I STARTED FEELING THAT WAY, TOO.
ONE LOVELY DAY, WHILE I WAS LOOKING AT THE SKY, I SUDDENLY FELT LIKE I COULD FLY.
SO I JUMPED AND FELL FROM THE SECOND FLOOR OF OUR HOUSE.
WERE YOU OKAY...?
I BROKE MY LEG.
AT THAT TIME, I LEARNED FROM MY MOTHER...
WHAT MY NAME MEANT.

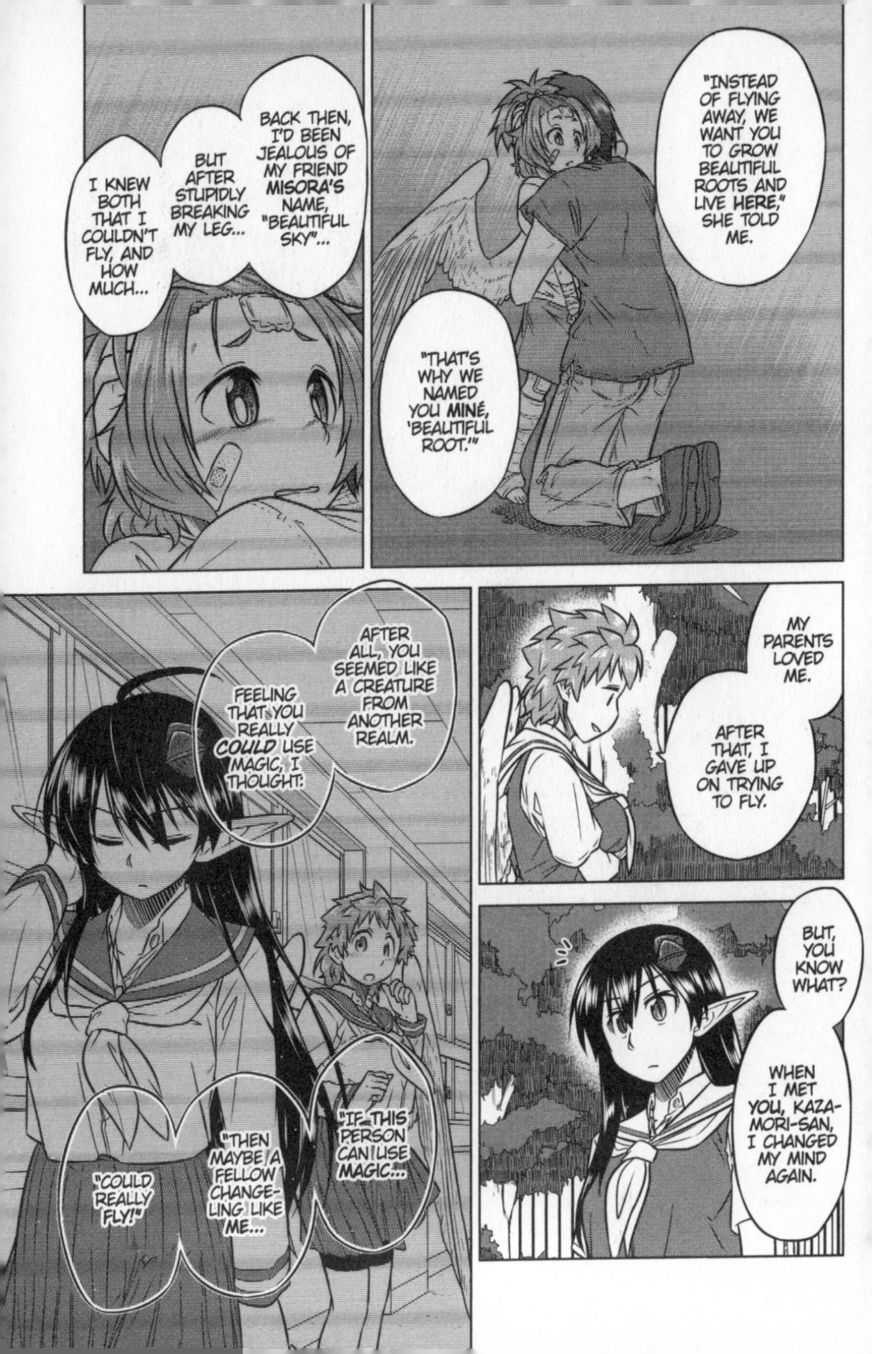
"INSTEAD OF FLYING AWAY, WE WANT YOU TO GROW BEAUTIFUL ROOTS AND LIVE HERE," SHE TOLD ME.
"THAT'S WHY WE NAMED YOU MINÉ, 'BEAUTIFUL ROOT.'"
BACK THEN, I'D BEEN JEALOUS OF MY FRIEND MISORA'S NAME, "BEAUTIFUL SKY"...
BUT AFTER STUPIDLY BREAKING MY LEG...
I KNEW BOTH THAT I COULDN'T FLY, AND HOW MUCH...
MY PARENTS LOVED ME.
AFTER THAT, I GAVE UP ON TRYING TO FLY.
BUT, YOU KNOW WHAT?
WHEN I MET YOU, KAZA-MORI-SAN, I CHANGED MY MIND AGAIN.
AFTER ALL, YOU SEEMED LIKE A CREATURE FROM ANOTHER REALM.
FEELING THAT YOU REALLY COULD USE MAGIC, I THOUGHT:
"IF THIS PERSON CAN USE MAGIC...
"THEN MAYBE A FELLOW CHANGE-LING LIKE ME...
"COULD REALLY FLY!"

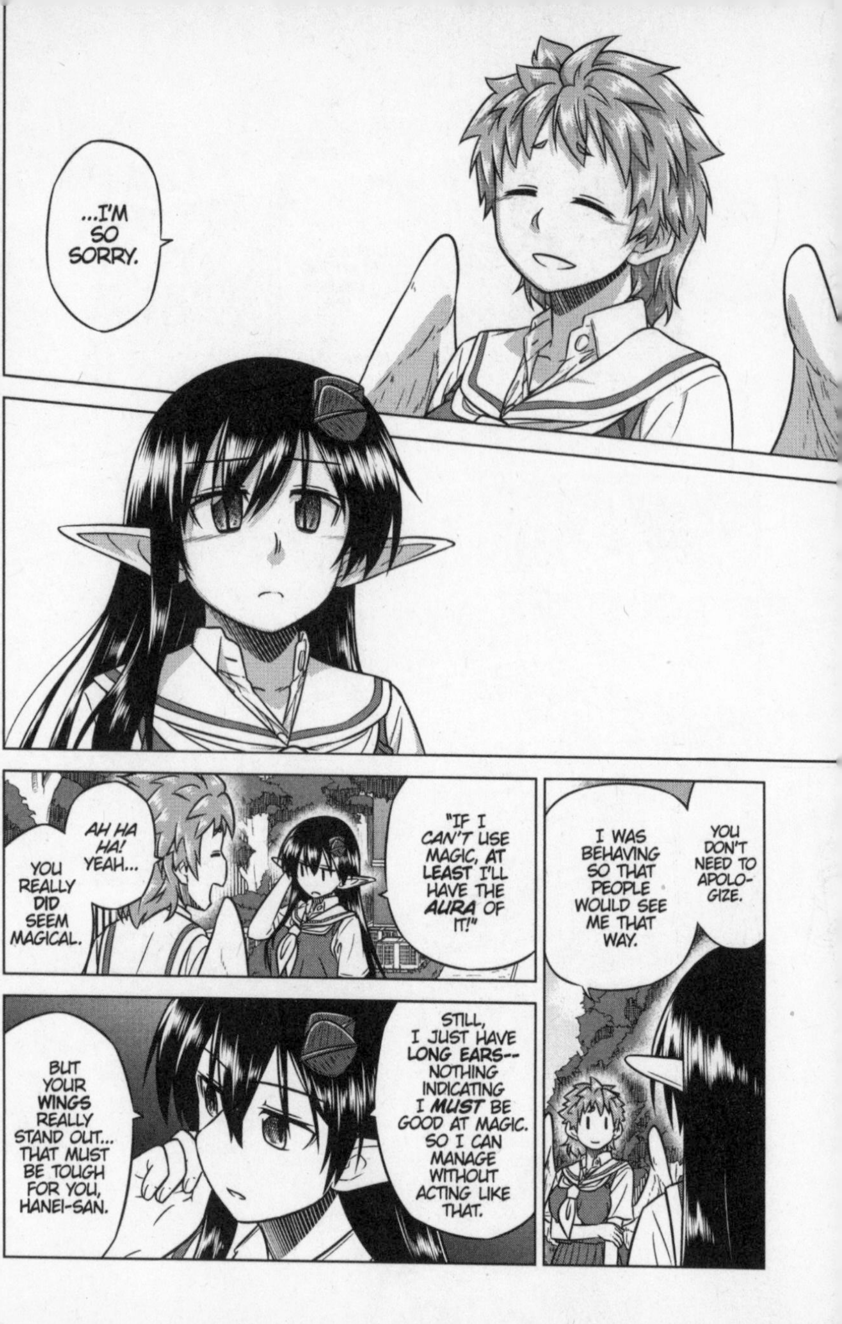
...I'M SO SORRY.
YOU DON'T NEED TO APOLO-GIZE.
I WAS BEHAVING SO THAT PEOPLE WOULD SEE ME THAT WAY.
"IF I *CAN'T* USE MAGIC, AT LEAST I'LL HAVE THE ***AURA*** OF IT!"
AH HA HA! YEAH...
YOU REALLY DID SEEM MAGICAL.
STILL, I JUST HAVE **LONG EARS**--NOTHING INDICATING I ***MUST*** BE GOOD AT MAGIC. SO I CAN MANAGE WITHOUT ACTING LIKE THAT.
BUT YOUR WINGS REALLY STAND OUT... THAT MUST BE TOUGH FOR YOU, HANEI-SAN.

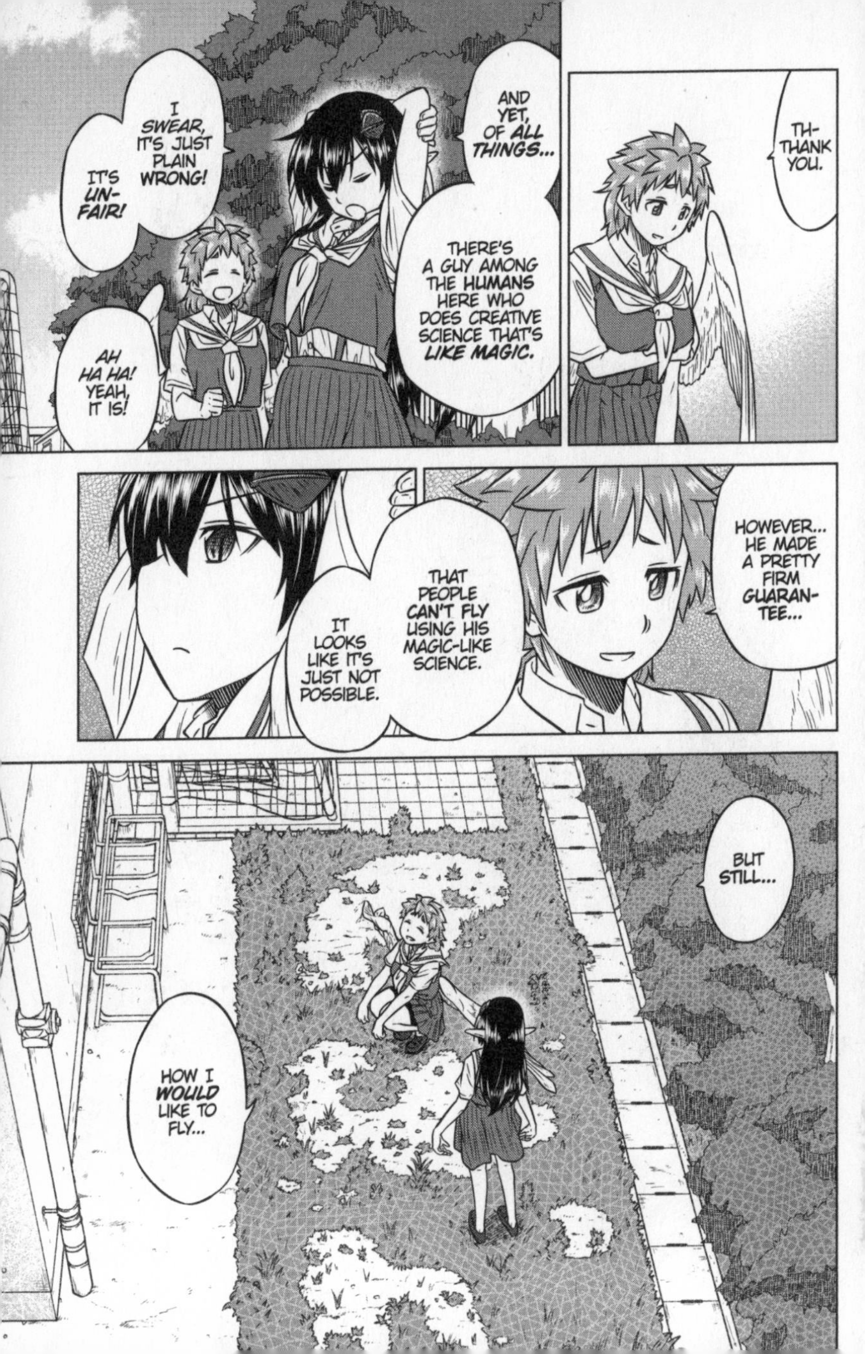
TH- THANK YOU.
AND YET, OF ALL THINGS...
THERE'S A GUY AMONG THE HUMANS HERE WHO DOES CREATIVE SCIENCE THAT'S LIKE MAGIC.
I SWEAR, IT'S JUST PLAIN WRONG!
IT'S UN-FAIR!
AH HA HA! YEAH, IT IS!
HOWEVER... HE MADE A PRETTY FIRM GUARAN-TEE...
THAT PEOPLE CAN'T FLY USING HIS MAGIC-LIKE SCIENCE.
IT LOOKS LIKE IT'S JUST NOT POSSIBLE.
BUT STILL...
HOW I WOULD LIKE TO FLY...

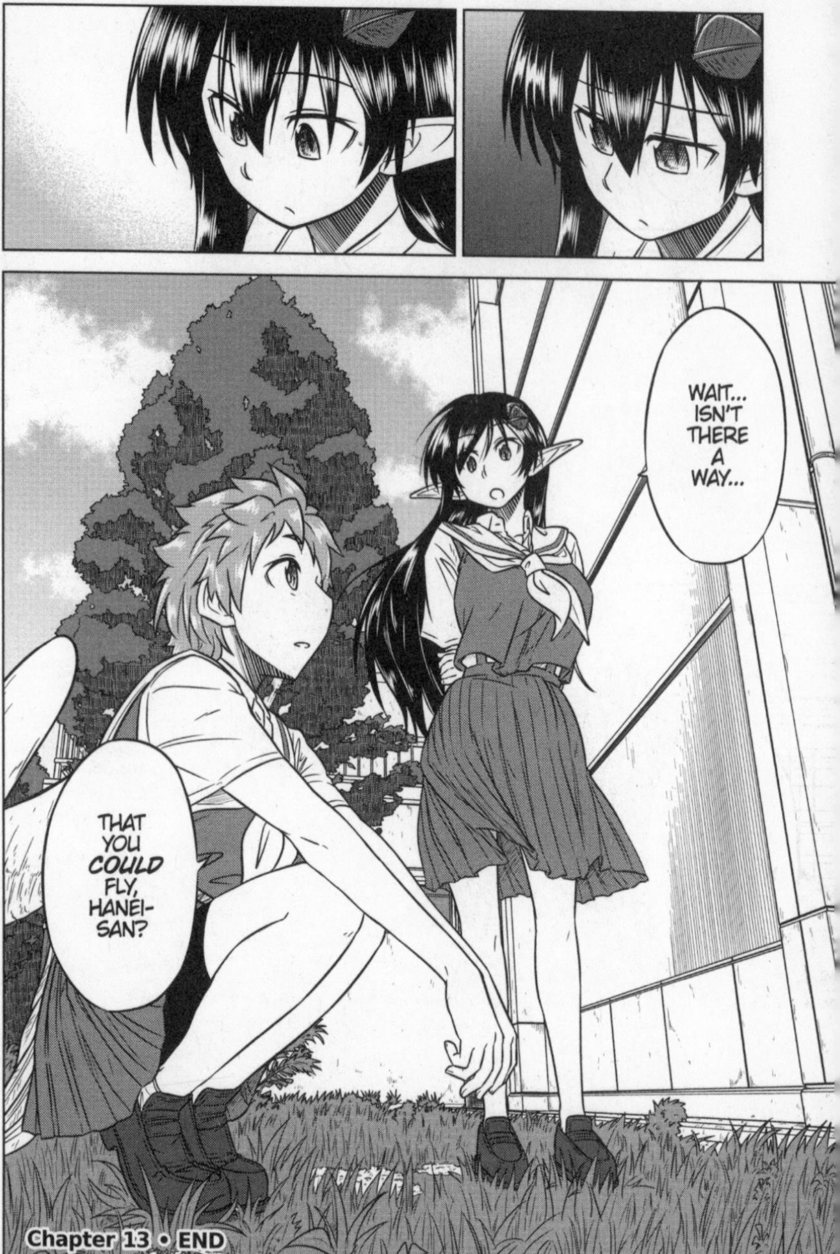
WAIT... ISN'T THERE A WAY...
THAT YOU COULD FLY, HANEI-SAN?
Chapter 13 • END

Chapter 14: Hanei-san Flies

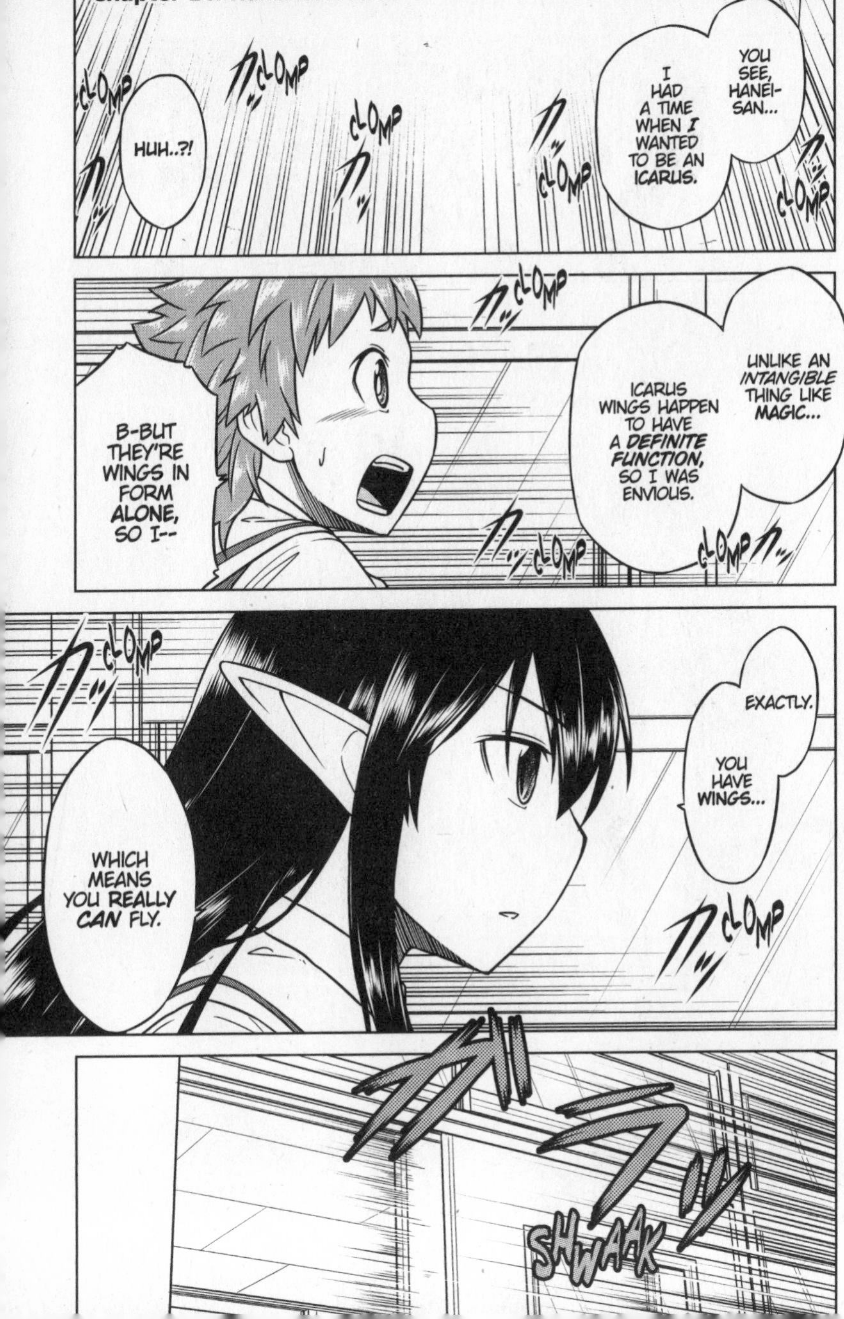
YOU SEE, HANEI-SAN...
I HAD A TIME WHEN *I* WANTED TO BE AN ICARUS.
CLOMP
CLOMP
CLOMP
CLOMP
CLOMP
HUH..?!
UNLIKE AN *INTANGIBLE* THING LIKE MAGIC...
ICARUS WINGS HAPPEN TO HAVE A *DEFINITE FUNCTION*, SO I WAS ENVIOUS.
CLOMP
CLOMP
CLOMP
B-BUT THEY'RE WINGS IN FORM ALONE, SO I--
EXACTLY.
YOU HAVE WINGS...
CLOMP
CLOMP
WHICH MEANS YOU REALLY *CAN* FLY.
SHWAAK

Chapter 14: Hanei-san Flies

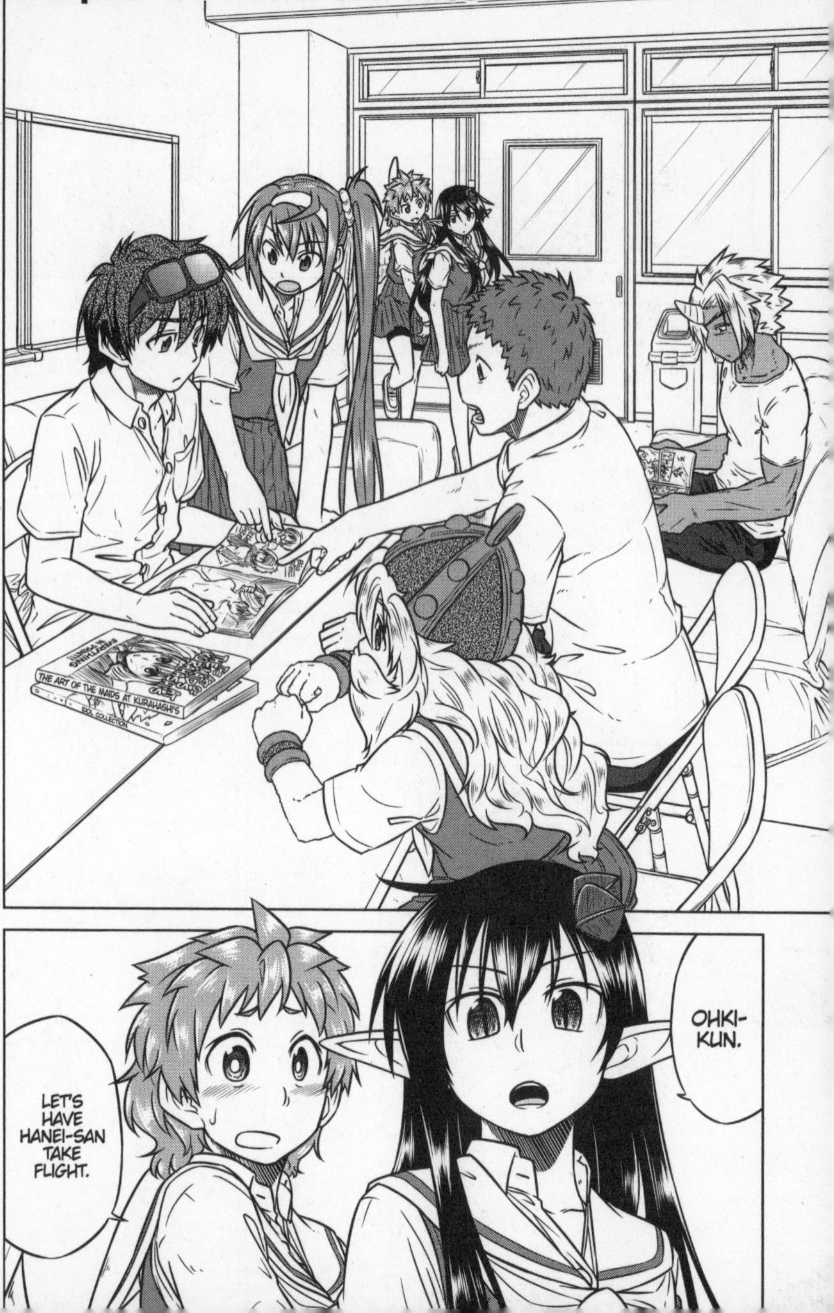
THE ART OF THE MAIDS AT KURAHASHI'S
IDOL COLLECTION
OHKI-KUN.
LET'S HAVE HANEI-SAN TAKE FLIGHT.

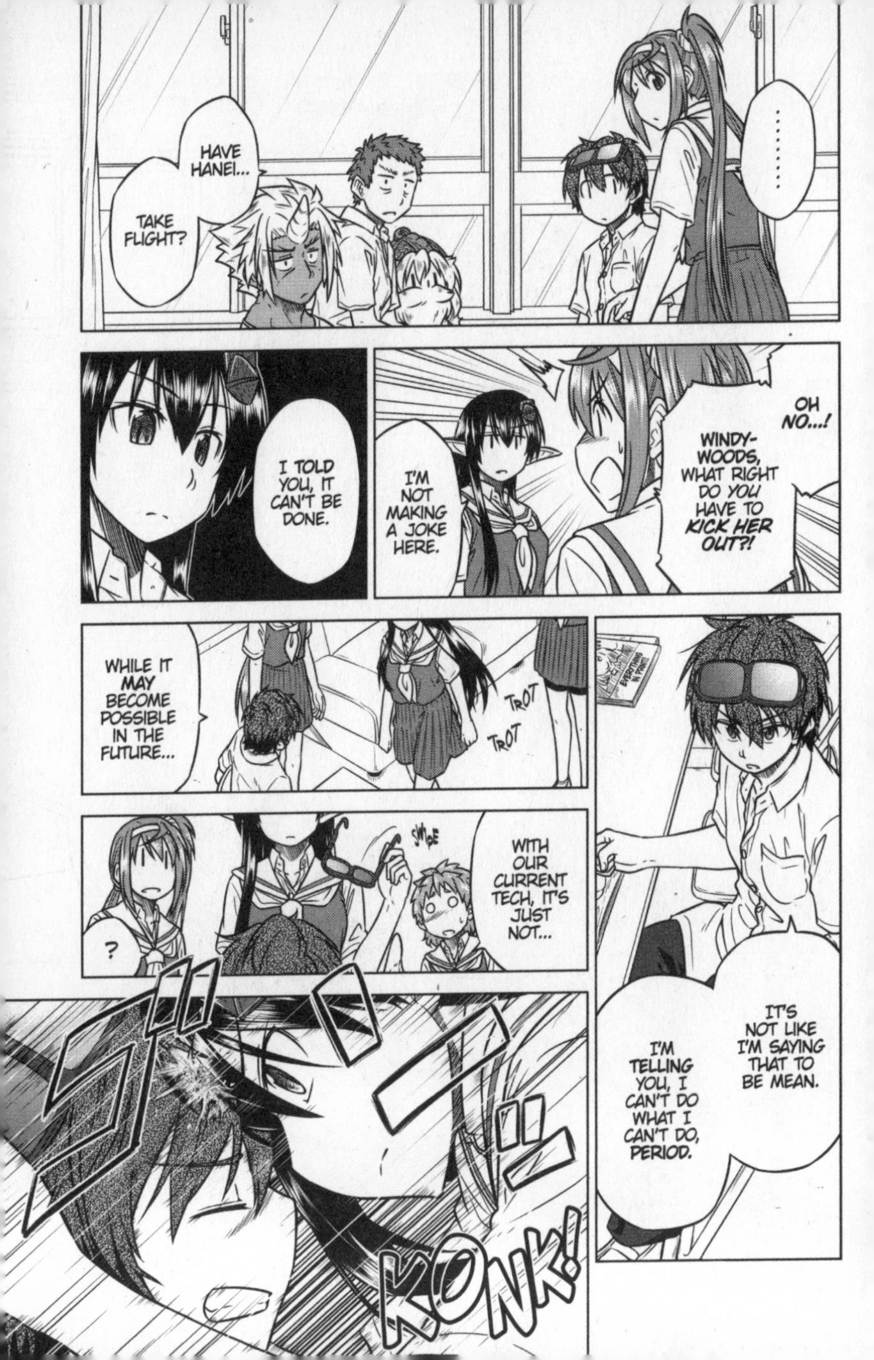
......
HAVE HANEI...
TAKE FLIGHT?
OH NO...!
WINDY-WOODS, WHAT RIGHT DO YOU HAVE TO KICK HER OUT?!
I'M NOT MAKING A JOKE HERE.
I TOLD YOU, IT CAN'T BE DONE.
EVERYTHING IN PRINT!
IT'S NOT LIKE I'M SAYING THAT TO BE MEAN.
I'M TELLING YOU, I CAN'T DO WHAT I CAN'T DO, PERIOD.
WHILE IT MAY BECOME POSSIBLE IN THE FUTURE...
TROT
TROT
SWIPE
WITH OUR CURRENT TECH, IT'S JUST NOT...
?
KONK!

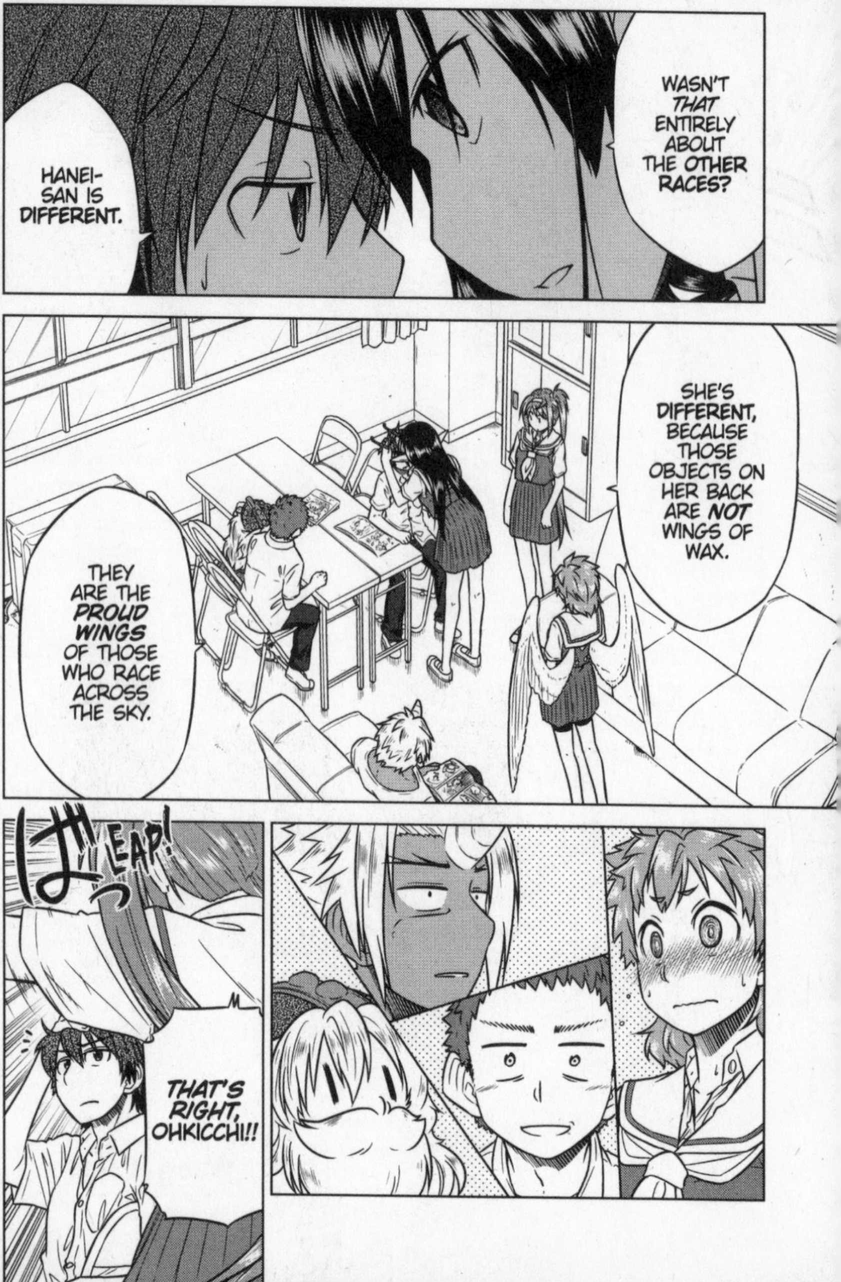
WASN'T THAT ENTIRELY ABOUT THE OTHER RACES?
HANEI-SAN IS DIFFERENT.
SHE'S DIFFERENT, BECAUSE THOSE OBJECTS ON HER BACK ARE NOT WINGS OF WAX.
THEY ARE THE PROUD WINGS OF THOSE WHO RACE ACROSS THE SKY.
ばっ LEAP!
THAT'S RIGHT, OHKICCHI!!

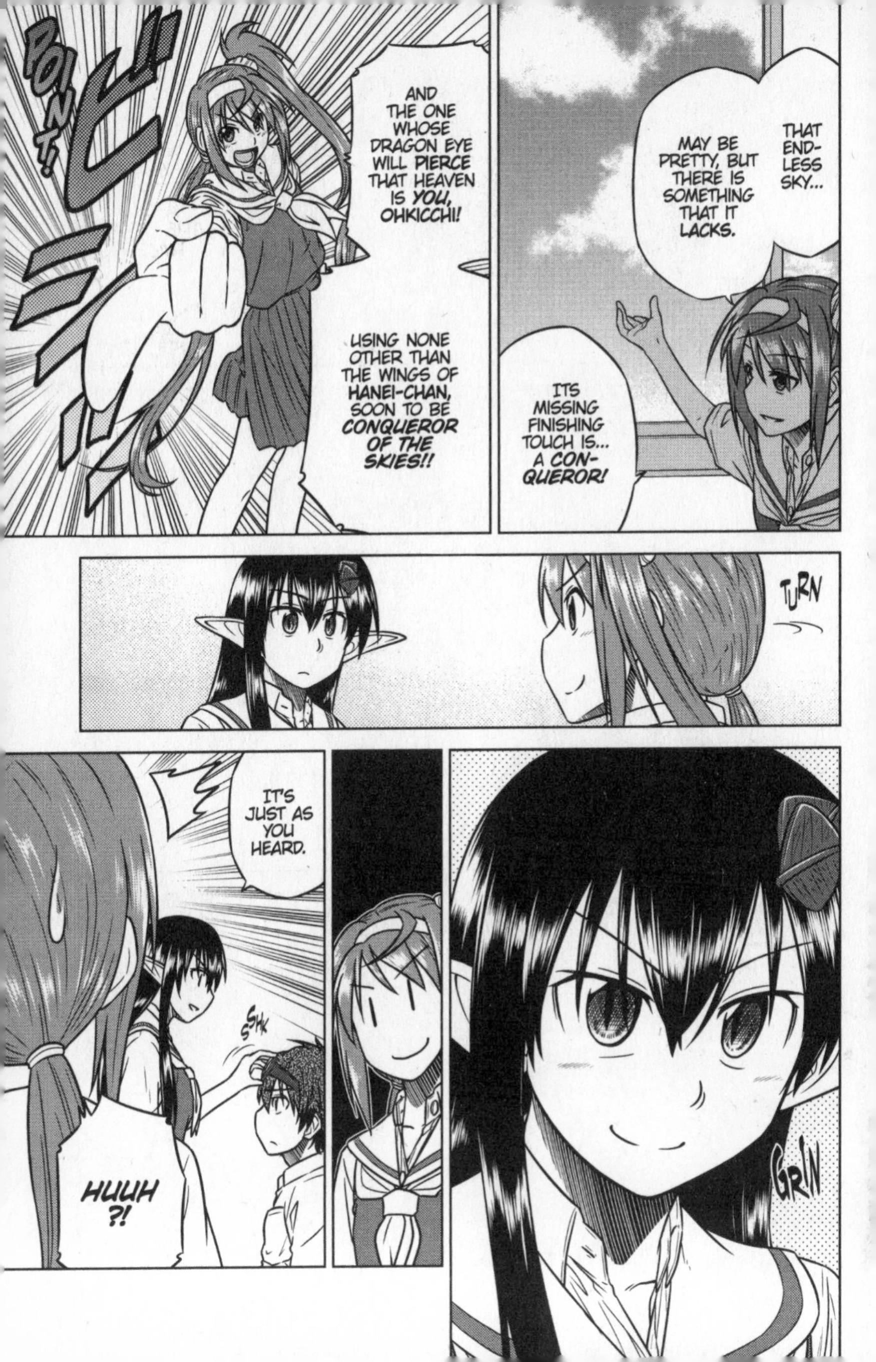
THAT END-LESS SKY...
MAY BE PRETTY, BUT THERE IS SOMETHING THAT IT LACKS.
ITS MISSING FINISHING TOUCH IS... A CON-QUEROR!
AND THE ONE WHOSE DRAGON EYE WILL PIERCE THAT HEAVEN IS *YOU*, OHKICCHI!
POINT!
USING NONE OTHER THAN THE WINGS OF HANEI-CHAN, SOON TO BE ***CONQUEROR OF THE SKIES!!***
TURN
GRIN
IT'S JUST AS YOU HEARD.
SSHK
HUUH ?!

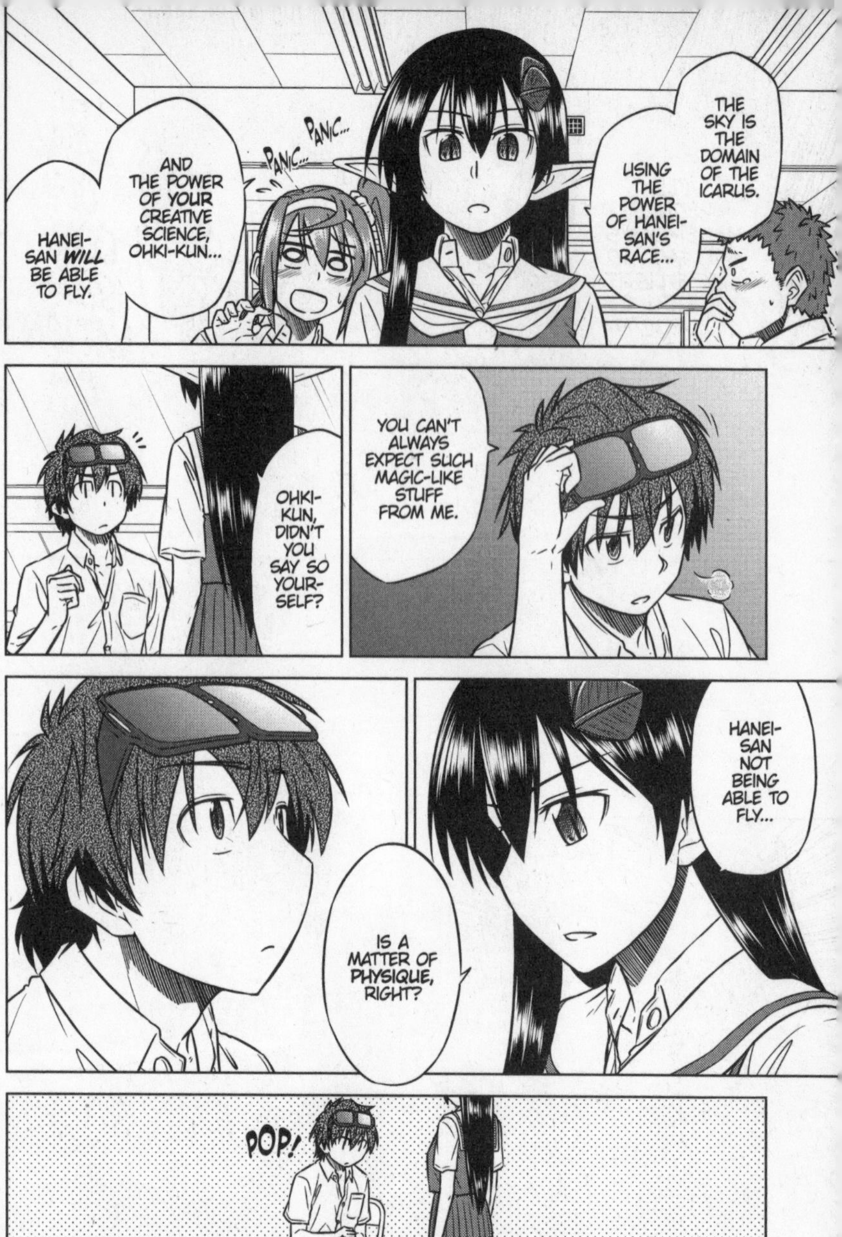
THE SKY IS THE DOMAIN OF THE ICARUS.
USING THE POWER OF HANEI-SAN'S RACE...
PANIC... PANIC...
AND THE POWER OF YOUR CREATIVE SCIENCE, OHKI-KUN...
HANEI-SAN WILL BE ABLE TO FLY.
YOU CAN'T ALWAYS EXPECT SUCH MAGIC-LIKE STUFF FROM ME.
OHKI-KUN, DIDN'T YOU SAY SO YOUR-SELF?
HANEI-SAN NOT BEING ABLE TO FLY...
IS A MATTER OF PHYSIQUE, RIGHT?
POP!

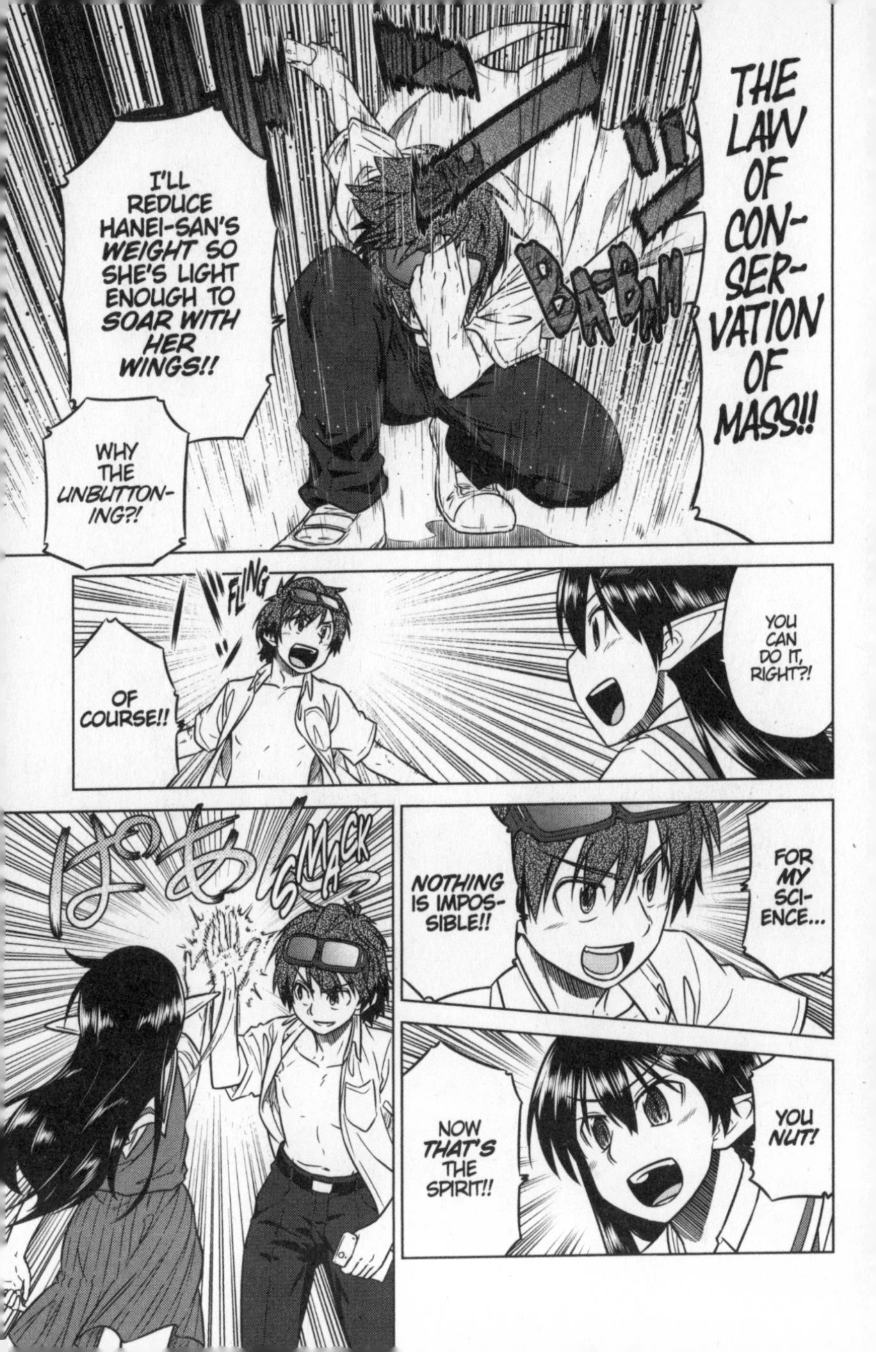
THE LAW OF CON-SER-VATION OF MASS!!
BA-BAM
I'LL REDUCE HANEI-SAN'S WEIGHT SO SHE'S LIGHT ENOUGH TO SOAR WITH HER WINGS!!
WHY THE UNBUTTON-ING?!
YOU CAN DO IT, RIGHT?!
FLING
OF COURSE!!
FOR MY SCI-ENCE...
NOTHING IS IMPOS-SIBLE!!
YOU NUT!
NOW THAT'S THE SPIRIT!!
SMACK

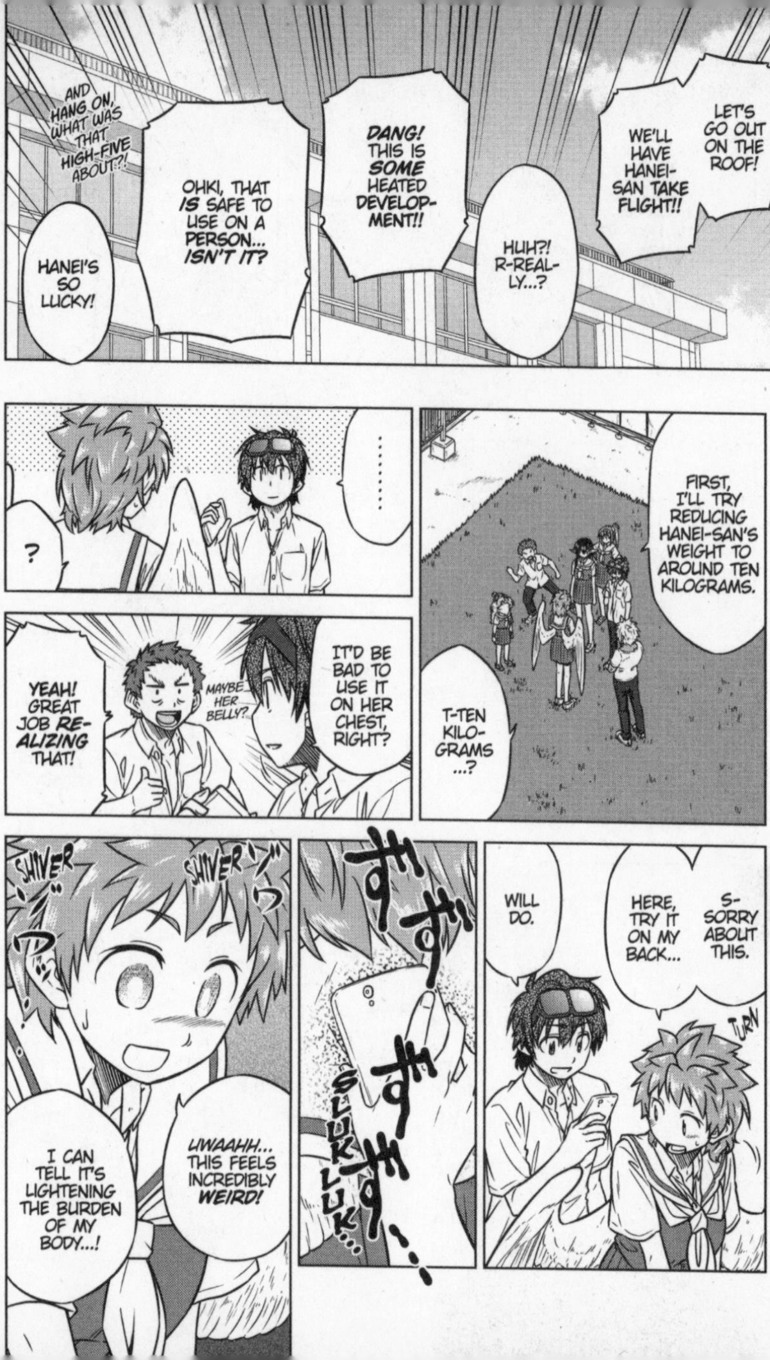
LET'S GO OUT ON THE ROOF!
WE'LL HAVE HANEI-SAN TAKE FLIGHT!!
HUH?! R-REALLY...?
DANG! THIS IS SOME HEATED DEVELOPMENT!!
OHKI, THAT IS SAFE TO USE ON A PERSON... ISN'T IT?
AND HANG ON, WHAT WAS THAT HIGH-FIVE ABOUT?!
HANEI'S SO LUCKY!
FIRST, I'LL TRY REDUCING HANEI-SAN'S WEIGHT TO AROUND TEN KILOGRAMS.
T-TEN KILOGRAMS ...?
......
?
IT'D BE BAD TO USE IT ON HER CHEST, RIGHT?
MAYBE HER BELLY?
YEAH! GREAT JOB REALIZING THAT!
S-SORRY ABOUT THIS.
HERE, TRY IT ON MY BACK...
WILL DO.
TURN
SLUK LUK...
SHIVER
SHIVER
UWAAHH... THIS FEELS INCREDIBLY WEIRD!
I CAN TELL IT'S LIGHTENING THE BURDEN OF MY BODY...!

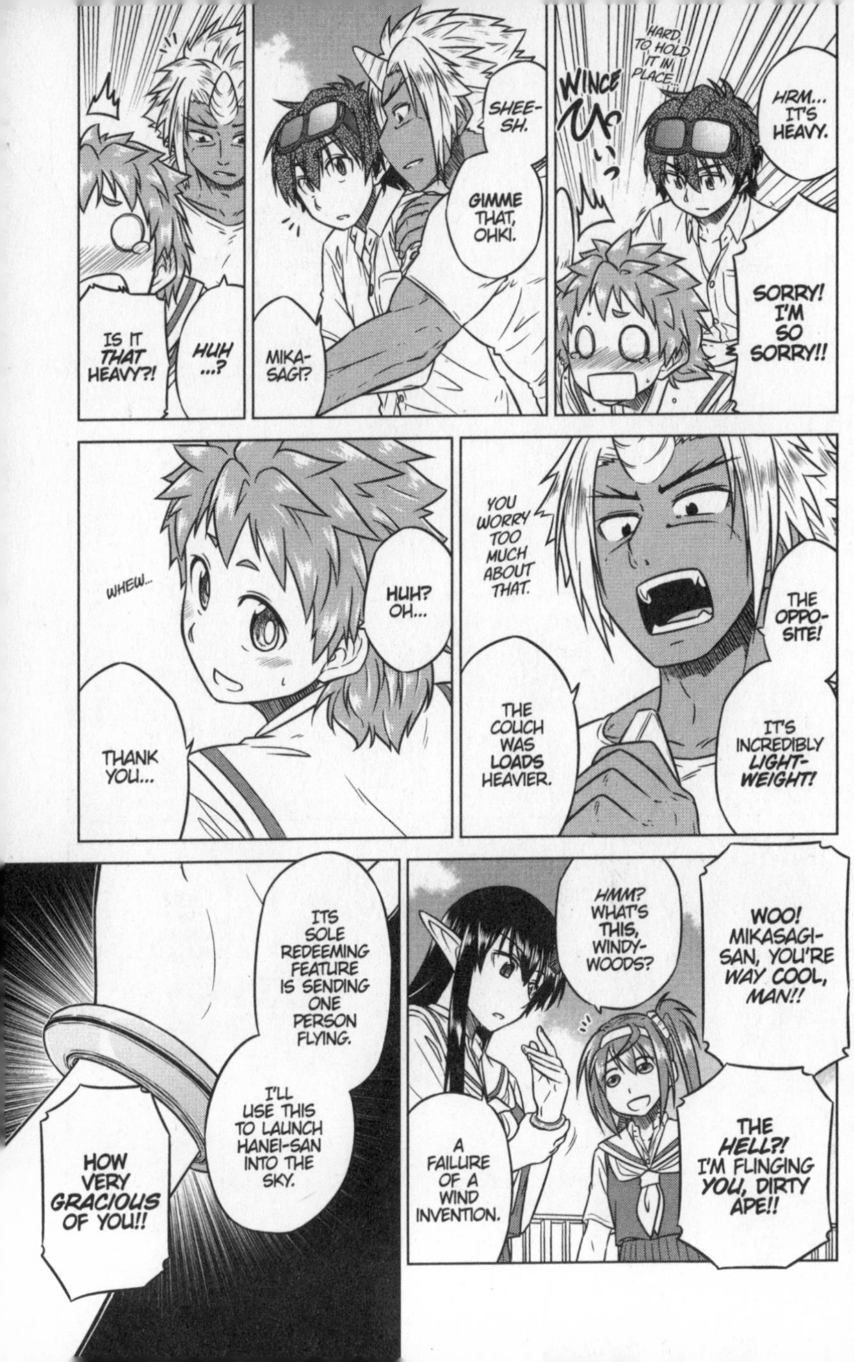
HRM... IT'S HEAVY.
HARD TO HOLD IT IN PLACE...
WINCE
SORRY! I'M SO SORRY!!
SHEE-SH.
GIMME THAT, OHKI.
MIKA-SAGI?
HUH...?
IS IT THAT HEAVY?!
YOU WORRY TOO MUCH ABOUT THAT.
THE OPPO-SITE!
IT'S INCREDIBLY LIGHT-WEIGHT!
THE COUCH WAS LOADS HEAVIER.
HUH? OH...
WHEW...
THANK YOU...
WOO! MIKASAGI-SAN, YOU'RE WAY COOL, MAN!!
HMM? WHAT'S THIS, WINDY-WOODS?
THE HELL?! I'M FLINGING YOU, DIRTY APE!!
A FAILURE OF A WIND INVENTION.
ITS SOLE REDEEMING FEATURE IS SENDING ONE PERSON FLYING.
I'LL USE THIS TO LAUNCH HANEI-SAN INTO THE SKY.
HOW VERY GRACIOUS OF YOU!!

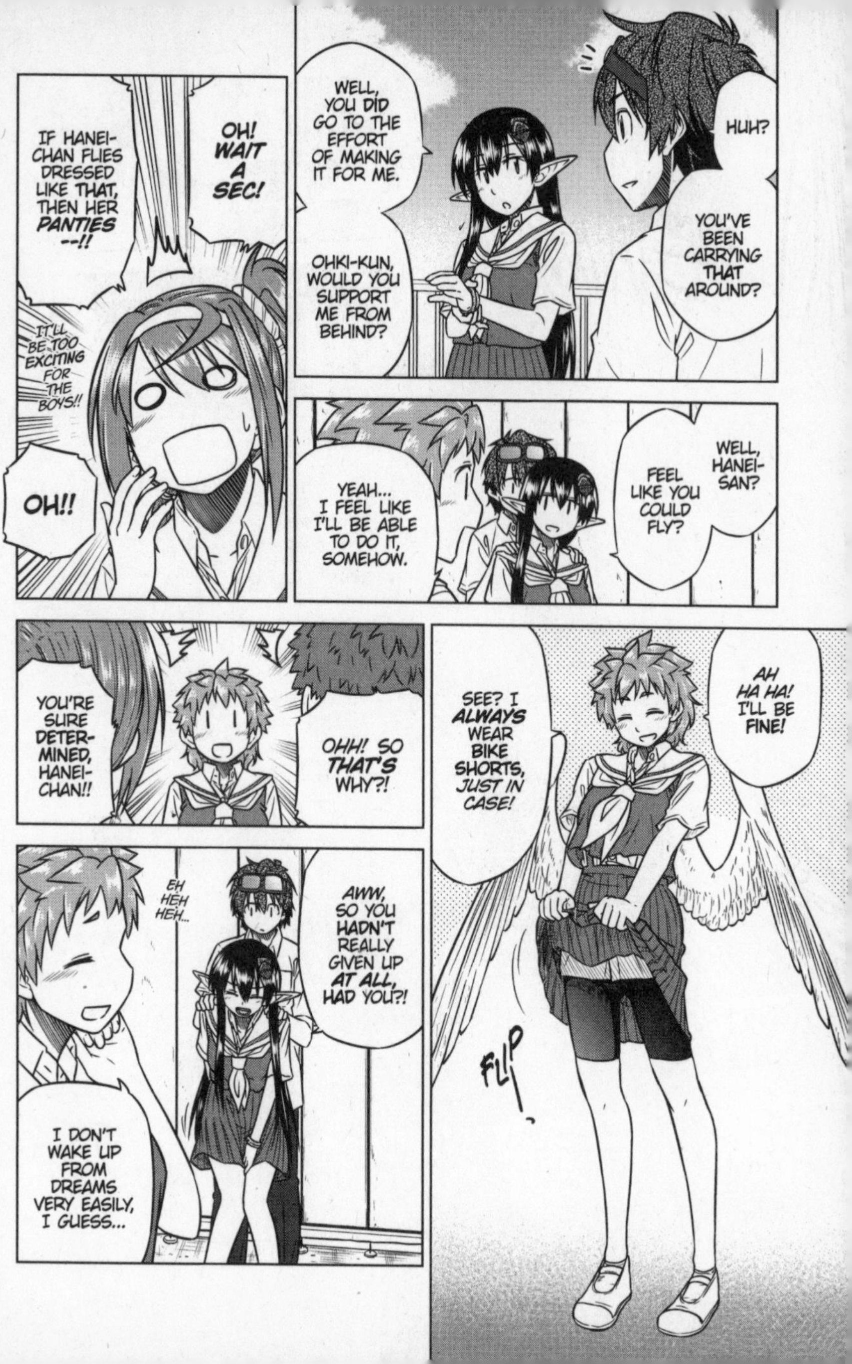
HUH?
YOU'VE BEEN CARRYING THAT AROUND?
WELL, YOU DID GO TO THE EFFORT OF MAKING IT FOR ME.
OHKI-KUN, WOULD YOU SUPPORT ME FROM BEHIND?
WELL, HANEI-SAN?
FEEL LIKE YOU COULD FLY?
YEAH... I FEEL LIKE I'LL BE ABLE TO DO IT, SOMEHOW.
OH! WAIT A SEC!
IF HANEI-CHAN FLIES DRESSED LIKE THAT, THEN HER PANTIES--!!
IT'LL BE TOO EXCITING FOR THE BOYS!!
OH!!
AH HA HA! I'LL BE FINE!
SEE? I ALWAYS WEAR BIKE SHORTS, JUST IN CASE!
FLIP
OHH! SO THAT'S WHY?!
YOU'RE SURE DETERMINED, HANEI-CHAN!!
AWW, SO YOU HADN'T REALLY GIVEN UP AT ALL, HAD YOU?!
EH HEH HEH...
I DON'T WAKE UP FROM DREAMS VERY EASILY, I GUESS...

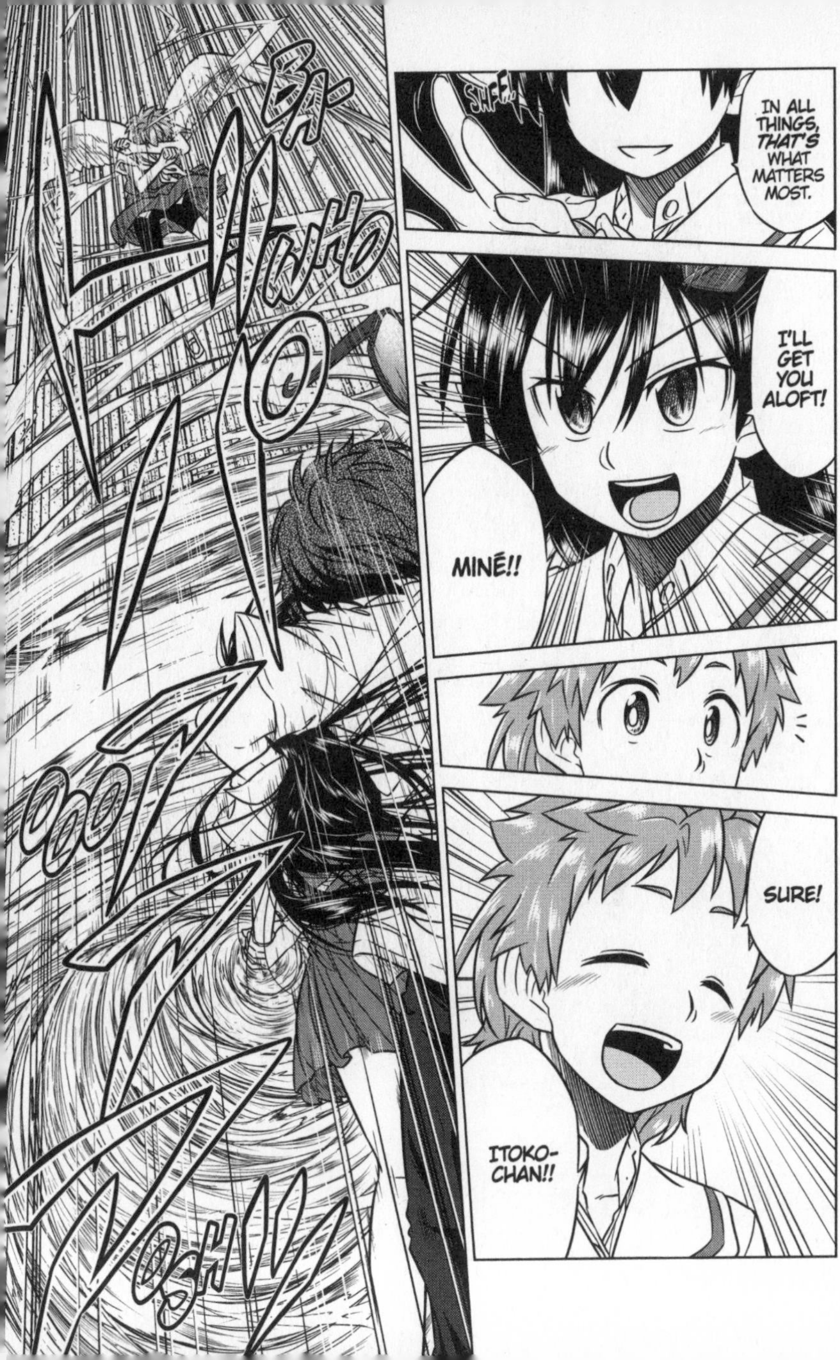
SHFF...
IN ALL THINGS, *THAT'S* WHAT MATTERS MOST.
I'LL GET YOU ALOFT!
MINÉ!!
SURE!
ITOKO-CHAN!!

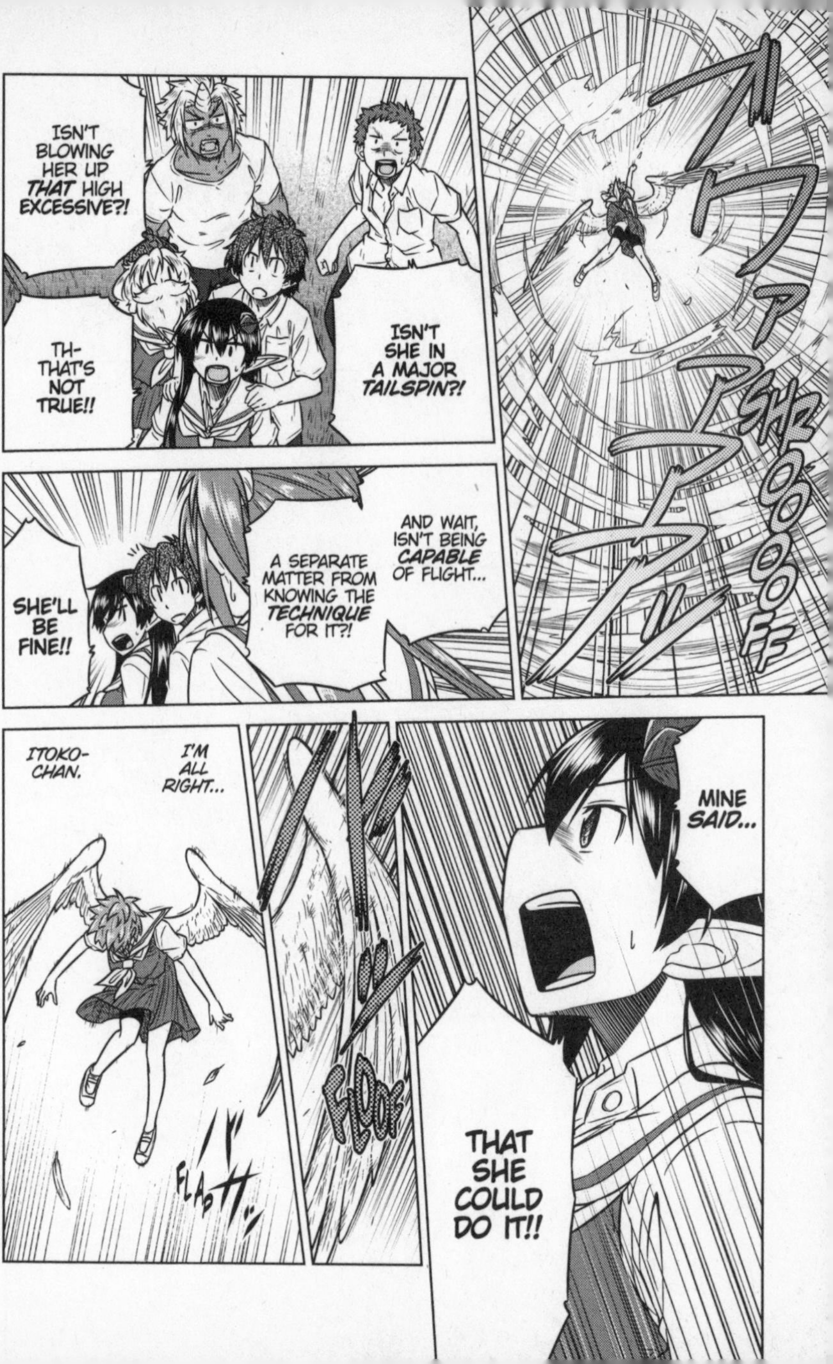
SHPOOOOOFF
ISN'T BLOWING HER UP *THAT* HIGH EXCESSIVE?!
ISN'T SHE IN A MAJOR *TAILSPIN*?!
TH- THAT'S NOT TRUE!!
AND WAIT, ISN'T BEING *CAPABLE* OF FLIGHT...
A SEPARATE MATTER FROM KNOWING THE *TECHNIQUE* FOR IT?!
SHE'LL BE FINE!!
MINE SAID...
THAT SHE COULD DO IT!!
FLOOF
ITOKO-CHAN.
I'M ALL RIGHT...
FLAP

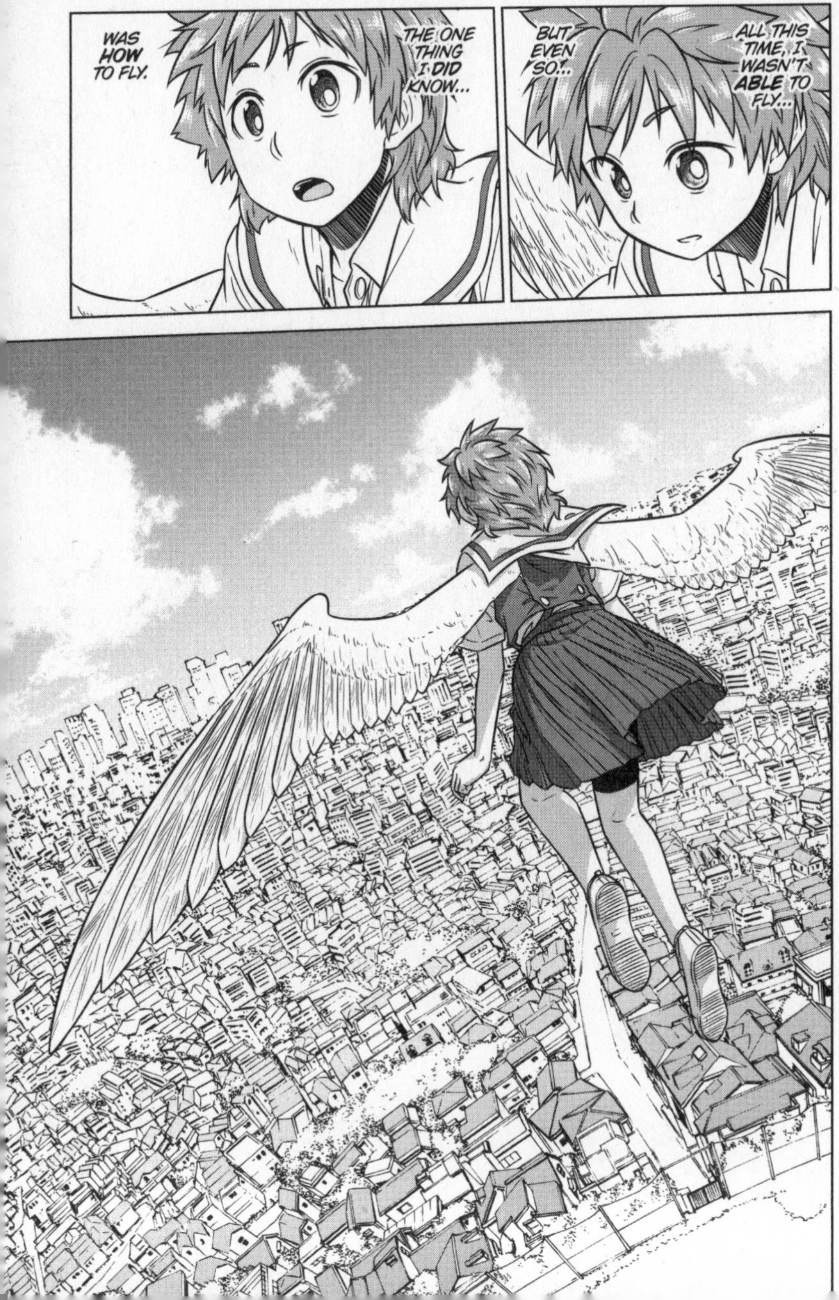
ALL THIS TIME, I WASN'T **ABLE** TO FLY...
BUT EVEN SO...
THE ONE THING I **DID** KNOW...
WAS **HOW** TO FLY.

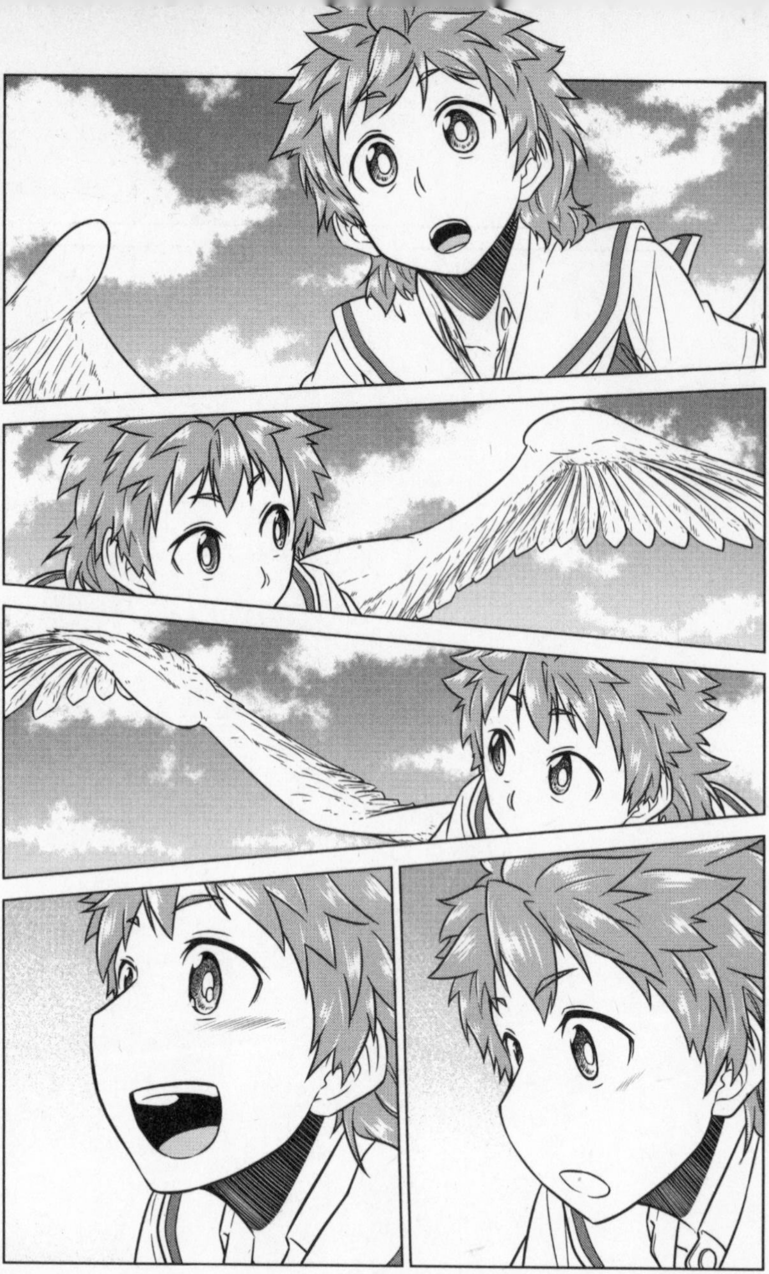

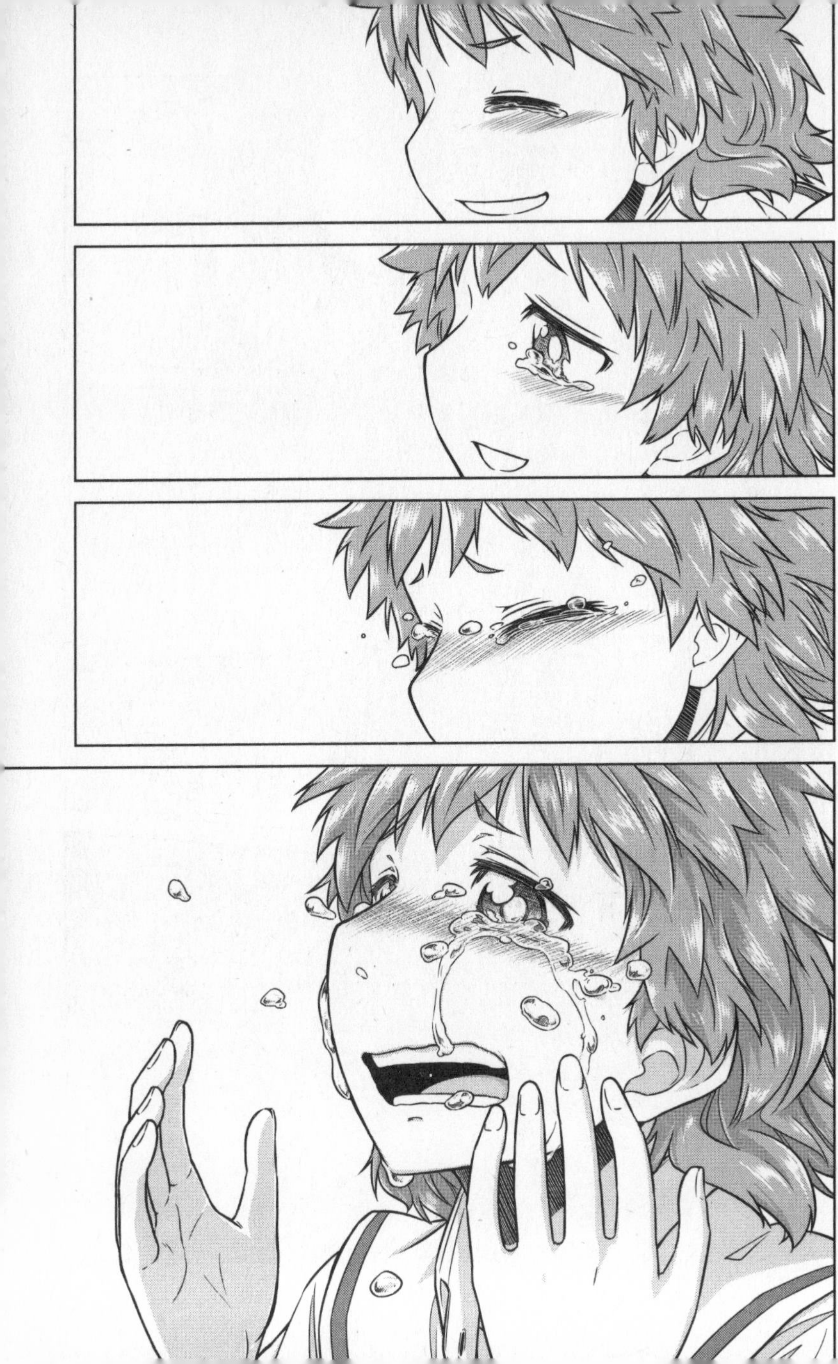

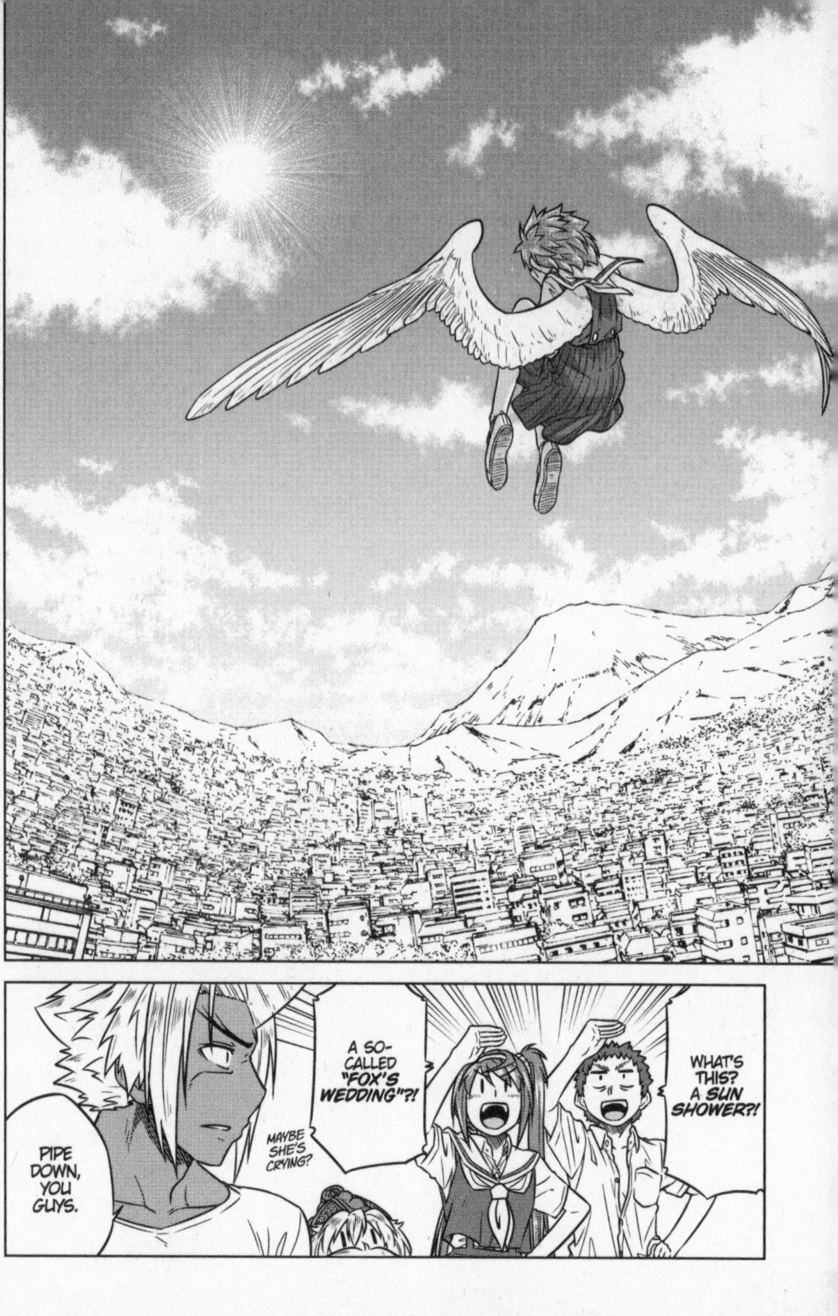
WHAT'S THIS? A SUN SHOWER?!
A SO-CALLED "FOX'S WEDDING"?!
MAYBE SHE'S CRYING?
PIPE DOWN, YOU GUYS.

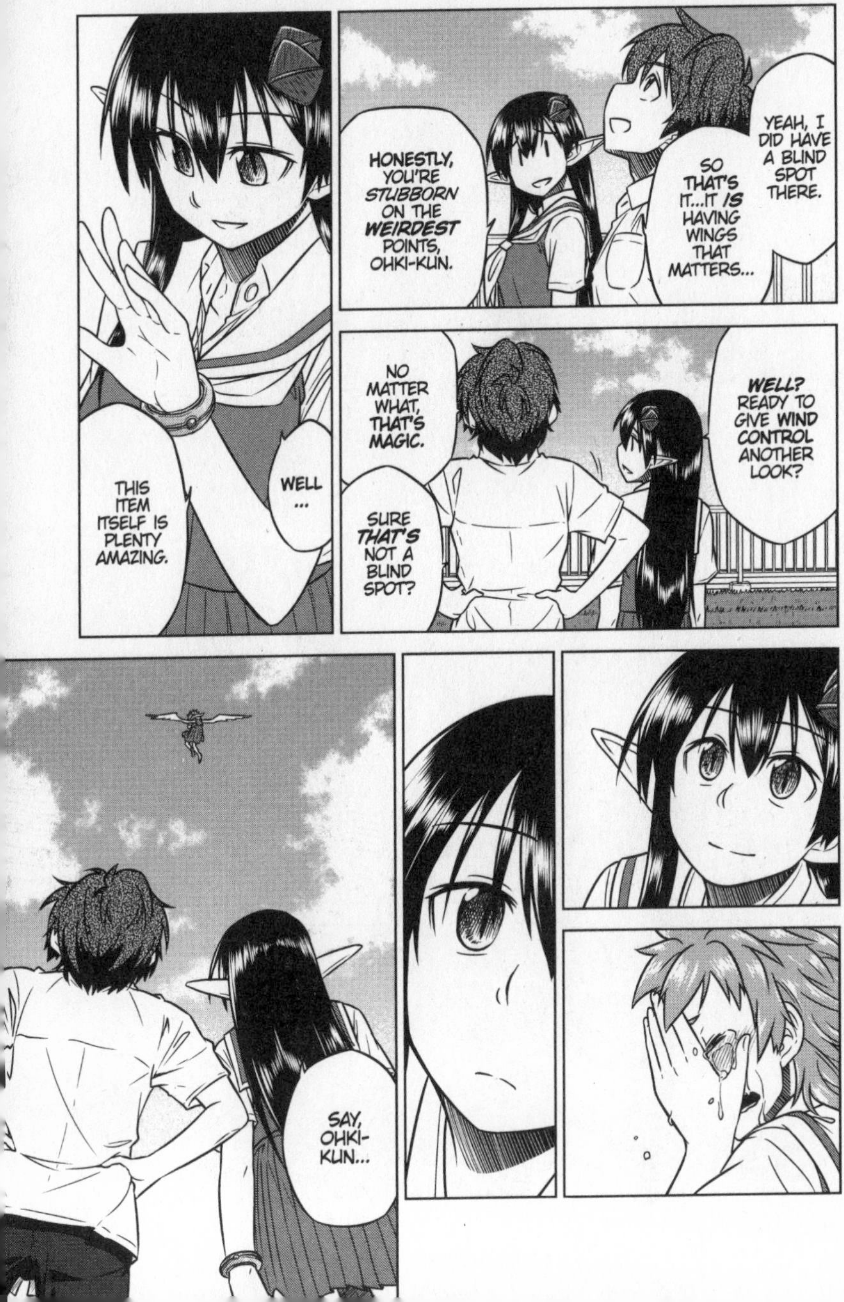
YEAH, I DID HAVE A BLIND SPOT THERE.
SO THAT'S IT...IT IS HAVING WINGS THAT MATTERS...
HONESTLY, YOU'RE STUBBORN ON THE WEIRDEST POINTS, OHKI-KUN.
WELL? READY TO GIVE WIND CONTROL ANOTHER LOOK?
NO MATTER WHAT, THAT'S MAGIC.
SURE THAT'S NOT A BLIND SPOT?
WELL...
THIS ITEM ITSELF IS PLENTY AMAZING.
SAY, OHKI-KUN...

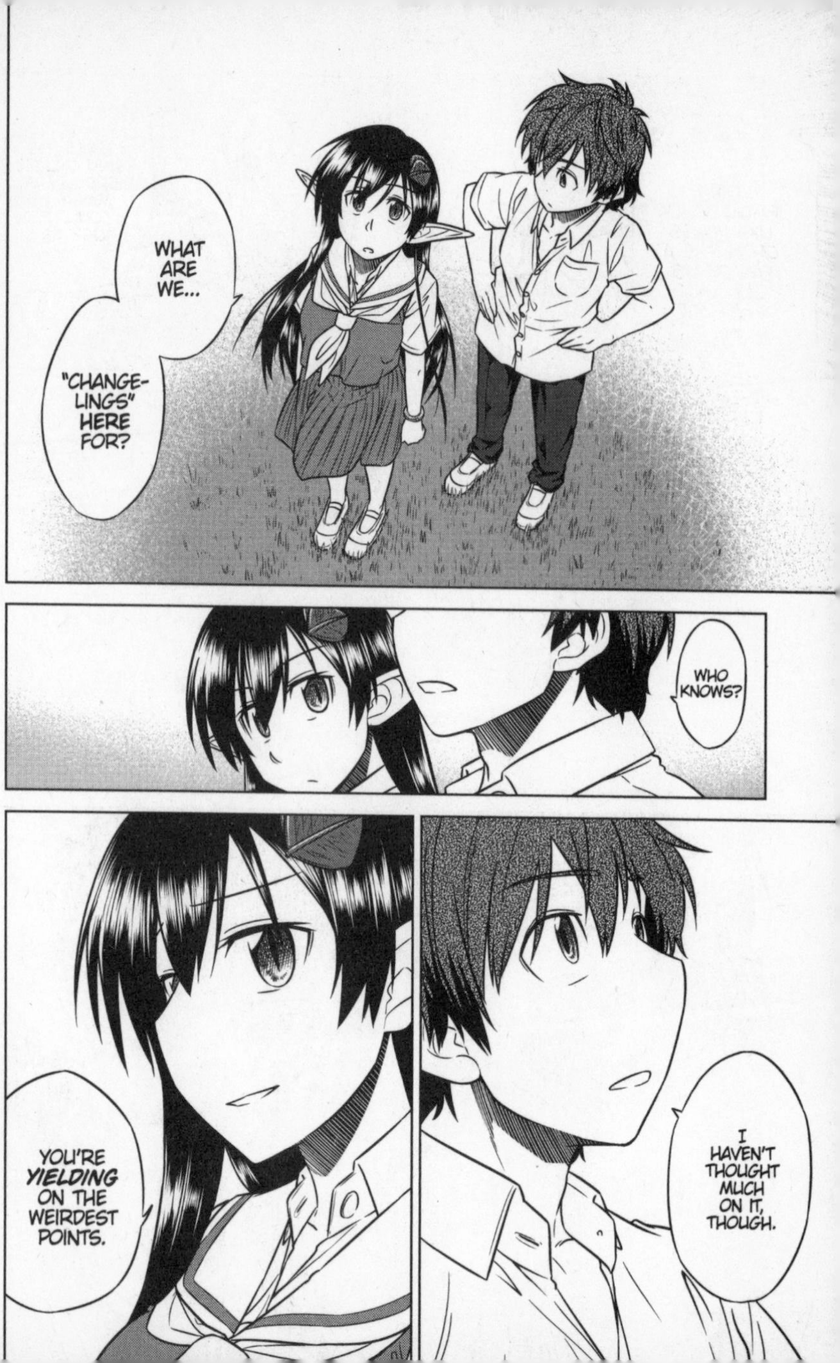
WHAT ARE WE...
"CHANGE-LINGS" HERE FOR?
WHO KNOWS?
I HAVEN'T THOUGHT MUCH ON IT, THOUGH.
YOU'RE *YIELDING* ON THE WEIRDEST POINTS.

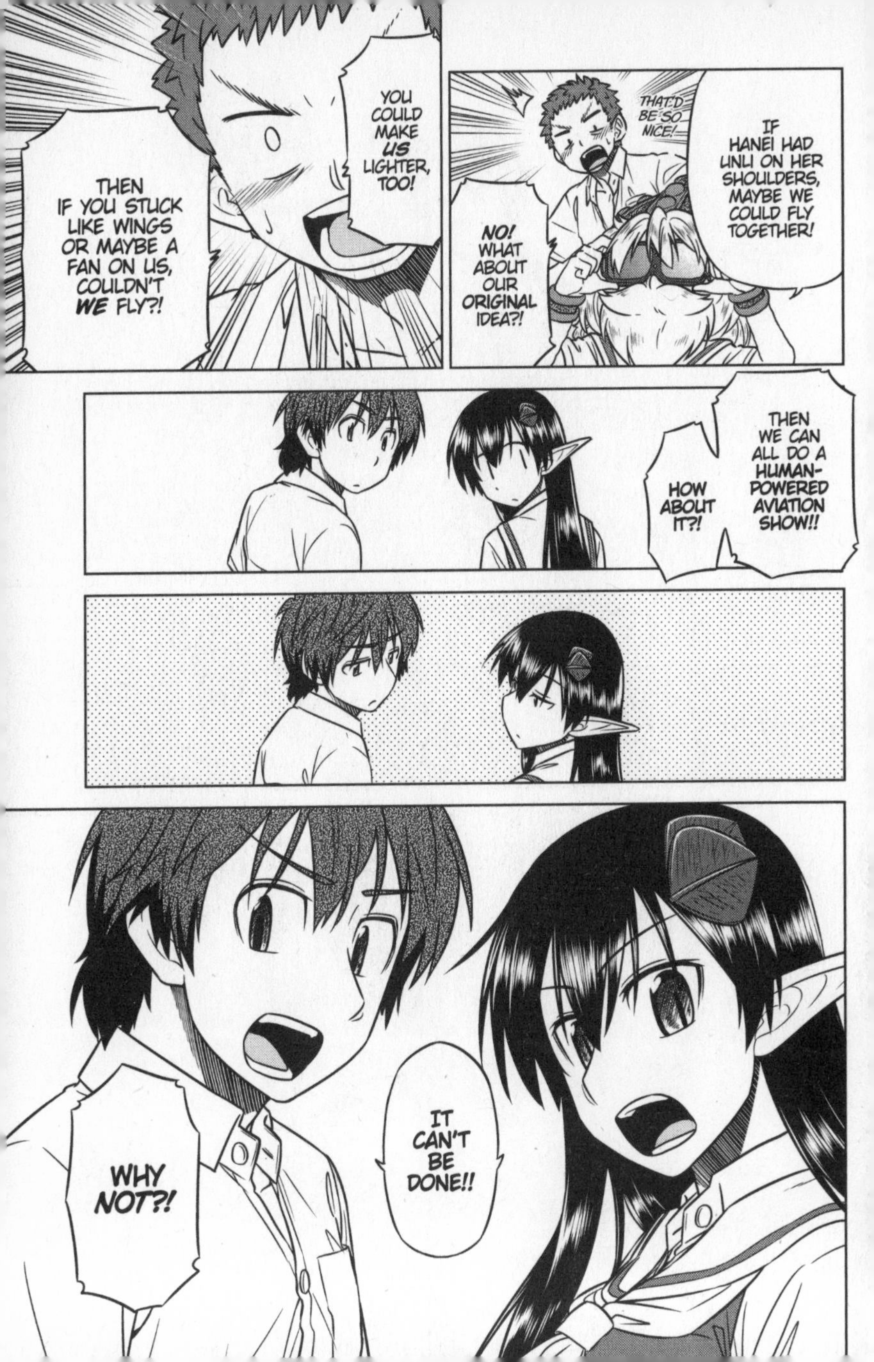
IF HANEI HAD UNLI ON HER SHOULDERS, MAYBE WE COULD FLY TOGETHER!
THAT'D BE SO NICE!
NO! WHAT ABOUT OUR ORIGINAL IDEA?!
YOU COULD MAKE US LIGHTER, TOO!
THEN IF YOU STUCK LIKE WINGS OR MAYBE A FAN ON US, COULDN'T WE FLY?!
THEN WE CAN ALL DO A HUMAN-POWERED AVIATION SHOW!!
HOW ABOUT IT?!
IT CAN'T BE DONE!!
WHY NOT?!

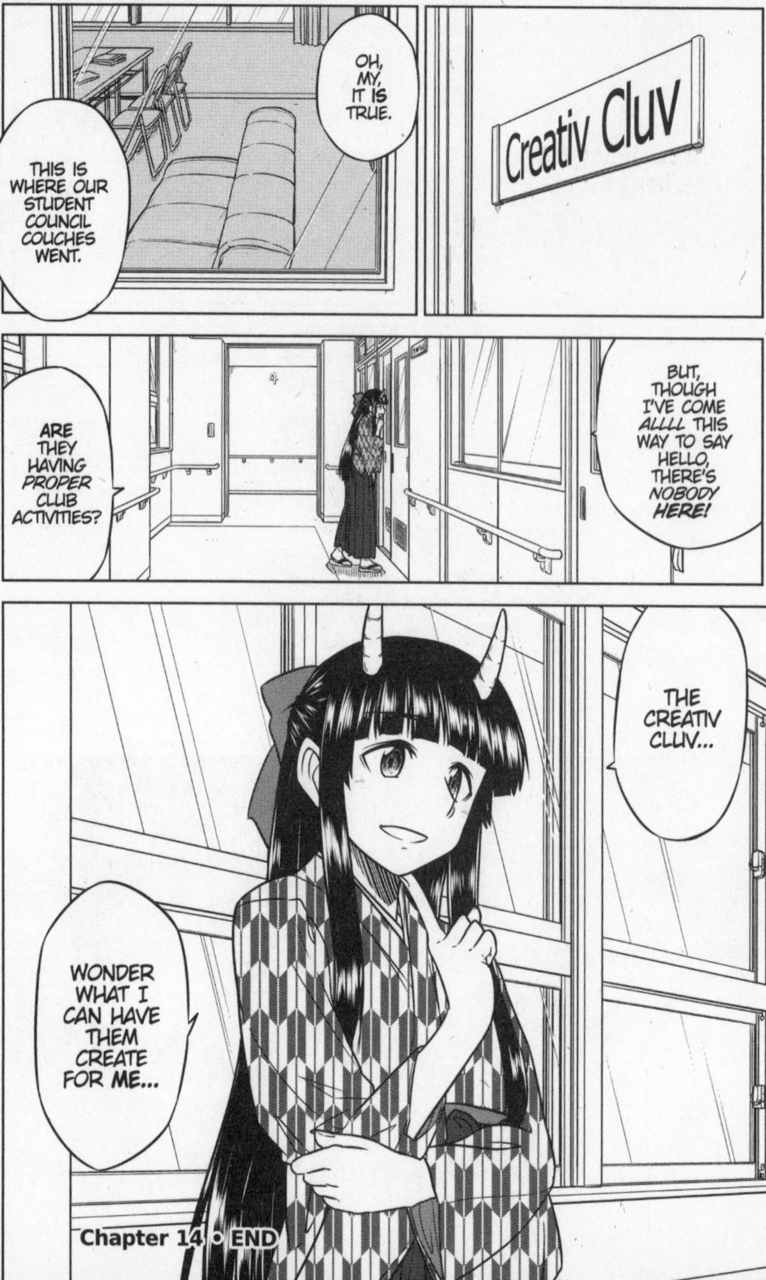
Creativ Cluv
OH, MY, IT IS TRUE.
THIS IS WHERE OUR STUDENT COUNCIL COUCHES WENT.
BUT, THOUGH I'VE COME *ALLLL* THIS WAY TO SAY HELLO, THERE'S *NOBODY HERE!*
ARE THEY HAVING *PROPER* CLUB ACTIVITIES?
THE CREATIV CLUV...
WONDER WHAT I CAN HAVE THEM CREATE FOR ME...

Chapter 14 • END

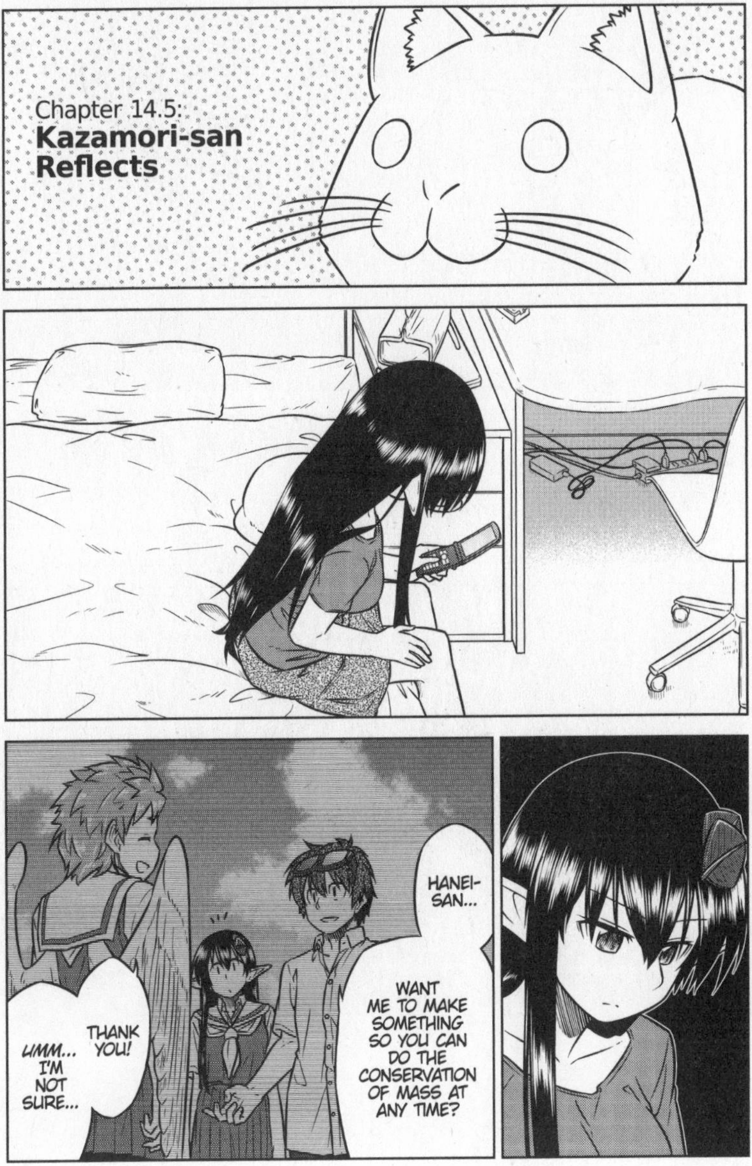
Chapter 14.5:
Kazamori-san Reflects
HANEI-SAN...
WANT ME TO MAKE SOMETHING SO YOU CAN DO THE CONSERVATION OF MASS AT ANY TIME?
THANK YOU!
UMM... I'M NOT SURE...

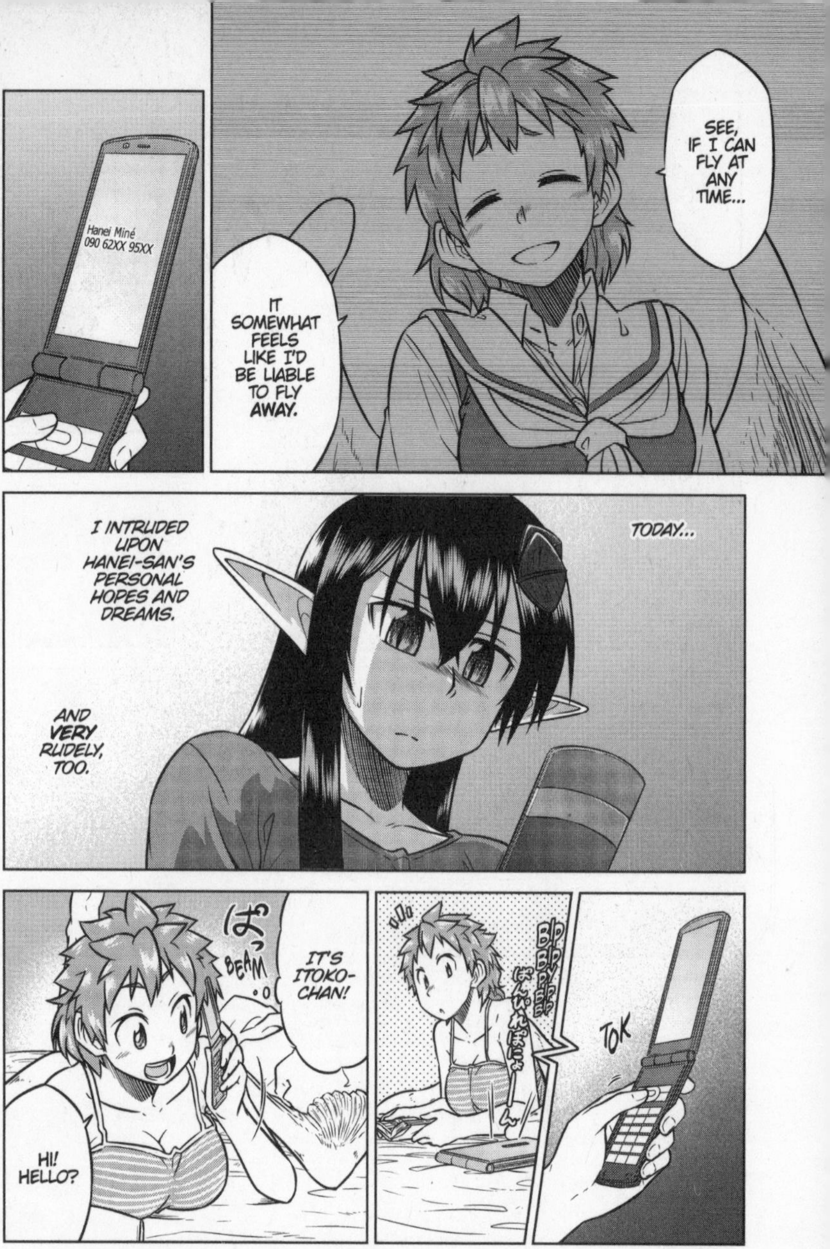
SEE, IF I CAN FLY AT ANY TIME...
IT SOMEWHAT FEELS LIKE I'D BE LIABLE TO FLY AWAY.
Hanei Miné
090 62XX 95XX
TODAY...
I INTRUDED UPON HANEI-SAN'S PERSONAL HOPES AND DREAMS.
AND VERY RUDELY, TOO.
TOK
BIP BIP BIP BIP
ぱっ
BEAM
IT'S ITOKO-CHAN!
HI! HELLO?

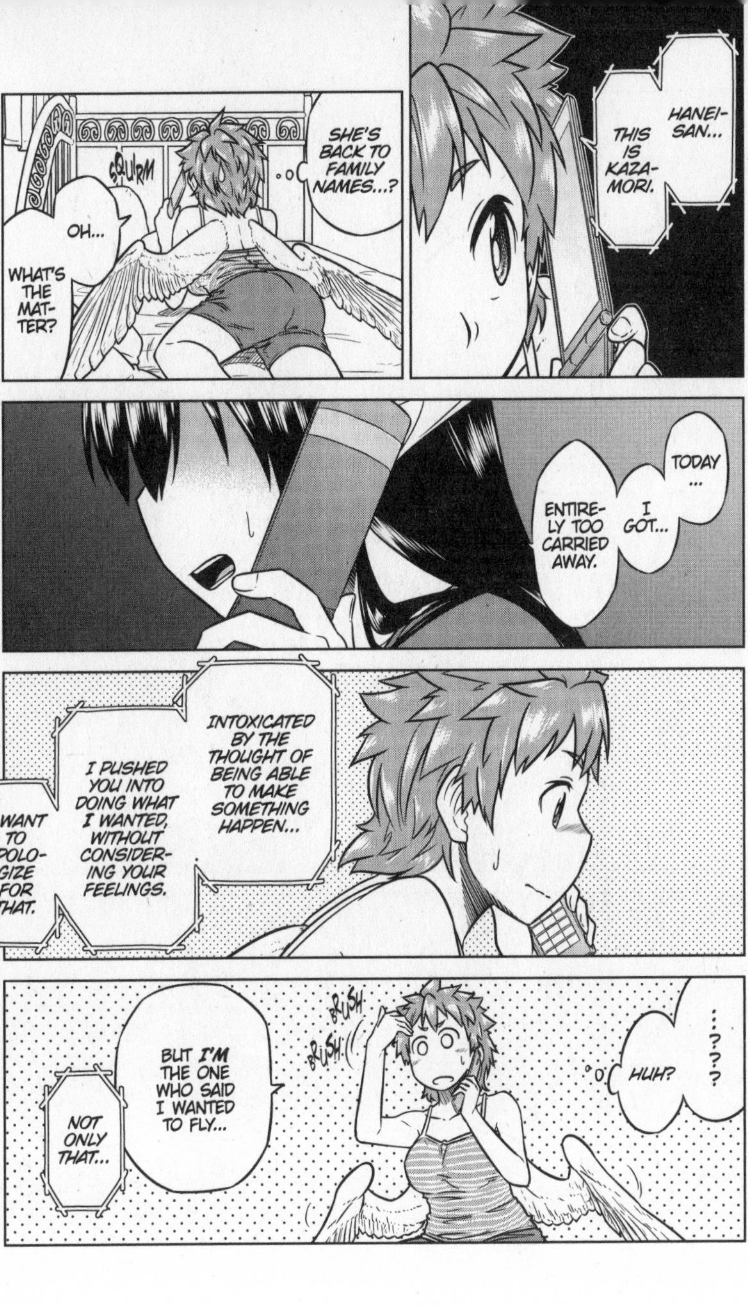
HANEI-SAN... THIS IS KAZAMORI.
SHE'S BACK TO FAMILY NAMES...?
SQUIRM
OH... WHAT'S THE MATTER?
TODAY... I GOT... ENTIRELY TOO CARRIED AWAY.
INTOXICATED BY THE THOUGHT OF BEING ABLE TO MAKE SOMETHING HAPPEN...
I PUSHED YOU INTO DOING WHAT I WANTED, WITHOUT CONSIDERING YOUR FEELINGS.
I WANT TO APOLOGIZE FOR THAT.
...???
HUH?
BRUSH
BRUSH
BUT I'M THE ONE WHO SAID I WANTED TO FLY...
NOT ONLY THAT...

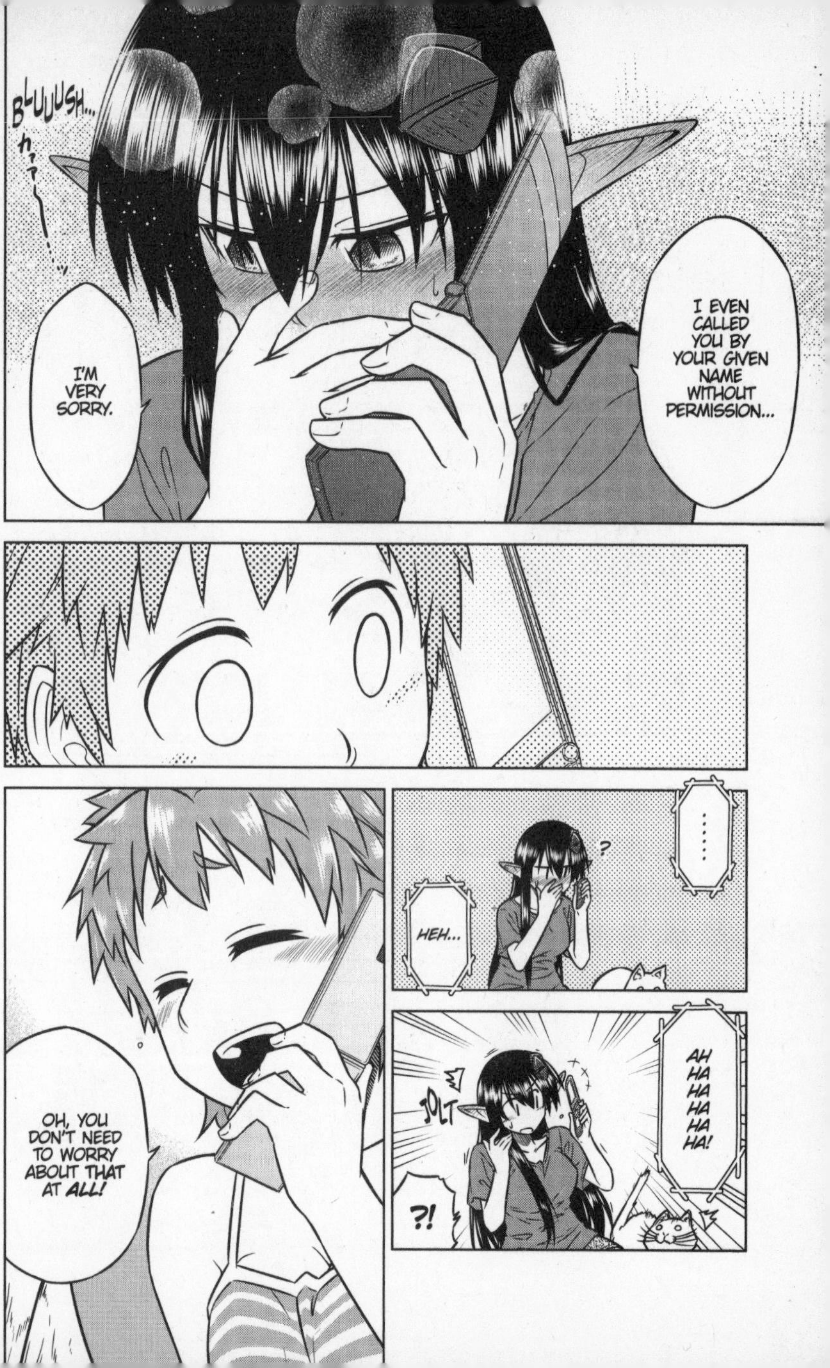
I EVEN CALLED YOU BY YOUR GIVEN NAME WITHOUT PERMISSION...
I'M VERY SORRY.
BLUUUSH...
......
?
HEH...
AH HA HA HA HA HA!
JOLT
?!
OH, YOU DON'T NEED TO WORRY ABOUT THAT AT ALL!

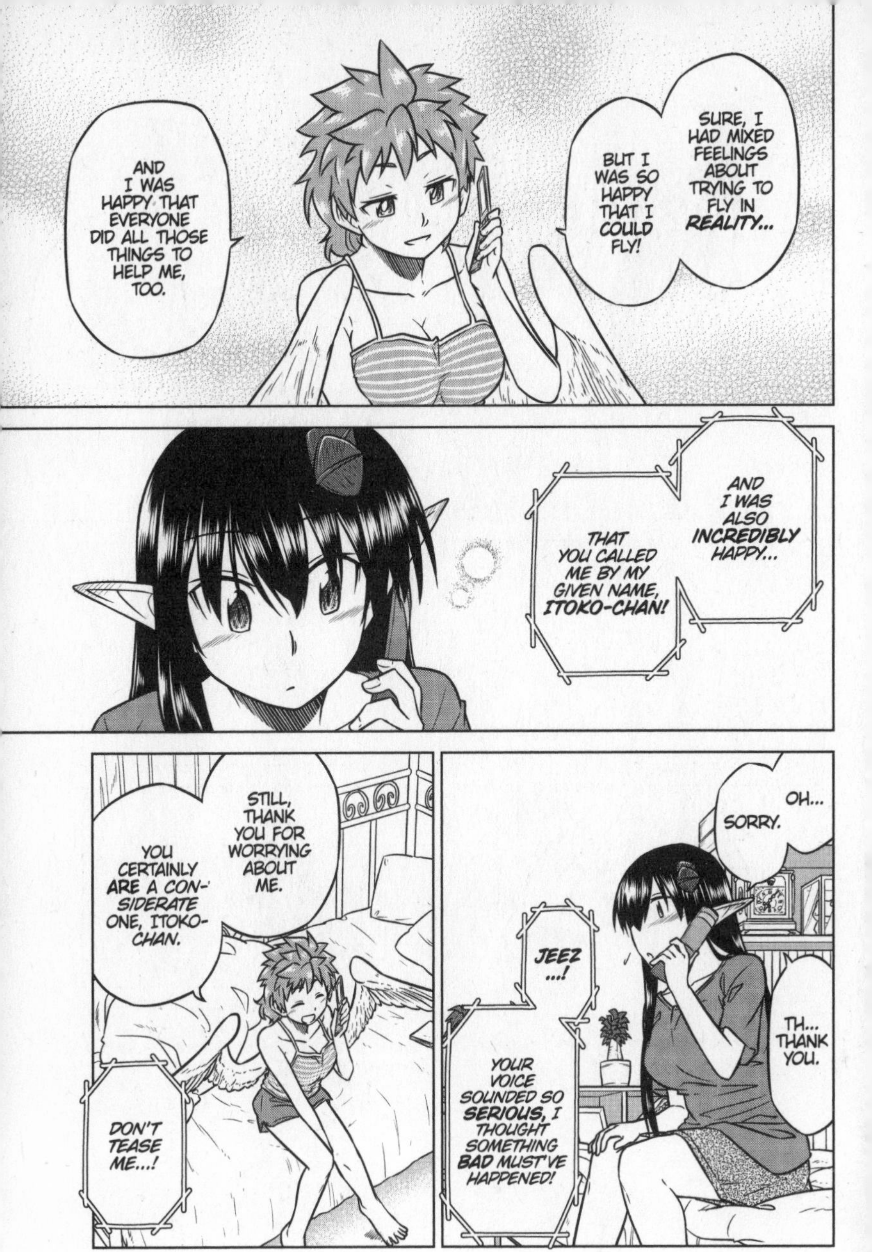
SURE, I HAD MIXED FEELINGS ABOUT TRYING TO FLY IN REALITY...
BUT I WAS SO HAPPY THAT I COULD FLY!
AND I WAS HAPPY THAT EVERYONE DID ALL THOSE THINGS TO HELP ME, TOO.
AND I WAS ALSO INCREDIBLY HAPPY...
THAT YOU CALLED ME BY MY GIVEN NAME, ITOKO-CHAN!
OH... SORRY.
TH... THANK YOU.
JEEZ ...!
YOUR VOICE SOUNDED SO SERIOUS, I THOUGHT SOMETHING BAD MUST'VE HAPPENED!
STILL, THANK YOU FOR WORRYING ABOUT ME.
YOU CERTAINLY ARE A CON-SIDERATE ONE, ITOKO-CHAN.
DON'T TEASE ME...!

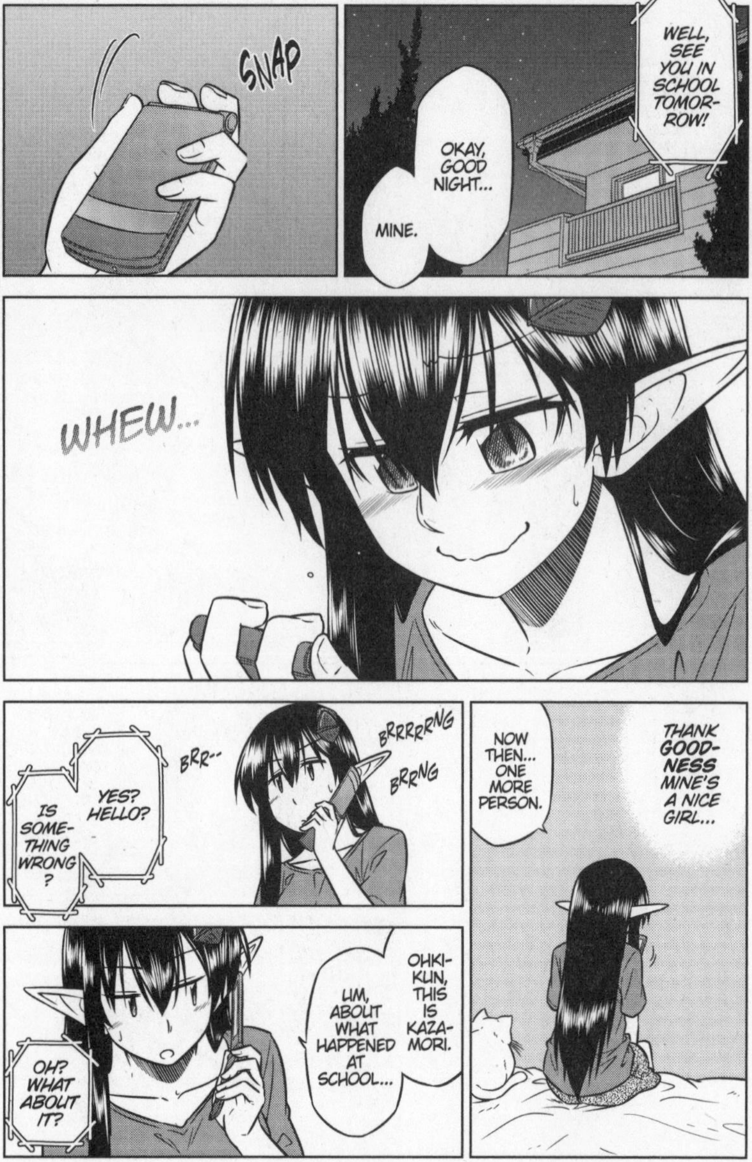
WELL, SEE YOU IN SCHOOL TOMOR-ROW!
OKAY, GOOD NIGHT...
MINE.
SNAP
WHEW...
THANK GOOD-NESS MINE'S A NICE GIRL...
NOW THEN... ONE MORE PERSON.
BRRRRRNG
BRRNG
BRR--
YES? HELLO?
IS SOME-THING WRONG?
OHKI-KUN, THIS IS KAZA-MORI.
UM, ABOUT WHAT HAPPENED AT SCHOOL...
OH? WHAT ABOUT IT?

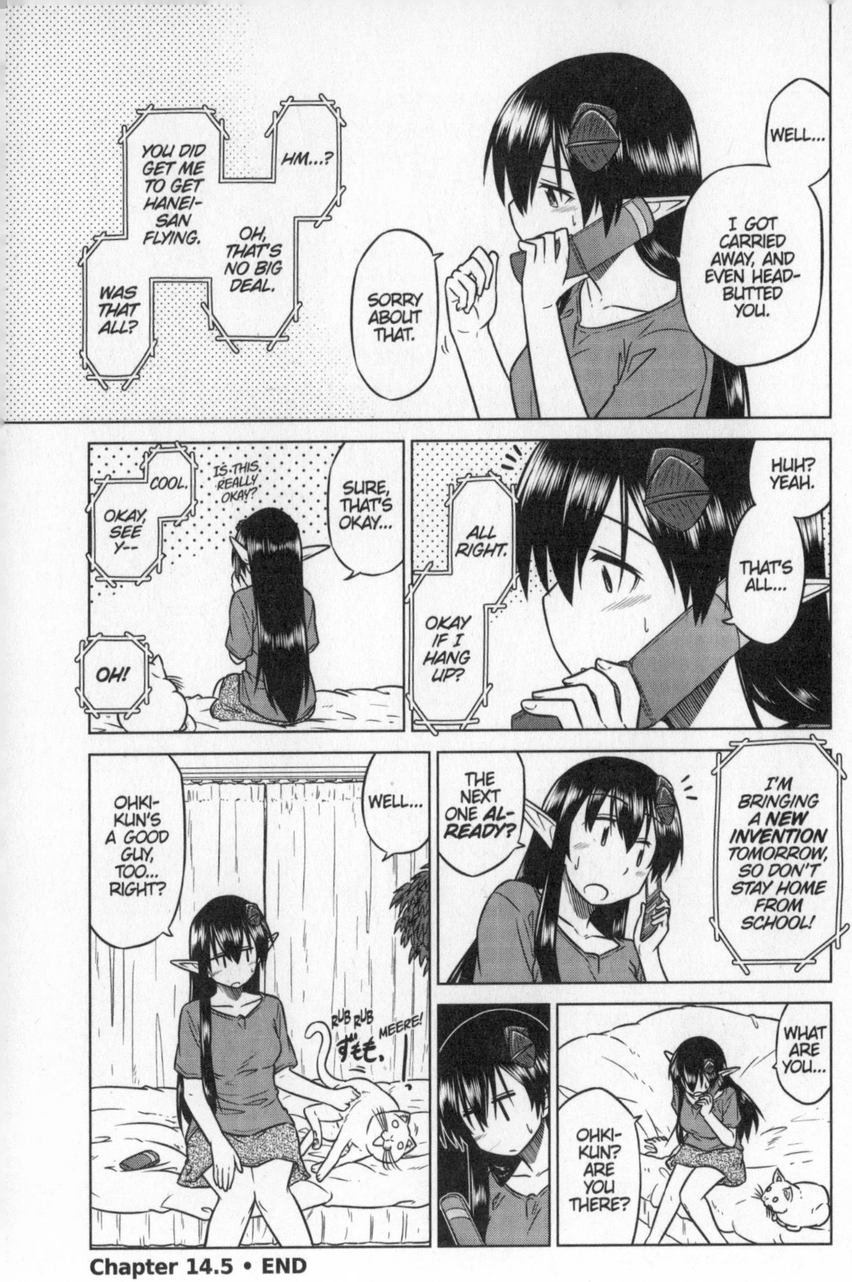
WELL...
I GOT CARRIED AWAY, AND EVEN HEAD-BUTTED YOU.
SORRY ABOUT THAT.
HM...?
YOU DID GET ME TO GET HANEI-SAN FLYING.
OH, THAT'S NO BIG DEAL.
WAS THAT ALL?
HUH? YEAH.
THAT'S ALL...
ALL RIGHT.
OKAY IF I HANG UP?
SURE, THAT'S OKAY...
IS THIS REALLY OKAY?
COOL.
OKAY, SEE Y--
OH!
I'M BRINGING A NEW INVENTION TOMORROW, SO DON'T STAY HOME FROM SCHOOL!
THE NEXT ONE AL-READY?
WHAT ARE YOU...
OHKI-KUN? ARE YOU THERE?
WELL...
OHKI-KUN'S A GOOD GUY, TOO... RIGHT?
RUB RUB
ずもも、
MEERE!

Chapter 14.5 • END

ITOKO-CHAN...

WHEN YOU WANTED TO SAY, "LET'S BE FRIENDS," BUT COULDN'T...

TO SAVE APPEARANCES, YOU HAD IT CONVEYED VIA OHKI-KUN.

AND NOW, YOU EVEN TAKE STUFF LIKE THIS SO SERIOUSLY...

YOU'RE JUST SO CUTE...!

TRMBL

TRMBL

I WONDER WHAT YOU'RE NORMALLY LIKE WITH OHKI-KUN...

SIGH-

She ends up going there.

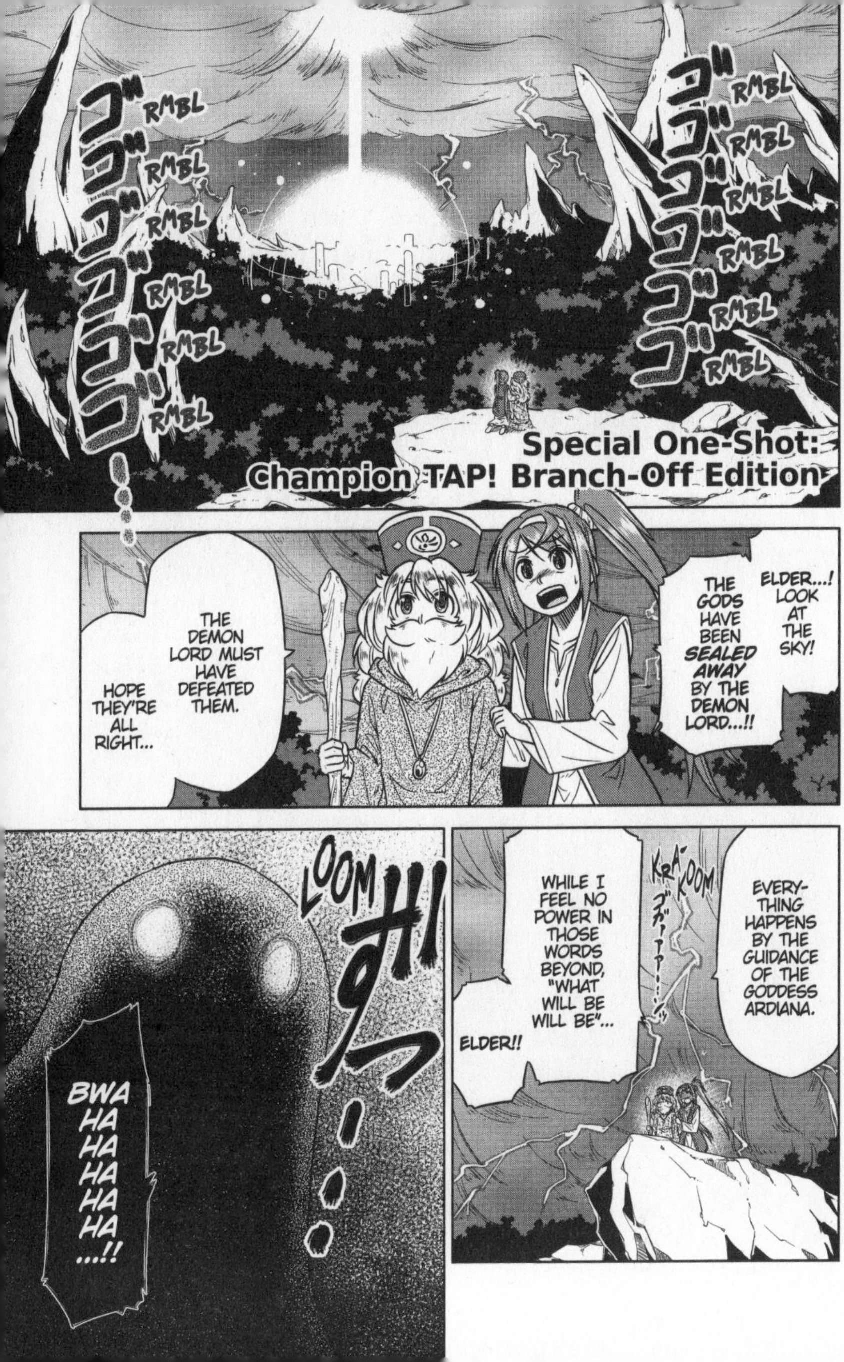
RMBL RMBL RMBL RMBL RMBL RMBL
RMBL RMBL RMBL RMBL RMBL RMBL
Special One-Shot: Champion TAP! Branch-Off Edition
ELDER...! LOOK AT THE SKY!
THE GODS HAVE BEEN SEALED AWAY BY THE DEMON LORD...!!
THE DEMON LORD MUST HAVE DEFEATED THEM.
HOPE THEY'RE ALL RIGHT...
EVERY-THING HAPPENS BY THE GUIDANCE OF THE GODDESS ARDIANA.
KRA-KOOM
WHILE I FEEL NO POWER IN THOSE WORDS BEYOND, "WHAT WILL BE WILL BE"...
ELDER!!
LOOM
BWA HA HA HA HA HA...!!

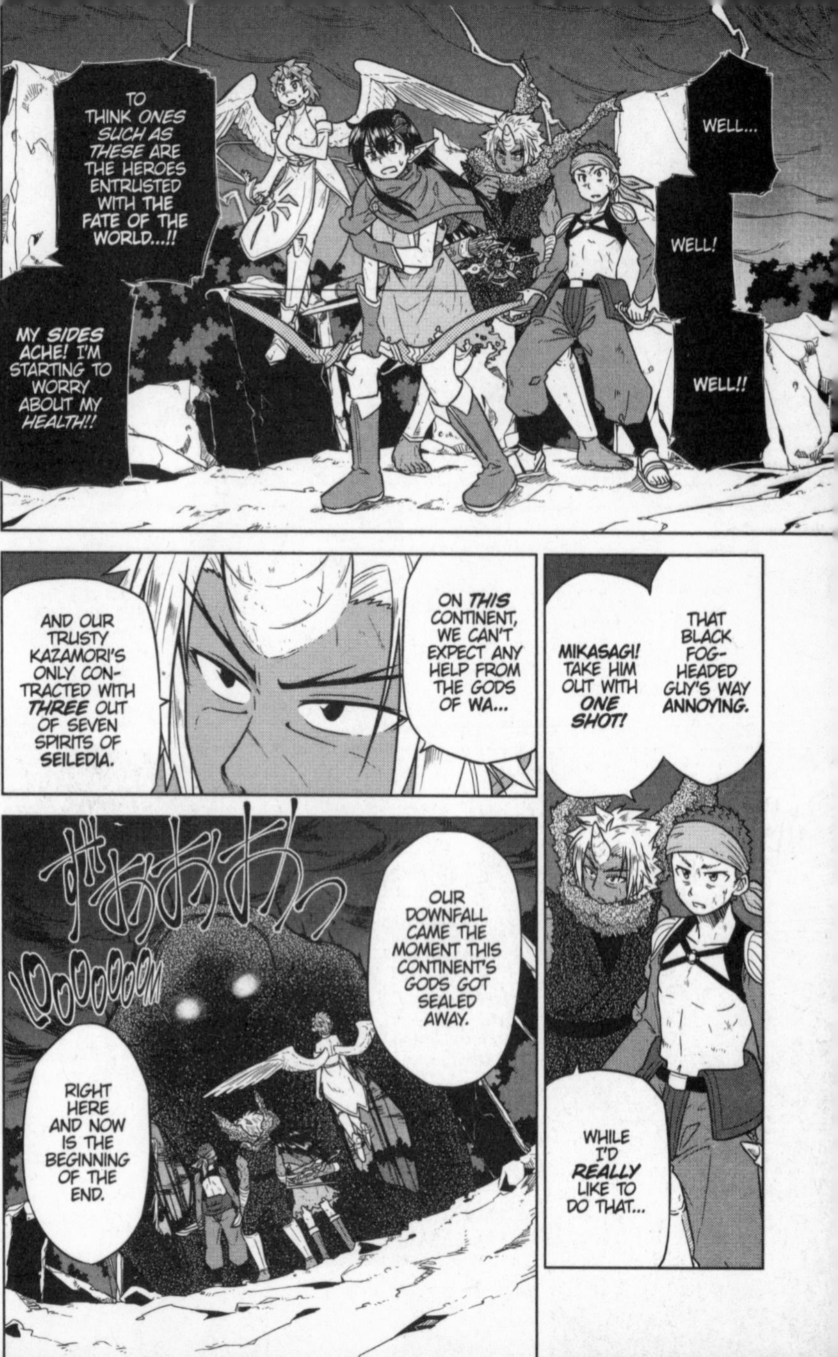
WELL...
WELL!
WELL!!
TO THINK ONES SUCH AS THESE ARE THE HEROES ENTRUSTED WITH THE FATE OF THE WORLD...!!
MY SIDES ACHE! I'M STARTING TO WORRY ABOUT MY HEALTH!!
THAT BLACK FOG-HEADED GUY'S WAY ANNOYING.
MIKASAGI! TAKE HIM OUT WITH ONE SHOT!
WHILE I'D REALLY LIKE TO DO THAT...
ON THIS CONTINENT, WE CAN'T EXPECT ANY HELP FROM THE GODS OF WA...
AND OUR TRUSTY KAZAMORI'S ONLY CONTRACTED WITH THREE OUT OF SEVEN SPIRITS OF SEILEDIA.
OUR DOWNFALL CAME THE MOMENT THIS CONTINENT'S GODS GOT SEALED AWAY.
RIGHT HERE AND NOW IS THE BEGINNING OF THE END.

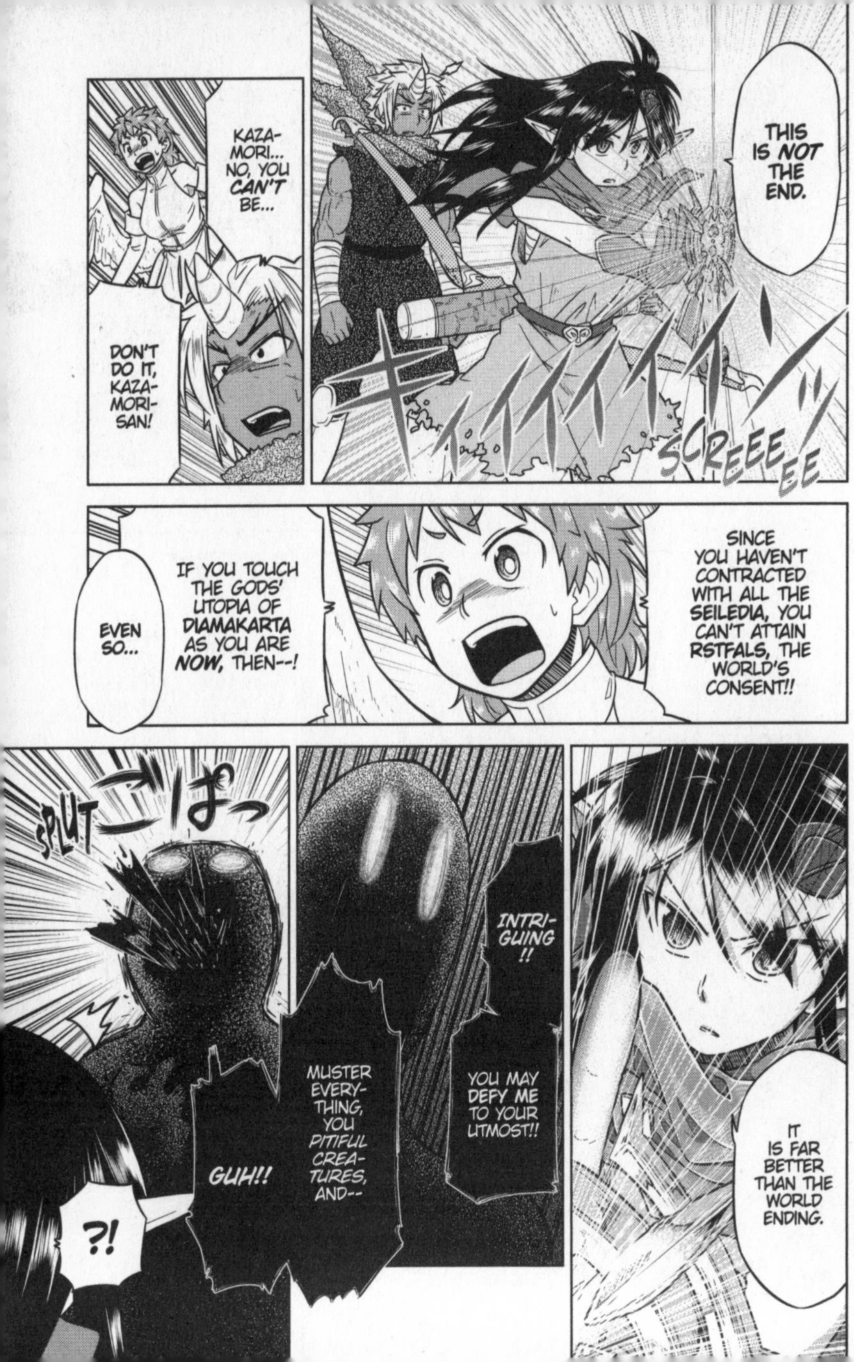
THIS IS *NOT* THE END.
SCREEEEEE
KAZAMORI... NO, YOU *CAN'T* BE...
DON'T DO IT, KAZAMORI-SAN!
SINCE YOU HAVEN'T CONTRACTED WITH ALL THE SEILEDIA, YOU CAN'T ATTAIN RSTFALS, THE WORLD'S CONSENT!!
IF YOU TOUCH THE GODS' UTOPIA OF DIAMAKARTA AS YOU ARE *NOW*, THEN--!
EVEN SO...
IT IS FAR BETTER THAN THE WORLD ENDING.
INTRIGUING!!
YOU MAY DEFY ME TO YOUR UTMOST!!
MUSTER EVERYTHING, YOU *PITIFUL CREATURES,* AND--
SPLUT
ごぱっ
GUH!!
?!

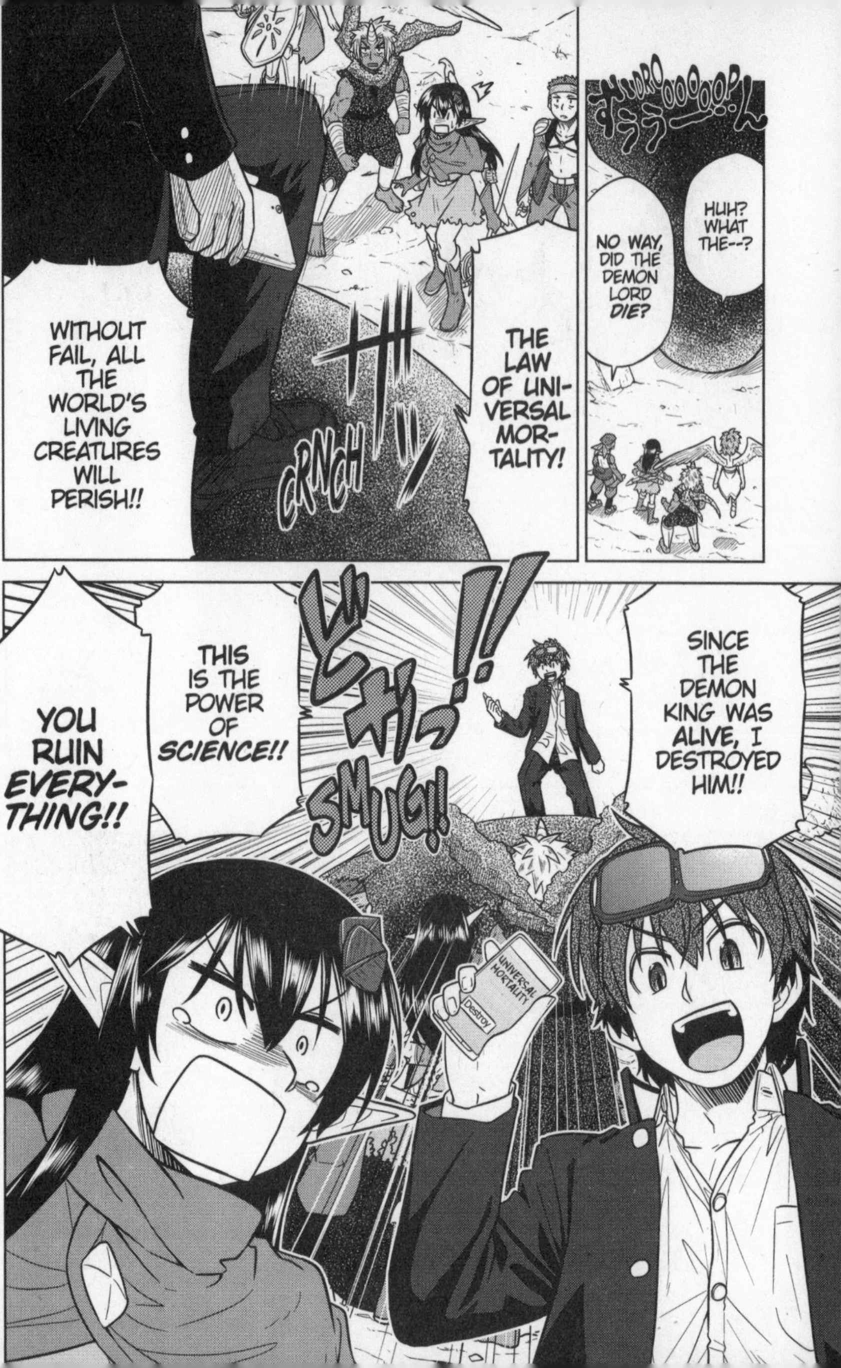
DROOOOOOP!
HUH? WHAT THE--?
NO WAY, DID THE DEMON LORD DIE?
THE LAW OF UNI-VERSAL MOR-TALITY!
WITHOUT FAIL, ALL THE WORLD'S LIVING CREATURES WILL PERISH!!
CRNCH
SINCE THE DEMON KING WAS ALIVE, I DESTROYED HIM!!
SMUG!!
THIS IS THE POWER OF SCIENCE!!
YOU RUIN EVERY-THING!!
UNIVERSAL MORTALITY
Destroy

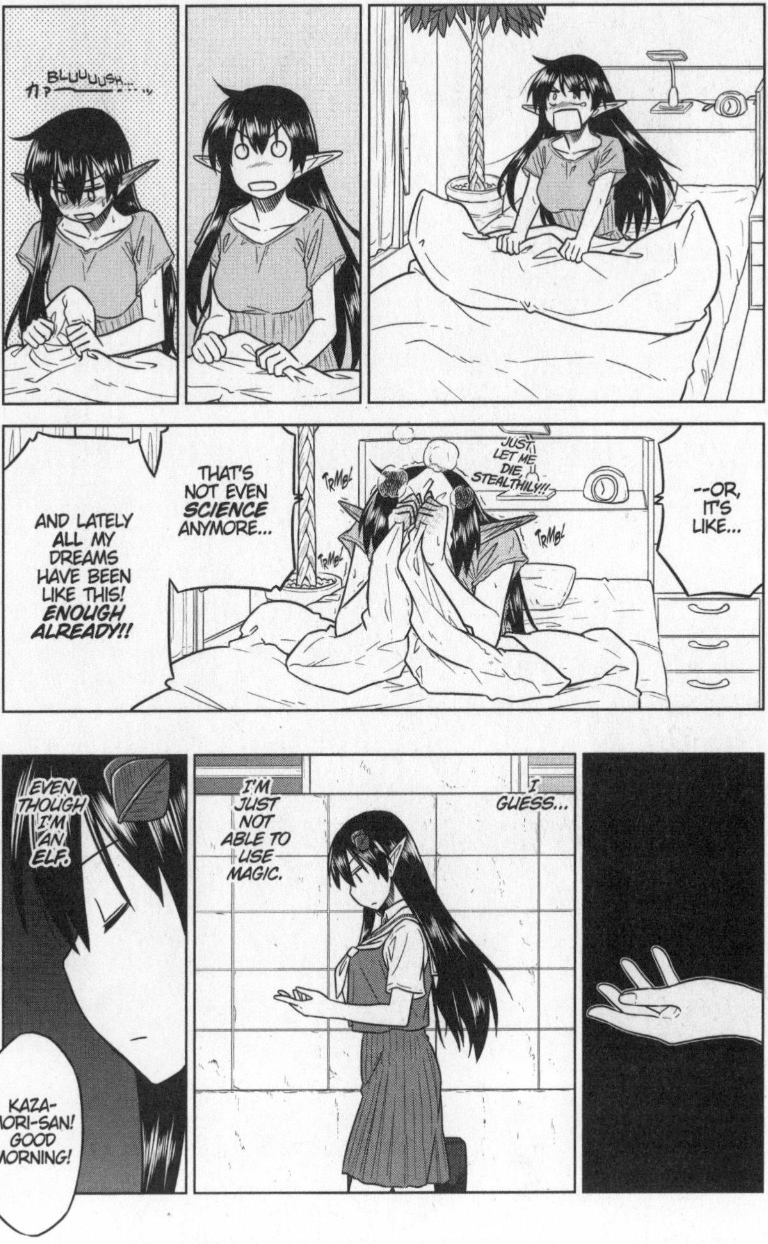
BLUUUUUSH...
--OR, IT'S LIKE...
JUST LET ME DIE, STEALTHILY!!!
TRMBL
TRMBL
TRMBL
THAT'S NOT EVEN SCIENCE ANYMORE...
AND LATELY ALL MY DREAMS HAVE BEEN LIKE THIS! ENOUGH ALREADY!!
I GUESS...
I'M JUST NOT ABLE TO USE MAGIC.
EVEN THOUGH I'M AN ELF.
KAZA-MORI-SAN! GOOD MORNING!

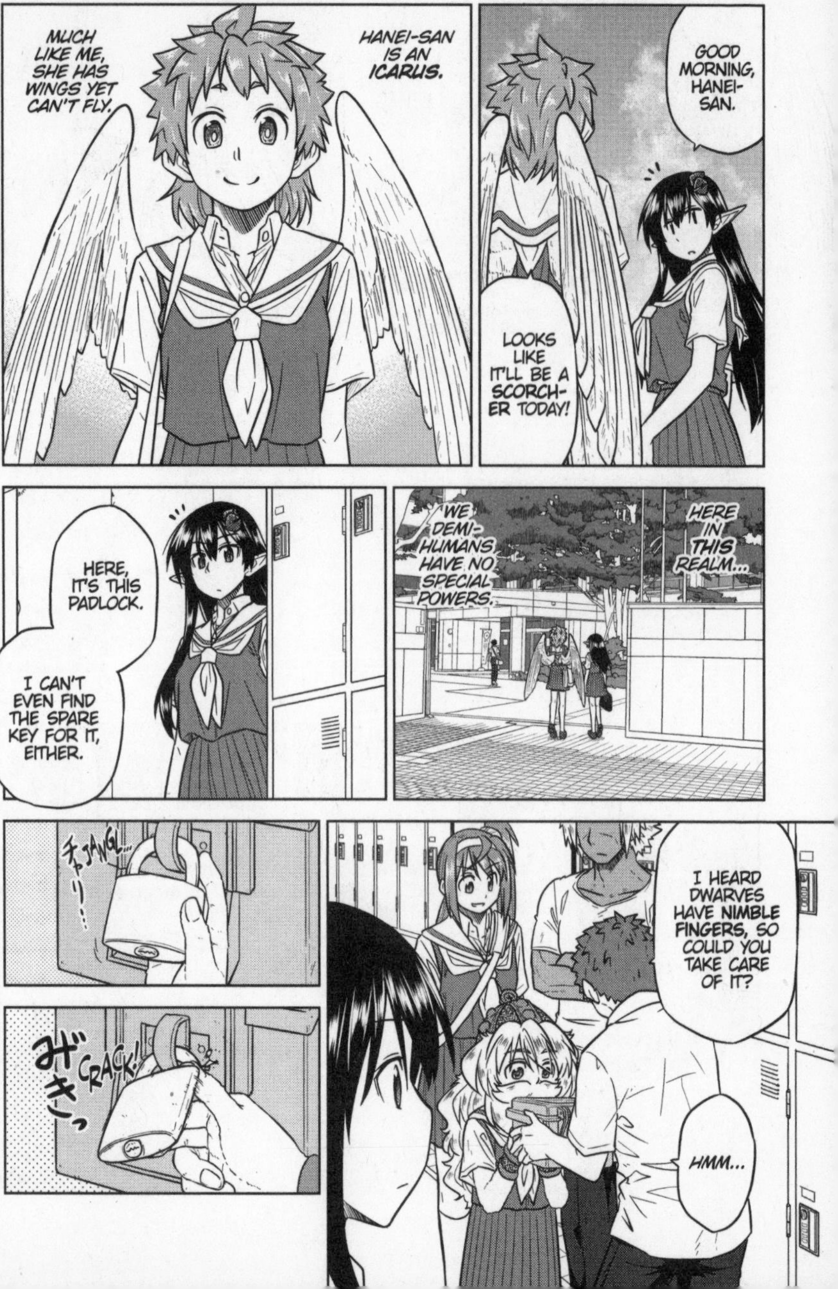
GOOD MORNING, HANEI-SAN.
LOOKS LIKE IT'LL BE A SCORCHER TODAY!
HANEI-SAN IS AN ICARUS.
MUCH LIKE ME, SHE HAS WINGS YET CAN'T FLY.
HERE IN THIS REALM...
WE DEMI-HUMANS HAVE NO SPECIAL POWERS.
HERE, IT'S THIS PADLOCK.
I CAN'T EVEN FIND THE SPARE KEY FOR IT, EITHER.
I HEARD DWARVES HAVE NIMBLE FINGERS, SO COULD YOU TAKE CARE OF IT?
HMM...
チャリ...
JANGL...
みきっ
CRACK!

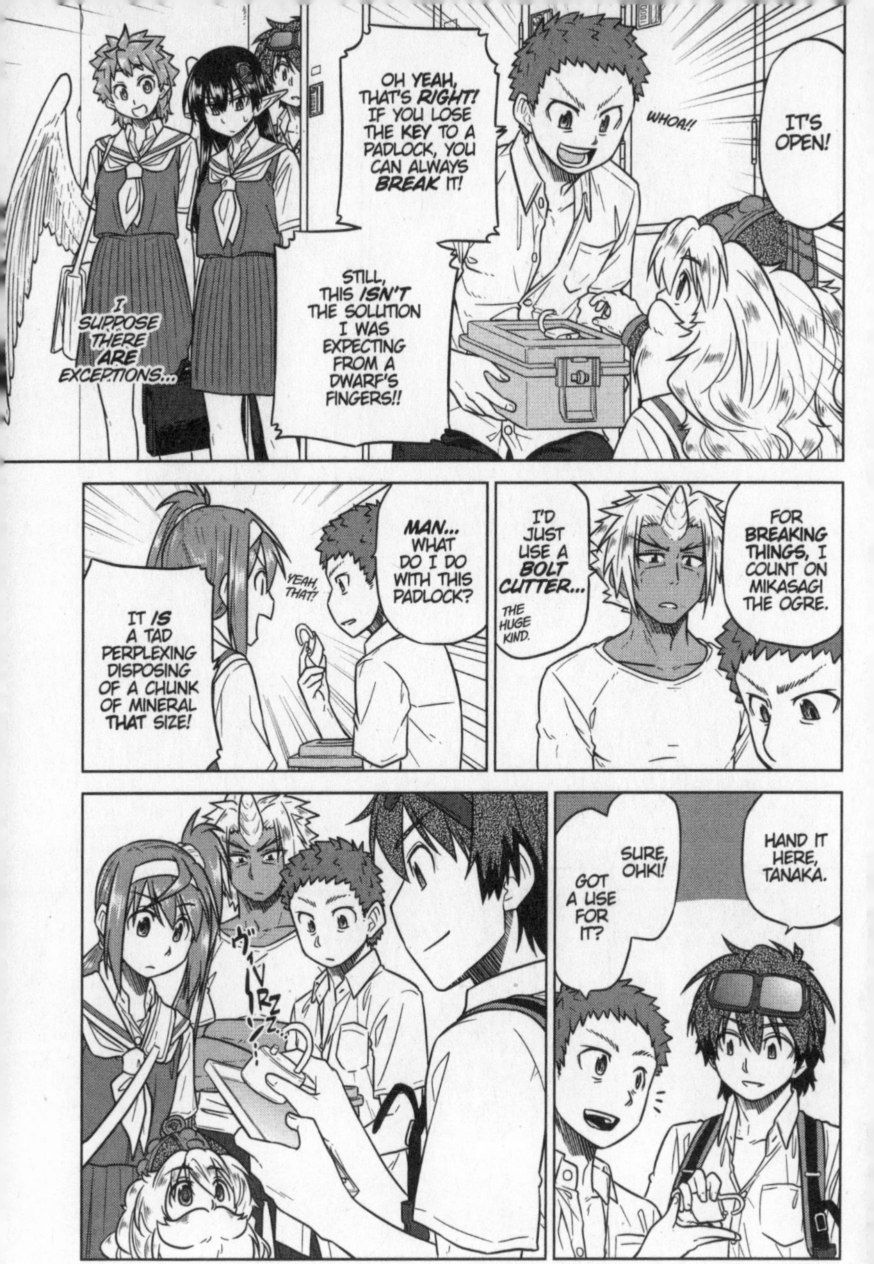
IT'S OPEN!
WHOA!!
OH YEAH, THAT'S **RIGHT!** IF YOU LOSE THE KEY TO A PADLOCK, YOU CAN ALWAYS **BREAK** IT!
STILL, THIS **ISN'T** THE SOLUTION I WAS EXPECTING FROM A DWARF'S FINGERS!!
I SUPPOSE THERE **ARE** EXCEPTIONS...
FOR BREAKING THINGS, I COUNT ON MIKASAGI THE OGRE.
I'D JUST USE A **BOLT CUTTER...**
THE HUGE KIND.
MAN... WHAT DO I DO WITH THIS PADLOCK?
YEAH, THAT!
IT **IS** A TAD PERPLEXING DISPOSING OF A CHUNK OF MINERAL THAT SIZE!
HAND IT HERE, TANAKA.
SURE, OHKI!
GOT A USE FOR IT?

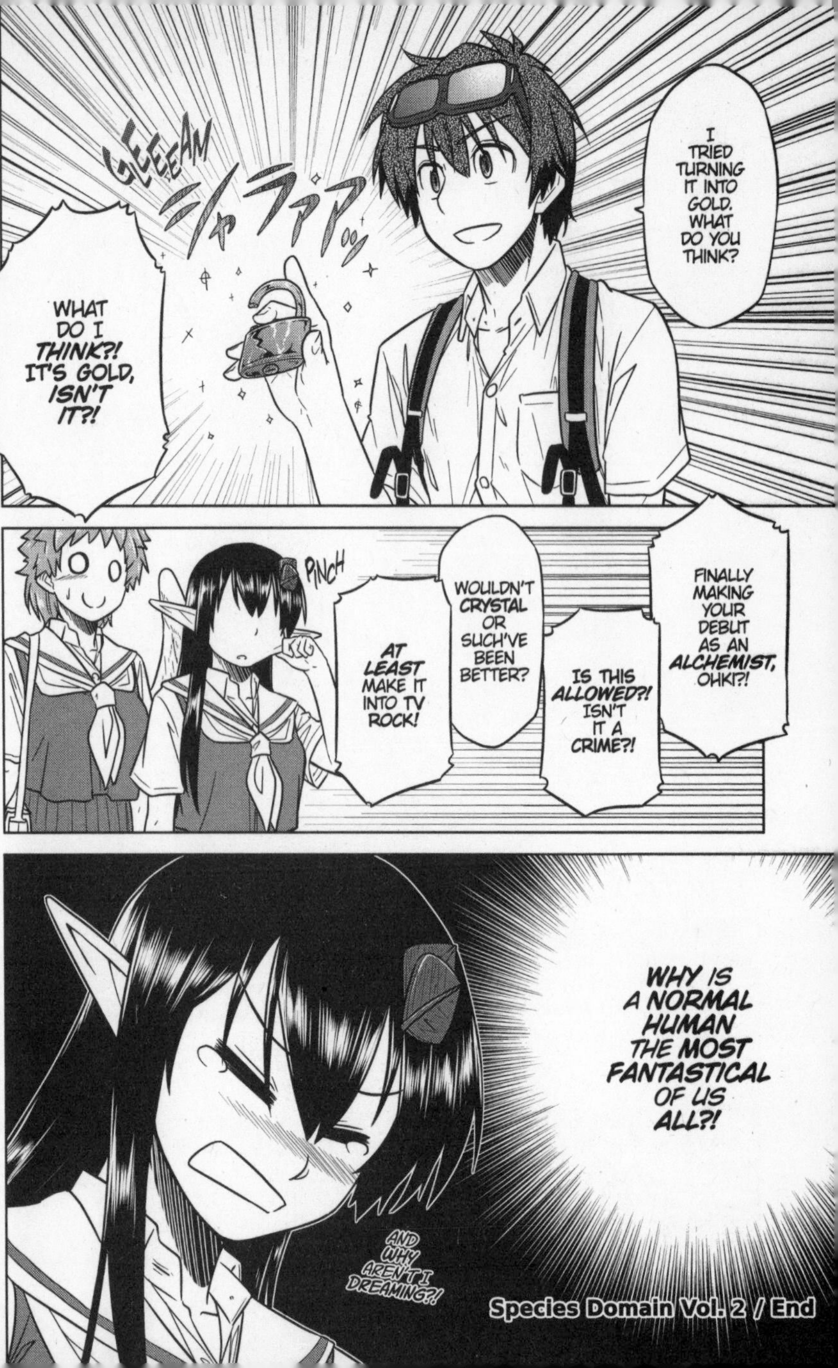
I TRIED TURNING IT INTO GOLD. WHAT DO YOU THINK?
GLEEEAM
シャァァッ
WHAT DO I THINK?! IT'S GOLD, ISN'T IT?!
FINALLY MAKING YOUR DEBUT AS AN ALCHEMIST, OHKI?!
IS THIS ALLOWED?! ISN'T IT A CRIME?!
WOULDN'T CRYSTAL OR SUCH'VE BEEN BETTER?
AT LEAST MAKE IT INTO TV ROCK!
PINCH
WHY IS A NORMAL HUMAN THE MOST FANTASTICAL OF US ALL?!
AND WHY AREN'T I DREAMING?!
Species Domain Vol. 2 / End

Species
スピーシーズドメイン
Domain

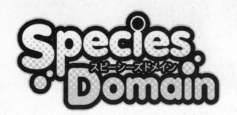

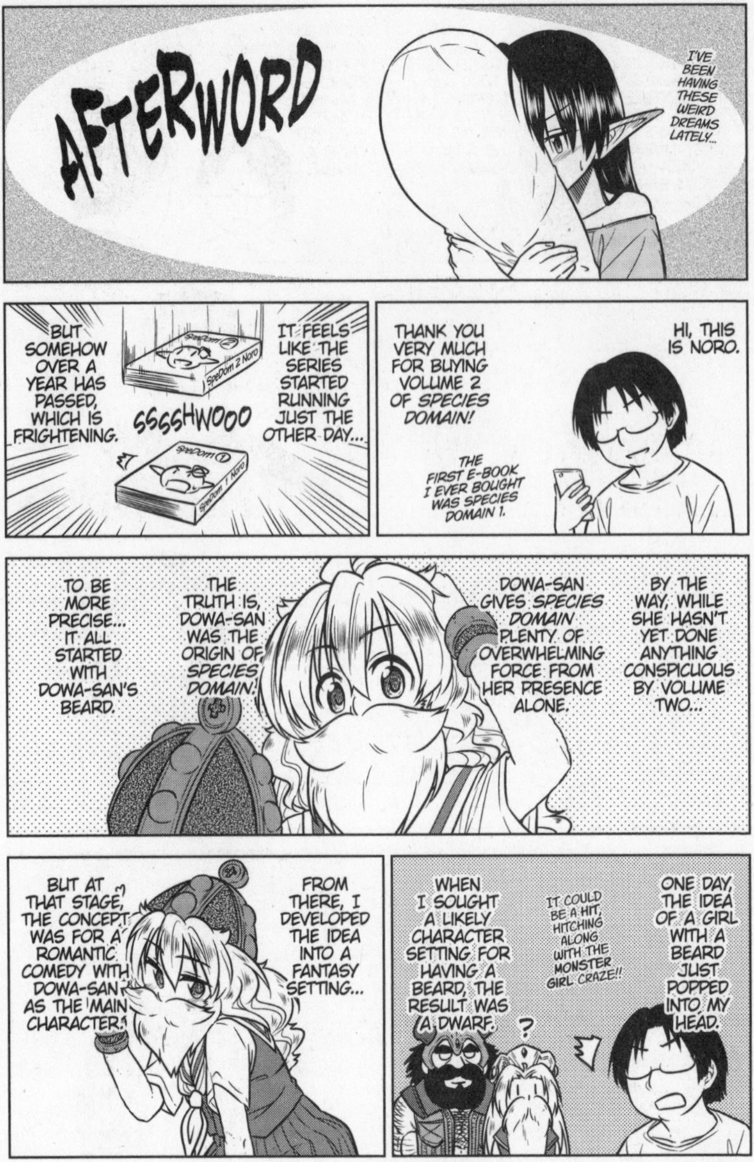
AFTERWORD
I'VE BEEN HAVING THESE WEIRD DREAMS LATELY...
HI, THIS IS NORO.
THANK YOU VERY MUCH FOR BUYING VOLUME 2 OF *SPECIES DOMAIN*!
THE FIRST E-BOOK I EVER BOUGHT WAS SPECIES DOMAIN 1.
IT FEELS LIKE THE SERIES STARTED RUNNING JUST THE OTHER DAY...
SpeDom 2 Noro
BUT SOMEHOW OVER A YEAR HAS PASSED, WHICH IS FRIGHTENING.
SSSSHWOOO
SpeDom 1 Noro
BY THE WAY, WHILE SHE HASN'T YET DONE ANYTHING CONSPICUOUS BY VOLUME TWO...
DOWA-SAN GIVES *SPECIES DOMAIN* PLENTY OF OVERWHELMING FORCE FROM HER PRESENCE ALONE.
THE TRUTH IS, DOWA-SAN WAS THE ORIGIN OF *SPECIES DOMAIN*!
TO BE MORE PRECISE... IT ALL STARTED WITH DOWA-SAN'S BEARD.
ONE DAY, THE IDEA OF A GIRL WITH A BEARD JUST POPPED INTO MY HEAD.
IT COULD BE A HIT, HITCHING ALONG WITH THE MONSTER GIRL CRAZE!!
WHEN I SOUGHT A LIKELY CHARACTER SETTING FOR HAVING A BEARD, THE RESULT WAS A DWARF.
?
FROM THERE, I DEVELOPED THE IDEA INTO A FANTASY SETTING...
BUT AT THAT STAGE, THE CONCEPT WAS FOR A ROMANTIC COMEDY WITH DOWA-SAN AS THE MAIN CHARACTER.

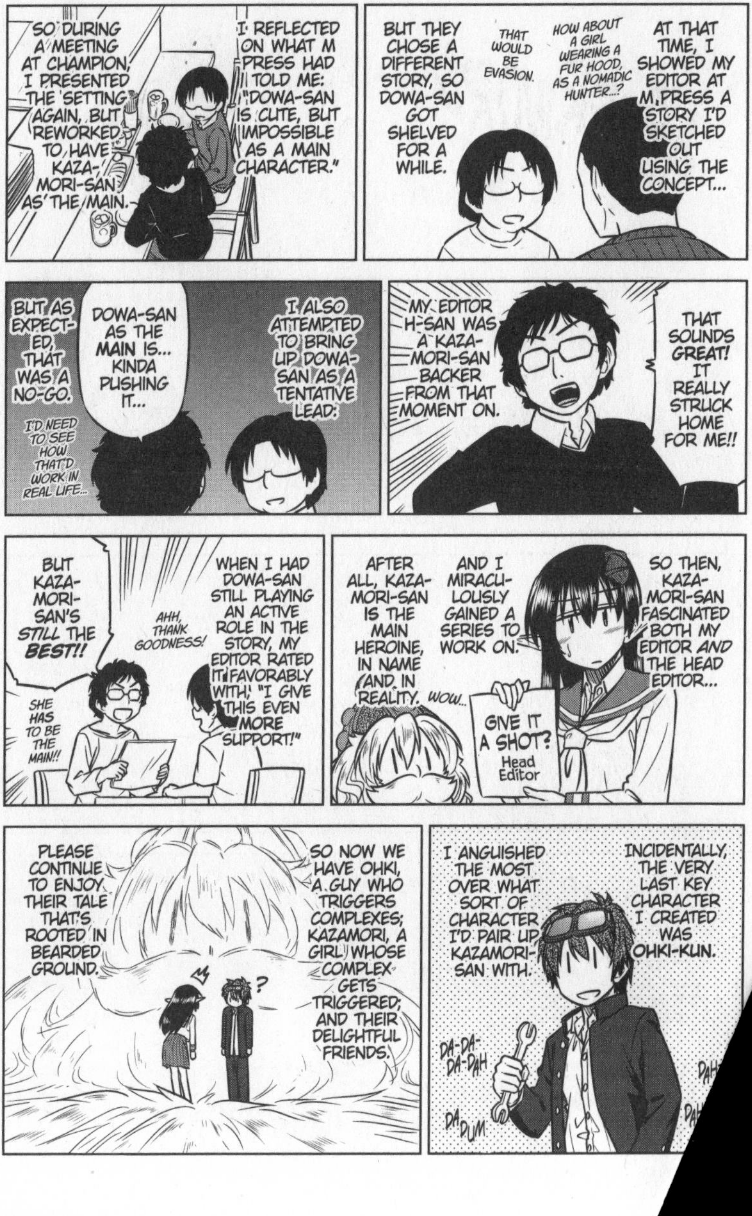
AT THAT TIME, I SHOWED MY EDITOR AT M PRESS A STORY I'D SKETCHED OUT USING THE CONCEPT...
HOW ABOUT A GIRL WEARING A FUR HOOD, AS A NOMADIC HUNTER...?
THAT WOULD BE EVASION.
BUT THEY CHOSE A DIFFERENT STORY, SO DOWA-SAN GOT SHELVED FOR A WHILE.
I REFLECTED ON WHAT M PRESS HAD TOLD ME: "DOWA-SAN IS CUTE, BUT IMPOSSIBLE AS A MAIN CHARACTER."
SO DURING A MEETING AT CHAMPION, I PRESENTED THE SETTING AGAIN, BUT REWORKED TO HAVE KAZA-MORI-SAN AS THE MAIN.
THAT SOUNDS GREAT! IT REALLY STRUCK HOME FOR ME!!
MY EDITOR H-SAN WAS A KAZA-MORI-SAN BACKER FROM THAT MOMENT ON.
I ALSO ATTEMPTED TO BRING UP DOWA-SAN AS A TENTATIVE LEAD.
DOWA-SAN AS THE MAIN IS... KINDA PUSHING IT...
BUT AS EXPECT-ED, THAT WAS A NO-GO.
I'D NEED TO SEE HOW THAT'D WORK IN REAL LIFE...
SO THEN, KAZA-MORI-SAN FASCINATED BOTH MY EDITOR AND THE HEAD EDITOR...
AND I MIRACU-LOUSLY GAINED A SERIES TO WORK ON.
GIVE IT A SHOT? Head Editor
AFTER ALL, KAZA-MORI-SAN IS THE MAIN HEROINE, IN NAME AND IN REALITY.
WOW...
WHEN I HAD DOWA-SAN STILL PLAYING AN ACTIVE ROLE IN THE STORY, MY EDITOR RATED IT FAVORABLY WITH, "I GIVE THIS EVEN MORE SUPPORT!"
AHH, THANK GOODNESS!
BUT KAZA-MORI-SAN'S STILL THE BEST!!
SHE HAS TO BE THE MAIN!!
INCIDENTALLY, THE VERY LAST KEY CHARACTER I CREATED WAS OHKI-KUN.
I ANGUISHED THE MOST OVER WHAT SORT OF CHARACTER I'D PAIR UP KAZAMORI-SAN WITH.
DAH
DAH
DA-DA-DA-DAH
DA DUM
SO NOW WE HAVE OHKI, A GUY WHO TRIGGERS COMPLEXES; KAZAMORI, A GIRL WHOSE COMPLEX GETS TRIGGERED; AND THEIR DELIGHTFUL FRIENDS.
PLEASE CONTINUE TO ENJOY THEIR TALE THAT'S ROOTED IN BEARDED GROUND.

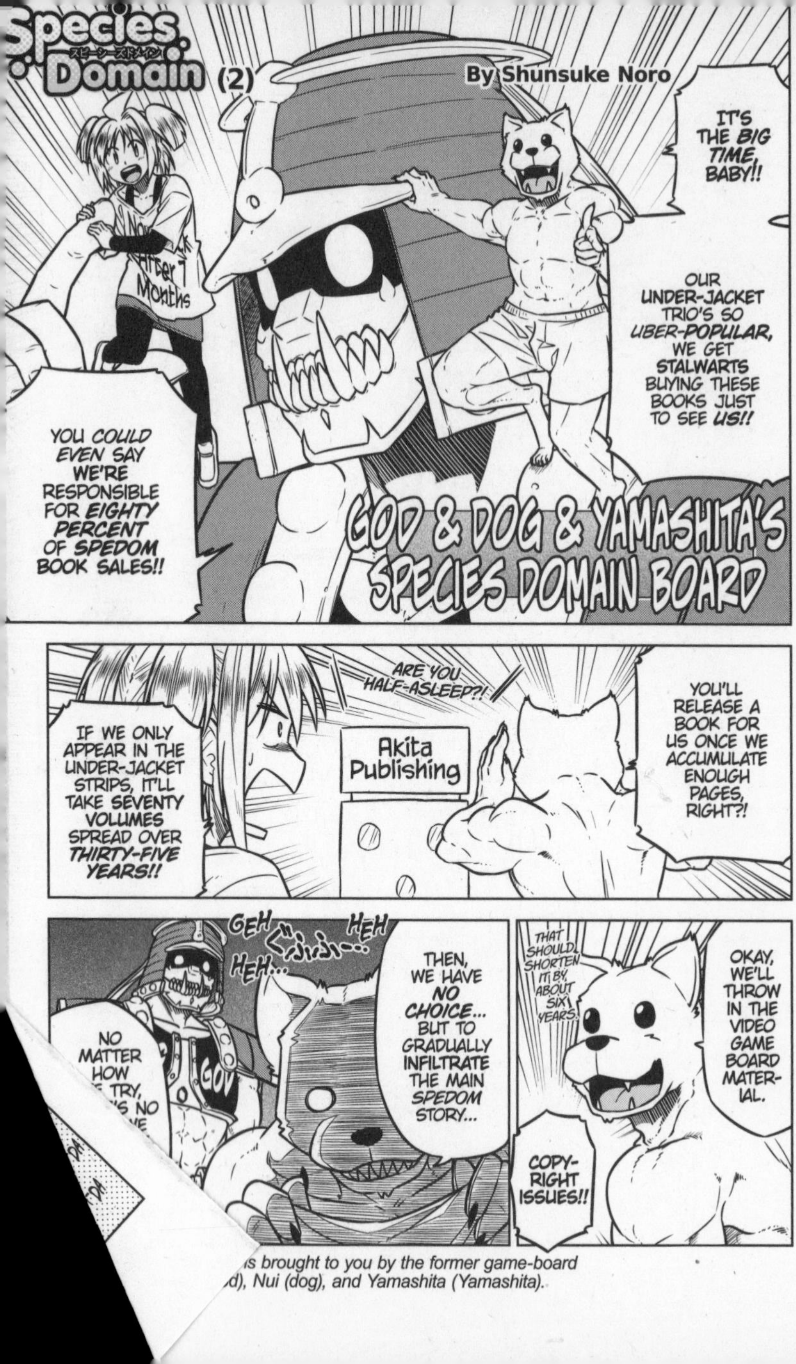
Species Domain (2)
スピーシーズドメイン
By Shunsuke Noro
IT'S THE BIG TIME, BABY!!
OUR UNDER-JACKET TRIO'S SO UBER-POPULAR, WE GET STALWARTS BUYING THESE BOOKS JUST TO SEE US!!
YOU COULD EVEN SAY WE'RE RESPONSIBLE FOR EIGHTY PERCENT OF SPEDOM BOOK SALES!!
GOD & DOG & YAMASHITA'S SPECIES DOMAIN BOARD
YOU'LL RELEASE A BOOK FOR US ONCE WE ACCUMULATE ENOUGH PAGES, RIGHT?!
ARE YOU HALF-ASLEEP?!
Akita Publishing
IF WE ONLY APPEAR IN THE UNDER-JACKET STRIPS, IT'LL TAKE SEVENTY VOLUMES SPREAD OVER THIRTY-FIVE YEARS!!
OKAY, WE'LL THROW IN THE VIDEO GAME BOARD MATERIAL.
THAT SHOULD SHORTEN IT BY ABOUT SIX YEARS.
COPY-RIGHT ISSUES!!
GEH HEH HEH...
ぐふふー…
THEN, WE HAVE NO CHOICE... BUT TO GRADUALLY INFILTRATE THE MAIN SPEDOM STORY...
NO MATTER HOW

...is brought to you by the former game-board ...d), Nui (dog), and Yamashita (Yamashita).